Backbench Opinion
in the House of Commons 1945–55

Backbench Opinion
in the House of Commons 1945–55

BY

HUGH B. BERRINGTON

Professor of Politics, University of Newcastle upon Tyne

PERGAMON PRESS

OXFORD · NEW YORK · TORONTO
SYDNEY · BRAUNSCHWEIG

Pergamon Press Ltd., Headington Hill Hall, Oxford

Pergamon Press Inc., Maxwell House, Fairview Park, Elmsford,
New York 10523

Pergamon of Canada Ltd., 207 Queen's Quay West, Toronto 1

Pergamon Press (Aust.) Pty. Ltd., 19a Boundary Street,
Rushcutters Bay, N.S.W. 2011, Australia

Vieweg & Sohn GmbH, Burgplatz 1, Braunschweig

First edition 1973

Library of Congress Cataloging in Publication Data

Berrington, Hugh.
Backbench opinion in the House of Commons, 1945–55.

1. Great Britain. Parliament. House of Commons.
2. Conservative Party (Great Britain). 3. Labour
Party (Great Britain). I. Title.
JN675 1945.B46   328.42   73–79
ISBN 0–08–016748–9

Printed in Great Britain by A. Wheaton & Co., Exeter

To Catherine

Contents

Preface and Acknowledgements

EVEN though this book deals with an earlier period, it is essentially a sequel to *Backbench Opinion in the House of Commons, 1955–59*. Techniques similar to those used in the earlier study have been employed in this work. The use of Early Day Motions (EDMs) as a source of information about the opinions of backbench MPs has been heavily attacked: this study, whilst relying to a considerable degree on the same source, makes substantial use of free votes and floor revolts. The striking way in which the evidence of the latter confirms inferences drawn from the study of EDMs goes far to show that many of the criticisms of the use of the EDM as a source-material were misguided.

Much of the research for this work was completed by 1962. For several reasons, including my own departure from Keele to Newcastle upon Tyne, the actual writing up of the material was deferred. One of the penalties of divorcing the process of research from the act of writing is that many promising lines of inquiry, which only become apparent when drafting is under way, have to be explored, and other lines of inquiry have to be investigated anew. For this reason, a considerable amount of further research became necessary, and this, too, contributed to the delay.

There is, of course, considerable disparity in the amount of space devoted to the two parties. This reflects no special preference for one party or the other, but is the inevitable result of the differences in their nature. There were few open revolts and relatively few important EDMs tabled on the Conservative side during the first three post-war parliaments. Inevitably a disparity of data is reflected in an imbalance of attention. Conservatives should perhaps be grateful that the chronicler of internal party discord has, in their case, relatively little material on which to work.

A study of this kind requires an enormous amount of detailed work, and for this reason my first thanks are due to the Nuffield Foundation, whose generosity made this work possible. With my thanks go my apologies that there should have been such a long delay in the completion of the manuscript.

David Bartholomew left Keele in 1960 for Aberystwyth and then went to the University of Kent and then to LSE as Professor of Statistics. I left Keele in 1965, and Professor Finer went to Manchester in 1966. As a result of the dispersion of the original team it was agreed that I should be responsible for the completion of the present book. I must express my special gratitude to Professor Finer and Professor Bartholomew for their confidence, and for the benefit of their continued collaboration, encouragement, and advice.

Many people have contributed in one way or another to this study. In particular, my thanks are due to our research officers, John Thompson and Betty Thirsk, who between them undertook with great zeal and efficiency most of the detailed work in the first stage of research. I must also thank Miss Pat Heneage, formerly of the University of Keele, and Mr. H. V.

Madison of the University of Keele, who carried out the statistical tests on the results of the first stage. I am also grateful to Stoke Corporation, and especially to Mr. Edwards, for their help in the provision of both manpower and facilities in making the preliminary tabulations, and to Aubrey Noakes who supplied us with the basic raw material for our task by supplying copies of all the EDMs (and signatures thereto) which were tabled during the 10-year period of our study.

Many people helped in the second stage, and I must express my thanks to Norman Mallabar, John Hartas, Robin Haggart, Neill Nugent, and Eva Philipson, who undertook a considerable amount of manual sorting; to Mrs. Rule, Mrs. V. Maddison and Eva Philipson who typed and re-typed successive drafts of the script; to Tony Breakell and Pat Stace for the preparation of certain diagrams; to John Kennedy, Betty Gittus, and Susan Webber for their continued patience and help in discussing statistical problems, and also to Susan Webber and Victor Jupp for carrying out a large number of statistical tests.

I am also grateful to Professor Richard Rose of the University of Strathclyde for granting me permission to read his doctoral thesis on "The relation of socialist principles to foreign policy", the influence of which is not to be measured merely by the number of direct citations; to Mrs. G. Hutton (*née* Bremner) for permission to quote from her doctoral thesis on "The analysis of British parliamentary thought concerning the United States in the post-war period"; to Mark Franklin, another explorer of the EDM jungle, for permission to read and quote from his doctoral thesis and for much stimulating discussion of the problems involved in validating the use of EDMs; and to Patrick Seyd for permission to quote from an unpublished article and for similar stimulating discussion.

My thanks are also due to Dr. W. S. Mitchell, the Librarian at the University of Newcastle upon Tyne, and to Mr. S. Stewart, the Librarian at the University of Keele, and their staffs; to Mr. F. B. Singleton, Librarian of the *Guardian*; to Mr. D. C. L. Holland, Librarian of the House of Commons Library; and to the Librarian and his staff at the City Library, Newcastle upon Tyne, for their help and co-operation.

I must also thank my colleagues and friends Vincent Wright, Tim Gray, David George and Ben Pimlott for reading (and re-reading) the manuscript; them again and Iain McLean for many helpful comments; and Harold Lever, MP, and John Mackintosh, MP, for their advice and help.

Lastly, but certainly not least, I must thank my wife, Catherine, to whom this book is dedicated, for her enthusiasm, encouragement, and forbearance, for the practical help she gave me in the preparation of certain diagrams, and for accepting so patiently my frequent absences from home whilst this book was being written.

It should be superfluous to add that no one mentioned bears any responsibility for the judgements and opinions expressed in this book.

Let me finally add that a computer (expensive or otherwise) has been used only for one stage of this study, namely the carrying out of chi-squared tests.

Hugh Berrington

CHAPTER 1

Introduction

"... we have to be numerate as well as literate." (R. H. S. CROSSMAN, MP, House of Commons, 15 July 1963.)

"All my life I have thought if you explain something sensibly then a person will understand. I retain that belief even now, though I have frequently been disproved." (R. H. S. CROSSMAN, *Sunday Times*, 25 May 1969.)

"Quantitative method is one among various means of discovering truth." (STUART RICE, *Quantitative Methods in Politics*.)

The use of quantitative methods and statistical techniques in the study and practice of British politics has been a recent, and to some a not altogether welcome, development. The political parties are ambivalent about this change; whilst the central organizations of the parties make increasing use of privately commissioned opinion surveys, party spokesmen often profess a haughty scepticism about the polls, particularly when their findings are unfavourable. Old-fashioned hunch is preferred to new-fangled inquiry. The study of election results (popularly known as psephology) arouses similar misgivings and encounters the same hostility. Resistance to these innovations has several causes. A lack of understanding of the claims and objectives of quantitative methods, a fear that the autonomy of the individual is threatened by the assumptions and findings of new techniques of political investigation, a need to protect reassuring prejudices and congenial images from new and disturbing information, sheer occupational *amour-propre*, and perhaps even a congenital distaste for figures help to explain the animosity felt by some for the application of quantitative methods to the study of political behaviour.[1]

The chief use of quantitative techniques in the academic study of British politics has hitherto lain in the field of election results and mass communications. Constituency studies such as

---

[1] The attitude of some political observers and practitioners to opinion surveys affords a notable illustration of vocational defensiveness. The occasional failure of the polls is greeted with a chorus of pleasure, whilst their extraordinary run of success is ignored. Truman's victory over the pollsters in 1948 has worn a deep groove into the psyches of many politicians and journalists; the highly accurate predictions of 1972 and 1968 are overlooked. Similarly, the precision of Gallup's forecast in the British General Election of 1945, a forecast which confuted the expectations of almost every political observer of note, is rarely mentioned; the falsification of the pollsters' predictions in 1970 has been the subject of repeated and, it seems, delighted comment. Many commentators have expressed concern at the apparent facility with which the parties have adopted these new techniques; in retrospect, what is surprising is that it took politicians so long to recognize the potential utility of survey research. An opinion poll may provide only an estimate of public opinion and the measurement of that opinion is subject to a number of hazards; but the hazards which beset other, more informal measures of opinion are usually much greater.

1

Marginal Seat,[2] *How People Vote*,[3] and *Constituency Politics*[4] have helped to develop, along with the work of commercial polling organizations, the study of voting behaviour on a systematic basis; more recently, Butler and Stokes, *Political Change in Britain*,[5] using the panel technique and a national sample, have greatly enriched our knowledge of electoral motivation; and studies such as Trenaman and McQuail, *Television and the Political Image*,[6] and Blumler and McQuail, *Television in Politics*,[7] have clarified our understanding of the political influence of the mass media.

In the United States, quantitative methods have also been applied extensively to the study of behaviour in Congress and the State legislatures.[8] Duncan MacRae has applied similar techniques to the assemblies of the French Fourth Republic.[9] Not surprisingly, the looser discipline and more fluid structure of the American and some of the French parties have enabled scholars to use the published records of votes cast on the floor of the Chamber by Congressmen and Deputies. Historians have employed the same techniques to the study of pre-twentieth-century parliaments in Britain.[10]

The richness of the data available from some sources (such as the roll-call votes of the American Congress) has enabled sophisticated statistical treatment to be applied, and has provided precise answers to questions that had hitherto been answered impressionistically, if at all. Thus it has been possible to distinguish blocs of Senators and Representatives who vote alike on most issues;[11] to relate voting and party loyalty to the nature of the Congressman's constituency—its ethnic composition, its occupational make-up, and its degree of urbanization; and to identify groups supporting different kinds of policies—such as supporters and opponents of social welfare measures, internationalists, and isolationalists.[12]

Not surprisingly, the rigid party voting which grew up in this country in the late nineteenth century discouraged the employment of similar methods in Britain. The division lists, as has been said hundreds of times before, reproduce the details of a ritual satisfying to the Whips but usually offer nothing of interest to the inquirer except that Labour Members have voted with the ayes and the Conservatives with the noes or vice versa. "Yet day after day and night after night, we MPs go through the ancient rituals of party warfare. . . . . at an abnormally late hour, we form up in two well-ordered processions, bow our way through the lobbies of our ancient temple, and depart."[13] The strict discipline which has been observed in the division lobbies, and the absence of any provision for recording deliberate abstentions as distinct from

---

[2] R. S. Milne and H. C. Mackenzie, *Marginal Seat*, London, 1958.

[3] M. Benney, A. H. Gray, and R. Pear, *How People Vote*, London, 1956.

[4] F. W. Bealey, J. P. Blondel, and W. McCann, *Constituency Politics*, London, 1965.

[5] D. Butler and D. Stokes, *Political Change in Britain*, London, 1969.

[6] J. Trenaman and D. McQuail, *Television and the Political Image*, London, 1961.

[7] J. Blumler and D. McQuail, *Television in Politics*, London, 1968.

[8] See, for instance, Julius Turner, *Party and Constituency*, Baltimore, 1951; D. MacRae, Jr., *Dimensions of Congressional Voting*, Los Angeles, 1958; D. Mayhew, *Party Loyalty Amongst Congressmen*, Cambridge, Mass., 1966.

[9] D. MacRae, Jr., *Parliament, Parties and Society in France, 1946–1958*, London and New York, 1967.

[10] See, for example, W. O. Aydelotte, Voting patterns in the British House of Commons in the 1840's. *Comparative Studies in Society and History*, vol. V, 1962–3.

[11] For example, D. Truman, *The Congressional Party*, New York, 1959.

[12] See, for example, MacRae, Jr., *op. cit.*, and L. Rieselbach, The demography of the Congressional vote on foreign aid, 1939–58, in *American Political Science Review*, 1964.

[13] C. P. Mayhew, *Party Games*, London, 1969, p. 110.

involuntary absences, has made it difficult to apply the same techniques to the behaviour of British MPs.[14]

Yet no observer of British politics doubts, or can doubt, that the parliamentary parties are often divided, and sometimes bitterly divided, amongst themselves. In the Labour Party these cleavages have usually, though not invariably, been related to a dispute between a dissident Left, and a normally dominant Right. In the Conservative Party the divisions are more elusive, more subtle, less well publicized, and less frequently invested with the same acrimony —but they are certainly there.

In assessing the strength of different opinion blocs, or their relationship to the social structure of the parties, commentators have had, perforce, to rely on impressions derived from newspaper reports, on personal conversations with MPs, and on leaks from meetings of the parliamentary parties. In 1961 an attempt was made in *Backbench Opinion in the House of Commons, 1955–59*[15] to surmount the difficulties posed by the reticence of the parliamentary division lists. To do this, resort was had to a hitherto untapped source—backbench motions, known officially as Early Day Motions (EDMs). These motions are resolutions, tabled by backbenchers who usually solicit signatures from their parliamentary colleagues. Wilfred Fienburgh's description of the EDMs and their purpose can hardly be bettered. "The placing of motions on the Order Paper is a recognized parliamentary gambit. Unless a motion is sponsored by the government or official Opposition it is not expected to be discussed. It is a device whereby Members advertise their views, and no one, neither Whips nor Front Bench, can prevent a Member from using this channel."[16]

There were, and still are, no formal restrictions on the tabling of EDMs in the Conservative Party but Labour Members are obliged to consult the Whips before tabling a motion. The obligation to consult, however, does not carry with it an obligation to accept the Whips' advice. The EDMs remain—for both parties—one of the least controlled mechanisms for expressing opinions.

Some motions are trivial and attract few signatures; others are simply means for airing the personal crotchets of individual MPs. Some, however, deal, either implicitly or directly, with important issues of public policy, and draw considerable support. In the fifties the number of EDMs tabled in a session often rose to a hundred or more; in a parliament of normal length there might well have been from 400 to 500, and some of these would have raised questions of great political significance. If anything, the number tabled has grown in recent years; in the Session of 1968/9, no fewer than 443 were put down.[17]

The aim of the earlier study was to identify, from these motions, where Members, within each of the two parliamentary parties, stood on the issues of the day, and to discover whether, and to what extent, distinctive political opinions were related to such characteristics as occupation, education, and age. How did the large public school contingent within the Conservative

---

[14] The division lists of the 1966 Parliament offer more scope for the use of quantitative techniques than those of earlier years as party discipline in this Parliament appears to have been noticeably looser, especially on the Labour side, than in the earlier post-war period. Moreover, several issues of great substance were the subject of free votes. For the latter, see P. G. Richards, *Parliament and Conscience*, London, 1970.

[15] S. E. Finer, H. B. Berrington, and D. J. Bartholomew, *Backbench Opinion in the House of Commons, 1955–59*, London, 1961.

[16] W. Fienburgh, *New Statesman and Nation* (*NS & N*), 26 Feb. 1955.

[17] Mark Franklin, *Voice of the Backbench: Patterns of Behaviour in the British House of Commons* (Ann Arbor University Microfilms), Cornell University Ph.D., contains a valuable account of the significance of EDMs.

Party react to questions of foreign and economic policy or penal reform? How far was it correct to view the conflict between Left and Right in the Parliamentary Labour Party as one between university-educated intellectuals and manual-worker trade unionists?

The pattern and purpose of this book closely follows that of the earlier study. Expressions of backbench opinion, which occurred in the three parliaments sitting between August 1945 and April 1955, and which lend themselves to aggregate analysis, have been examined; those which seemed to be of political significance constitute the raw material for this study. These backbench manifestations include EDMs, amendments to the Address, floor revolts, an open letter, and free votes. The EDMs supply by far the largest source of data; but in these three parliaments there were considerably more floor revolts than in the 1955–9 House, and this has permitted the analysis of divisions and of abstentions, alongside EDMs and other lists of signatories, both for their intrinsic interest and where appropriate as a way of confirming findings drawn from backbench motions.

The primary aims of this study are to examine the relationship between the social backgrounds of Members within each party and any distinctive political attitudes they may have had; and, secondly, to investigate the relationship between different "opinion blocs".

It must be emphasized that this is not primarily a study of the attitudes of individuals or parliamentary opinion leaders; the evolution of opinion on foreign policy, at the level of individual spokesmen in the parliamentary parties, has been treated at length, with great skill, by both Rose and Epstein.[18] The present study deals essentially with the attitudes of *aggregates* rather than with those of particular spokesmen, though naturally the opinions of the latter are often cited for purposes of illustration.

This kind of study has certain implications. The composition of the parliamentary parties affects the nature of the decisions made, either directly, on the rare occasions when free votes are taken, or indirectly, through the weight and character of the forces, within the backbench parties, to which the party leaders are exposed. Opinion on the death penalty, for example, seems within each party to have been closely related to Members' level of education. Labour MPs were far more hostile than Conservatives to capital punishment; but within each party graduates were more likely than non-graduates to favour abolition. On the Labour side there is a strong tendency for the proportion of graduates to increase; this development, quite apart from simple changes of individual opinion (undoubtedly important in the period 1948–55) must tend to strengthen abolitionist sentiment within the party. Many commentators have seen, in the decline of trade union strength within the PLP, an illustration of the more indirect way in which changes in the social composition of the parliamentary parties can affect the outlook of the parties, and can, in the absence of countervailing forces, influence the character of governmental decisions.

Studies of this kind enable us in addition to test what may be called "implicit hypotheses" about the structure of the parties and the relationship between their structure and political attitudes. For many years it was axiomatic that Labour's left-wing ideologues could be identified with the upper middle-class intellectual section of the party; more recently, the Labour Party's failure to carry through wholeheartedly socialist policies whilst in office has been attributed in part to its gradual embourgeoisement. In much the same way, the strength of Conservative opposition to penal reform has often been ascribed, especially by left-wing critics, to the authoritarian character of public-school education. Analysis of aggregate data enables us to see

[18] R. Rose, The relation of socialist principles to foreign policy, Unpublished D.Phil. thesis, Oxford, 1958, and L. Epstein, *Britain—Uneasy Ally*, Chicago, 1954.

what truth, if any, there is in these hypotheses, and to examine the relationship between changes in the social composition of the parties and the distribution of opinion within them.

Moreover, this sort of inquiry may broaden our understanding of the manner and help us to appraise the extent to which Parliament functions in a *representative* way. Though it would be an exaggeration to say that our MPs are self-selected, such a statement contains an element of truth. It is an irony that representatives in a democracy are likely, in many respects, to be grossly unrepresentative of those who elect them. It is well known that the Conservative Party in Parliament is drawn from an extraordinarily narrow social stratum; but the Labour Party —if not equally exclusive in its social composition—has for many years been blatantly untypical of its rank-and-file electors. Furthermore, MPs are, apart from the wide occupational and educational gap between them and their voters, likely to be unrepresentative of their electors in a more fundamental, broadly psychological, sense. Political life demands special skills and special interests which, by definition, are unlikely to be found amongst ordinary people; and the kind of men and women who stand as Labour candidates though, in strictly occupational or educational terms, somewhat closer to the broad mass of the electorate than the Conservatives, may, psychologically speaking, be even more distant from them.

The issue of penal reform once again provides a convenient example; although almost every opinion poll stubbornly discloses a large majority of voters in favour of the death penalty, the Parliamentary Labour Party is overwhelmingly hostile. Studies of Parliament and other representative bodies which focus largely on the more conspicuous characteristics like occupation and education have usually ignored the question of the psychological representativeness of legislatures and local councils. Left-wing critics have, perhaps rightly, emphasized the narrow range of classes and interests from which Conservative candidates are recruited, but it is perhaps also true that important sections of the PLP are drawn from an equally narrow and, in some sense, even less representative constituency. We may agree with Donald Matthews that it is misleading to assume that "a group must literally be represented among the political decision makers to have influence or political power", yet it remains true that the exaggerated representation of some groups, and the virtual absence of others, must be reflected in the nature of the decisions taken. The House of Commons is not only an assembly of representatives from the nation at large; often it more closely resembles a congress of ambassadors from certain special and highly politicized groups. It may function well, by virtue of its composition, as a body which represents certain specific constituencies, e.g. middle-class left-wing intellectuals or Old Etonians; to the extent that it does, it may function badly as a legislature representative of the country. To say this is not to deny that what Bagehot called the teaching duties of Parliament are as important as its representative function.

Studies of backbench opinion have implications, too, for the cohesion of the parliamentary parties. Lipset[19] has argued that a society's unity will be enhanced if various lines of cleavage such as class, religion, language, and moral values cut across each other, and that conversely, divisions will become more bitter and harder to resolve if these differences accumulate and reinforce each other. In the earlier book it was shown that in the PLP occupation, education and sponsorship reinforced each other so as to produce three separate cultures, each associated with a distinctive pattern of political opinions. It is hardly surprising that the unity of the Labour Party should have been so precarious nor that Labour should have contrasted so sharply with the Conservatives where the lines of cleavage—both social and attitudinal—tended to be

[19] S. Lipset, *Political Man*, London, 1960.

dispersed rather than cumulative. Furthermore, the Labour Party was distinguished by families of attitudes; not only social characteristics but political opinions tended to reinforce each other; left-wing opinions on defence tended to go hand in hand with left-wing views on the ownership of industry. The Labour Party's occupational structure, and the values and opinions linked with each occupational or educational group, made it as much an alliance of separate parties as a single entity.

British parties, moreover, are curious accretions of distinct and, sometimes, inimical historical traditions. Labour has inherited part of the strain of nineteenth-century radical individualism once associated with the left-wing of the Liberal Party; it has had somehow to combine this tradition with that of twentieth-century managerial collectivism, whose historic source is to be found in the Fabian Society; it has had to marry a Marxist or quasi-Marxist dialectic with the prophetic scriptures of the early Independent Labour Party. The Conservative Party presents a more subtle texture, woven however from scarcely less diverse threads such as Tory paternalism, whiggism, and, again, radical individualism. The analysis of backbench attitudes may help us to see how far these separate strands can be discerned today, and in what form, and through what groups, they continue to be represented.

Lastly, the findings of such studies may be significant both for comparison with general political, or more narrowly legislative, recruitment in other countries and for changes in British parliamentary recruitment over time. The resemblance between Labour's "miscellaneous occupations" and Kornhauser's "freelance intellectuals" is striking; it would certainly be enlightening to know to what extent Labour's left-wing rebels were drawn from the same social groups as the Liberal dissidents of the late nineteenth and early twentieth centuries. To what extent is Britain's "permanent opposition" drawn from the same social groups?

The great stumbling-block to the acceptance of the EDM as a valid source of information about MPs' opinions seems to lie in the apparently fortuitous way in which some of the signatures are obtained. The fortuitous element consists partly in the *motives* of the signatories (or non-signers), partly in the *circumstances* in which names are collected, and sometimes in both. An EDM, we are told, may be signed or not signed for motives which have little to do with its merits. One Member might sign an EDM to oblige a colleague, and another might refuse to sign out of dislike of one of the sponsors. There are Members who are willing to sanctify almost any cause with their signatures, and others who are reluctant to sign any motion of any kind. Some may sign, without appreciating the full significance of an EDM, and be prepared to retract their support when the arguments against the proposal are set out more fully. So, the late Sir Edward Fellowes, citing a report in *The Times* that only 26 Labour MPs were prepared at a meeting of the PLP to vote for a motion which had gained no less than 54 signatures, expressed disquiet at the use of motions "as a basis of calculation" when Members "after hearing the arguments were apparently unwilling even to hold up their hands".[20,21]

[20] *Parliamentary Affairs*, vol. 15, p. 244, 1962.

[21] Sir Edward overlooked two possibilities. First, the Member's initial action in associating himself with some protest or demand may be a more accurate indicator of his real preferences than withdrawal under pressure from the leadership or as a response to the appeal of party loyalty. Secondly, some or all of the 28 Members who signed the motion but did not vote for it at the party meeting may have been absent. Meetings of the Parliamentary Labour Party are often badly attended. It is also significant that a Member should have joined in a protest even if he later recanted. If in a group of 100 people 50 sign a protest and 25 of them later withdraw, these 25 are still distinguished, in one important respect, from the 50 who never signed at all.

Fortuitous circumstances may also affect the collection of signatures. Some Members will be absent from the House when names are being enrolled; some motions, blessed with fervent and thrustful sponsors, may obtain more signatures than others, intrinsically more popular, tabled by less eager Members.

A combination of circumstance and motive can also affect the subscription of signatures. An enthusiastic signer, away from the House for illness or some other reason, would take steps to find out what motions had been tabled during his absence and to sign those deemed appropriate, whilst a less diligent colleague would simply let such occasions pass.

Considerations of this kind doubtless explain why critics of the earlier study found it hard to acquiesce in the thesis propounded. As one prominent politician put it: ". . . the reasons why Members add their names to motions are many and mysterious and [that] it would be unwise to assume that you can estimate the intensity of MPs' convictions by adding up the number of motions they sign."[22]

Unfortunately, such critics were unable to distinguish between an assessment of the predominant attitudes of a particular *category* of Members and the appraisal of attitudes of particular *individuals*. Social science, by its very nature, is not primarily concerned with individuals but with classes, groups, and categories. The problem of individual motivation is common to the whole field of social science. An opinion survey, for example, may disclose the by now familiar relationship between social class and voting choice. Working-class people will (in normal times) divide preponderantly for Labour, and middle-class voters heavily for the Conservatives. From such a finding we infer that there is some connection between social class and party affiliation. In fact the motives of particular electors may vary widely. A few voters may be impressed by the qualities of the local candidate; some may be reacting to a local incident like the closure of a works, or to a personal event such as the loss of a job. Some individuals may even lie to the interviewer out of fear or a desire to please, a wish to appear to be going with the dominant trend of opinion, or simple cussedness.

This diversity of motives does not in itself invalidate the inferences that are drawn from opinion surveys about the relationship between class and party support. Every pollster is aware that *systematic* distortions can arise, obscuring the true relationship between social characteristics and voting behaviour, and in a well-conducted poll care is taken to eliminate or minimize these factors. Certain types of voters such as the less well educated may misunderstand the meaning of a question or tend to answer "yes" regardless of the question's content. Similarly, pollsters are aware of the problem of those sample members who cannot be interviewed—who are on shift work or are often away from home or of those who simply refuse to co-operate with the interviewer. Difficulties will arise if these voters are distributed disproportionately amongst different social or political groupings: in other words, if there is some *systematic* distortion at work. In the same way, if lying to interviewers were predominantly concentrated amongst, say, middle-class women, the inferences that are drawn about the connection between class and party choice, and sex and party choice, might be fallacious. Nevertheless, if interview responses of this kind, or "fortuitous" motives for choosing a certain party are randomly distributed amongst the voters, no difficulty arises. The fact that Mr. Brown or Mrs. Green tells lies to the pollster is irrelevant to the pollster's purpose.

Similar problems were faced by the authors of the earlier study. Like the opinion pollsters, they were primarily concerned with the behaviour of categories rather than of individuals. A

---

[22] R. H. S. Crossman, *The Guardian*, 15 Dec. 1961. Franklin (*op. cit.*) found there was no tendency for "high signers" to give their signatures indiscriminately.

Labour MP has a number of observable characteristics; he may have been educated at a public school, gone to an ancient university, become a professional man, and entered Parliament as a constituency party sponsored candidate in the election of 1945. The authors were essentially interested in such an MP as a member of a series of categories, not as an individual—though as will become clear later in this chapter, EDMs are perhaps a better guide, at least in the Labour Party, to the political opinions of individual Members than the authors themselves suspected at the time. If such a Member as has been described signs motions, with which he does not agree, for frivolous reasons, or abstains from signing from those with which he does agree, for equally frivolous reasons, *his behaviour does not in itself affect the validity of conclusions which may be made about the categories to which he belongs.* If those Labour MPs who were educated at public schools or were sponsored by constituency parties or belonged to the 1945 intake behaved like this to a grossly disproportionate extent, then the conclusions would, of course, be seriously affected. The critics produced no evidence to show that this had occurred. In the earlier study the authors assumed that the "fortuitous" signers and the "fortuitous" non-signers were randomly distributed throughout the different social categories that were employed. Only one characteristic—age—seemed to be affected by disproportionate non-signing; the oldest Members—the over-sixties—seemed to sign less frequently than others, and it is possible, therefore, that some of the findings about the behaviour of specific age groups may have been less securely grounded than others; though, as will be discussed later, even this proviso refers only to the quantitative tables—those based on the *number* as distinct from the *type* of motions signed.

We can never be entirely sure that a particular motion was not affected by a disproportionate concentration of fortuitous signing or fortuitous abstention from signing amongst some social categories; but the importance of this diminishes as the number of motions included in any particular attitude scale increases. The risk of some kind of *systematic* bias can never be entirely discounted; but sceptics have an obligation to explain in detail why a particular attitude scale is faulty, not to reject all of the findings in a general and arbitrary way.

Examples have, indeed, been found where there are grounds for suspecting that there *has* been some systematic distortion in the collection and subscription of signatures. In the 1950–1 Parliament the reactions of Conservatives to 21 distinct issues (not all of them politically important) were examined. In 14 of these 21 an association was found between year of entry into Parliament and signature of the appropriate motions; and in all but one of the 14, the new intake of Members elected in 1950 signed most frequently. It may well be that the Members of this new, distinctive, and talented generation signed more enthusiastically, *regardless of the topic*, than the older Members. There remains the possibility that the association is real, that Members of the 1950 intake *were* more concerned about the various matters expressed through EDMs than their colleagues. Given the uncertainty, however, little emphasis has been placed on the analysis, by year of entry, of the quantitative scales for the Conservatives in the 1950–1 Parliament. Apart from the 1950–1 Parliament, distortions of this sort do not seem to have been important. Where it has been possible to construct qualitative scales—scales based on the *kind* and not on the *number* of motions studied—the problem does not arise; for granted some types of Members may sign motions more often than others, we still have to ask why they signed one *kind* rather than another.

In the same Parliament, the sponsorship of motions seems to have provided another example of a systematic distortion in the collection of names. In late 1950, Michael Foot and others tabled an EDM urging high-level negotiations with Russia; a few days later another EDM, expressing the same demand, was put down by Ellis Smith. The type of Members signing the two motions diverged considerably; the Foot EDM appealed disproportionately to the Professionals and the Miscellaneous Occupations, the Ellis Smith motion to the Workers.[23] This same topic furnished a similar instance of the effects of sponsorship in the next Parliament. The Bevanite EDMs on the subject were signed preponderantly by one kind of Member; those with a mixed sponsorship by another sort. Clearly a very important systematic bias arose in these cases. We cannot completely overlook the possibility that this occurred on other issues, but the fact that alternative EDMs were not tabled, as they were on negotiations with Russia, suggests that no substantial and distinctive group of Members, anxious to voice some protest or express some demand, were deterred from doing so by the names of the sponsors. The question of a more subtle systematic bias arising from the influence of formal and informal reference groups in the House is discussed later.

The critics seemed unaware that something needed to be explained; associations were repeatedly found, often at a high level of statistical significance, between social characteristics such as occupation or education, and political attitudes[24] such as pacificism, or anti-colonialism, or opinions on penal reform. Such associations were unlikely to have occurred by chance; and the odds against their occurring by chance could be precisely calculated. If EDMs were predominantly signed for "fortuitous" reasons—for motives of personal friendship, for the desire to repay old favours, for an inability to say "no" to any request—it is unlikely that particular occupational groups would subscribe more heavily than others to EDMs, and even more implausible that one occupational group would subscribe generously to motions on, say, defence, and that another group would give disproportionate support to motions on social welfare. In the Labour Party, Members drawn from the Miscellaneous Occupations group took a distinctly more pacificistic stand than Workers, or Members from the established professions. Workers, on the other hand, subscribed more liberally to social welfare motions. Amongst Conservatives, public-school MPs—contrary to popular legend—were less likely to sign motions calling for the restoration of judicial corporal punishment. From this evidence the authors inferred that the Miscellaneous Occupations were more pacificistic than their fellows; that Workers were more interested in domestic bread-and-butter questions than were other Labour Members; and that non-public-school Conservatives favoured a more severe policy towards some kinds of delinquents than did their public-school-educated colleagues. Possibly some more recondite explanation of these statistical associations might have been advanced; perhaps Etonians did not sign the motions in favour of the restoration of corporal punishment because they were absent in large numbers when these motions were tabled; perhaps they were all at Ascot or attending the Fourth of June celebrations; perhaps disproportionate numbers of Trades Unionists were attending miners' galas when the pacificistic EDMs were put down; but none of the sceptics chose to offer specific explanations of this sort.

In the field of both the social and natural sciences, there are situations in which certain phenomena can be explained by reference to more than one possible cause, and in which the available knowledge does not permit a conclusive and definitive explanation. In such a situation,

---

[23] See Chapter 5 for a discussion of these EDMs.

[24] Social psychologists often use the term "attitude" in a highly specific way; in this, as in the previous study, it has been used in a much looser sense to indicate belief in the sentiments expressed in a particular EDM or group of EDMs. The problem arises as to whether the same EDM may not attract signatures subscribed by people wishing to voice different attitudes. This involves the problem of scaling which is discussed in some detail in Annex 1.

until further knowledge becomes available, the student has to choose the most plausible hypothesis. To the authors of *Backbench Opinion* it seemed more plausible to ascribe the associations between a particular social characteristic and the signature of distinctive EDMs to a real association between social characteristic and attitude, than to any other cause.

The critics seemed to be implying that *fortuitous* signature and non-signature of EDMs could lead to a *systematic* distortion in the results. Such an implication needs only to be stated for its absurdity to be recognized.

The problem can be illustrated by a simple example. Let us suppose that the reader were to take his holiday at a British seaside resort during the summer season; he might observe that there seemed to be a quite disproportionate number of cars with Manchester registration markings, but few bearing Sheffield numbers. Suppose, then, that he tried to carry out a more systematic inquiry: he might discover, after eliminating all those cars with local registration numbers, that half of the cars in the town's car parks at a specific time of day had Manchester numbers, whilst only 1 in 10 came from Sheffield. He might then go on to infer that this seaside resort was a popular holiday place for people living in the Manchester area but had little appeal to those in Sheffield.

The sort of criticism, however, that has been directed against the use of EDMs and similar sources might be made against this conclusion. The reasons why cars bear particular registration numbers are indeed "many and mysterious". That a particular car has a Manchester registration number, it might be argued, is no guarantee that this car actually belongs to someone now living in Manchester. The owner might himself live in Norwich and have bought the car secondhand; he might previously have lived in Manchester and later moved to Norwich; he might have borrowed the car from a man living in Manchester; or he might even, on payment of a fee, have obtained a special registration number. No doubt some of the cars with Manchester numbers would belong to people of this sort. It would, however, be most implausible to believe that |it was only cars with the Manchester numbers which were affected in this way. Are no Sheffield cars bought secondhand? Do the inhabitants of Sheffield never lend their cars to friends? Do they never move to different parts of the country? It would indeed be strange if none of the Sheffield cars belonged to drivers elsewhere. The reader might also notice that although Manchester is bigger than Sheffield, the disparity between the number of Manchester and Sheffield cars is out of all relation to the difference in population.

He would, therefore, be on good ground in rejecting the view that his figures could be explained by fortuitous occurrences of the sort mentioned. Most people would accept the common-sense interpretation that his statistics could best be explained by the conclusion that people from the Manchester area were more likely than the people of Sheffield and its neighbourhood to spend their holidays at this resort.

Having disposed then of the fallacy that systematic differences might be attributed to the idiosyncratic behaviour of individual car owners, he would have to meet the argument that the kind of systematic difference which he established could be explained in other and perhaps more plausible ways. It might be that people from Sheffield coming to this resort were more likely to travel by train than those coming from Manchester. On the face of it this is a rather unlikely explanation, but the reader could assess its plausibility by seeing whether the statistics of car ownership in the two towns were sufficient to explain the difference in his figures. Another critic might argue that the reader's figures could be explained because of some contrast in the holiday habits of the visitors from Sheffield and those from Manchester. Perhaps people om Manchester are more likely to go shopping or promenading at a particular time, and this might account for the disproportionate number of Manchester cars in the town's car parks. This seems a rather far-fetched explanation, but the reader could check its validity by asking his critic for evidence to support this alternative and less plausible explanation, and if need be he could carry out his counts at different times. A much more plausible explanation could lie in local differences in holiday times. Perhaps Manchester people take their holidays early in the season and workers in Sheffield later. Again, the force of this argument could be assessed by making the count at different weeks during the summer.

The problems raised by the use of EDM data do not differ in principle from those in the example just cited. A particular MP may sign a motion with which he does not agree, or fail to sign one of which he does approve, for fortuitous reasons, just as a particular car can bear a Manchester registration number without its owner necessarily living in the Manchester area. In this study it has usually been inferred that where members of a particular social category sign a motion in disproportionate numbers, this is because the motion is especially attractive to that category. Alternative explanations of this systematic difference may be advanced; but we have to ask whether they are more or less reasonable in the particular instance than the assumption generally made in this study.

If the likelihood of an association occurring by chance is rejected (and this probability can be measured), only three explanations of the association can be tenable. Either, as the authors proposed, the association between social characteristic and political attitude is real; or there has been some error in the construction of the scales; or, alternatively, some *systematic* bias has occurred in the process of collecting signatures. Perhaps Members of a particular type habitually signed more often than their colleagues; perhaps Members of a particular type objected to the sponsors of a certain EDM; or perhaps Members absent from the House when the motions were tabled were drawn disproportionately from specific groups. There may, indeed, have been situations in which one, or more, of these conditions applied; but in choosing the more complex rather than the simpler explanation the onus is on the critics to answer why.

Nor, indeed, were the critics apparently impressed (and gave no sign of being aware) that, where possible, the study attempted to verify the validity of findings based on EDMs by reference, where available, to divisions on similar issues. Thus the behaviour of Labour MPs in the free vote on the Street Offences Bill of 1959, a Bill which raised issues of a libertarian character, corresponded closely with the behaviour of Members as revealed by the civil liberties scale. As Bartholomew and Bassett have put it: "In spite of the many and mysterious reasons for signing (or not signing) the underlying relationship can still be discerned through the web of random distortions".[25]

Similarly, the sort of Conservatives who voted for the re-introduction of birching were the same as those (the relatively small number) who signed EDMs calling for the restoration of judicial corporal punishment; the sort of Conservatives who signed EDMs calling for the abolition of the death penalty were the same as those who voted for its abolition in 1956. Even the Conservative social policy scale (a scale to which less importance and certainty were attached than to any other in the book) corresponded with the behaviour of Conservative Members in the Office Charter Bill of 1959. All this evidence, drawn from the division lists, on free votes, corroborated the findings of the EDMs.

[25] D. J. Bartholomew and E. E. Bassett, *Let's Look at the Figures: The Quantitative Approach to Human Affairs*, London, 1971, p. 34.

DEFENCE AND FOREIGN POLICY EDMs, 1955–9

The most trenchant vindication of the EDM as a source-material, at least for the Labour Party, is afforded by a comparison of the attitudes of Labour MPs as revealed by EDMs relating to defence and foreign policy with their behaviour in the numerous floor revolts on these issues.

Between 1951 and 1955 and from 1960 to 1961 the Labour Party experienced no fewer than eight major floor revolts—all of them in the field of defence and foreign affairs.[26] The EDMs in the 1955–9 Parliament which were most closely related to the substance of these floor revolts were those on pacificism and foreign policy; these were also the most ideologically charged areas of controversy.

Members were first divided, on the basis of their behaviour in the floor revolts, into two broad categories—Rebels and Non-Rebels. To classify for inclusion in the Rebel category a Member had simply to vote against (or where appropriate to abstain in a vote on) the leadership's policy on at least one of the eight occasions. The Rebels were next classified according to their frequency of rebellion and then according to their consistency. Members who were backbenchers during the whole period from November 1951 to March 1961 and who rebelled at least once between 1951 and 1955 but not in 1960–1, or vice versa, have been called Non-consistent Rebels. Thus someone like Mr. Donnelly, who took part in the March 1952 Bevanite revolt but not in any one of the four revolts after 1959, has been regarded as a Non-consistent Rebel. Members who were backbenchers throughout the years 1951 and 1961 and who rebelled at least once in each period have been called Consistent Rebels. These terms are used for the convenience of the reader and do not, of course, express any judgement on the opinions held.

Two additional complications were caused by the failure of some Members to sign any of the relevant foreign policy EDMs and by the fact that some Members did not serve on the backbenches throughout the whole period. Members were, therefore, also classified according to whether or not they were committed, according to the EDMs, on foreign policy. Seventy-six of our 227 Members did not sign any of the relevant foreign policy motions, and their views have, therefore, been gauged on the issue of pacificism alone. Members have also been divided according to their length of backbench service. Some were there for the whole of the November 1951 to March 1961 period, some retired in 1959, and some were not elected until after 1951.

Table 1, which shows the relationship between participation in floor revolts and signature of the relevant defence and foreign policy EDMs, has been designed so that the groups which according to the EDMs were predominantly Left (i.e. Left on at least one issue and Centre or Left on the other) appear on the left of the table, whilst those groups which were predominantly Right (i.e. Right on at least one and Centre or Right on the other) appear, appropriately enough, on the right of the table.

It is at once apparent that a Left position on the basis of the EDMs is closely related to Members' participation in floor revolts. In Table 1, 25 of the 29 classed as Left on the EDMs had taken part in 3 or more revolts. In contrast, only 4 of the 56 classed as Right took part in 3 or more revolts, whilst 39 participated in none at all. Even more marked is the relationship between a Member's placing on the EDMs and the consistency of rebellion. Twenty-five of the 29 Rebels on the Left were consistent, i.e., they took part in at least one of both

---

[26] Details of these rebellions can be found in Annex 1.

TABLE 1. PACIFICISM (P), FOREIGN POLICY (FP), and FLOOR REVOLTS IN THE LABOUR PARTY

Members Continuously on Backbenches, November 1951 to March 1961

No. of rebellions	Left on both scales	Left P Centre FP	Left FP Centre P	Total Left	Centre on both scales	Left P Right FP	Right P Left FP	Centre P Right FP	Centre FP Right P	Right on both scales P	Total Right	Total
6–8	9	—	2	11	—	—	—	—	—	—	—	11
3–5	8	2	4	14	2	1	—	3	—	1	4	21
1–2	2	1	1	4	4	—	—	3	3	7	13	21
Nil	—	—	—	—	2	—	—	2	10	27	39	41
Total	19	3	7	29	8	1	—	8	13	35	56	94

Data grouped. Total Left against total Right. 1 and 2, 3–5 and 6–8 combined. $\chi_1^2 = 37 \cdot 319$. Significant at $0 \cdot 1\%$.

	Left on both scales	Left P Centre FP	Left FP Centre P	Total Left	Centre on both scales	Left P Right FP	Right P Left FP	Centre P Right FP	Centre FP Right P	Right on both scales P	Total Right	Total
Consistent Rebels	17	2	6	25	2	1	—	1	—	—	1	29
Non-consistent Rebels	2	1	1	4	4	—	—	5	3	8	16	24

Consistent against Non-consistent. $\chi_1^2 = 28 \cdot 138$. Significant at $0 \cdot 1\%$.

series of floor revolts—those happening in the 1951–5 Parliament and those taking place between 1959 and 1961. On the other hand, only 1 of the 17 Rebels on the Right was consistent.

A similar conclusion emerges from a scrutiny of those uncommitted on foreign policy. Three of the 4 Left Pacificists were Rebels as against 6 of the 14 Centre Pacificists and only 9 of the 25 Right Pacificists.

An examination of those Members who were on the backbenches for only part of the period corroborates the striking correspondence between rebellion in the House and signature of EDMs, provided by Table 1. Members who sat throughout the 1951–5 Parliament but who were defeated or retired in 1959, could have taken part in a maximum of four floor revolts. Only one of the EDM left-wingers, amongst those committed on foreign policy, obeyed the Party Whip throughout, as against 11 of the 17 right-wingers.

Like those who sat from 1951 to 1959, Members who were elected in 1955 and sat through until March 1961 could have taken part in four of the selected floor revolts at most. Amongst those committed on foreign policy, 8 of the 15 EDM left-wingers rebelled on two occasions or more, as against none of the 15 right-wingers.

The correspondence between overt rebellion and the EDM data is not absolute. Crude tables such as these cannot fully capture the subtleties of parliamentary attitude and behaviour. The data covers more than 9 years, and in that time some Members certainly modified their beliefs. Thus Desmond Donnelly, who took part in three floor revolts between 1951 and 1954, broke with the Bevanites in the latter year and moved sharply towards the Right.[27]

[27] Mr. Donnelly was expelled from the Labour Party in 1968 and joined the Conservatives in 1971.

Others, like Harold Lever who had voted with the Bevanites against the scale of British re-armament in 1952, were, except on the issue of rearming Germany, general supporters of the leadership in the later struggles. Arthur Irvine, another ally of Bevan in 1952, later moved away from the Left.[28] Then there were those who, like John McGovern, might retain some lingering traces of a pacifist past, but whose attitude to the Soviet Union was far more hostile than that of most of the Left. Moreover, some normally loyal Members of the Centre and Right might disobey the Whip on a single floor revolt because of a particular aspect of the issue under debate. More than a dozen Members, never otherwise linked with the Left, supported Frank Beswick's clause which sought to prohibit the manufacture of thermonuclear bombs without the prior approval of Parliament.[29] Some, if not all of them, supported the clause, not because of a special antipathy to the British manufacture of nuclear weapons but because of a belief that Parliament should first be consulted. Again, the abstention of the 72, over the party's nuclear defence policy in December 1960, attracted, in addition to the unilateralists, some normally loyal MPs who did not want to defy annual conference.[30] Then there were those Members, not generally seen in the company of the Left, whose horror at the destructive capacity of nuclear weapons brought them into conflict with the Front Bench. In addition there were others, prepared to sign EDMs critical of official policy and prepared to vote for left-wing motions at the Parliamentary Party's meetings, who were not willing to flout the party's instructions on the floor of the House. Finally, of course, there were those who were unable to participate in a specific floor revolt because of absence.

What is so striking, given these potentialities for divergence between the behaviour of Labour MPs in floor revolts and the opinions expressed through signature of EDMs, is the extraordinary similarity between the two measures. The significance of this correspondence can hardly be exaggerated. Nearly all the Members scored as left wing on the basis of the relevant EDMs participated in some rebellions; most of those assessed as right wing maintained perfect discipline. Especially noteworthy is the behaviour of the Consistent Rebels. Most of them subscribed to left-wing EDMs. Those rebels who, on the EDM data, belonged to the Centre and Right, were overwhelmingly Non-consistent.

EDMs AND DIVISIONS, 1945–55

There is, moreover, ample evidence from the EDMs of the Parliaments of 1945–55 to confirm the value of backbench motions as a source-material. In the Labour Party, findings from EDMs on foreign affairs, capital punishment, conscription, and hunting have been set against the results of floor revolts, free votes, and abstentions. In the Conservative Party it has been possible to compare the results obtained from EDMs on corporal punishment and MPs' salaries, with free votes on these subjects. In every case there has been a close correspondence between the verdict of the EDMs and that of the division lists. Members who signed left-wing EDMs on foreign affairs were much more likely to abstain in key foreign-policy votes than their colleagues. Members who signed EDMs expressing concern at capital punishment were more likely than their fellows to vote for abolition.

[28] See, for example, his letter to his constituency party reported in the *Daily Telegraph*, 3 Mar. 1960.
[29] HC Deb. 526, c. 1795.
[30] At the Scarborough Conference of 1960, unilateralist resolutions had been carried against the leadership's wishes.

Evidence of this kind clearly meets one objection to the use of the EDM as a source-material; but the persistent sceptic might still argue that it does not wholly remove his sense of diquiet. Accepting that there is a relationship between signing and voting, it would still be possible for a disproportionate number of Members *of a particular kind* to express an opinion through an EDM and to behave in a contrary way in the division lobbies, or for a significantly disproportionate number of Members *of a particular kind* not declaring an attitude through an EDM but doing so by abstention or an adverse vote on the floor of the House. It can, however, be confidently said that, with rare exceptions, this does not happen. Members who sign distinctive motions are more likely to express these sentiments in the division lobbies than Members who do not; and in nearly every case conclusions drawn about the attitudes of particular social groups, from the evidence of the EDMs, are consistent with inferences made about the attitudes of the same groups from abstentions, floor revolts, or free votes. Full details for each of the subject areas mentioned are given in later chapters: what can be categorically affirmed is that the signatures appended to EDMs are not meaningless jumbles of names. Nor are these lists so contaminated by names collected in a haphazard way as to be worthless for purposes of analysis. Signature of motions can, over a reasonable time span, often provide a highly accurate indication of the opinions of individual MPs; study of the opinions of social categories and the relationship between one opinion bloc and another rests on even more secure foundations.

The assumption made by the authors of the earlier study that "fortuitous" signers and non-signers were drawn randomly from the various social and ideological groups into which the parties were divided has, as far as Labour is concerned, received abundant confirmation. For the Conservatives, fewer comparisons are possible with EDM data, since there were fewer cleavages expressed in significant floor revolts and free votes. The evidence that is available, however, bears out the utility of the EDMs. Those who are impressed by the apparently casual nature of the signing of motions do not take account of the extent to which the subscription of signatures yields, in the gross, a meaningful pattern of conduct. To decry the value of the information yielded by EDMs is to prefer a prejudice to a fact.

It is also possible to trace the extent to which Members who sign one EDM in a given subject area also sign another. This can be done with a measure known as Yule's Q, which is described in detail in Annex 1. The value of Yule's Q for various combinations of motions within each subject area is given in the appropriate section of this book. It may, at this point, be noted that EDMs on world government, on equal pay, on Europe, and on education in the Labour Party yielded high or relatively high values of Q, indicating that the signatories were drawn from relatively compact groups. The anti-Soviet EDMs in the Labour Party in the 1951–5 Parliament, and the motions on social welfare and colonial brutality in the same Parliament, display much less cohesion.

ATTITUDES AND INFORMAL GROUPINGS

It seems clear, therefore, that the patterns of signing reflect something of a systematic kind; the signatures taken in the gross, mean something. The question is whether they reflect opinions, considered as purely psychological phenomena, or whether they reflect some other factor as well.

One possibility which has been canvassed[31] is that EDMs are not so much indicators of

[31] By Mark Franklin of Strathclyde University.

opinion *per se* as of the groupings of trust and respect which are to be found in the House of Commons. Thus we might expect informal friendship groups to arise as well as the more formal bodies like the Trade Union group of the PLP, whose members would be drawn to one another, partially at least, by common beliefs, and which would in turn generate, or help to reinforce, a special group attitude. It would not be surprising if such groups comprised men coming preponderantly from particular type-classes. The existence of such groups would account for the association between the opinions expressed in EDMs and social characteristics; members of such groups, drawn predominantly from the same social milieu and sharing the same position in the party spectrum, would tend to sign one another's motions.

According to this view, EDMs are indicators not of attitudes as such but of the membership of informal groups whose adherents tend to hold common attitudes. The implication is that Members outside the group holding similar attitudes would have been less likely to sign the relevant EDMs because, not being members of the group, they would have been less likely to be asked.

Clearly such an explanation could account for the associations which have been found. But informal groups, based on shared beliefs and composed mainly of men from the same type-class, are likely to be politically more significant than mere aggregates of Members who happen to share an attitude; and the effect of such an explanation is to enhance the political importance of the associations which have been found.

A view not dissimilar to that given above has been expressed by the well-known political correspondent, Alan Watkins: "Motions are a method not so much of influencing the government as of buying cheap and risk-free popularity from one's colleagues."[32] Watkins may be right to argue that EDMs are sometimes signed as a way of buying cheap popularity from colleagues; but we have then to ask why a Member should be anxious to buy popularity from one set of colleagues rather than another, the more so as this goodwill is sometimes purchased at the cost of the Front Bench's favour. What attracted him to a friendship group consisting of unilateralists rather than to one composed of education enthusiasts? Again, if Watkins's explanation accounted for all EDM signatures, the political significance of EDMs and the inferences made from them would be increased—not reduced.

Opinions are usually formed and expressed within a specific social context. Although we use the term free votes to indicate those divisions in which the party Whips are not applied, few divisions can be regarded as completely free and unconstrained. Except on the most trivial issues, a Member is always likely to incur some cost—be it only in terms of damaged friendship (by voting and speaking in a particular way); most votes are cast under some constraint.

The attitudes revealed by EDMs, or indeed by floor revolts, are not, therefore, to be interpreted as signifying a kind of raw opinion unmodified by the subtle pressures found in any social situation. Nevertheless, it would be equally wrong to regard a Member's signature to a particular EDM as representing nothing more than the influence of parliamentary reference groups. As has been shown, opinions as revealed by EDM signature are reflected in division-lobby behaviour. Members who signed EDMs criticizing the Labour Party's foreign and defence policies were much more likely than others to cast adverse votes or to abstain on foreign and defence policy questions; and the social groups prominent in the expression of an attitude through EDMs were similarly conspicuous in floor revolts.

It might be objected that this correspondence between EDM signatures and rebellion might be true only of the Labour Left and not of Members in general, and that extremism was a

[32] A. Watkins, All loyalists now, *NS & N*, 26 Dec. 1969.

group phenomenon which manifested itself both in EDM signing and in division lobby revolts; some backbenchers might hold the same opinions but not partake in either activity.

Evidence which has been presented in this study shows, however, that the connection between the signature of EDMs and votes in the division lobbies was not confined to the left wing of the Labour Party. Hunting, capital punishment, and conscription all provide examples of a close relationship between EDM signing and division-lobby votes; a similar relationship was found on the Conservative side on birching and MPs salaries.

Moreover, on some issues within the Labour Party no associations were established between opinions and social characteristics. Attitudes to health and education or European unity, for instance, cut across most structural groupings; it seems difficult, therefore, to argue that the correspondence between EDMs and floor revolts is just a product of group activity which expresses itself jointly through both channels, producing similar results unless it is postulated that, on motions like those dealing with health and education, a number of separate friendship groups came together. The latter explanation is plausible—but if it is true we have to ask why the same process should not have occurred with the motions on foreign policy, social security, or colonialism.

Two further criticisms which were voiced frequently reflected the disquiet of some observers at the use made of EDMs. The first and most widely quoted concerned the publication of a list of the 50 Labour MPs who, according to the EDM data, were the most Left Members of the Parliamentary Labour Party.

During a long discussion of the syndrome of British socialism, a number of different elements of this syndrome which had been expressed in EDMs were identified; these elements comprised pacifism, neutralism in foreign policy, anti-colonialism, libertarianism, humanitarianism and zeal for social welfare. During this discussion it was observed that different sections of the party laid a varying emphasis upon these elements. The Trade Unionists were more concerned with improvements in social welfare, the Miscellaneous Occupations MPs with pacifism and anti-colonialism, and the intellectual Professional section with humanitarian penal reform. At the end of this disquisition a list appeared of those Members who, on average over the whole range of issues, could be regarded as the most Left. Support for social welfare changes is not conventionally regarded as one of the distinguishing marks of the Labour Left; and the range of issues entering into the definition helped to include in the list of 50 a number who would not, by any conventional definition, have been regarded as Left. To make it clear that the authors were aware of this, a footnote was included pointing out that some Members, not normally thought of as belonging to the Left, qualified for inclusion by virtue of their heavy emphasis on social welfare motions.

Now the definition of Left adopted is doubtless unusual; and it is certainly legitimate for anyone to criticize the usefulness of such a definition or the value of a list derived from it. What was strange was the difficulty that some critics had in distinguishing between the validity of a definition and the validity of a source-material—in this case the EDMs. The "deviant" names did not find their way into the list because of faults in the data; they were there because of one particular and perhaps inadequate definition. Any critic has the right to question and, if he wishes, to condemn such a definition; what he cannot legitimately do is to use this definition as a means of discrediting the source.

A second object of criticism was the finding that in the Conservative Party the attitudes of Members educated at Oxford seemed to diverge sharply from those of Cambridge-educated MPs. Some critics, with whom there can be no special quarrel, thought that the information was not helpful. Others seemed to find in this strange distinction a further cause for rejecting EDMs as a valid source-material for backbench attitudes.

An association between two factors does not imply a direct causal relationship between them; it implies (assuming that chance be discounted) that a connection *of some kind* exists. Such a connection may be supplied by a third and perhaps unidentified factor. No such link could, in fact, be distinguished (though that is not to say it does not exist); and it is readily conceded that no more direct explanation for this difference of attitude between graduates of the two older English universities was offered. Yet such an inability cannot cancel the obligation of the researcher to report findings which may appear curious or even bizarre: "what is irrelevant and obvious in one context may illuminate something important in another."[33] The differences between Oxford and Cambridge Conservatives repeatedly recurred; it is stretching coincidence too far to believe that a meaningless and fortuitous distinction was *repeatedly* thrown up by the EDM data. It was also found on free votes such as that on Mr. Silverman's Bill to abolish the death penalty in 1956. The same strange cleavage was found in earlier sessions (e.g. 1945–50) and even in the vote which helped to overthrow Neville Chamberlain in May 1940.[34] Had similar differences been found between the attitudes of Oxford and Cambridge graduates, on the one hand, and the graduates of provincial and Scottish universities on the other, some heads at least would have nodded sagely in assent. However odd this particular finding, it would have been wrong to have suppressed it.

A final criticism which may be mentioned was the familiar complaint that the authors had undertaken a lot of work to prove the obvious. Inevitably, quantitative analysis will always confirm some widely held beliefs. It would say little for traditional observation if it did not. None of the authors supposed that the inferences made about the political attitudes of trade unionists were particularly novel; but the figures do permit a comparison to be made with the responses of trade unionists in the early post-war years, and show that although trade unionists were significantly more right wing than other groups between 1955 and 1959, they were, from the Labour leadership's viewpoint, a substantially less dependable force than they had been in the 1945 House. The distinction between the two chief middle-class components of the Parliamentary Labour Party—the Miscellaneous Occupations and the Professions—seemed so obvious that it was ignored altogether. Moreover, it is hardly consistent to complain at one and the same time that the authors had "proved the obvious" and relied on faulty data.

QUANTITATIVE AND QUALITATIVE SCALES

Backbench motions sometimes deal with matters that are subjects of deep and often passionate controversy within the parties—nuclear weapons and foreign policy, say, on the Labour side; capital and corporal punishment and policies towards Europe and the Commonwealth on the Conservative side. Such EDMs usually lend themselves to the construction of qualitative scales. Members of the same party sign motions advocating different policies. With qualitative scales a Member's location will be determined by the *kind* of motion he signed.

Many EDMs, however, espouse causes that arouse little if any dissent within a particular party. Some Members may feel more strongly about a question than others, but all—or almost all—agree on the issue. The numerous motions on pensions and national assistance

[33] J. P. Nettl, *Political Mobilisation*, London, 1967, p. 55.

[34] J. G. Rasmussen, Party discipline in war-time: the downfall of the Chamberlain Government, in *Journal of Politics*, 1970.

scales and on the health and education services which were tabled by Labour backbenchers in the 1951 Parliament afford a good illustration. It may be presumed that few, if any, disapproved of increases in social welfare payments or agreed with the restrictions imposed on the development of the education services; but Members almost certainly varied in their enthusiasm for higher social security payments or the advance of education. In cases like these, quantitative scales have been constructed, and Members' keenness has been gauged by the number of motions they signed. What is being asserted is that, in general, Members who feel more intensely in favour of a specific policy are more likely to sign motions which express support, either directly or indirectly, for such a policy. It does not follow that the social composition of the most enthusiastic Members will precisely duplicate that of the Members who give a broad, if tepid, assent to the proposed course of action; there are, however, virtually no findings based on behaviour in free votes or floor revolts which are in contradiction to findings based on an analysis of EDM signatories.[35]

CLASSIFICATION OF MEMBERS AND STATISTICAL TESTS AND MEASURES

Members in each party have been divided into appropriate social categories. Thus Labour MPs were classified according to such factors as age, education, occupation, and sponsorship. Conservatives were classified in a broadly similar way but, as will be seen, the differences in the structure of the parties imposed some variation in the categories used for Members of the two parties.

The distribution of Members in the various social groups expressing different attitudes has been inspected, and a standard statistical test of association—the chi-squared test—has been applied to see whether differences in the support for particular attitudes displayed by the various social categories are statistically significant.

Were there not a widespread suspicion of statistical techniques amongst the lay public it would be superfluous to emphasize that the purpose of the chi-squared test is not to enable the research worker to squeeze, illicitly, more dramatic and interesting conclusions out of his figures than the facts warrant. On the contrary: the object or such a test is to prevent the student from making inferences about behaviour that can be reasonably ascribed to chance. The chi-squared test is a hurdle the data has to jump—not a springboard to enable it to overcome an inner weakness. Looking at a table such as Table 10 (p. 64) we are able to see that signatures on foreign policy motions were associated with Members of particular type-classes. The signatures were not random, and by calculating chi-squared we can show what the odds are against this distribution of signatures being thrown up by chance.

The chi-squared test begins by assuming that the subscription of signatures is quite random. From this assumption it is possible to calculate the number in any social group who would have signed a motion or train of motions. The test then compares these "expected frequencies" with the actual distribution of signatures. If the differences are small they will be attributed to chance. If they are larger it will be assumed that the variations are due to a genuine difference of opinion between various social categories within the party.

The level of statistical significance indicates the probability of the differences being caused by pure chance. Thus a significance at the 10 per cent level shows that the odds are at least 9 to 1 against differences being due to chance; a significance at the 5 per cent level of significance

---

[35] See the discussion on support for the abolition of the death penalty in Chapter 6 and Annex 3.

shows that the odds are at least 19 to 1; and a 1 per cent level of significance shows the odds to be at least 99 to 1.

If the possibility of a significant difference occurring by chance is rejected; if the scales used are appropriate (and the grouping of motions in scales poses perhaps the greatest problem in the use of this data); if no *systematic* distortion has occurred in the collection and subscription of signatures—then the assertion that a particular type-class of Members diverges in its attitude to some issue from other type-classes in the same party becomes not so much a question of opinion as one of fact. Where the table reaches the 10 per cent level of significance it has been assumed, as in the previous study, that a relationship of some kind can be regarded as having been provisionally established. Where the table reaches the 5 per cent level of significance or better, a relationship has been regarded as having been firmly established. It has been assumed that all other differences can plausibly be attributed to chance fluctuations, though, even where no significant difference has been established, it has sometimes seemed worth while to report particular figures.

Where significant differences have been found amongst Members with different social characteristics it has been normally assumed that this is because Members within a given social category favoured to a disproportionate extent the attitudes expressed in the motion or vote. This judgement in no way prevents those who disagree with this conclusion in any particular case from substituting their own private explanation of the association which has been found.

Reference has already been made to Yule's Q which can be used in certain circumstances for scaling purposes but has been more frequently employed to assess the degree to which Members signing one motion on a given topic signed motions dealing with similar issues. If the value of Q is positive for a pair of motions it means that there was a tendency for the signatories of one motion to sign another. If it was both high and positive it means that there was a strong tendency in this direction. The value of $1 \cdot 0$ would mean that all Members signing the motion with fewer signatures also signed the motion with more. A value of zero means there is no tendency at all for the signatories of one motion to sign the other. A negative value means that Members who signed one motion tended not to sign the other.

A NOTE ON REFERENCES TO EDMs

For convenience, EDMs have been referred to by the number allotted to them on the Order Paper of the House of Commons and the year in which the session began. Thus, EDM 40, tabled on 22 March 1948, is referred to as 40/47, the session having begun in the previous autumn. A problem arises with EDMs tabled in the Parliament of 1950/1 as two sessions began in 1950—one in March and one in October. The solution adopted has been to put the suffix 51 denoting the session October 1950 to October 1951 in *italics*. Thus, EDM No. 5, tabled on 20 November 1950, is referred to as EDM 5/*51*: such EDMs are distinguished from those tabled in the session October 1951 to October 1952, where the suffix is put in roman type.

An amendment to an EDM will be referred to by the suffix A, e.g. EDM 33A/47.

Again, as in the earlier study, description of, and comment upon, the more important and interesting findings, have been separated from a full discussion of the statistical techniques used, and the way the scales have been constructed. The essentials of this study are contained within the first nine chapters; scholars who wish to know about the techniques employed, and further details about the distribution of opinions, will find them in the Annexes at the end of the book.

CHAPTER 2

Government, Party, and Early Day Motions

"Neither party, for a long time at least, will be able to govern in the spirit, or according to the wishes, of its extreme supporters: a Conservative Government will not be such as Mr. Newdegate would wish; a Liberal one must be far short of what Mr. Trevelyan or Sir Charles Dilke would prefer. Any extreme Government would be plainly contrary to the wishes of the nation. . . .

"There is nothing new in such a state of politics." (WALTER BAGEHOT, *Not a Middle Party but a Middle Government.*)

The apparent omnipotence of the Executive in the twentieth century and the decline of the independent-minded Member have for long been mourned by observers of British political life. The freedom of the private Member in the nineteenth century, the seeming importance of debate, the responsiveness of governments to the plenary House, have often been adverted to with nostalgic regret. "In Bagehot's day", wrote Richard Crossman, echoing an oft-voiced theme, "the private member was genuinely free to defy the whip, genuinely responsible to his own conscience and his constituents, and genuinely at liberty, within wide limits, to speak as he wished. It was this independence of the private member that gave the Commons its collective character and made it the most important check on the executive."[1]

The nature of backbench independence in the nineteenth-century parliaments has been widely misunderstood. Although party discipline was lax by modern standards,[2] government defeats were relatively infrequent except in those situations where a minority administration held office. Backbench revolts, especially on the Liberal side, tended to come from the extreme wing of one party and, in these circumstances, were usually met by an otherwise united House. Governments could often rely on the support of the opposition leaders in meeting criticism or in enacting laws. The Conservative Front Bench could count on a united Liberal Party to help in voting down the demands of diehard Tories; and the Liberal leadership could frequently depend on Conservative support against the claims of the radicals.

Backbench rebellions in the twentieth century often fall into a similar pattern, with the Labour Party occupying the position of the Liberals. It is illuminating to examine not merely the number of backbench protests but their direction. The revolts of the Labour Left and the reactionary Right clearly have a significance which differs from that of the protests of Labour moderates or Conservative progressives.

A preliminary examination of political factionalism in Britain suggests that intra-party rebellions can be divided into three kinds. There are rebellions in which the left wing of the

---

[1] R. H. S. Crossman, Introduction to W. Bagehot, *English Constitution*, London, 1963, pp. 42–43.

[2] Perhaps more strictly, one should say, by the standards prevailing until the 1966 Parliament.

Labour Party or a right-wing[3] faction on the Conservative side protest at some consensus policy. The revolts against Ernest Bevin's foreign policy in the late forties and against the Labour Party's defence policies in the fifties were of this type; on the Conservative side examples are provided by the demonstration of the Suez Group in 1954 and the recurrent calls for the restoration of judicial birching. In contrast to these rebellions are those which occur when the moderate members of one party aim, either tacitly or openly, to achieve the same ends as the opposite party. The protests of some Conservatives against the Anglo-French attack on Egypt and the attempts of others to amend Henry Brooke's Rent Bill belong to this category. Such rebellions are clearly more significant, in terms of political effects, than the former kind of revolts, for "moderate" rebels who carry their convictions as far as the division lobbies can help defeat their own government. It is not easy to cite examples of this sort from the Labour Party; the nearest parallel when Labour was in government was furnished by the fortuitous alliance between the predominantly left-wing critics of the Prices and Incomes Bill and the Conservative Opposition in the 1966 Parliament. Again, in 1971, Labour's marketeers voted in strength with the Conservative Government against their own party; on this occasion the revolt can be described as "moderate" in content as well as in form, for most of the marketeers were drawn from the party's right wing.

A third type are those rebellions in which a backbench coalition, drawn from both parties, confronts another coalition embracing the leadership of both parties. Sometimes the rebels of the two parties are prompted by different motives, as in the campaign against British entry into the Common Market in 1967–8, or as in the successful attempt to destroy the Labour Government's Bill to reform the House of Lords in 1969. On other occasions the dissidents may not merely seek the same end but may do so for broadly similar reasons, as illustrated by the bipartisan opposition to the Labour Government's Nigeria policy. The situation which arose from the Labour Bill to restrict the entry of U.K. passport holders, such as Kenya Asians, in 1968 provides another example.

Such a classification is based on the *form* taken by the revolts rather than on the *content* of the demands posed by the dissidents. Usually, but not invariably, form and content will coincide; protests from a section of one party against a generally united House will usually represent extreme policies. Revolts by a breakaway faction from one party, seeking ends similar to those of the other, will normally represent moderate demands. Occasional exceptions can be found; the adventitious alliance between left-wing Labour rebels and the Conservative Opposition against statutory control of wages provides a good, if rare, illustration.

This kind of classification can be applied with little difficulty to divisions in which rebellion of some sort occurred. Divisions in the nineteenth-century House can be categorized in this way.[4] Unfortunately it is not possible to classify EDMs in this manner, as Members from both sides are not obliged, as they virtually are in a division, to declare their position; in particular, the Opposition Front Bench is under no constraint to show its hand. Moreover, an EDM enjoying some support amongst backbenchers of both parties may be canvassed only amongst the Members of one. In classifying EDMs, therefore, the main emphasis must lie on the *content* of the demand. Such a method puts a considerable strain on personal judgement; nevertheless,

[3] Terms such as "right-wing" factions or "diehard sections" have been used in relation to the Conservative Party because it is difficult to trace the existence of anything resembling a coherent and cohesive Conservative "right wing" except in the limited area of foreign policy.

[4] See H. Berrington, Partisanship and dissidence in the nineteenth-century House of Commons, *Parliamentary Affairs*, vol. 21, 1968.

with all its defects it may help to illuminate the nature of the cleavages revealed through the medium of the Order Paper. This emphasis on content does not exclude some attention being paid to the form of the EDM. A motion which attracts signatures from both sides can be clearly distinguished from those drawing support from only one.

A classification of EDMs illustrates the nature of the motions put down, and may also help to throw light on differences in the pattern of revolts between the two parties.

The kind of categorization which can be applied to divisions is, moreover, too crude to be applied to EDMs because of the large number of motions which elude such a simple classification. Nevertheless, this way of classifying backbench pressures can furnish the basis for one more elaborate.

Under such a system,[5] *Extremist* motions are defined essentially by their content; these are EDMs in which a section of one party protest against a policy shared both by their own leaders and the whole of the opposite party. *Quasi-Extremist* EDMs were, like the Extremist category, supported exclusively by members of one party and, though not strictly opposed to Front Bench policy, had some affinity, by virtue of their sponsorship and the nature of their demands, with the Extremist EDMs.

The *Centre-Oriented* category is very similar to the "moderate" type of rebellion mentioned earlier in that such motions made some criticism, explicit or implied, of official party policy of a kind similar to that being made by the opposite party. It is not essential for such EDMs to have won support from both sides; it suffices that backbenchers from one party were prepared to put down a motion which, in effect, criticized the policy of their own leaders.

Crossbench EDMs were those attracting a stipulated minimum of support from both sides which were not clearly contrary to the official line of the party; in these respects they differ from the Centre-Oriented motions. Moreover, in order to qualify as a Crossbench EDM, a motion (or amendment) had to receive at least sixteen signatures with not less than six coming from each party. The terms Centre Oriented and Crossbench do not refer strictly to the EDMs as such but to the EDMs in relation to a particular party. The same EDM can be classified as Centre Oriented with respect to one party because it criticized *that* party's policy, and as Crossbench with regard to the other.

Convergent EDMs resemble the revolts in which backbenchers from both parties pressed demands opposed by the leaders of both. In this they resemble the campaign against the Labour Government's attempt to enter the Common Market or the bipartisan attack on the Labour Government's Lords Reform Bill.

Partisan EDMs were motions signed exclusively by Members of one party whose views were either consonant with official party policy or, in line with the party's traditions and prejudices, were not at variance with the current Front Bench view. Many of these consisted of squibs put down as part of the normal party warfare.

This leaves a large residual category of *Neutral* EDMs, which usually expressed pressure-group demands (often those of a territorial group) or were manifestos giving voice to worthy and innocuous sentiments.

The distribution of EDMs amongst these categories is shown in Tables 2 and 3.

It can hardly be stressed too much that the actual allocation of EDMs to the various categories is a subjective exercise; nevertheless, making every allowance for the vagaries of personal judgement, certain features are conspicuous. The score for each category differs according to

[5] Only motions which are signed by not less than 10 Members were included. Amendments were treated as full EDMs. The term Members for purposes of this definition includes only Labour and Conservative MPs.

TABLE 2. THE LABOUR PARTY

1945–50 Parliament

	Extremist	Quasi-Extremist	Convergent	Partisan	Crossbench	Centre-Oriented	Neutral	Total
1945–6	7	—	—	—	5	1	—	**13**
1946–7	4	—	—	—	5	—	—	**9**
1947–8	15	1	—	—	1	1	3	**21**
1948 (short session)	—	—	—	—	1	1	—	**2**
1948–9	7	1	—	1	4	1	2	**16**
Total	33	2	—	1	16	4	5	**61**

1950–1 Parliament

	Extremist	Quasi-Extremist	Convergent	Partisan	Crossbench	Centre-Oriented	Neutral	Total
1950	2	1	1	—	1	—	4	**9**
1950–1	6	3	2	3	6	—	3	**23**
Total	8	4	3	3	7	—	7	**32**

1951–5 Parliament

	Extremist	Quasi-Extremist	Convergent	Partisan	Crossbench	Centre-Oriented	Neutral	Total
1951–2	3	3	—	16	3	—	21	**46**
1952–3	—	5	—	10	6	—	31	**52**
1953–4	2	5	—	9	5	—	14	**35**
1954–5	3	1	—	13	3	—	8	**28**
Total	8	14	—	48	17	—	74	**161**

whether or not a party was in government; and, irrespective of this factor, there are important contrasts between the two parties.

During the 6 years of the Labour Government it is clear that the two parties put the EDM to different purposes. The number put down by the two sides in these years was much the same— 93 by Labour and 98 by the Conservatives. But the latter used the Order Paper to score party points to a much greater extent, putting down 33 Partisan EDMs to Labour's 4. The number of Neutral EDMs tabled by Conservatives was also considerably greater than those put down by Labour. The most glaring difference, however, concerns the Extremist and Quasi-Extremist categories. Labour tabled 45 of these against 7 for the Conservatives. The luxuriant spread of Partisan and Neutral EDMs on the Labour side after 1951 tempers the contrast afforded by the earlier years, suggesting that the differences between the parties may be due less to permanent distinctions of party style than to their status as governing or opposition parties. Yet even in 1951–5 the absolute differences in the tally of Extremist and Quasi-Extremist motions are suggestive, Labour scoring 22 to the Conservatives 12. In short, Labour tended to use the

TABLE 3. THE CONSERVATIVE PARTY

1945–50 Parliament

	Extremist	Quasi-Extremist	Convergent	Partisan	Crossbench	Centre-Oriented	Neutral	Total
1945–6	—	—	—	6	6	—	5	17
1946–7	1	2	—	5	6	—	1	15
1947–8	—	—	—	2	2	1	3	8
1948 (short session)	—	—	—	—	1	—	—	1
1948–9	—	—	—	3	6	—	6	15
Total	1	2	—	16	21	1	15	56

1950–1 Parliament

	Extremist	Quasi-Extremist	Convergent	Partisan	Crossbench	Centre-Oriented	Neutral	Total
1950	2	—	1	4	1	—	4	12
1950–1	2	—	2	13	6	—	7	30
Total	4	—	3	17	7	—	11	42

1951–5 Parliament

	Extremist	Quasi-Extremist	Convergent	Partisan	Crossbench	Centre-Oriented	Neutral	Total
1951–2	5	—	—	5	2	2	4	18
1952–3	3	2	—	3	6	—	5	19
1953–4	2	—	—	2	4	2	7	17
1954–5	—	—	—	—	3	—	3	6
Total	10	2	—	10	15	4	19	60

Order Paper to ventilate differences within their own party and especially to advertise the nostrums of the left wing. The Conservatives, to a much greater degree, employed it as a weapon in the daily battle between the parties.[6]

Though numerous Crossbench EDMs were tabled, there were few Centre-Oriented motions, those in which a section of one party clearly supported, against the guidance of their leaders, the policy of the other.

Amongst the Extremist and Quasi-Extremist motions tabled by Labour when in office may be noted a demand to protect racial and religious minorities, an EDM calling for the

[6] The greater reliance on informal or semi-formal channels of communication in the Conservative Party means that fewer internal conflicts are ventilated through the medium of either EDMs or floor revolts. Enoch Powell has referred to the way in which Conservative governments of the fifties repeatedly gave way to backbench pressure "where, nevertheless, the whole operation, which seemed so embarrrassingly obvious to the participants in it, entirely escaped the Opposition's notice" (Enoch Powell, 1951–1959 Labour in opposition, *Political Quarterly*, cited by R. J. Jackson in *Rebels and Whips*, London, 1968, p. 19). For a view that the style of backbench rebellion in the Conservative Party may be becoming more like that of Labour, see A. King, The changing Tories, *New Society*, 2 May 1968.

abolition of conscription, 3 calling for the transformation of the United Nations into a World Government, 2 on the control of atomic energy, and another criticizing the government's Palestine policy. In opposition there were several criticizing or seeking to postpone German rearmament. Amongst the Conservatives, 4 of the 16 called for the re-introduction of birching, 3 criticized the administration of the nationalized industries, 1 called for the breaking off of negotiations with Egypt over the future of the Suez Canal base, and another asked the government to delay the introduction of a system of allowance for MPs.

Partisan EDMs were rare on the Labour side until 1951 when they appeared in profusion. These usually sponsored the claims of Labour's client groups—pensioners, tenants, and the various categories of workers covered by the Gowers Committee Report—or criticized reductions in the social services or the standard of living. The Conservative Partisan motions, put down in opposition, usually involved criticisms of the administration of post-war controls (e.g. petrol rationing), or the nationalized industries, or sponsored the demands of the party's own clientele such as agriculture, and members of the armed forces; in office they tended to be ripostes at Labour EDMs, scoring simple party points.

The Crossbench EDMs are less easy to characterize; several consisted of attacks on Communist practices in eastern Europe, others championed the claims of groups such as retired civil servants and war pensioners, another called for self-determination for the South Tyrol, two urged that fresh attention should be given to the Channel Tunnel, others pressed the claims of prisoners of war—both British and enemy—whilst one called for an inquiry into the marriage laws.

The Convergent EDMs were few. Two sponsored the cause of World Government (largely Labour EDMs which gained a few Conservative signatures), and one called for the introduction of equal pay in the Civil Service. The Centre-Oriented motions were not numerous either; Labour's included two calling for a review of war pensions and another pressing the government to give facilities for the discussion of the Analgesia in Childbirth Bill. Those on the Conservative side embraced an amendment attacking European federation, one which called for the reduction of purchase tax on textiles, another which urged the introduction of equal pay in the civil service, and another pressing the claims of disabled war veterans.

Neutral EDMs on the Labour side, which proliferated after 1951, covered a wide range of topics; there were regional demands such as references to unemployment in Scotland and broadcasting in the north-east and Wales; some sectional claims, such as those of blitzed towns, victims of silicosis, and road transport; protests at abuses of colonial power as well as such trivial matters as restaurant facilities in the House of Commons.

The Neutral EDMs in the Conservative Party followed a similar pattern; there were Scottish demands, the claims of agriculture and forestry, and such miscellaneous political demands as a call for house-purchase grants and an end to the earnings rule for pensioners.

Table 4 shows the distribution of EDMs by subject-matter. Again, the personal and subjective character of the allocation of EDMs to their respective categories must be stressed.

The lack of any objective criterion for assessing the relative importance of the motions means that the figures are inevitably distorted by the presence of a large number of minor and indeed trivial EDMs. The Suez motion of 1954 and the Bevan EDM on German rearmament in 1955 were clearly of vastly greater significance than motions about television services in the north-east or the activities of the Kitchen Committee of the House of Commons. Yet, even as they stand, the figures, with all their limitations, both endorse the picture given by more impressionistic study, and confirm the pattern of factional revolts which prevailed under the superficially very different circumstances of the late nineteenth-century parliaments.

TABLE 4. LABOUR AND CONSERVATIVE EDMs BY SUBJECT-MATTER

	Labour			Conservative		
	1945–50	1950–1	1951–5	1945–50	1950–1	1951–5
Social welfare	2	3	29	1	4	4
Territorial pressure groups	3	4	25	15	5	6
Other pressure groups	8	2	17	8	2	6
Foreign and defence	26	13	40	9	11	19
Economic, taxation, industry	4	—	5	6	4	1
Humanitarian, libertarian, moral	14	2	13	3	6	5
House of Commons (procedural, etc.)	1	6	14	4	2	8
Other	3	2	18	10	8	11
Total	61	32	161	56	42	60

Most of these categories are self-explanatory; the territorial pressure group class refers to motions which represented the claims of a section concentrated in a particular area, such as Scotland or north-east England or connected with some specific kind of constituency, such as agricultural divisions. Other pressure group EDMs represent the claims of more widely scattered interests.

"I notice [said Mr. Crossman, speaking in the debate on the London and Paris Agreements in November 1954] that foreign affairs debates do now tend to take an L-shaped pattern. The whole of one side of the House and the top half of the other are both on one side in a debate, while the lower half below the Gangway on one side of the House is on the opposite side in the debate. It may be hon. Members below the Gangway opposite or my hon. Friends below the Gangway on this side, but one group or the other comprises the militant opposition".[7]

In this statement Mr. Crossman described succinctly a familiar pattern of parliamentary schism—an alliance between the whole of one party and the leadership and more conforming followers of the other against a section of the latter party.

British government displays a continuing tension between the demands of national leadership and the claims of party. A Minister normally relies on the support of his party in the House of Commons for the passage of legislation and to repel the criticism of the opposition. Nevertheless, he often finds himself unable to reciprocate the support he receives in the division lobbies by acceding to the wishes of his followers. A Minister always occupies a dual role; as a party leader he shares and must be sensitive to the special demands of his party; but as a Minister, confronted by the need for workable solutions to immediate problems, surrounded and advised by men who do not share his special party stance, he will be drawn to decisions which owe little or nothing to his party creed. If, as with the Labour Party, the party professes an ideology or allegiance to certain moral values of unchanging importance, he will find the conflict between the claims of party and those of the national or administrative interest even more acute.

It is commonplace to say that the most important differences today are found, not between

[7] HC Deb. 533, c. 475.

the two main parties, but within each; and more obviously, however narrow the divergence between the two Front Benches, there is clearly a wide gulf between the left wing of the Labour Party and diehard sections of the Conservative Party. In the nineteenth century it was not unusual to find the two Front Benches voting in the same lobby, opposing an extreme faction of one party. In modern Britain the same pattern is found in many political controversies even though it is not possible to trace it in the division lobbies. On many issues an informal coalition, dominated by the moderate elements on each side, prevails.

Bagehot, writing in 1874, observed that though a middle party was impossible, a middle government—"a Government which represents the extreme of neither party, but the common element between the two parties"—was inevitable. Neither party could govern in the spirit of its extreme supporters; and though moderate men could not set up a party of their own, they could, in 1874, decisively enjoin their will on both parties.[8]

British government goes through periods when party government is in the ascendant, as between 1906 and 1914 and to a much lesser extent between 1945 and 1950, and times when "consensus politics" are dominant, as in the years since 1950. Moreover, even in decades when the parties are bitterly divided on some issues, there are certain to be questions on which a tacit Front Bench coalition imposes its will. So, even though the parties fought each other strongly over the nationalization measures of the 1945 Labour Government, there was virtual agreement between the leadership of the two parties on foreign affairs and defence.

Mr. Crossman saw the conflict as lying as much between the Tory diehards and the Front Bench coalition, as between the latter and the Labour Left. The greater number of Extremist and Quasi-Extremist EDMs on the Labour side suggest, however, that dissension between the left wing of the Labour Party and the bipartisan establishment is the more normal situation. The Labour Left stands as the permanent opposition. Whoever governs, the Left are out of power. In this they resemble, in an uncanny way, the radical wing of the late-nineteenth-century Liberal Party. Moreover (though it is not possible to trace this difference through the EDMs of this period), moderate revolts do occur, albeit rarely on the Conservative side, whilst they are very unusual in the Labour Party.[9] Again, the rebellions of the nineteenth century provide an instructive parallel. On the Conservative side demonstrations by moderate sections of the party were at least as numerous, and usually more so, than rebellions from the diehards. In the Liberal Party, extremist revolts predominated.[10]

The persistence of this pattern over the last 70 years, despite the apparent extent of political change, suggests that enduring factors are at work. A Labour government has to function within the context of an *élite* opinion which lies substantially to the "right" of opinion in the Labour Party. Whether or not this *élite* opinion reflects certain objective and ineluctable constraints is not, in this context, relevant. In turn, a Labour government, and a Labour shadow cabinet, occupy a position well to the "right" of the centre of gravity of the party. In short, a Labour government has to maintain an uneasy balance between the demands of party ideology and its role of national leadership.

Just as a Labour government can be perceived as being to the right of the party's centre of gravity, so a Conservative government can be seen to stand to the left of the Conservative centre of gravity—though the gap between the two is much less than the corresponding gap

---

[8] *The Economist*, 17 Jan. 1874.

[9] Ignoring one man rebellions like those of Alfred Edwards or Desmond Donnelly.

[10] See H. Berrington, Partisanship and dissidence in the nineteenth-century House of Commons, *Parliamentary Affairs*, Vol. 21, 1968.

in the Labour Party. A Conservative government has, therefore, fewer diehard rebellions to contend with; but this relative exemption is purchased at the price of rather greater discontent on the Left of the party.[11] A Conservative government, moreover, does not merely lie closer to the centre of its own party; it also lies nearer to *élite* opinion. The nature of government in modern Britain obliges a Labour government, if it is to be true to its national obligations, to court the discontent of its Left. Because the Conservative Party as a whole lies closer to the dominant attitudes and assumptions of British society, a Conservative government is freer to pursue policies congenial to its backbench following. Even here there are important constraints; the diehards of Suez, the birching lobby, and the critics of the nationalized coal industry were all in conflict with the received truths of the Front Bench consensus, and Conservative governments had to incur their hostility just as Labour governments had to resist the Left. The differences between the two parties are, nevertheless, substantial.

Relations between Britain and Egypt between 1952 and 1957 illustrate the way in which Conservative governments respond now to *élite* opinion (or the reality which it expresses) and at other times to the demands of party. Military and diplomatic advice appears to have been united in pressing the government to reach agreement with the Egyptians on the evacuation of the Suez Canal base in 1954. The Conservative Government's responsiveness to this advice led them to fall foul of the diehard imperialists, enrolled in the celebrated Suez Group. Churchill's Government, able to keep the loyalty of most Conservative MPs, and with nothing to fear from the Labour Party, was able to overcome the diehard opposition. In 1956 the Eden Administration, in attacking Egypt, rallied the Conservative Right but alienated important sections of *élite* opinion, strained the loyalty of its own Left, and outraged the Labour Party. Then, in 1957, by withdrawing from Port Said, and eventually recommending British ships to use the nationalized Canal, the government again lost the goodwill of the Right. When government policy moved towards the right it sacrificed the allegiance of the Conservative Left, and incurred the criticism of *élite* spokesmen. When it moved towards a position of Front Bench consensus, it frayed the patience of the diehards.

The Suez affair illustrates the way in which, on occasion, Conservative policy oscillates between the national and the party centres of gravity. A Labour government has a more serious task; its policies are like threads stretching more or less permanently across a gap set by the Labour Left at one end and *élite* opinion (or objective reality as Labour's enemies would aver) at the other. A Labour government which bows to the insistent clamour of administrative feasibility and practical necessity, must lose the acquiescence of the Left. It is not surprising that the threads should so often snap.

This brief reconnaissance of the EDMs of three post-war parliaments illustrates the great diversity in subject-matter and motive, represented by backbench motions. It also emphasizes certain lasting distinctions between the two parties, both of style and intra-party conflict. Differences of style may in themselves reflect contrasting social backgrounds; and to the social composition of the Parliamentary Labour Party we must now turn.

[11] It must be emphasized that the composition of the left in the Conservative Party tends to vary from issue to issue.

CHAPTER 3

The Social Composition of the Labour Party

"The newcomers were at sea, and there were so many newcomers—345—that the old hands were reduced to a wild wonder and uncertainty about their own bearings. . . .

". . . to lift one's eyes along the rear benches was to encounter a chaos of anonymous faces; youthful faces, faces expressing all the confidence of early middle age; a number of women's faces, one almost girlish. But who were they? There was one handsome bearded face that had clearly more of the sea about it than Bloomsbury. And there were still more of them, quite a hundred, standing at the Bar, even standing on the Bar—a breach of order. They were all hopelessly surplus to the seating accommodation."

(HARRY BOARDMAN writing in the *Manchester Guardian*, 2 August 1945, on the first meeting of the new Labour-controlled Parliament.)

1945–55

The Labour Party's sweeping and unexpected victory in the General Election of 1945 was accompanied by important, though not spectacular, changes in the structure of the backbench party. The Parliamentary Party more than doubled in size to nearly 400 Members. More than 200 of the Labour MPs elected in 1945 had gained their seats in the July poll; most of them had never served in Parliament before. The party broke new ground by winning constituencies in the suburbs and in areas of light industry. Yet the effect of all these changes on the social and occupational structure of the party was considerable rather than dramatic. The manual workers constituted less than a quarter of the new MPs it is true, but then they had comprised only two-fifths of the backbenchers who had served in the previous Parliament. The infiltration of university graduates and professional men into the party had begun long before 1945; and though their strength increased as a result of the election they remained a minority. Professional men numbered a third of the new intake as compared with under a fifth of the pre-1945 remnant.

Educationally, the Parliamentary Party showed the same trend towards moderate embourgeoisement. University graduates numbered more than a third of the newcomers compared with less than a quarter of the old Members. The elementary-educated who constituted more than two-fifths of the pre-1945 party fell to less than a third amongst the new entrants.

Even the regional make-up of the new Members did not diverge too sharply from that of the older men. The traditional areas of Labour strength—Wales, Scotland, the north-west, and the north—accounted for 60 per cent of the pre-1945 backbenchers, and for as many as 43 per cent of the new Members.

Only in two respects did the newcomers differ very markedly from their predecessors—in sponsorship and, not surprisingly, in age. The trade-union-sponsored Members totalled half of the older entrants but only a quarter of the new, whilst the proportion of constituency-party-sponsored candidates rose from less than two-fifths to two-thirds. Sixty-four per cent of the old guard were over 60 in 1945 as against 17 per cent of the newcomers; only 9 per cent of the returning Members were under 50 compared with just over half of the new.

The Labour Government, then, was faced by a backbench party whose occupational, educational, and regional structure differed substantially, but not spectacularly, from that of the Parliamentary Party in the old Parliament; and by a backbench party which was very much younger than its predecessor. The main difficulty the government would confront would lie in the sheer size and inexperience of the new intake, most of whose Members were coming into Parliament for the first time and who outnumbered the old hands by more than 3 to 1, and also in the relatively small proportion of trade-union-sponsored candidates amongst them.

In terms of social and educational backgrounds there was a substantial continuity between the old and the new; in terms of individuals there had been a transformation.

Table 5 compares, in summary form, the more important background characteristics of the senior Members, those, that is, who had been Members at the dissolution in 1945 and who were not appointed to government office, with those of the new backbench intake.

Three hundred and ninety-three Labour MPs had been elected in July 1945; to this must be added 33 who were elected at byelections, together with three Members, elected on the ILP or Common Wealth ticket, who joined the Labour Party during the lifetime of the 1945 Parliament.[1] From these, for comparability purposes, we must exclude those Members who held government office for all or most of the Parliament, for Ministers and others holding government office cannot sign backbench motions or participate in floor revolts. To these have been added a few Members who were in Parliament for too short a time to have had the opportunity of signing many significant EDMs. In addition a handful of Members not holding office who held or had held politically sensitive posts and who failed to sign *any* politically relevant motions, have been discarded—men like Sir Charles Edwards, the former Labour Chief Whip, and Arthur Moyle, PPS to the Prime Minister. The point of these exclusions is to ensure that backbenchers who signed any particular motion, or train of motions, are compared only with those who were not debarred from signing either by the requirements of office or non-membership of the House. The result of these exclusions is to give a total of 352 MPs.

These 352 MPs have been classified in various ways. *Occupation* has long been regarded as one of the most important dividing lines in the Labour Party. Occupation here means the Member's occupation during the 1945–50 Parliament, or if he had none, his last occupation before election. *Workers* embraces manual workers and includes full-time trade union officials who had been manual workers before taking a paid trade union appointment. They numbered just over a quarter of the backbench party. The *Professions*, constituting almost a third of the party, consisted of members of recognized professions such as doctors, lawyers, and school and university teachers. Just over a third were barristers or solicitors, and about the same number were teachers or university lecturers. Doctors and dentists accounted for a tenth, and the remainder—professional soldiers, architects, electrical engineers, clergymen, and others—comprised nearly a fifth. The *Business* section was a small and heterogeneous group consisting of managers and proprietors, and included the owners of small businesses such as hairdressers and booksellers. Three-quarters of the men included in the Business group were company directors or had held office in either the co-operative retail societies or the CWS. The *Miscellaneous Occupations* totalled nearly a quarter of the backbench party. Two-fifths of them were

[1] One Independent Labour Member, Mr. D. N. Pritt, a former Member of the Party, who had been expelled from it, has also been included.

TABLE 5. THE RUMP AND THE 1945 INTAKE

		Pre-1945 rump (%)	1945 intake (%)
(a)	*By occupation*		
	Workers	42	23
	Miscellaneous Occupations	27	25
	Business	6	16
	Professions	18	34
	Unknown	6[a]	3[a]
(b)	*By sponsorship*		
	Trade Union	50	26
	Co-operative	5	7
	CLP	38	67
	Unknown	6[a]	—
(c)	*By education*		
	Elementary	43	28
	Elementary/Secondary+	13	10
	Secondary and Public School only	11	17
	University	23	36
	Women	1	7
	Unknown	9	2
(d)	*By university*		
	U1 (public school and Oxford or Cambridge)	5	12
	U2 (public school and other university)	5	5
	U3 (secondary school and Oxford or Cambridge)	—	3
	U4 (secondary school and other university)	11	14
	Unknown	1[a]	1[a]
(e)	*By age*		
	> 60	64	17
	51–60	21	25
	41–50	6	35
	< 41	3	17
	Unknown	6	5[a]
(f)	*By region*		
	Metropolitan	21	21
	Scotland, Wales, Lanc., Cheshire, and the North	60	43
	Rest	20[a]	36

[a] Apparent discrepancies in addition due to rounding.

journalists or authors; a quarter had held miscellaneous clerical posts. Some difficulty arose about the classification of trade union organizers for whom there was no evidence of previous manual working-class employment. Eventually they were classed with the Miscellaneous Occupations, constituting a fifth of this group. The remaining fifth had varied backgrounds; mention may be made of four who were full-time political organizers, and of five who were lecturers not attached to a university or the WEA.

Educationally the party has been divided into five groups. Women form a small separate class; the *Elementary/Secondary+* group consisted of Members with an elementary and/or secondary school education who went on to further formal training, such as teacher-training college or technical college. The *Secondary* school group includes the small number of public-school men who did not go to university.

The *Elementary* school and *University* classes are self-explanatory; but, as in the previous study, the University Members have been divided into four subgroups. U1 consists of those Members who attended a public school and went on to either Oxford or Cambridge; U2 of public-school Members who went to some other university; U3 of secondary-school Members who went to Oxford or Cambridge; and U4 of the secondary-school men who went on to one of the other universities.

The sponsorship categories are clear. *Trade Unionist* MPs consist of all those Members whose candidature had been formally sponsored by a trade union, the co-operators of those sponsored either by the Co-operative Party or the RACS, with the constituency party Members accounting for the rest.

The Members were also classified according to five other criteria—age,[2] year of first entry into Parliament, size of majority,[3] and war service. Figures 1–5 show, in diagrammatic form, the structure of the backbench party by occupation, education, sponsorship, age and year of entry into Parliament (political seniority).

Not surprisingly, there was a strong (though not perfect) tendency for the occupational, educational, and sponsorship boundaries to coincide. Four-fifths of the Workers were trade-union sponsored. Nearly a quarter of the Miscellaneous Occupations class were likewise sponsored—a significant difference from the situation in the 1955–9 Parliament. On the other hand, only a handful of the Business and Professions groups were sponsored by the unions.

Conversely, nearly half of the CLP-sponsored Members were from the Professions, most of the remainder being drawn in fairly equal numbers from the Business and Miscellaneous Occupations group.

There was the similar and expected coincidence between the educational and occupational groupings. Two-thirds of the Workers were elementary educated and only one was a university graduate (though a further six had had some form of post-secondary training). The Miscellaneous Occupations and Business classes showed the widest educational spread; a third of the former and a quarter of the latter were drawn from the elementary educated; whilst university graduates supplied a quarter of the Miscellaneous Occupations and a third of the Business sections. In contrast, three-quarters of the professional men were graduates.

Some of the most intriguing interrelationships were found amongst the university graduates. If the intellectuals of the Labour Party can be defined as the university graduates, it is clear that the intellectuals were not a homogeneous group.

For purposes of comparison, all the graduates who had been to a public school or to Oxford or Cambridge, or had done both of these (i.e. the U1's, U2's, and U3's) were contrasted with those who had been to a secondary school and a provincial Scottish or Welsh university (the U4's).

The U4's were considerably older than their fellow graduates; nearly half of them were over

---

[2] Members' ages were taken as at 31 Dec. 1949.

[3] This classification has a strong overlap with those of occupation, sponsorship, and education, and is not a very useful measure. Nevertheless, a breakdown of Members by size of majority was made and is occasionally referred to in the text.

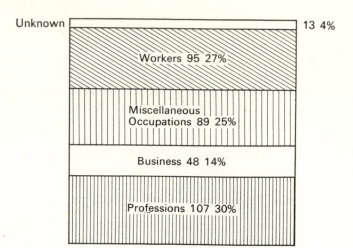

FIG. 1. The Labour Party, 1945–50: by occupation.

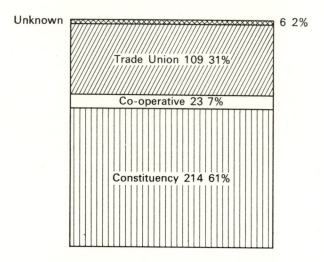

FIG. 2. The Labour Party, 1945–50: by sponsorship.

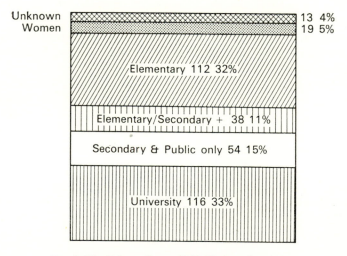

FIG. 3. The Labour Party, 1945–50: by education.

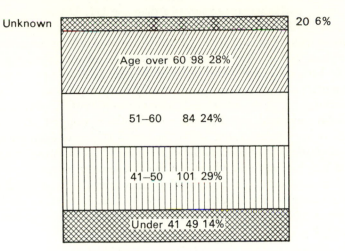

FIG. 4. The Labour Party, 1945–50: by age.

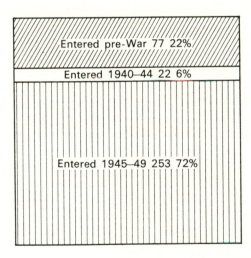

FIG. 5. The Labour Party, 1945–50: by political seniority.

50, compared with a seventh of the U1, U2, and U3 group. Less than a fifth of them had served in the armed forces as against three-fifths of the other university Members. The U4's tended to have had rather more parliamentary experience than the U1, U2, and U3 classes; nearly a third had come into Parliament before 1945, whilst this was true of only a sixth of the U1's, U2's and U3's. Most striking of all, perhaps, were the regional differences; nearly a third of the U4's sat for Scottish or Welsh constituencies; only *one* of the other university groups did so.

The relationship between age and year of entry has already been mentioned; but there was also a fairly strong relationship between age and year of entry, on the one hand, and occupation, sponsorship, and education, on the other hand. About two-fifths of the over-60's were Workers and Trade Unionists compared with less than a tenth of the youngest age group, the under-41's. A fifth of the oldest Members, but half of the under-41's, were from the Professions. The four age groups drew in roughly equal numbers from the Miscellaneous Occupations. Similar links were found between age and education; the Elementary educated were concentrated disproportionately amongst the over-60's, the University graduates amongst the younger MPs.

The relationship between year of entry and factors such as occupation was less close, as has already been indicated. Nearly a quarter of the 1945 class were Workers—the proportion of pre-war Members being a third.

We find, therefore, that as in the 1955–9 Parliament, there were two distinct cultural groupings, and a third, more heterogeneous and less certain. There was the Trade-Union-sponsored working-class group, most of whose Members had received an elementary education; a professional CLP-sponsored group which consisted largely of university men; and the Business and Miscellaneous Occupations, whose Members came from a wide range of educational backgrounds and whose sponsorship characteristics were more mixed than those of either the Professions or the Workers. These interrelationships are presented in diagrammatic form in Figs. 6–8.

According to the information available, just under a quarter of the backbenchers had served in the armed forces. It may be that some of the older Members who had served in the First World War did not mention this[4] in the standard reference works. Nearly half of the Members claiming war service were under 41; nearly all of them were first elected in 1945. Over half were university graduates; half were professional men; and most of the remainder was drawn from the Miscellaneous Occupations and the Business group. Most, too, were sponsored by the CLPs.

Yet though there was a strong tendency for the occupational, educational, and sponsorship boundaries to coincide, the relationship was never exact. For this reason the behaviour of a specific occupational group will not necessarily be reflected in the response of the corresponding educational group. If, for instance, we find the reactions of the Workers diverging from those of the Elementary educated, the cause will lie in the distinctive attitudes of those elementary-school Members who were not Workers, or of those Workers who had proceeded beyond an elementary education.

Table 5 compared the composition of the pre-war rump of the party with the new intake of 1945. Table 6 gives the composition of the whole backbench Labour Party by occupation, education, university background, sponsorship, age, year of entry into Parliament, war service, and region.

[4] According to McCallum and Readman, *British General Election of 1945*, London, 1947, 101 Labour MPs had served in the armed forces either in the First World War or the Second or both. Their figures refer to all Labour MPs, whilst those cited above refer only to backbenchers.

FIG. 6. Sponsored and non-sponsored Members for 1945–50: by occupation.

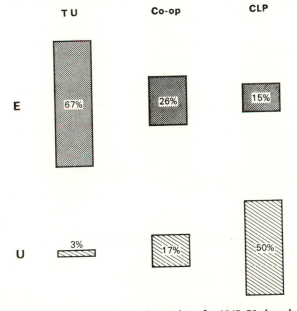

FIG. 7. Sponsored and non-sponsored Members for 1945–50: by education.

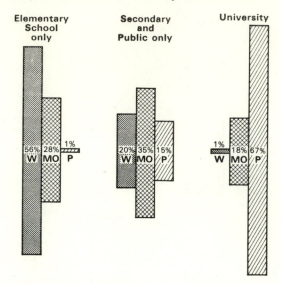

FIG. 8. Educational distribution of the Labour Party 1945–50.

TABLE 6. THE LABOUR PARTY, 1945–50

		No.	%
(a)	*By occupation*		
	Workers	95	27
	Miscellaneous Occupations	89	25
	Business	48	14
	Professions	107	30
	Unknown	13	4
		352	100
(b)	*By sponsorship*		
	Trade Union	109	31
	Co-operative	23	7
	CLP	214	61
	Unknown	6	2
		352	100[a]
(c)	*By education*		
	Elementary	112	32
	Elementary/Secondary+	38	11
	Secondary and Public School only	54	15
	University	116	33
	Women	19	5
	Unknown	13	4
		352	100

[a] Apparent discrepancies in addition due to rounding.

TABLE 6   (*continued*)

	No.	%
(d) *By University background*		
U1 (public school and Oxford or Cambridge)	37	11
U2 (public school and other university)	19	5
U3 (secondary school and Oxford or Cambridge)	9	3
U4 (secondary school and other university)	48	14
Unknown	3	1
	116	33[a]
(e) *By age*		
> 60	98	28
51–60	84	24
41–50	101	29
< 41	49	14
Unknown	20	6
	352	100[a]
(f) *By year of first entering Parliament*		
Pre-1939	77	22
1940–44	22	6
1945–9	253	72
	352	100
(g) *By war service*		
Civil Defence or Ambulance	18	5
Armed Forces	81	23
None	250	71
Unknown	3	1
	352	100
(h) *By region*		
Metropolitan	73	21
South-east	32	9
Eastern	16	5
Northern	55	16
Midlands	53	15
Western	14	4
Lancashire and Cheshire	53	15
Wales	19	5
Scotland	36	10
Ulster	1	—
	352	100

[a] Apparent discrepancies in addition due to rounding.

Regions were defined as follows:

Metropolitan: All constituencies lying wholly or largely in the Metropolitan Police Area.

South-east: All constituencies (other than those classified as Metropolitan) in Essex, Bedfordshire, Hertfordshire, Kent, Surrey, Sussex, Hampshire, Berkshire, and Oxfordshire.

Eastern: Norfolk, Suffolk, Huntingdonshire, Cambridgeshire, Isle of Ely, and Lincolnshire (except for Rutland and Stamford).

Northern: Northumberland, Cumberland, Westmorland, Durham, and Yorkshire.

Midlands: Staffordshire, Warwickshire, Herefordshire, Shropshire, Derbyshire, Nottinghamshire, Leicestershire, Northamptonshire, and the constituency of Rutland and Stamford.

Western: Cornwall, Devon, Dorset, Somerset, Gloucestershire, and Wiltshire.

Lancashire and Cheshire: Self-explanatory.

Wales: All constituencies in Wales and Monmouthshire.

Scotland: Self-explanatory.

Ulster: Self-explanatory.

THE 1950–1 AND 1951–5 PARLIAMENTS

The Labour Party limped back to office in 1950 shorn of nearly 80 seats and with its overall majority cut to 6. It limped out of office in 1951, losing in the process a further 22 seats. These losses, however, had little effect on the balance of social forces within the Parliamentary Party.

As the composition of the backbench party in the 1950–1 Parliament differed little from the 1951–5 Parliament, the figures for the two parliaments have been combined (except for age and year of entry into parliament) to form Table 7 in order to avoid unnecessary repetition. In Figs. 9–13, however, the composition of the party is shown diagrammatically, and for this

TABLE 7. THE LABOUR PARTY, 1950–1 AND 1951–5

	%
(a) By occupation	
Workers	30
Miscellaneous Occupations	23
Business	12
Professions	32
Not known	3
	100
(b) By sponsorship	
Trade Union	35
Co-operative	8
CLP	57
	100
(c) By education	
Elementary	33
Elementary/Secondary+	11
Secondary	14
University	36
Women	5
Not known	1
	100

TABLE 7 *(continued)*

	%
(d) *By school and university*	
U1 (public school and Oxford or Cambridge)	11
U2 (public school and other university)	6
U3 (secondary school and Oxford or Cambridge)	3
U4 (secondary school and other university)	16
Not known	1
	37
(e) *By war service*	
Civil Defence or Ambulance	5
Armed Forces	23
None	72
	100
(f) *By region*	
Metropolitan	17
South-east	5
Eastern	3
Northern	18
Midlands	19
Western	4
Lancashire and Cheshire	14
Wales	9
Scotland	12
	100

1950–1

	No.	%
(g) *By age*[a]		
> 60	69	29
51–60	72	30
41–50	66	27
< 41	31	13
Unknown	3	1
	241	100
(h) *By year of first entering Parliament*		
Pre-war	47	20
1940–4	15	6
1945–9	146	61
1950	33	14
	241	100

[a] Members' ages were taken as at 31 Dec. 1951.

TABLE 7 (*continued*)

1951–5

	No.	%
(i) *By age*[a]		
> 60	79	31
51–60	87	34
41–50	62	24
< 41	21	8
Unknown	5	2
	254	100
(j) *By year of first entering Parliament*		
Pre-1945	56	22
1945–9	151	59
1950	28	11
1951–3	19	7
	254	100

[a] Members' ages were taken as at 31 Dec. 1955.

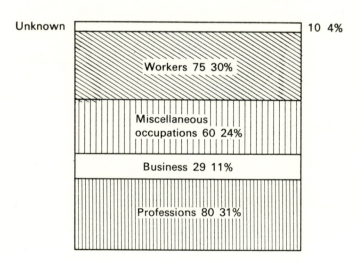

FIG. 9. The Labour Party, 1951–5: by occupation.

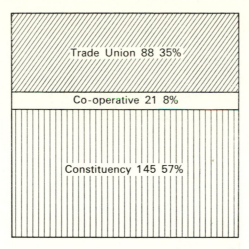

FIG. 10. The Labour Party, 1951–5: by sponsorship.

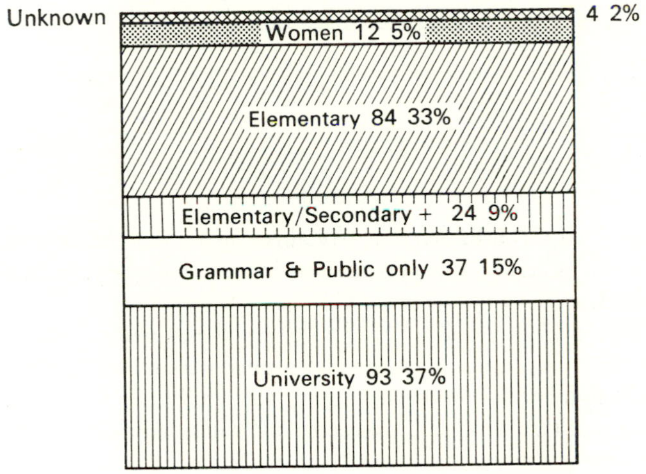

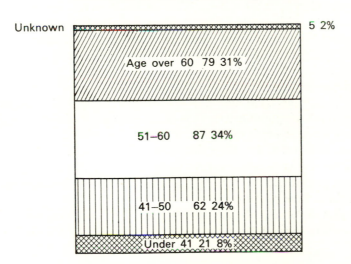

FIG. 11. The Labour Party, 1951–5: by education.

FIG. 12. The Labour Party, 1951–5: by age.

43

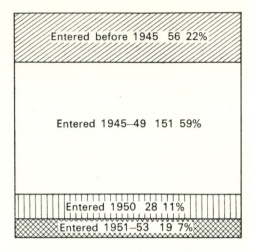

Fig. 13. The Labour Party, 1951–5: by political seniority.

purpose the figures for the 1951–5 Parliament have been used. On the former basis the representation of both the Workers and the Professions increased slightly, with the Professions keeping their narrow lead.

The proportion of Trade Unionists improved a little at the expense of the CLP sponsored and the Co-operators. In contrast, amongst the educational groups, the University graduates increased their strength slightly whilst the Elementary educated marked time. What had happened was that the effects of two distinct movements had cancelled each other out. There was the long-term trend towards the embourgeoisement of the Parliamentary Party—the secular tendency for the number of Labour candidates drawn from the professions, the white-collar groups, and business to increase at the expense of the manual-worker element. Against that is the fact that the Trade Unionist working-class Members occupied (and still do) to a disproportionate extent the safer Labour seats. Thus, whilst the processes of retirement and replacement helped the middle-class section of the party, the defeated Members were drawn predominantly from that same group.

Yet in all, the differences between the backbench party of the 1945 Parliament and that of the 1950–1 and 1951–5 Parliaments were minor. The separation of the three cultures within the party was, however, if anything, more acute than in the Parliament of 1945. By 1951 88 per cent of the Workers were trade-union sponsored; the percentage of trade unionists amongst the Miscellaneous Occupations fell to 12. More than two-thirds of the Workers, and almost the same proportion of Trade Unionists were Elementary educated, whereas 82 per cent of the Professional men were graduates. More than half of the CLP-sponsored had been to a university, and nearly half of them were professional men. The Trade Union Worker MPs were also considerably older than the others; 85 per cent of the Workers were over 50 compared to 58 per cent of the Miscellaneous Occupations and 49 per cent of the Professions. The differences within the University group remained, though the contrast in age and war service was somewhat less marked than in 1945. Nothing that had happened in the two elections since 1945 had done anything to blend the party into a more integrated whole or to soften the edge of the cultural cleavages. A diagrammatic representation of the sponsorship position and educational distribution from 1951 to 1955 is shown in Figs. 14–16.

Figure 14 shows the proportion of each sponsorship group comprised by the various occupational groups, i.e. 75% of the Trade Unionists were Workers.

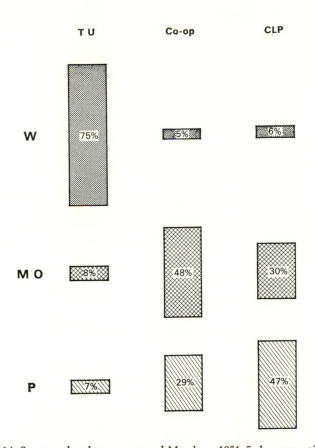

FIG. 14. Sponsored and non-sponsored Members, 1951–5: by occupation.

Figure 15 shows the proportion of each sponsorship group comprised by the two main educational categories, e.g. 66% of the Trade Unionists were Elementary educated.

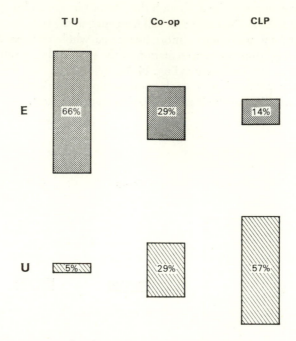

FIG. 15. Sponsored and non-sponsored Members, 1951–5: by education.

Figure 16 shows the proportion of the two main educational categories comprised by the three occupational groups, e.g. 61% of the Elementary educated were Workers.

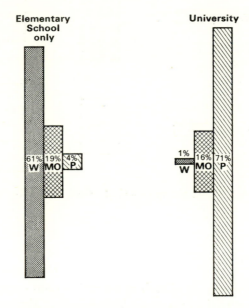

FIG. 16. Educational distribution of the Labour Party, 1951–5.

CHAPTER 4

The Labour Party: Foreign Affairs and Defence, 1945–50

"There is always a tendency on the part of some people in the Labour Party to oversimplify foreign affairs." (CLEMENT ATTLEE quoted in FRANCIS WILLIAMS, *A Prime Minister Remembers*.)

"The war which has devastated Europe for four and a half years is over, and millions have perished, but the heathen deities of Militarism and Secret Diplomacy which exacted the sacrifices have still to be slain." (F. SEYMOUR COCKS (later Labour MP), *E. D. Morel: The Man and his Work*, 1920.)

"Anglo-American world policy in fact is not so much a policy as a series of retreats and rearguard actions by die-hard defenders of Capitalism, who can be forced to acknowledge defeat but will go on preparing for war. . . ." (K. ZILLIACUS, MP, *I Choose Peace*, 1949.)

The Labour Left's attitude to Ernest Bevin's foreign policy did not manifest a consistent pattern over the years or, indeed, a coherent doctrine at any one time. Rather, criticisms of government policy varied both in force and persistence, and were based upon beliefs which were not always free of contradiction and uncertainty. This is hardly surprising given the diversity of the historic strands of which the Labour Left and, indeed, the Labour Party itself is composed. Like the nineteenth-century Liberals, the Labour Party can be aptly described as "a gathering of the discontented"; what unites the Labour Party, as with the Liberals before them, is often a negative response towards the dominant institutions and values. In no area is this more true than in the realm of foreign affairs; and nowhere do the inconsistencies and contradictions become more apparent. Left-wing criticism (or more accurately criticisms) of traditional foreign policy is drawn from a rich diversity of sources, some of which long preceded the rise of socialism and the creation of working-class political organizations.

The oldest of these sources was closely identified with the political radicalism of the mid and late nineteenth century which, so far from being linked to a programme of domestic collectivism, was usually associated with a policy of free trade and *laissez-faire*. A single phrase, "power politics", sums up the object of radical attack. To radical critics (the dissenters in A. J. P. Taylor's phrase) the pursuit of selfish national advantage, the creation of sectional alliances, the maintenance of the balance of power, and the accumulation of national armaments were the begetters of discord between nations and the cause of war. "Power politics", moreover, were seen not as the prosecution of a genuine national or popular interest but as something designed to safeguard and extend the privileges of the ruling national *élite*. A sharp distinction was drawn between the interests of the people—"the common man"—and their governors.

Radicals saw the content of traditional policy as being closely connected with the form in which it was carried out. "Power politics" was to them the international policy of an aristocracy which managed affairs through the medium of its Cabinet representatives or the Foreign Office itself without either adequate publicity or genuine parliamentary control. For radicals, aristocractic or official management of foreign policy was a formula for national rivalry and war, democratic control a necessary and perhaps sufficient condition of universal peace.

This distinctively radical view of foreign policy has tended to merge in the twentieth century with the specifically socialist criticism of imperialism. For the socialist, and especially the Marxist, foreign policy reflected the wishes and needs not so much of the political *élite* as of the broader property-owning class. The makers of foreign policy—both official and political—proceeded on the assumptions of the dominant bourgeoisie. Investors, unable to obtain an adequate return on their capital at home, found a profitable outlet in the undeveloped world. Railways were laid down in East Africa, mines sunk in Rhodesia, tin was extracted in Bolivia, rubber planted in Malaya. Producers, lacking markets in their own country, exported to the underdeveloped world which paid for these in cheap raw materials. The critics of capitalism saw investors and producers driven by the demands and contradictions of the system to seek new opportunities for the employment of capital, new markets for surplus manufactures, and new sources of commodities. The political power was called in to protect the investments of the rentier and the markets of the exporter from the risk of native disturbance or the aggression of other capitalist states. The rivalry in armaments and diplomacy of the Great Powers sprang from their relationship as economic competitors. The jealousies and enmities that had culminated in the First World War were the inevitable result of the economic organization of society. Britain and Germany were competitors in trade and rivals in investment before they became antagonists in arms. In the same way, 20 years later, the territorial expansion of Nazi Germany was seen as coming from an economic imperative. Moreover, armament programmes were seen as the resort of an economic system which, unable to consume in peaceful ways all that it could produce, was compelled to solve its problem of unemployment and over-production by the creation of weapons of destruction and the enrolment of conscript armies. Only the replacement of capitalism by socialism could save mankind from the recurrent clashes of competing imperialisms. Even Clement Attlee appeared to share much of this analysis. Writing in 1937 he declared, in an oft-quoted passage: "There is a deep difference of opinion between the Labour Party and the Capitalist parties on foreign as well as on home policy, because the two cannot be separated. The foreign policy of a Government is the reflection of its internal policy. Imperialism is the form which Capitalism takes in relation to other nations."[1]

The theory of imperialism had emphasized the hostile interests of the property-owning classes in the industrialized countries of the world. A third tendency, however, which appeared during the thirties and the Second World War, stressed not ruling-class rivalry but ruling-class collaboration. Fascism was seen as the instrument with which the ruling classes in Germany, Italy, Austria, and Spain had destroyed the threat to their domination which came from political democracy in general and working-class groups in particular. Some who took this view alleged that the ruling classes of Britain and France had actively encouraged the rulers of Nazi Germany and Fascist Italy as a bulwark against Soviet Russia. Frightened by the growth of communism, the rulers of the Western states hoped to use fascist power to destroy the threat of social revolution in the rest of Europe.

"In the field of foreign policy [wrote Tom Horabin, then a radical Liberal, but later a

---

[1] C. R. Attlee, *The Labour Party in Perspective*, London, 1937.

Labour MP] the Tory Dictatorship had two objectives in view to achieve its grand design of safeguarding the privileges of wealth. It wished to destroy Soviet Russia as the symbol of revolution, and it was determined to create impregnable barriers in Europe against the spread of revolution across the western border of Soviet Russia."[2]

In a less extreme form it was argued that the Conservative governments of the thirties had tacitly allowed the growth of fascist strength as a barrier to and a possible suppressor of Russian communism. F. Elwyn Jones,[3] in attempting to explain Mr. Chamberlain's foreign policy, put this succinctly in his book *The Battle for Peace*: "What is the explanation? It is the sympathy of reactionaries in England with reactionaries abroad."[4] This theme, in either its more melodramatic or its more sober form, was publicized in numerous popular publications which appeared during the war, such as the Gollancz Yellow Books, and was echoed in the years after 1945.

The pursuit of "power politics", the rivalries of imperialist states, competition in the manufacture of ever-increasing armaments, the collaboration (tacit or open) of ruling classes frightened by the threat of social revolution—these were what socialist critics saw in the conduct of foreign policy. To these may be added a fourth contribution, which had some affinity to the radical distrust of "power politics"—a widespread antipathy to militarism. According to this view, the military spirit rather than a particular form of political control or economic organization was the enemy of peace. "Some people here", said the veteran pacifist Rhys Davies, MP, at the Labour Party Conference of 1949, "imagine that the great conflict of the age is between Capitalism and Socialism. That is only a small part of the problem that afflicts mankind. The real issue is between the military class and the civilian population all over the world."[5] Militarism, then, was seen as transcending the opposition between capitalism and socialism. Indeed, historically, pacifism—like the suspicion of "power politics"—was often found amongst those who were innocent of any trace of collectivism. "There never was a time", exclaimed Alfred Illingworth, a Liberal MP, later the special object of the hostility of the ILP, "when the armaments of Europe were so bloated and so enormous, and who would deny that there never was a moment before when less confidence existed between nations."[6] But, despite its connection with *laissez-faire* and free trade, pacifism and, in particular, hostility to conscription, has registered a strong appeal amongst some sections of the British Labour Movement. The Labour Party officially opposed rearmament in the early 1930's and compulsory national service as late as May 1939, and elements of the party continued to criticize rearmament down to the time of Munich.

Given the diversity of opinion it was not easy for the party in the inter-war years to construct a foreign policy which would satisfy all its sections. After 1918 the party officially supported the League of Nations and collective security, a policy which reflected the radical rather than the specifically socialist components of its thinking. Even here it must be recalled that the radical dislike of "power politics" sometimes carried with it opposition to foreign entanglements and a desire for isolation incompatible with a genuine belief in collective security. But generally the party saw, in a strong and effective League, the answer to the international anarchy of the years before the First World War. Armed force, whose use was illegitimate for a national government

[2] T. Horabin, *Politics Made Plain*, London, 1944.
[3] Attorney-General in the Labour Governments of 1964 and 1966.
[4] F. Elwyn Jones, *The Battle For Peace*, London, 1938.
[5] *LPCR (Labour Party Conference Report), 1949*, p. 159.
[6] HC Deb., 3rd series, 177, c. 262. Illingworth was speaking in 1883.

pursuing its own selfish interests, could be justified if employed at the orders of the League. Yet both the pacifist and the specifically socialist approaches to foreign policy were hard to square with collective security. Unconditional pacifists could no more accept the use of sanctions at the instructions of the League than they could endorse expenditure for the defence of empire. Extreme socialists found it difficult to believe that collective security could be effective in a world of capitalist states. The dynamic of imperialism, or perhaps the common interest of the ruling classes in crushing the social revolution, would make nonsense of a policy whose success depended on capitalist governments loyally agreeing to and faithfully executing the League's recommendations.

British socialists, when they looked at the problems of foreign policy, prayed not to one god but to several. The diverse elements might acquire a gloss of unity when blended in the rhetoric of the conference platform; their disparate nature became all too clear under the stress of crisis or the test of events.[7]

Yet, despite this diversity, many socialists thought it axiomatic that a Labour government's foreign policy should differ, radically and perhaps fundamentally, from that of the Conservative Party. Socialists might disagree with one another about the exact nature of a socialist foreign policy; few on the Left of the party doubted that such a policy should be distinctive. Ernest Bevin's much misquoted "Left can speak to Left" was echoed, often in ways of which Bevin never approved, by the Left. The Labour Government's relationship with socialist governments abroad would differ radically from its relationship with capitalist countries. To many, though not to all, on the Left, the Soviet Union appeared as the exemplar of a socialist society; whatever temporary or local divergences might appear between the two countries, it was unthinkable that a Labour Britain could ever treat Russia as just another foreign country. A socialist Britain and a socialist Russia would be ideological partners whose friendship, though it might be disturbed by occasional and local disputes, would never be shaken, like that of capitalist states, by major conflicts of economic interest. A Labour Britain would collaborate, in a special and intimate way, with socialist Russia, and encourage socialist forces in those countries where they had not yet achieved power.

From 1940 to 1945 Labour, as one of the parties forming the coalition, shared responsibility for the war-time Government's foreign policy. There were, nevertheless, vocal critics on the Left, both inside and outside the party, who strongly opposed some of the government's decisions. British policy towards Italy provoked discontent on the Left in 1944; Mr. Churchill was alleged to be conniving at the reinstatement of monarchical and reactionary elements within the country. British intervention in Greece aroused more bitter and more persistent criticism. Churchill's apparently friendly references to General Franco in 1944 also not unnaturally excited some ill-feeling in left-wing circles. Some saw in the conduct of British policy a continuation of what, it was alleged, had been the dominant tendency in pre-war foreign policy —a desire to shore up the privileged and propertied classes against the demands of the common people. This analysis of Britain's actions and motives was widely voiced in resolutions and speeches from the floor at the party conference of 1945. ". . . the British Government's policy now and for the future of certain liberated countries in Europe, particularly Belgium, Greece, Italy and Poland is more concerned with the preservation of vested interests than for the welfare, liberty, equality or social security of these peoples" declared a resolution moved by Jack

---

[7] The divergent strands were, of course, sometimes embodied in the attitudes of the same individual. Thus Kingsley Martin, for many years Editor of the *New Statesman and Nation*, represented a notable convergence of what were, historically speaking, different elements.

Stanley of the Constructional Engineering Union.[8] "In Greece, in Belgium, and in Italy the British imperialists have shown that they will not tolerate the emergence of Socialism in Europe, but that, on the contrary, they are prepared to back up the forces of reaction with British bayonets",[9] asserted Mr. Leigh Davis of Willesden. Another delegate, Mr. Pugh of Westbury, complained that Mr. Attlee, in opening the debate on international affairs, had not applied a socialist analysis to the world situation. "It was an analysis that might have been applied by a very good Liberal statesman in those days of the League of Nations when people believed sincerely that a League of capitalist governments would prevent war."[9]

It is not surprising, given the commitment of the party's leaders to the foreign policy of the Coalition Government, that foreign affairs played little part in the election campaign. The official policy statement of the Labour Party called for a consolidation of "the great war-time association of the British Commonwealth with the U.S.A. and the U.S.S.R.",[10] and for the formation of "an International Organization capable of keeping the peace in years to come". Germany and Japan, so the statement said, must be deprived of all power to make war again. Only once did the section on international affairs strike a partisan note: "in the years leading up to the war the Tories were so scared of Russia that they missed the chance to establish a partnership which might well have prevented the war."[10] The wartime euphoria induced by the alliance of the Big Three still persisted in certain quarters.

The similarity of the approach to foreign affairs offered by the leaders of the two parties[11] was not fully shared by rank-and-file candidates. Between these there were differences, at least in tone; Labour candidates emphasized collective security through the United Nations; Conservatives the importance of national power.[12]

Both Attlee and Bevin at the Labour Party Conference in May appeared to endorse the foreign policy of the Coalition and to dampen the hopes of their more militant supporters, and when Bevin made his first Commons' speech as Foreign Secretary in the Debate on the Address in August it became clear that there would be little change in the conduct of foreign affairs. "The basis of our policy [said Mr. Bevin] is in keeping with that worked out by the Coalition Government. . . . It rests in the main on agreement and co-operation between the great Powers."[13] Such a broad statement, of course, was not incompatible with meeting the specific discontents of the Left, but when he went on to deal with particular countries such as Greece, Mr. Bevin indicated that there would be no change in policy. He charged that the governments set up in Bulgaria, Rumania, and Hungary did not represent the majority of the people: ". . . the impression we get from recent developments is that one kind of totalitarianism is being replaced by another."[14] As for Spain, he rejected intervention by foreign powers on the ground that this would probably strengthen, and not weaken, General Franco's position.[15]

The recurring freelance criticism of the Coalition's foreign policy found an echo in the speeches of Labour backbenchers which gave a warning of troubles and disillusionment to come. Three new MPs—Lyall Wilkes, Michael Foot, and John Platt-Mills—spoke of intimidation and terror in Greece.[16] Mr. Peart averred that a Labour government would give a lead to the removal of suspicion and distrust between Britain and Russia.[17] Michael Foot, perhaps the

---

[8] *LPCR, 1945*, p. 109.   [9] *Ibid.*, p. 112.   [10] *Let Us Face the Future.*

[11] "It is curious, however, that the foreign policy of the two parties was remarkably similar in spite of this differing emphasis" (R. B. McCallum and A. Readman, *The British General Election of 1945*, London, 1947, p. 49).

[12] *Ibid.*, p. 97.

[13] HC Deb. 413, c. 287.   [14] *Ibid.*, c. 291.   [15] *Ibid.*, c. 296.

[16] *Ibid.*, cc. 305–11, 337–8, 385–7.   [17] *Ibid.*, c. 360.

most consistent and conspicuous libertarian in post-war British politics, clearly disturbed by signs of dictatorship in eastern Europe, appealed to the House to understand the bitterness aroused in liberated Europe by the collaboration of "the rich and powerful elements"[18] with the Nazis. Towards the end of his speech Foot foreshadowed a theme that was to play a prominent part in left-wing thinking—the idea of the Third Force. A democratic and socialist Britain combining conceptions of political liberty not known in Russia and of economic democracy not shared by the United States could offer a unique example to the world.

These expressions of backbench disquiet were echoed in some left-wing journals. In what was in the main a guardedly favourable comment on Bevin's speech, the *New Statesman* argued that there was a danger of certain passages of his speech being interpreted as a sign that he had already given way unduly to American pressure. "Was it really necessary [asked this journal] to identify ourselves with the American protests against the political set up in Bulgaria, Rumania and Hungary and to vie with Mr. Byrnes in formalistic adherence to parliamentary democracy as a universal panacea?"[19] Nor did the *New Statesman* find Mr. Bevin's references to Greece reassuring, and explained them by saying that in forming his judgement on Greece the Foreign Secretary had not had available to him all the essential information.[19] Three weeks later the same journal said that the Russians and the left-wing parties throughout Europe had waited to see what would happen when Labour achieved power. "Was Labour Socialist in the sense that it would regard reaction as a worse enemy than Communism? Everywhere east of Prague and Vienna, Mr. Bevin's speech brought hope to those Right wing parties whose power seemed to have been smashed by the German defeat, and dismay to the Left."[20] It was the misunderstandings and fears of Anglo-American policy which poisoned the atmosphere in southeastern Europe. Mr. Bevin had so far confirmed and not broken down these fears.

In its next issue, during the London meeting of the Council of Foreign Ministers, the same journal, in a mood of near despair, hinted at the need for a Third Force. America carried out a unilateral policy in the Far East, Russia in eastern Europe. "Unless there is to be real United Nations collaboration . . . we have no option but to draw together with the Dominions and our similarly situated European near neighbours in active self-preservations",[21] a view which was repeated in more explicit terms a fortnight afterwards.

War-time optimism about post-war co-operation between the three Great Powers soon faded. Serious difficulties had been apparent during the war, and while important decisions were taken at the Potsdam Conference of the Big Three in July 1945, the solution of other controversies was simply deferred. Although agreement was later reached on some minor issues during the next 18 months, the crucial problem of the German peace settlement remained; and, behind each particular quarrel lay the pattern of a general and widening conflict between East and West.

In the early months and years of the Labour Government there was widespread restiveness amongst Labour backbenchers at the course of British foreign policy. This restiveness was most marked amongst those who both then and later were identified with that loose and almost amorphous grouping, "the Left"; but it was also shared by some who soon renounced their left-wing identity and by others who were never regarded as members of the Left. Many Labour backbenchers put a sympathetic construction on Soviet policy; Russia's actions, so they said, were prompted by justified fears for her own security. The Allied invasion of 1919, Western policy in the thirties, and the German attack of 1941 had made the Russians, acutely and legiti-

[18] HC Deb. 413, c. 339.   [19] *NS & N*, 25 Aug. 1945.   [20] *NS & N*, 15 Sept. 1945.
[21] *NS & N*, 22 Sept. and 6 Oct. 1945.

mately, suspicious of the motives of other countries, especially the United States. If Russia would not co-operate, if she was both secretive and belligerent, this behaviour was natural in the light of her past experience. The onus was on the West to convince the Russians of their good faith and to show them that their fears were groundless.[22] Hence, any defensive, forestalling action by the West must be condemned. In winning Russia's confidence, Labour Britain had a special role and a unique opportunity. ". . . if we are to live in this world we must win the confidence of Russia, and I appeal to the Prime Minister to go out and seek Russia", declared S. Scholefield Allen in the autumn of 1945.[23]

Mrs. Barbara Ayrton Gould, a member of the party's National Executive, put the onus on Britain in a more explicit way.

> "In order to gain Russia's confidence we have got also to give them confidence. I want to suggest [she said] that, in order that we may get the only possible atmosphere to enable us to achieve peace, we should not go on insisting for the brief time available to us, on withholding from Russia and from other big nations that may be working on it the secret of the atomic bomb. . . ."[24]

Labour Members spoke repeatedly of the West's obligation to persuade Russia of their sincerity, "If we are to allay the suspicion which has been spoken of, it can only be done by proving *our*[25] sincerity",[26] asserted Fred Lee, whilst Lyall Wilkes, speaking 3 months later, said that he preferred to believe that "Russian policy today is a policy of self-defence".[27]

Elevated hopes about the intentions of Russia and the eastern Communist parties led some Members to unrestrained optimism.

> "O, it is excellent,
> To have a giant's strength; but it is tyrannous,
> To use it like a giant"

quoted John Mack of Newcastle under Lyme, adding "Russia has no intention of doing that".[28] John Haire, after returning from a visit to Hungary, disagreed with the idea that the Communist Party "is about to take over Hungary in a Communist 'putsch'. There is no suggestion of that; the four Communist Members in the Cabinet work in close co-operation with the other members . . .".[29]

Some backbenchers saw the main danger to peace arising not from Russia's desire for expansion but from the needs of capitalist America to find new export markets, new investment outlets, and new sources of raw materials.

> "The threat to security [argued Fred Peart, later to become the acme of Labour respectability] may come from other quarters. It may come from the desire of certain nations who seek economic interests in other parts of the world. . . . I am suspicious and disturbed about American monopoly capitalism which seeks to gain a stranglehold on many parts of the world."[30]

William Warbey saw in the demand of James Byrnes, American Secretary of State, for the opening up of the Danube basin, "a desire prompted by the dictates of American business".[31]

---

[22] See also R. Rose, The relation of socialist principles to foreign policy, Unpublished D.Phil. thesis, Oxford, 1958.

[23] HC Deb. 416, c. 639.   [24] *Ibid.*, c. 656.   [25] Author's italics.   [26] HC Deb. 416, c. 667.

[27] HC Deb. 419, c. 1235.   [28] HC Deb. 416, c. 626.   [29] HC Deb. 423, c. 1902.

[30] HC Deb. 416, cc. 690–1.

[31] For similar views to Warbey's see the speech of K. Zilliacus, HC Deb. 427, c. 1720.

". . . he meant that any American private business man should be free to go in with his investments and get a hold upon the internal economy, the industries and trade of those countries, . . .
and to prevent those countries, even if they so desired, establishing a planned socialist economy
and control of their foreign trade."[32] Such considerations lay behind the American resolve to
contain the spread of communism. "If it cannot split open the closed Socialist economies, then
it is going to prevent other Socialist economies from being established."[33] "The second effect
of this policy of the pressure groups in the United States", affirmed Tom Horabin, then a
Liberal, "is that they realise that to maintain their position inside their own country they have
to export their unemployment abroad . . . at the present moment the United States is pursuing
a policy of ruthless economic imperialism."[34]

Since the Russian Revolution, many on the Left have emphasized the ideological hostility of
capitalist to socialist states and many left-wing critics of the government's foreign policy often
differed in the stress they put upon the economic dynamic behind American policy and the
ideological motives. Sometimes they saw the two motives as complementing and reinforcing
each other. American business was hostile to the establishment of closed socialist economies, for
narrowly economic reasons, and was credited, for broader ideological purposes, with a wish
to hold back and if possible destroy communism. Zilliacus, from the extreme Left, saw the
Soviet Union as the spearhead of the social revolution in Europe; the road to peace lay in
the acceptance of this revolution, not in formulating plans for its containment and overthrow.
"The issue we have to face is the fact of the social revolution in the world, and what we are
going to do about it, what our attitude is towards it. On our decision on that issue depends
whether there will be peace between us and the Soviet Union or whether there is to be a third
world war."[35] Again, at the Labour Party Conference of 1948, when moving a long resolution
on foreign policy, Zilliacus complained that the government's foreign policy was not
Labour's policy but a continuation of that of Mr. Churchill and Mr. Eden in the war-time
coalition.

> "Mr. Churchill has also claimed again and again [said Zilliacus] that the Government
> shared his attitude towards Communism in Europe and Mr. Churchill's attitude is inspired
> by craven fear and fanatical hatred of the revolutionary workers of Europe . . . we must
> either co-operate [continued Zilliacus] with the working-class leadership of Europe, such
> as it is, as it really exists in fact, or else we will be driven into the position of getting ready
> with Mr. Churchill to fight the Socialist revolution in Europe."[36]

Those critics who emphasized the ideological motive behind Western policy to Russia often
saw Anglo-American policy as prompted by a resolve to maintain capitalism by force of arms.
Official Western claims about the defence of freedom and democracy were regarded as shabby
excuses to justify the strengthening of an economic system based on private ownership and
exploitation. By the autumn of 1946 backbench disquiet at the Labour Government's foreign
policy had developed into strong and sometimes violent criticism. The Labour Government
was accused of becoming the *de facto* ally of the American administration. Britain was no
longer playing the role of mediator between East and West, no longer discharging that special
role of conciliator for which she was so uniquely fitted. She was aligning herself with the
United States and within her own special sphere of influence she was supporting reactionary and

[32] HC Deb. 423, cc. 2068–9.   [33] *Ibid.*, c. 2068.   [34] *Ibid.*, c. 2061.
[35] HC Deb. 427, cc. 1712–13. See also HC Deb. 416, c. 828 and K. Zilliacus, *I Choose Peace*, London, 1949.
[36] *LPCR, 1948*, p. 186.

semi-fascist regimes. "I am suggesting", said Lyall Wilkes in October 1946, "that so far as Greece, Palestine, Spain, and other countries are concerned, British foreign policy at the moment is suffering from paralysis and is failing to perform the function which we hoped it would perform."[37] Others charged the government in even stronger terms. "His [Ernest Bevin's] policy is to seek out in every land where his writ runs that party which for certain will oppose the Soviet Union and the Communists and he backs that party to the hilt",[38] accused John Platts-Mills, later to be expelled from the Labour Party. "So here", said Zilliacus, speaking on the controversy over the Danube basin, "we have the Labour Government openly and directly supporting an offensive of American big business against the Socialist economies of Eastern Europe."[39]

A few Labour Members appeared to believe that it should be the task of British policy to assist the "social revolution" in Europe and to work in concert with the Soviet Union. Many more wanted Britain to detach herself from both the Russian and American blocs and to develop, in alliance with other "socialist" countries of western Europe and the Commonwealth, a Third Force, which would offer an alternative to the world other than absorption by the American colossus or the Russian giant. Others still argued that British policy should be based on collective security through the United Nations, an opinion which the government claimed to share. Some went further, and saw in world government the answer to Britain's dilemma and the world's agony. "I asked the electors of South Ayrshire", said the pacifist Emrys Hughes, "to send me here to support this idea of World Government as an alternative to the old traditional struggle of power politics";[40] or as Henry Usborne, the most prominent crusader for world government in Parliament put it, when moving the Address in November 1946: "Yet we, the common people of Britain . . . recognize that in this atomic age there is only one form of security for any of us; that is, the security, not of force but of effective international law, and the order which can be based upon it."[41]

The hostility of left-wing MPs to Bevin's policy did not preclude sharp disagreement amongst themselves. Michael Foot, after rejecting the idea of an Anglo-American alliance as "the shortest way to create the gulf across which the next war will be fought", also dismissed the view that

> ". . . the way to get peace is to agree to all the proposals which are made by the Soviet Union. . . . We should have to abandon our interests over a large part of Europe and the Middle East and break many of the pledges we have given, particularly in regard to the Poles . . . and hand over Trieste to the Yugoslavs. . . . Only if the surrender is abject and complete can we be certain of getting conciliation with the Russians, and if the surrender is abject and complete we may as well abandon all principles of democratic Socialism for which we stand in this country. Each issue [said Foot] should be judged on its socialist merits."[42]

In the same speech, alluding to the problem of Germany, Foot urged a total revision of the Potsdam Agreement: ". . . it is impossible to pursue a policy of keeping a country down and, at the same time, . . . of trying to build it up."[43] In the same debate, however, Julius Silverman, later to rebel with Foot in the famous Amendment to the Address of November 1946, argued that whatever the economic troubles of Germany, the cause "certainly is not the Potsdam agreement".[44] In the same way John Haire's defence of conditions in Hungary, to which

[37] HC Deb. 427, c. 1594.   [38] *Ibid.*, c. 1543.   [39] *Ibid.*, c. 1720.   [40] HC Deb. 419, c. 1186.
[41] HC Deb. 430, c. 11.   [42] HC Deb. 423, c. 1931 ff.   [43] *Ibid.*, c. 1930.
[44] *Ibid.* c. 1915.

reference has been made, seemed to encounter some scepticism from Richard Stokes,[45] who like Haire, was to sign the Amendment to the Address 5 months later.[46]

Government statements did not admit that the hopes of Big Three co-operation had irretrievably failed. The differences were treated as specific disagreements rather than as evidence of a universal schism. It was not the British Government but the Leader of the Opposition who publicly raised the banner of the Cold War. Speaking at Fulton, Missouri, in the hearing of President Truman, Mr. Churchill spoke of the "iron curtain" which had descended across Europe from the Baltic to the Adriatic. Peace would best be secured by the "fraternal association" of the English-speaking states, which required not only mutual friendship and understanding but continued military co-operation.

The government refused either to endorse or to repudiate Mr. Churchill's sentiments, and disclaimed any previous knowledge of the speech. Nevertheless, a newly elected Labour MP, William Warbey, tabled an EDM which strongly criticized Churchill's proposals for a military alliance as calculated to do injury to good relations between Great Britain, the United States, and Russia and as "inimical to the cause of world peace". The motion, which was signed by 120 Labour MPs, went on to affirm that peace and security could be maintained not by sectional alliances but by progressively strengthening the power and authority of the United Nations.[47] Many of the signatories were to become strong critics of Bevin's foreign policy, but some soon accepted the apparent inevitability of the government's course.

During 1946 signs of restiveness grew amongst the Labour Left, both in the House of Commons and outside, as evidence increased of British and American co-operation in the realm of foreign policy. There were hostile speeches in Parliament, in the Party Conference, and critical comment in the left-wing press. The first substantial parliamentary demonstration did not occur, however, until the autumn of 1946.

In late October, 21 Members, including Crossman, Foot, and Sydney Silverman, wrote to the Prime Minister about their disquiet at "the trend of the Government's foreign policy".

The letter put, in summary form, nearly all the dissident objections to the government's policy. In its analysis of the world situation and the prescriptions it offered, the letter paid some kind of homage to almost every element in the thinking of the dissident Left. The backbenchers proclaimed the idea of the Third Force; British social democracy, they affirmed, could provide a genuine middle way between American free enterprise and Russian totalitarianism. Whilst they acknowledged the difficulties under which the government worked, and the burden of inherited obligations, the critics complained that little had been done to establish the "middle way" in a "dynamic and positive manner". By her example, and the vigorous pursuit of socialist policies at home and abroad, the letter went on, Britain could bridge the antagonism between the United States and Russia; it would be possible to live in terms of friendship with both. Whilst the success of the Americans in establishing political democracy commanded the respect of the writers, so did "the Soviet Union's Socialist achievements in the economic field". Moreover, the pursuit of socialist policies by Britain both at home and abroad would "do much to encourage the Soviet Union in extending political and personal liberties once the danger of poverty and the fear of war have been overcome". British policies had not only alienated the new Communist societies, but had also discouraged democratic socialists in

[45] HC Deb. 423, c. 1903.
[46] Stokes, a Roman Catholic, can best be described as a radical humanitarian. He became Lord Privy Seal in the 1950 Government and was later strongly identified with the Right Wing of the party.
[47] EDM 36/45.

countries where Western socialism would, with British assistance, have been ripe for establishment.

Those with a Marxist or semi-Marxist view of the world could be satisfied by the reference to the "capitalist expansionist nature" of the American economy. The charge that the British Government had tacitly accepted the United States' "growing imperialist tendencies in all parts of the globe", and both in this and in her dealings with other countries such as Spain, Greece, and Germany seemed to be infected by an "anti-Red virus", echoed the thought of those who saw Anglo-American policy as a continuation of the anti-Communist strategy of the inter-war years. Labour's traditional belief in collective security and the hope of world government was reflected in the assertion that the safety of Britain and the Commonwealth must rest on the forces of the United Nations. For radicals, the letter denounced "power politics" and the British maintenance of "obsolete policies of Imperial defence". Similarly, the letter paid a minor tribute to the party's long pacifist tradition by averring that Britain's defence policies imposed a military burden on the country which could not be indefinitely sustained.

In its prescriptions, the letter pressed the government to aim at the elimination of all those forces in Europe, "social, economic or political", which had collaborated actively or passively with fascism. In countries such as Spain or Greece, Britain should set a "moral example to strengthen democratic Socialist resolve". The stress put on political, economic, and moral assistance reflected Labour's long-standing repugnance to the use of armed force, and the repeated theme of the "democratic Socialist example of Britain" testified to the left-wing tendency to think in terms of symbols and gestures rather than practical politics.

A deputation from the 21 MPs saw the Minister of State at the Foreign Office, Hector McNeil, on 12 November, the Foreign Secretary having gone to New York for the Foreign Ministers' Conference. Afterwards, the critics tabled an Amendment to the Address.[48]

Both the form and timing of the Amendment distinguished this incident from the normal run of parliamentary demonstrations. An Amendment to the Address is virtually a vote of censure upon the government of the day; and the disclosure of a revolt amongst government's backbench supporters during a meeting of Foreign Ministers of the Four Powers was hardly likely to strengthen the Foreign Secretary's hand.

The Amendment, which was eventually signed by 58 Members, called on the government to change its foreign policy so as to encourage and collaborate with those nations and groups which were striving to obtain "full Socialist planning and control of the world's resources"; such a change, asserted the Amendment, would provide "a democratic and constructive Socialist alternative to an otherwise inevitable conflict between American Capitalism and Soviet Communism in which all hope of World Government would be destroyed".[49] Its sponsors included Crossman, Foot, and Sydney Silverman. The next day the Parliamentary Labour Party, at the instigation of Attlee and Morrison, pressed for the withdrawal of the Amendment.[50] Nevertheless, the rebels persisted, and the Amendment was called by the Speaker on 18 November during the debate on the King's Speech.

Crossman, who moved the Amendment, distributed his censures equally between America and Russia. The latter, he asserted, had not co-operated, and bore much of the responsibility

[48] See Rose, *op. cit.*, p. 468. For the text of the letter and the list of signatories see the *Manchester Guardian*, 16 Nov. 1946.
[49] HC Deb. 430, c. 526.
[50] *Daily Telegraph*, 14 Nov. 1946.

for world tension. Nevertheless, America was pursuing an aggressive and imperialistic policy and Labour Britain had become closely identified with her. Crossman strove hard to dissociate his criticism of government policy from the issue of compulsory national service. He accepted that if British policy were re-cast on the lines advocated, the need for conscription would be greater—not less. He went on to expand on both the terms of the letter he and his 20 colleagues had sent to the Prime Minister and the Amendment. Everyone else in the world believed that Great Britain had lined up on the American side in this struggle. ". . . That is the reason for the widespread dispute with the Labour Governments of the people in Greece, Spain, France and other countries all over the world, who danced in the streets when the Labour Government came into power." The alignment of the Anglo-American bloc had destroyed the parties of the Centre and the Centre Left in Europe, such as France. He went on to press the policy of the British "middle way"; "a Socialist Britain which puts into effect an independent British policy and refuses to join any ideological bloc is the only power which can break the present deadlock and save this country and the world." Despite his acceptance of conscription, he found the *weight* of military commitments another reason for opposing the Anglo-American alliance. "We are being saddled with military commitments, including conscription, far too heavy to bear", and, anticipating the Bevanite critique of the 1951 rearmament programme, he added "no policy which demands military commitments and equipment which we cannot afford is tolerable or safe to this country or to democracy".

Crossman put three questions to the government. Would the government disavow the policy enunciated by Churchill in his Fulton speech? Had the government agreed to standardize the arms of British forces with those of the United States? Was the government holding staff conversations with the American General Staff?[51]

Of equal significance to Crossman's impartial allocation of blame was his attempt to separate the left-wing criticism of the government's foreign policy from the principle of conscription. Crossman's had been one of the few voices in the Labour Party during the thirties calling for rearmament and compulsory military service.

Crossman was followed by Joe Reeves, a Co-operator who, like many Labour backbenchers, saw a world government elected by the peoples of the world as the ultimate solution. Reeves, who later that day voted against conscription, represented the more pacificistic rather than the explicitly ideological strain in the Labour Left. The country's security, he asserted, did not lie in armies. "This country needs a positive peace policy . . . we can become the persistent and consistent advocate of peace throughout the world. We can be the actual peace force in the United Nations organization. Instead of seeking military alliances, let us find security by making the United Nations organization the instrument of our policy."[52] Jennie Lee's main criticisms were directed at Anglo-American policy in Germany, and in particular the way in which denazification had been carried out, or perhaps more appropriately, not carried out. Sydney Silverman suggested that Britain had no right to insist on governments being elected in a particular way in the states on Russia's borders, expressed intense admiration and affection for the socialist achievement of Russia, and asserted that the source of war could be found in economic disorder, citing the unemployment in Weimar Germany which had led to the rise of Hitler.[53]

At the end of the debate Crossman sought the leave of the House to withdraw the Amendment. Two ILP Members objected, however, with the result that a division was called. The two ILP Members acted as tellers for the Amendment but none of the rebels went into the lobby against the government. Three hundred and fifty-three voted for the government,

[51] HC Deb. 430, c. 526 ff.   [52] *Ibid.*, c. 543.   [53] *Ibid.*, c. 555 ff. and cc. 570–5.

including about a hundred Conservatives. Nevertheless, 130 Labour MPs, including all the signatories of the Amendment, did not vote in the division, many having deliberately abstained.

A few months later a pamphlet, *Keep Left*, supported by 15 MPs, most of whom had signed the Foreign Affairs Amendment, was published. In it the rebels explained their own programme in a detailed way. On the domestic front they had little quarrel with the government; they called, not for the implementation of full socialism in the classical sense but simply for an intensification of the government's present policies—an overall planning mechanism to be embodied in a Minister of Economic Affairs, tighter control of materials, controls over employment in non-essential industries, the cutting of luxury imports, and greater industrial democracy.

The tone of the pamphlet became much sharper when it discussed foreign affairs though even here the censure was qualified. "The real criticism of the Government's foreign policy is not that it has been Tory but that it has been only half-heartedly Socialist."[54] Again, Soviet responsibility for this condition was emphasized; nevertheless, whatever the reason, "Britain had been driven into a dangerous dependence on the USA."[55] Despite the confusion of British policy, the contradiction between the decision to emancipate India and the intention to maintain the imperial presence in the Middle East, there ran "one single and disturbingly consistent note—a readiness to follow American strategic thinking".

In Spain and in Greece Britain had supported, openly or tacitly, fascist and semi-fascist regimes. In the Middle East, Britain, with American help, was building up an anti-Bolshevik bloc of reactionary Arab states, and in this process was attempting to sustain reactionary Arab governments against their peoples. Whilst acknowledging that Middle East oil was a legitimate British interest, it questioned the need for large British forces in the area. The job of "propping up" Greece and Turkey had been left to the Americans, and this increased the risk of friction with Soviet Russia. Again, a new British initiative was called for. "If matters are allowed to drift the seeds of the next war will grow fast in a hotbed of oil."

Britain, the authors recognized, could not break suddenly with America and throw in its lot with Russia; she should "regain her independence" so that she could deal "with the USA and USSR as equals and as friends". Yet the pamphlet saw that Britain was not strong enough to follow a strictly independent policy. The authors wanted to avoid the division of the world into two blocs; but Britain alone could not offer the alternative. Echoing the language of the Amendment to the Address they called for a European Socialist alliance based on Britain and France. "France and Britain are now partners in a common fate . . . working together, we are still strong enough to hold the balance of world power, to halt the division into a Western and an Eastern *bloc*, and so to make the United Nations a reality."[56] One way to foster this alliance would be to stimulate trade between the countries of Europe. Another would be to create a European defence alliance, to deter aggression "either by Germany or by any non-European power".[57] Britain and France should formally forswear staff conversations with either America or Russia.[57]

The German problem remained a great obstacle to European unity. To break the deadlock between America and Russia required a British initiative—an initiative which would meet the fears of France about future German aggression.[58]

In the Near and Middle East, Britain should announce a timetable for the withdrawal of her troops. Having done this and so "proved the sincerity of our Socialist intentions", Britain should try to negotiate a settlement of the Great Power conflicts. She should propose that both

---

[54] *Keep Left*, London, 1947, p. 35.
[55] *Ibid.*, p. 37.   [56] *Ibid.*, p. 38.   [57] *Ibid.*, p. 40.   [58] *Ibid.*, p. 41.

the Dardanelles and the Suez Canal should be regarded as international waterways whose defence should be entrusted to the United Nations. Britain should also propose a four-power treaty which would guarantee the integrity of Persia and the Arab States and an agreement for the "equitable development and distribution" of Middle East oil.[59]

Thus the theme of the pamphlet, in the area of foreign affairs, lay in independence from the two power blocs, and, more specifically, in a detachment from any military alliance with the United States. A new socialist bloc, based on Britain, France, and apparently the Commonwealth, would prevent the polarization of the world into two alliances—one based on totalitarian communism, the other on unrestrained capitalism. A new democratic socialist "Third Force" would mediate between the two giants in external affairs, and the countries adhering to this Third Force would in their internal policies offer an alternative combining social justice with personal freedom. To this vision of the Third Force the pamphlet added in its proposals for the Dardanelles and the Suez Canal the familiar obeisance to the United Nations.

Hardly had the pamphlet been published, however, than its proposals had been made irrelevant by events, as its authors admitted in the successor pamphlet *Keeping Left* which appeared in January 1950.[60] The American Secretary of State, General Marshall, proposed that America should give economic help to Europe if the European nations could come together and agree on the best way of distributing this aid. The offer was made to both Communist and non-Communist countries. The foreign ministers of European countries, including Molotov, met in Paris in June 1947, but the Russians left the conference after a few days. The Czech Government, which had accepted the invitation to attend, also withdrew later under Soviet pressure.

General Marshall's offer transformed the view which many of Bevin's critics had of the United States. The change in the attitudes of the Left to America had already been well traced.[61] So generous an offer as the Marshall Plan seemed to refute the notion that the American Administration was under the control of big business. In *Keep Left* it was stated that "America, wedded to free enterprise had swung to the Right" (a reference presumably to the Republican victories in the Congressional elections of 1946): "Both the Democrat and Republican party machines [it went on] are dominated by Conservatives—short-sighted, reactionary, but supremely self-confident."[62] Then in 1948 Mr. Truman, campaigning on the Fair Deal programme, was re-elected to the presidency in one of the greatest electoral upsets of modern times. British socialists saw in the Fair Deal an American version—diluted and toned down, no doubt—of Labour's own programme. Sentiment on the Left moved markedly in favour of the United States. In the meantime the Czech coup had taken place, Yugoslavia had been expelled from the Cominform, and the Russians had blockaded the land routes to the western sectors of Berlin.[63]

So, in May 1948, Benn Levy, one of the signatories of the Foreign Affairs Amendment 18 months before, could argue:

"There is no longer a third choice. We must travel the Russian road or the American road

---

[59] *Keep Left*, London, 1947, pp. 43–44.   [60] *Keeping Left*, London, 1950.

[61] In L. Epstein, *Britain—Uneasy Ally*, Chicago, 1954, and Rose, *op. cit.*

[62] *Keep Left*, London, 1947, p. 35.

[63] See M. Bremner, An analysis of British parliamentary thought concerning the United States in the postwar period, Unpublished Ph.D. thesis, London, 1950, fol. 125: "However, faced with the direct question What should America do? many felt bound to say that they could see no feasible alternative policy. They are also somewhat more flexible in mind, and though reluctant to change their views about the Soviet Union appear to have been more able to do so." Bremner was speaking specifically of Labour's intellectuals. This revealing thesis is based on interviews with a sample of MPs.

... But if there are only these two choices, which choice are we to make? Are we to choose the American alignment which, it is widely feared, may jeopardise our Socialism, or the Russian alignment which, with the object lesson of Czechoslovakia in mind, we may reasonably believe would end in the loss of our democracy? For better or worse, the choice is made. ... If there was ever any doubt about that, Mr. Molotov removed it when he refused to participate or to allow his family of dependent nations to participate.[64] ... That is the choice that we are making and in my view it is the right choice."[65]

Despite the defection of numerous of Bevin's critics, a number of Labour MPs still hankered after an independent foreign policy. In March 1948, soon after the Communist coup in Czechoslovakia, Anthony Greenwood tabled an amendment to a European Unity motion which called for the "progressive transformation" of the United Nations Organization into a world government, and asserted that pending the establishment of such a world government Britain should try to act as a reconciling and mediating force between Russia and the United States, forthwith renouncing any military alliance or co-operation with either of the two Great Powers.[66] Thirteen Labour Members—8 of whom had associated themselves with the Amendment to the Address in November 1946—signed Mr. Greenwood's amendment. In July Sydney Silverman put down a motion signed by 19 other Labour Members which declared that "both the possibility and purposes of Western Union would be irretrievably compromised and undermined if either Western Union or its component states should enter into any military alliance or understanding with either Russia or America".[67]

It is easy to oversimplify the nature of the Labour Party's divisions, especially those relating to foreign affairs and defence. The crude dichotomy of an ideological Left thinking in terms of a total reconstruction of the economic and social order, and a pragmatic Right, concerned to modify and to adapt to existing conditions, has been projected on to the foreign policy debates within the Labour Party. The party has been depicted as being split between a relatively unified Left who see the achievement of lasting peace as depending on the fulfilment of the classic socialist goals at home and abroad, and a Right who have accepted a qualified *Realpolitik*, and are content to prosecute a traditional foreign policy based on British national interests and owing nothing to the claims of ideology. This ideological cleavage is often seen as reflecting a social division—the visionary socialists being recruited from the public-school educated, professional, intellectual members of the party, and the Right, whatever the character of its leadership, resting on the solid support of prosaic, working-class trade unionists.

Historically, such a stark distinction does not do justice to the complexity of socialist thinking on foreign policy. EDMs and other similar expressions of backbench feeling, on the grand question of Britain's alignment in the Cold War, as well as on subsidiary issues, such as western European union, may help to indicate to what extent, if any, such a pattern obtained in the heady years after 1945. In order to elucidate the nature of the conflict over foreign policy, the Amendment to the Address, the two "Third Force" EDMs, and a further motion, tabled in 1949, have been used to construct a General Foreign Policy Scale.

Those who signed either the Greenwood amendment or the Silverman motion have been designated as Left, for they were advocating a foreign policy independent of America's, even

---

[64] In the Marshall Plan for European recovery.
[65] HC Deb. 450, cc. 1135–6.
[66] EDM 33A/47.   [67] EDM 75/47.

after the Prague coup; Members who signed the Amendment to the Address[68] without adhering to either the Greenwood Amendment or the Silverman motion constitute the Centre Left, for they were Members who in the early years criticized Anglo-American collaboration but did not according to our data continue this censure after the events in Czechoslovakia. The Ultra Left consists of five Members—all of them expelled from the Labour Party—who subscribed to EDM 59/49,[69] a motion tabled in July 1949, 3 months after the signing of the NATO treaty, which viewed with alarm "the speeches and other material put out by the Government creating and inflaming hostility to the Soviet Union and other countries of Eastern Europe", warned that this policy would involve ever-increasing surrenders to American interests, and called on the government to return to and apply the policy for which they received their mandate in 1945.[70] For convenience these three groups can be collectively described as the Combined Lefts. The remaining Members, who account for the bulk of the backbench party, have been termed the Rest. Thus the party can be divided into the classes shown in Table 8.

TABLE 8. FOREIGN POLICY (GENERAL) SCALE

Ultra Left		Left		Centre Left		Rest		Total	
No.	%	No.	%	No.	%	No.	%	No.	%
5	2	26	9	39	14	216	76	286[a]	100

[a] The 286 Members consist of all those continuously on the backbenches from June 1946, when a motion against conscription was tabled, to July 1949 when the Ultra Left EDM was put down. By limiting the analysis to those Members who were backbenchers throughout this period it is easier to study the interrelationships between attitudes to conscription and different aspects of foreign policy.

The validity of this scale can be checked by comparing the responses of Members to EDMs and the Amendment to the Address with their behaviour in the division lobbies. One hundred and twenty-four Labour backbenchers were absent from the division on the Amendment to the Address in 1946 including all the 58 signatories of the Amendment; as the *New Statesman and Nation* commented, "the discipline of the rebels was a good deal better than that of the Government Whips".[71] One hundred and twelve were absent from the division on the NATO treaty, and a further six voted against it.

Unfortunately there is no accurate way of distinguishing the deliberate abstainers from the involuntary absentees—those who were ill, absent abroad, or away on business or some other commitment. However, it seems likely that most of the "dual abstainers"—those absent on both occasions—abstained deliberately. Some may have been involuntary absentees in both divisions; there are not likely to have been many. It is possible to trace which Members were present in the House on or near the days of the relevant divisions. In Annex 2 it is shown that only four of the 59 dual abstainers did not indicate they were in the House on or near the date

[68] Not, of course, an EDM, but serving a similar purpose.

[69] The five signatories of this motion had constituted themselves into the Independent Labour Group in June 1949.

[70] Presumably a foreign policy based on collective security and co-operation with Russia.

[71] *NS & N*, 23 Nov. 1946.

of at least one of the divisions. We would expect, therefore, the proportion of "dual abstainers" to diminish as we move across the scale from the Far Left to the Right. This expectation is confirmed (Table 9).

TABLE 9. FOREIGN POLICY (GENERAL) SCALE AND ABSTENTIONS
Number and Percentage of Dual Abstainers[a] in Each Class

Ultra Left		Left		Centre Left		Rest	
No.	%	No.	%	No.	%	No.	%
5	100	14	54	15	39	25	12

Ultra Left and Left combined. $\chi_2^2 = 49 \cdot 69$. Significant at $0 \cdot 1\%$.
[a] Dual Abstainers include the handful of Members who actually voted against the NATO treaty whilst abstaining on the Amendment to the Address in 1946.

To simplify Table 9, the figures showing the number in each category who were not dual abstainers have not been shown. These numbers have, of course, been used in calculating the level of significance.

The 26 Members on the Left adhered to a neutralist position even after the Czech coup, whilst the Centre Left comprised those men who proclaimed the Third Force idea, up until 1947, but later either openly or tacitly accepted the need for the Anglo-American alliance. Whatever these groups may have had in common, the differences between them were important and sometimes acute.[72]

The gap between the Ultra Left and the Centre Left is obvious enough; but the divergences between the latter and the Left were remarkably consistent. A rather higher proportion of the Left than of the Centre Left took part in each of two main Bevanite revolts of the 1951 Parliament.[73] The Left were markedly more hostile to conscription than the Centre Left, and were, apparently, much more disturbed about policy towards Germany.[74] A third of them signed the "Nenni telegram"[75] in April 1948 as against a tenth of the Centre Left.[76]

The Centre Left represented the mainstream of the intellectual Left and included the most talented, well-known, and articulate critics of official policy. The Left, on the other hand, were a motley platoon of irregulars, containing few men of national reputation.

The foreign policy dissidents conformed strikingly to the popular stereotype of the socialist intellectual. Both their Conservative and Labour critics seized on the middle-class, professional,

[72] In a formal sense the foreign policy propounded by the Ultra Left did not differ greatly from that of the Left. Indeed, spokesmen of the Ultra Left emphasized that they were simply proclaiming the foreign policy outlined by the Labour Party in the election campaign of 1945. The critical difference was one of spirit and tone.

[73] See below, pp. 100 and 111.

[74] See below, p. 66.

[75] A message of support sent to Signor Nenni, leader of the Italian Socialist Party, then in alliance with the Communists. The British Labour Party officially supported the Social Democratic Party of Signor Saragat.

[76] The association between attitude (Left against Centre Left) and signature of the Nenni telegram is significant at the $2 \cdot 5$ per cent level.

and university-trained character of the 1946 rebels.[77] The Left and the Ultra Left were drawn broadly from the same social groups.

> "But if one compares the past of the signatories [said Captain Harry Crookshank from the Conservative Front Bench in the debate on the Amendment to the Address] one will find that there are only two who describe themselves as ex-manual workers, only two belonging to the core, so long respected in this House, of the old Labour Party. This is a mutiny of the intellectuals. Here are the dentists, the doctors, the solicitors, the accountants, the professors, the dons, the Socialist capitalists, and the company directors. What is more, they appear to be mostly the intellectual new boys. In opening the doors so wide to the doctrinaire Socialists, I wonder if the Labour Party has not taken to its bosom a viper which will ultimately destroy it."[78]

Will Nally, a Labour opponent of the Amendment, chided the rebels in terms of earthy pragmatism: "I suggest that some of the hon. Members on this side of the House who are now rather foolishly jeering would do well and would learn more if they spent rather more time in working class pubs than in attending gatherings of the Bloomsbury Bolsheviks."[79]

The association between occupation and opinions on foreign policy is established at the very high level of 0·1 per cent—that is the odds against this distribution occurring by chance are less than one in a thousand (Table 10).

TABLE 10. LABOUR PARTY AND FOREIGN POLICY (GENERAL) BY OCCUPATION

	Ultra Left		Left		Centre Left		Rest		Total	
	No.	%	No.	%	No.	%	No.	%	No.	%
Workers	—		2	3	2	3	73	94	77	100
Miscellaneous Occupations	2	3	4	6	12	17	52	74	70	100
Business	—		3	7	6	14	33	79	42	100
Professions	3	3	16	19	17	20	50	58	86	100
Unknown	—		1	9	2	18	8	73	11	100
Total	5		26		39		216		286	

Data grouped. Ultra Left and Left combined. Business and Unknown omitted. $\chi^2_4 = 31 \cdot 50$. Significant at 0·1%.

These, then, were middle-class revolts. Within the middle-class the Professions occupied the most conspicuous place. More than 2 out of every 5 Professionals, as against a quarter of the Miscellaneous Occupations, were found amongst the three left-wing groups. The Workers mustered less than one-tenth of their number in the rebel camps. Not surprisingly, the educational and sponsorship divisions closely reproduced the occupational cleavage. Nearly half the University graduates—41 out of 88—were amongst the foreign policy critics, but only 6 of the Elementary-educated Members. Furthermore, the Oxford and Cambridge trained graduates (the U1's and U3's) figured more prominently amongst the rebels than those educated at pro-

[77] See also Rose, *op. cit.*   [78] HC Deb. 430, cc. 544–5.   [79] *Ibid.*, c. 552.

vincial, Scottish, or Welsh universities (the U2's and U4's). Nine-tenths of the Trade Unionists were on the Right as compared with less than three-quarters of the Constituency Party and Co-operative Members.

These demonstrations were also revolts of the young. More than half of the under-40's rebelled compared with less than a tenth of the over-60's.

The broad similarity between the backgrounds of the Ultra Left and Left, on the one hand, and the Centre Left, on the other, has already been mentioned; but amongst the University-trained rebels there was a sharp distinction between the U1's and U3's, and the U2's and U4's. The Oxford and Cambridge men were concentrated heavily on the Centre Left, whilst graduates from other universities were found preponderantly amongst Ultra Left and the Left.[80]

These findings are generally corroborated by a study of the backgrounds of the Dual Abstainers and the consistent supporters of the government. A detailed breakdown of the occupational and other social characteristics of these Members is given in Annex 2. There is a remarkable correspondence between the findings based on the Foreign Policy (General) Scale and behaviour in the division lobbies. The correspondence is the more striking because it is likely that involuntary abstention, due to sickness, would have been higher amongst the older Members, who were disproportionately drawn from the Workers, the Elementary educated, and the Trade Unionists—the groups least conspicuous in the Order Paper revolts.[81]

GERMANY

As uneasiness increased about Russia's intentions, so criticism of Ernest Bevin became less confident and more muted, and other left-wing EDMs received little support.

In Europe, Germany was the focal point of tension between East and West, but by 1948, when the tension became most acute, the Centre Left had largely muted its criticism of Bevin's foreign policy. There were four motions on Germany; two of these (EDMs 68/47 and 6/49) called for the international public ownership of German industry and the holding of a four-power conference to achieve this end. Two tabled during the Berlin blockade (73/47 and 5/49) called for or welcomed United Nations mediation. None drew many signatories, and only about forty MPs altogether signed one or more of them.

EDM 73/47, which called for United Nations mediation over the Berlin dispute, drew support from the Left, especially the pacifist Left, and the opponents of conscription. EDM 68/47, which called for the internationalization of German industry, also drew disproportionate support from the Left. EDMs 5/49 (United Nations mediation over the Berlin crisis) and EDM 6/49 (international public ownership of German industry) both represented the

[80] This difference is significant at 2·5 per cent level when Ultra Left and Left are combined and tested against the Centre Left. When the Left alone are tested against the Centre Left, the difference is significant at 10 per cent.

[81] The only exception concerns the University graduates. As a group, graduates were significantly more numerous amongst the abstainers than were the Elementary educated, but the difference between the U1's and U3's, and the U2's and U4's, was much less marked. The absence of any strong difference between the two university categories can be explained by a growth in support for the government's foreign policy between the foreign affairs debate on the Address in 1946 and the ratification of the Atlantic Pact in 1949. The U1's and U3's constituted 18 per cent of all those who abstained in 1946, but only 10 per cent of the 1949 abstainers; the U2's and U4's fell from 23 per cent to 20 per cent. See footnote 63 for Bremner's assessment of the flexibility of mind displayed by some Labour intellectuals.

TABLE 11. FOREIGN AFFAIRS (GENERAL) AND GERMANY

Foreign Affairs (General) scale	German EDMs							
	Signed two or more		Signed one		Signed nil		Total	
	No.	%	No.	%	No.	%	No.	%
Ultra Left	4	80	1	20	—		5	100
Left	4	15	11	41	11	44	26	100
Centre Left	—		2	5	37	95	39	100
Right	2	1	12	6	202	93	216	100
Total	10		26		250		286	

Data grouped. Ultra Left and Left combined, and signatories of two or more and one German EDM combined. $\chi_2^2 = 85\cdot3$. Significant at $0\cdot1\%$ level.

concern of the Ultra Left, the former motion also attracting opponents of conscription, and the latter the Left and a scatter of other Members.

The value of Yule's Q for the six possible pairs of motions varies from $0\cdot86$ for EDM 5/49 and EDM 6/49, to the low figure of $0\cdot38$ for EDM 68/47 and EDM 5/49. The justification for combining these motions, disparate in support and in one sense in subject-matter, lies not so much in who signed them as in who did not. There was a marked overlap between the signatories of the EDM on Germany and the foreign affairs rebels, but the signatories were drawn not from the Centre Left but from the Left and the Ultra Left (Table 11).

Similarly, the signatories of the German EDMs were drawn to a quite disproportionate extent from those who abstained on or opposed the government on the two key foreign policy votes of the Parliament. Only 4 of the Consistent Loyalists signed any motion as against 26 of the 59 Dual Abstainers (Table 12).

TABLE 12. FOREIGN POLICY ABSTAINERS AND GERMANY

Foreign policy	German EDMs							
	Signed two or more		Signed one		Signed nil		Total	
	No.	%	No.	%	No.	%	No.	%
Dual Abstainers	8	14	18	31	33	56	59	100
Rest	2	2	4	3	113	95	119	100
Consistent Loyalists	—		4	4	104	96	108	100
Total	10		26		250		286	

Data grouped. Signatories of two or more and one German EDM combined. $\chi_2^2 = 67\cdot044$. Significant at $0\cdot1\%$ level.

Examination of the educational and occupational backgrounds of the signatories does not reveal any statistically significant differences in support, which, given the small number of signatures, is hardly surprising. Such differences as are found are consistent with the Foreign Affairs (General) Scale. The signatories to the German motions were drawn, disproportionately, from the Professions, the CLP sponsored, and the University educated. What is clear is that the signatories to the German motion were drawn disproportionately from the Ultra Left, the Left, and the Dual Abstainers; the abstention of the Centre Left is striking.

Fears of war over Germany provoked 45 Labour MPs, led by the pacifist, Reginald Sorenson, to send an open letter to Ernest Bevin in August 1948. The signatories urged the government to take immediate steps to ensure fresh discussions between the various leaders of the Great Powers on their differences, including Germany, and emphasized the urgent need for a general peace settlement. ". . . although there is wide political divergence", ran the letter, "between the United States and the USSR, we believe you, as Foreign Secretary, are in a position to promote conciliation and forbearance between these Powers."[82] They also asked the government to initiate proposals for a wide measure of disarmament and to repudiate atomic warfare.

The letter represented a coming together of the Left and the opponents of conscription, which had already been reflected in the EDMs on Germany; thus, 10 of the 26 Members of the Left signed the letter as against only 1 of the 39 Centre Left MPs; 14 of the 35 hard core of opponents of conscription also signed together with 6 MPs who had opposed conscription on the second reading of the National Service Bill or in the debate on the Address in 1946. A further 5 signatories abstained in all three of the major divisions on conscription in 1946 and 1947. A scatter of 7 Members with no record of hostility to conscription or adherence to the Left or Centre Left, also signed the letter. Both this letter and the German EDMs foreshadowed a partial union of the Left and the pacifists which, in conjunction with the more specifically Centre Left group around Aneurin Bevan, was to become the Bevanite coalition during the early 1950's.

WORLD GOVERNMENT

The hope of a world authority, which would be able to arbitrate between nations and resolve disputes, has long been cherished by sections of the British Left. Like much of the inheritance of the Labour Movement, these hopes had originally been voiced by *laissez-faire* radicals. Richard Cobden was an early prophet of international arbitration.

The Union of Democratic Control and the Fabian Research Department both embraced the idea of a "League of Nations" in 1916, and the Labour Party itself called in 1917 for a Supranational Authority. At the end of the Second World War many socialists looked forward to the development of the United Nations Organization into a world government with real, if limited, powers. The invention of the atomic bomb quickened this interest. Outside Parliament, enthusiasts for an international authority with effective powers set up the Crusade for World Government.

Within Parliament three backbench motions were tabled on world federation. Two motions sponsored by Henry Usborne, the leading Labour advocate of world federation, called on the government to federate with any other nations willing to do so.[83] A third, put down by Ernest Millington, was strictly an amendment to a European Unity motion; this amendment looked

[82] See *The Times*, 6 Aug. 1948, and for the list of signatories the *Daily Herald* of the same day.
[83] EDMs 8/46 and 19/47.

forward to a European federation as part of an effective world government.[84] Nineteen Labour MPs signed two or three motions, and 60 signed one.[85]

There was no marked or statistically significant relationship between signature for the world government motions and criticism of Bevin's foreign policy. The Left were barely more favourable than the Right, though Mr. Usborne and his friends recruited rather more support amongst the Centre Left.

The differences between the reactions of the various social groups were not marked; the younger Members were more enthusiastic than the older, and the Professions rather more favourable to these motions than the Workers; similarly, the University graduates signed more than the Elementary educated, the Constituency sponsored than the Trade Unionists—but the gap was relatively small. No associations between social characteristics and support for world government were established, so what differences there were can be reasonably ascribed to chance. World government, in short, had a wider appeal to the party than a "socialist foreign policy".

In the session of 1950–1 three further "world government" EDMs were tabled. The sponsors of EDM 32/50 took the opportunity of the invasion of South Korea to call for the reform of the United Nations into an effective world government. EDM 35/51 virtually repeated this call, and EDM 52/50 looked to a federal union of the countries of the Commonwealth and the USA as the basis of a future world government. Altogether 66 Labour MPs signed one or more of these motions, and these MPs appeared to constitute a quite cohesive group, to judge from the very high values of Yule's Q obtained from the three pairs of EDMs.[86] Their social characteristics were similar to those of the signatories of the world government motion in the 1945 Parliament: the Workers signed less than the other occupational groups, the Trade Unionists less than the Co-operators and CLP sponsored. In this Parliament there was a statistically significant relationship between occupation and support for world government, the Workers being less keen than the other groups, and displaying less enthusiasm than in the earlier Parliament. But what is notable is the stability of these findings over two separate Parliaments— further evidence that signatures to EDMs are not a meaningless and haphazard collection of names. Only when Members are analysed by age does a divergence appear between the two periods, and, again, even this divergence is not statistically significant.

EUROPE

Of more importance was the campaign for European Unity. The European Movement began in 1946: Winston Churchill gave the cause of United Europe his blessing at the Zürich Conference of September 1946. The drive towards European union was prompted by a strange assortment of motives; much of the support for European unity within the Labour Party came from those who saw a united Europe as specifically socialist in character. As we have seen, the idea of an independent socialist western Europe had gained currency in the Labour Party when it became clear that the war-time co-operation of the Big Three had broken down. Russia would not co-operate, and collaboration with capitalist America was distasteful to the socialist conscience. Indeed, the *New Statesman* had espoused the cause of European unity on a socialist basis, as early as the autumn of 1945.[87]

[84] EDM 33A/47.
[85] The value of Yule's Q for three pairs of motions varies from 0·71 to 0·95.
[86] The values ranged from 0·89 to 0·92.   [87] *NS & N*, 6 Oct. 1945.

The Russian rejection of Marshall Aid and the Czech coup gave a new impetus to the plans for western European federation. In March 1948 a crossbench motion was tabled with Ronald Mackay and Robert Boothby as sponsors, which called for "immediate and effective co-operation between the countries of Western Europe", declared that the long-term policy should be a democratic federation of Europe, and urged the convening, as soon as practicable, of a constituent assembly to draft a constitution for such a federation.[88] The motion attracted nearly 200 signatures—more than half from the Labour ranks.

The Labour leadership was cautious of the movement for European unity and openly hostile to the more advanced proposals for federation. Already, before the tabling of the motion, the National Executive had sought to discourage party members from attending the Congress of the European Movement at The Hague, and in February 1948 it reaffirmed its decision. The federalist motion was, however, debated by the House on 5 May. Attlee, who had once averred that "Europe must federate or perish", displayed little enthusiasm for European union. The motion, he declared, though admirable in its general intentions, suggested that "these things can be got over rather more easily than is possible". Though the government were prepared with other powers to pool some degree of authority, he was not prepared, at present, to agree to all the propositions in the motion as being immediately practicable. Attlee went on to "heartily agree" with the idea of federation but then expressed disquiet at the suggestion that Britain should move closer to Europe than to the Commonwealth, ". . . we are not solely a European power but a member of a great Commonwealth and Empire."[89] In September an official party pamphlet *Feet on the Ground* spoke out against federation. "Any attempt to create a federation now would raise innumerable general issues. . . . Precious years would be wasted in wrangles which created disunity and contributed nothing to solving our difficulties."[90] This tone of caution was repeated and accentuated in a second party statement on Europe, published in June 1950.[91]

Eleven months later a second European motion (EDM 21/48) was put down. This, less sweeping in its demands, merely welcomed the establishment of the new European consultative organs, and suggested a basis for representation in the Consultative Assembly. The reduction in scope of the motion was accompanied by a diminution in support. Fewer than 60 Labour Members signed this motion; all but 9 of them had signed the federalist motion 18 months before.[92] However, more than 60 Labour MPs had by now apparently lost their zeal for European union.

Unlike the foreign policy, the appeal of European unity cut almost completely across the party's political and social boundaries. The Left and Centre Left responded almost as much as the Right. Indeed, Ronald Mackay, one of the most vocal partisans of a European federation, was one of the sponsors of Silverman's left-wing EDM on western union. The university graduates and the Elementary/secondary+ groups were on this evidence more pro-European than the Elementary and the Secondary educated, though the differences were not dramatic.

It seems likely, given the evolution of opinion in the Labour Party over the year, that the fall in the number signing the second, more moderate, motion, reflected a genuine recession in support for British association with Europe. Sixty-one Labour MPs who signed the earlier, federalist EDM, did not sign the later one; this recession affected the Workers, the Professions,

[88] EDM 33/47.
[89] HC Deb. 450, cc. 1317–19.
[90] Labour Party, *Feet on the Ground*, London, 1948, p. 20.
[91] Labour Party, *European Unity*, London, 1950.
[92] The value of Yule's Q for the two European motions is 0·86.

TABLE 13. EUROPE AND WORLD GOVERNMENT

World Government EDMs	European EDMs				
	Signers		Non-Signers		
	No.	%	No.	%	Total
Signers	42	37	40	23	82
Non-Signers	73	63	131	77	204
Total	115	100	171	100	286

$\chi_1^2 = 5 \cdot 796$. Significant at 2% level. Yule's $Q = 0 \cdot 31$.

and Business more or less proportionally; the Miscellaneous Occupations, however, contributed considerably less than their fair share to the ranks of the backsliders.

Support for the lesser goal of European unity might have been expected to have gone hand in hand with belief in the wider concept of world federation; and indeed, as Table 13 shows, there was a tendency for the two to go together. What, at first sight, is surprising is that the relationship was not stronger. This, in turn, can be explained by the suspicion with which some of the advocates of world government regarded the drive for European unity, for though some Europeans like Christopher Shawcross might see a united Europe as a step towards world government, some enthusiasts for a world authority saw a federation of Europe not as a stepping stone to a wider world federation but as a diversion from the grand vision. Said Wing-Commander Millington of the Europeans:

"they are seeking to merge the sovereignties of 16 or 17 States into one larger sovereignty with the door shut against the inclusion of any other peoples in the world who may wish to join with them. . . . But I believe that responsibility rests quite firmly upon the people of this country, above all, to try to plan that structure of a world organization with the door wide open to everybody in the world to co-operate. . . . That is why I and a group of hon. Members, who have an organization in this House, seek all the time to present here . . . the cosmic, the universal approach."[93]

The leading advocate of world federation, Henry Usborne, spoke in a similar vein, and quoted with approval Anthony Eden's remarks "it would be all right to create Western Union if it could be done inside an effective world authority".[94]

PALESTINE

There was recurrent friction and great bitterness between the government and sections of the Left as a result of the British Government's handling of the Palestine problem. Mr. Crossman had been a member of the Anglo-American committee appointed by Mr. Attlee and President Truman which in 1946 had recommended the early admission of 100,000 Jewish

[93] HC Deb. 450, c. 1310.   [94] *Ibid.*, c. 1368.

immigrants to Palestine—a recommendation which the British Government eventually refused to implement. Late in 1947 the United Nations Assembly voted for the ending of the British mandate and for the partitioning of the country, and with it the creation of two new states— one Jewish and one Arab. A Bill was introduced in March 1948 to deal with matters arising out of the termination of the British Administration, and left-wing and Jewish Members took the opportunity to make a general attack on the government's Palestine policy.

Keep Left had already stigmatized the British Government's Middle Eastern policy as an attempt to build up an anti-Bolshevik bloc of reactionary Arab states. The government's measures in Palestine were seen as part and parcel of their overall foreign policy. In the debate on the second reading, Warbey moved an amendment rejecting the Bill because the government had failed to provide for the orderly transfer of jurisdiction to the United Nations. The government's critics argued that the failure to provide for the transfer of authority would create a hiatus resulting in chaos and bloodshed when the British Government surrendered its own jurisdiction in the area.

Those who voted against the government were drawn almost exclusively from the Combined Lefts and the Jewish Members. Of 29 Members who voted against the government, and were continuous backbenchers from June 1946 to July 1949, 12 were drawn from the Left or the Ultra Left and 12 from the Centre Left. Of the remaining 5 Members, 4 were Jewish and 1, Seymour Cocks, was a radical critic of Bevin. In the Committee stage Warbey moved an amendment which specifically provided for the transfer of authority to the United Nations. Seventeen of the "continuous" Labour backbenchers voted for the amendment, and of these 11 came from the Combined Lefts; 3 more were Jewish, and another represented a constituency with a substantial Jewish population. A further amendment by Warbey sought to make possible the transfer of official property to United Nations, and this was supported by 12 Members, all but 1 of whom were members of the Combined Lefts.[95]

In addition it must be noted that many of those who rebelled on the Palestine issue were both left-wing and Jewish; thus, of the 24 Members of the Combined Lefts who voted against the second reading of the Palestine Bill, 9 were Jews.

EXPULSIONS IN EUROPE

After the German defeat in Europe, the Polish and Czech authorities expelled large numbers of Germans from their borders. These expulsions, which were carried out by ostensibly socialist governments, met with widespread hostility in Britain. To many socialists this policy of forcible repatriation savoured of Vansittart-like notions of "collective German guilt", and the misery that followed the implementation of this policy was an offence to their humanitarian precepts. In October, six MPs, consisting of three Labour Members, including Crossman, and three Conservative or "National" ex-Ministers, tabled a motion calling on the British Government to try to influence the east European governments responsible to stop further expulsions or at least to postpone them until the end of the winter. Amongst 157 signatories were nearly a hundred Labour Members. The Combined Lefts, interestingly enough, contributed greater support, proportionately, than the Foreign Policy Right, and within the Combined Lefts the Left mustered a higher percentage of Members than the Centre Left.[96] When the Left were

[95] HC Deb. 448, cc. 1246–1363, 2449–99 and 2908–34.
[96] Two of the five Ultra Left MPs also signed.

faced with a conflict between ideological predilection and humanitarian concern, the latter often won.[97]

Support for this motion was also related to world government; half of the signatories of the world government EDMs signed compared with a quarter of the non-signatories. Support for world government and concern for the victims of war in Europe went hand in hand.

CONSCRIPTION

In contrast to the professional and university dominated revolts against Bevin's foreign policy, the opponents of conscription drew their support from a cross-section of the party. The Labour Movement had long been hostile to compulsory military service in time of peace. This hostility, like the yearning for a "socialist international policy", was derived from several sources. Conscription was linked, symbolically, with imperialist adventure and a belligerent foreign policy. It offended the radical passion for individual liberty; it alarmed Trade Unionists, who saw in it the threat of industrial conscription; and, naturally, it outraged a small section of the party, the absolute pacifists, who totally and unconditionally repudiated the use of force in international affairs.

The Labour Government took some time to decide upon its conscription policy. They recognized that conscription must stay for the immediate post-war period so that inescapable commitments could be met. In June 1946 the government published a White Paper which promised that the period of compulsory military service would be gradually reduced, but they did not decide until late in 1946 to introduce conscription as a regular peace-time practice. Soon after the publication of the June White Paper, 88 Labour MPs and 5 Liberals signed an EDM tabled by Rhys Davies[98] which welcomed the promise of a gradual reduction in the period of conscription, but went on to assert that military conscription in peace-time was alien to British traditions and should be brought to an end as soon as possible.[98]

In November the opponents of conscription again raised the issue, tabling an amendment to the Address which was debated immediately after the Foreign Affairs Amendment and pressed to a division. Forty-seven Labour MPs together with some Liberals voted against the government.

In March 1947 a further Defence White Paper[99] was published; a motion approving the White Paper was sponsored by the Prime Minister and other Ministers. To this motion Woodrow Wyatt, then a member of the "Keep Left" group, tabled an amendment which did not attack the principle of conscription—some of the amendment's signatories were explicit supporters of compulsory service—but did call for a further review of the country's military commitments "so as to reduce the burden on our manpower and financial resources". Of the 28 signatories, 15 had signed the Foreign Affairs Amendment 4 months before.

In March, too, the National Service Bill, which provided for an 18-month term of military service, was published. The pacifist, Rhys Davies, tabled an Amendment (not an EDM) calling for the rejection of the Bill. Seventy-seven Labour MPs signed the Amendment. When the Bill was given its Second Reading on 1 April, 74 Labour backbenchers (including 61 of those who had signed the Amendment) voted against it. Moreover, Mr. Crossman, who had

---

[97] For a discussion of the dilemma posed to socialists by the expulsions and one way in which the dilemma could be resolved, see V. Gollancz, *Our Threatened Values*, London, 1946.
[98] EDM 53/45.   [99] Cmd. 7042.

supported the Bill on Second Reading, announced that he and his colleagues would press for a reduction in the period of national service during the committee stage.

The government, faced by a revolt and confronted by the prospect of further defections in committee, gave way. The period of national service was reduced to 12 months, and when the Bill came up for Third Reading some of the critics had evidently been mollified; the number of rebels fell from 74 to 39. The partial victory of the rebels was short-lived; in October 1948 the period of service was lengthened to 18 months and in 1950 to 2 years.

The debates on conscription reveal the diversity of motives which led so many Labour MPs into the division lobbies against their own Ministers. Pacifists like Victor Yates might themselves use economic or military arguments to support what was essentially an ethically or emotionally based repugnance. Thus in the debate on his Amendment to the Address, opposing the retention of compulsory military service, Yates argued that the invention of the atomic bomb had made conscript armies out of date, and that conscription involved a waste of manpower which could be better deployed in industry and the work of reconstruction. To these arguments based, as he put it, on "common sense", he added three more familiar propositions. Conscription would stimulate, not discourage, competition between nations in military preparedness. Military discipline fostered an unhealthy conformism, and to deny a man the freedom to direct his own life was morally wrong. Unlike Crossman, he refused to separate the issues of conscription and foreign policy. Conscription could not solve our international difficulties.[100] Scollan, who followed, gave religious reasons as the main grounds of his objection,[101] but in the debate on the Second Reading of the National Service Bill he relied to a considerable extent on the economic arguments against compulsory service.[102] Both Mikardo and Seymour Cocks also spoke against the Bill on economic grounds, the former complaining that the government would give no appreciation of the economic, as distinct from the financial, cost of national service.[103] Stamford warned any trade unionists who intended to vote for the Bill "to do so with their eyes wide open to the industrial implications of their action, and recognize clearly where the logic of conscription must inevitably lead".[104] Herbert Butler emphasized that he was not a pacifist; he opposed conscription because of the way in which it wasted the time of young men and brought so much uncertainty into their lives.[105]

Ethical and economic arguments thus loomed large; to these were added fears of industrial conscription, the threat to individual liberty, and the sheer inconvenience to those called up.

Some Members, however, opposed conscription unequivocally because of its implications for foreign policy. Ernest Millington, a member of the Keep Left group, expressed his fear that the purpose of the Bill was "to put an iron glove on the fist of the Foreign Secretary which he is so fond of shaking at the leaders of the USSR".[106] Similarly, Zilliacus, who voted against both the Second and Third Readings of the Bill, wrote in the *New Statesman* that though he did not object in principle to conscription he voted against the government because young men might be required to give their lives for bad causes, to support the government's decisions in Greece or Palestine, or as "cannon fodder" for Wall Street's campaign against world socialism.[107]

Against such attacks on conscription from the Left, men like Crossman and Wigg argued that

---

[100] HC Deb. 430, c. 594 ff.   [101] *Ibid.*, c. 605.   [102] HC Deb. 435, c. 1913.
[103] *Ibid.*, cc. 1889 and 1942 ff.   [104] *Ibid.*, c. 1896.   [105] *Ibid.*, c. 1881.
[106] *Ibid.*, c. 1932.
[107] *NS & N*, 5 Apr. 1947. Zilliacus mentioned the claims of economic solvency as another reason for opposing the Bill.

the two problems of foreign policy and defence must not be confused. "If a Socialist Government in Britain were to repudiate conscription", they wrote in the *New Statesman*, "it would forfeit the confidence of France and every country in Europe . . . it is a political necessity for a Socialist Britain conscious of its duty to Europe."[108] "We should [added Crossman during the debate] keep defence and foreign policy separate and realize that the strength of Great Britain, even under a Tory Government, may be of value for the liberty of Europe." But Crossman also thought the proposed period of service fixed in the Bill at 18 months was too long; as in the struggle over rearmament 4–5 years later, he did not question the principle of defence forces, only the level.

However opposition to conscription is measured—whether on the evidence of EDM 53/45 or the floor revolts—it is significant that it cut across almost all the occupational, sponsorship, and educational boundaries within the party;[109] hostility to conscription was located, with roughly equal strength, amongst both young and old, amongst the newly elected, and the pre-war entrants. The Professions, the CLP sponsored, and the University graduates barely differed from the Workers, the Trade Unionists, and the Elementary educated. One significant divergence occurred within the University contingent. The U4 (secondary school and provincial universities) group signed the EDM in much greater numbers, proportionately speaking, than the other three University classes (U1, U2, and U3). The same difference, reaching a high degree of significance, was found in the floor votes against conscription. Another difference was found when the reactions of those Members who had served in the armed forces were compared with those who had not. Not unexpectedly, the Members with war service were more favourable to conscription than those without. Again, the same divergence was found in the floor votes.

Within the Labour movement, Scotland and Wales have been noted for their traditional pacificism; it is not surprising, therefore, that three-fifths of the Welsh and nearly two-fifths of the Scots signed the EDM compared with little more than a quarter of the Members representing English constituencies. This regional distinction was also found in the floor revolts.

The 35 who opposed the Third Reading of the National Service Bill can be regarded as the pacifist hard core.[110] Like the broader group of rebels hostile to conscription, these 35 tended to be drawn, in their due proportions, from the various social categories of which the party was composed, although Members from the Professions were more prominent amongst the 35 than MPs from the other occupational groups. Similarly, the over-50's and the men without war service were better represented than the younger Members and those who had served in the forces.

The Conscription Motion, EDM 53/45, affords a further opportunity for comparing findings based on parliamentary motions with behaviour on the floor of the House. There were three big revolts in the division lobbies against the government's conscription policy—that on Victor Yates's amendment to the Address supported by 47 backbenchers; the rebellion of the 74 on Second Reading; and the demonstration of the 39 irreconcilables on Third Reading. Altogether 76 Labour MPs took part in at least one of the three floor revolts; 87 signed the motion.

[108] *NS & N*, 29 Mar. 1947. More precisely, Crossman and Wigg seemed to mean not that issues of foreign policy and defence should not be confused, but that opposition to Bevin's policy should not be confused with opposition to conscription.

[109] See also Rose, *op. cit.*

[110] In fact, 39 Labour MPs actually voted against the Third Reading but 4 of them have been excluded from consideration as they were not in Parliament for the whole period of the study—i.e. June 1946 to July 1949.

In the year that elapsed between the tabling of the EDM and the passage of the National Service Bill, opinions had crystallized. Some of the signatories of the EDM voted for the government's Bill; some who had not signed the EDM flouted the Whip's advice and voted against conscription. Of the 87 signatories of the EDM, more than half, 49, went into the lobbies against the Whip on at least one of the three occasions; they were joined by a further 27 MPs who had not signed. Thirty-eight of the EDM signatories did not vote against the government in any of the three important divisions on the floor of the House. Of these 38, no fewer than 12 abstained on each of the three occasions and a further 9 abstained on two of the three. Table 14 shows the highly regular relationship between EDM signing and division lobby behaviour.

TABLE 14. CONSCRIPTION—SIGNING AND VOTING

EDM 53/45	Against Third Reading		Against Second Reading or against government on Address		Abstained all three times		Abstained twice		Rest		Total
	No.	%	No.	%	No.	%	No.	%	No.	%	
Signers	27	77	22	54	12	46	9	24	17	12	87
Non-Signers	8	23	19	46	14	54	28	76	130	88	199
Total	35	100	41	100	26	100	37	100	147	100	286

Data grouped: voters against Third and Second Reading and three times abstainers combined; abstained twice and Rest combined. $\chi^2_1 = 54\cdot124$. Significant at $0\cdot1\%$ level.

Substantial numbers of the signatories of EDM 53/45 did not vote against conscription on the floor of the House, and a considerable number of non-signers did; nevertheless, occupational and other breakdowns of the Members who voted against compulsory national service yield remarkably similar results to those obtained from the EDMs. Only in respect of age is there any serious discrepancy with the 41–50 age group contributing proportionately fewer to the voters than they had to the signatories, and the over-60's rather more. With this one exception, the resemblance between the social backgrounds of the EDM signers and of the voters against conscription is marked.[111]

A sharp distinction then can be drawn between the critics of the government's foreign policy and the opponents of conscription. The first group were drawn overwhelmingly from the University educated and the Professions, especially from Members educated at public schools and/or Oxford or Cambridge; the second group constituted a cross-section of the party; virtually all the various classes within the party were represented in their due proportions. There remains the intriguing contrast found amongst the University men themselves; the U1, U2, and U3 classes—graduates who had all been educated at public school and/or Oxford or Cambridge displayed much less hostility to conscription than the U4's (non-public school and provincial university). In turn, the U4's figured much less prominently amongst the critics of

[111] See Annex 2 for detailed figures.

Ernest Bevin's foreign policy than their more educationally privileged fellows. In much the same way Celtic radicalism was, if anything, slightly underrepresented amongst Bevin's opponents, but its spokesmen were conspicuous in the floor revolts against conscription.

If the opponents of conscription were drawn (the University and Celtic members apart) from a cross-section of the party, two important groups in this controversy were drawn disproportionately from particular elements of the PLP. Six members of the "Keep Left" faction led by Woodrow Wyatt and including Crossman had put down an amendment to the Prime Minister's motion calling for approval of the Defence White Paper, accepting the White Paper but urging a further review of Britain's military commitments so as to reduce the strain on the country's manpower and financial resources.[112] It will be recalled that Crossman, whilst accepting conscription, had called for a reduction in the length of service. The 28 Members who signed the amendment were drawn, like the Foreign Policy rebels, mostly from the University educated, middle-class section of the party; amongst the University men the Members who had been to a public school or one of the two ancient English universities were prominent; the Professions and Miscellaneous Occupations were conspicuous, the Workers few in number.

Moreover, amongst those who actually voted against conscription there was a contrast between the 26 "ideological pacifists" (a convenient short-hand term for Members who both opposed conscription and expressed criticism of the government's foreign policy) and the remaining 50 division-lobby opponents of compulsory service. Overwhelmingly, the "ideological pacifists" were drawn from the Professions and Business, and from the University graduates. Amongst the other Members voting against conscription, the Miscellaneous Occupations, the Elementary educated, and—to a lesser extent—the Workers, were conspicuous. Furthermore, the 23 Third Reading rebels who did not take part in any of the foreign policy demonstrations were much older than the Foreign Policy critics. Only five were graduates; pacificism in its purest form was derived from an earlier and largely non-intellectual tradition.

The relationship between opinions on conscription and on foreign policy was complex (Table 15).

The vocal support given by men like Crossman and Wigg to the principle of conscription has already been mentioned. It is hardly a surprise therefore that there was virtually no difference between the Centre Left and the Rest in their attitudes to conscription; but there was a sharp divergence between the Ultra Left and Left, on the one hand, and the rest of the party, on the other.

TABLE 15. FOREIGN AFFAIRS AND CONSCRIPTION

Foreign Affairs	Opposed conscription		Abstained or supported		Total	
	No.	%	No.	%	No.	%
Ultra Left and Left	16	52	15	48	31	100
Centre Left	10	26	29	74	39	100
Rest	50	23	166	77	216	100
Total	76		210		286	

$\chi_2^2 = 11 \cdot 15$. Significant at 1% level.

[112] EDM 16A/47. See also p. 72.

TABLE 16. FOREIGN POLICY ABSTENTIONS AND CONSCRIPTION

| | Foreign Policy | | | | | |
| Conscription | Dual Abstainers | | Rest | | Total | |
	No.	%	No.	%	No.	%
Voted against conscription	26	34	50	66	76	100
Not voting against conscription	33	16	177	84	210	100
Total	59		227		286	

$\chi^2_1 = 11 \cdot 66$. Significant at 1% level.

Furthermore, when the irreconcilables who voted against the Third Reading of the Bill are examined, we find that a third of the combined forces of the Ultra Left and Left defied the Whips against a tenth of the remainder of the party.

At first sight it seems as though the anti-conscription men were more prone to abstain on the two great foreign policy divisions than the rest of the party, for a third of them abstained in both divisions as against a sixth of those who, on conscription, did not openly rebel. This first impression, however, is somewhat misleading; further inspection shows that the higher abstention rate of the opponents of conscription can be ascribed entirely to the distinctive performance of one specific element within their ranks—the foreign policy critics or "ideological pacifists". Nearly two-thirds of the latter abstained on both the NATO treaty and the Foreign Affairs Amendment; however, the remaining opponents of conscription resembled in their behaviour the rest of the party, less than a fifth of them abstaining on these votes (Table 17).

TABLE 17. FOREIGN POLICY LEFTS, DUAL ABSTAINERS AND CONSCRIPTION

| | Voting Against Conscription | | | | | |
| | Dual Abstainers | | Rest | | Total | |
	No.	%	No.	%	No.	%
Ultra Left, Left, and Centre Left	16	64	9	36	25	100
Others	9	18	42	82	51	100
Total	25		51		76	

$\chi^2_1 = 16 \cdot 329$. Significant at 0.1% level.

It has been shown how the open letter to Ernest Bevin, of August 1948, calling for great-power discussions on Germany, attracted the signatures of the Left and of the pacifists. It is not surprising, therefore, that the German EDMs attracted a disproportionate share of the opponents of conscription (Table 18).

TABLE 18. GERMANY AND CONSCRIPTION

German EDMs	Opposed conscription		Abstained or supported government		Total	
	No.	%	No.	%	No.	%
Signed two or more	5	50	5	50	10	100
Signed one	11	42	15	58	26	100
Signed nil	60	24	190	76	250	100
Total	76		210		286	

Data grouped. Members signing two or more and one German EDM, combined. $\chi_1^2 = 6 \cdot 741$. Significant at 1% level.

There were those who, like Seymour Cocks,[113] thought that a system of collective security would mean a reduction, and not an expansion, of national forces; and presumably this hope, amongst other factors, helps to explain the relationship between enthusiasm for world government and hostility to conscription. However, there was no significant association between opinions on conscription and views on Europe. If anything, the opponents of compulsory service were less European-minded than its supporters (Table 19).

TABLE 19. WORLD GOVERNMENT AND CONSCRIPTION

World Government EDMs	Opposed conscription		Abstained or supported government		Total	
	No.	%	No.	%	No.	%
Signed two or more	10	53	9	47	19	100
Signed one	20	33	40	67	60	100
Signed nil	46	22	161	78	207	100
Total	76		210		286	

$\chi_2^2 = 10 \cdot 026$. Significant at 1% level.

CONCLUSION

The Labour Government was able to carry through its programme of domestic change with little dissent from its backbench supporters. There were occasional demands for more drastic nationalization measures, criticism of the way in which nationalization had been carried out, and sporadic calls for more vigorous socialist planning, but these hardly constituted a serious challenge to the party leadership. During the long period of post-war austerity the Conservative attack became more and more intense, and the Labour backbenchers consolidated behind

[113] HC Deb. 435, c. 1889.

the government. Not until the formulation of the policy for the next election was under way did the old dispute between messianic nationalizers and pragmatic interventionists recur—and when it did the differences were relatively little publicized.

Party harmony, however, stopped short at the English Channel. In foreign affairs the government was subjected to keen and sometimes violent criticism from sections of its own backbenchers; nevertheless, the critics diminished both in number and intellectual force as Soviet policy became increasingly intransigent and as America, in contrast, displayed the benevolent face of economic aid and political co-operation.

Over conscription, an essential adjunct of the government's foreign policy, the critics were rather more numerous, and drawn with rough equality from all sections of the party. Despite the retreat of April 1947, however, the government was able later to revert to its earlier plan of a 2-year term.

The outstanding feature of the revolts over defence and foreign policy was the strict separation between the two issues. Any distinctive connection between opposition to conscription and hostility to the government's foreign policy was confined to the Left and the Ultra Left. The Centre Left were no more likely to harbour critics of conscription than the Right. The most articulate of the Centre Left spokesmen, Richard Crossman, had been a voice for realism in the conscription debates of 1939. During this Parliament the only convergence between the pacifists and the ideological Left occurred on the far fringes of the latter.

Throughout the debates on foreign policy, the party was haunted by the ghosts of its past. To many, Russia with all its faults was the territorial symbol of socialism, America the homeland of capitalism. Reasons for the aggressive intentions ascribed to America by the Left could be found in the rhetoric of British socialism of the preceding 40 years or more. America was capitalist, America was imperialist; her need to find new markets for the surplus that could not under the laws of capitalist production be consumed at home, the greed of her factories for new supplies of raw materials, the search for new investment outlets—all of these would impel her towards the classic postures of belligerent empire. Often combined with this Marxist or quasi-Marxist analysis went the embellishments of the thirties; America was leading a great anti-socialist crusade with Labour Britain as a willing auxiliary. Once again, the ruling classes of western Europe had resolved to contain and, if possible, destroy socialist Russia; to do this they had invited, or at least acquiesced in, the extension of America's armed power beyond the Atlantic.

Often mixed with this explicitly socialist analysis was the rhetoric of radical protest against balance of power politics and that of pacifist opposition to militarism. Yet, as has been seen, pacifist feeling was pronounced only on the fringes of the Left; the more orthodox Centre Left had no special affinity for pacifism, and, indeed, was soon induced by the march of events to relax its hostility to the course pursued by Ernest Bevin. Indeed, by 1949 Crossman could declare at Labour Party Conference: "We can be proud of four years of foreign policy."[114] It is, moreover, remarkable how few of the Centre Left subscribed to the EDMs on Germany, which expressed both pacificist and left-wing sentiments. The intransigence and belligerence of Stalin's Russia, the apparent benevolence and social idealism of Truman's America, proved to be the best party managers that Ernest Bevin could wish for.

Considerable support was expressed for the cause of world government, an objective long in line with Labour and radical thinking. Yet the championing of a goal so remote from the day-to-day world of diplomacy and politics could hardly embarrass the Labour leadership.

[114] *LPCR, 1949*, p. 193.

The sudden enthusiasm for a federal Europe was short-lived; in 1948 and again in 1950, the government could safely contain or canalize whatever zeal there might be for European union, diverting it to such harmless channels as the Council of Europe. Here, too, events abroad came to the aid of the party managers; the swing to the Right in western Europe in the late forties killed much of the excitement originally evoked, in socialist circles, by the prospect of a united Europe. The government could carry out its policy of military alliance with the United States and western Europe; it could, at the same time, maintain an attitude of cautious detachment from the more far-reaching plans for European integration without suffering a substantial backbench rebellion.

Part of the credit for the facility with which the government was able to avoid a confrontation with its backbench critics must go to the Centre Left. By resolutely divorcing the issue of foreign policy from that of conscription, they denied themselves the chance to mobilize emotions and sentiments which had been cherished in the Labour movement for generations. Effectively they isolated themselves from the main stream of traditional radicalism. Of course, after the middle of 1947 (and certainly after the Czech coup) they no longer wished to challenge the government's foreign policy except on relatively narrow questions like that of Palestine. The Centre Left showed themselves to be more flexible and more attuned to the immediate realities of power than their older colleagues amongst the Left; coming to maturity as they had during the thirties and the Second World War, they did not display the repugnance to military preparedness felt by so many of their fellows.

The pacifists, on their side, were chary of their own distinctive humanitarian attitudes being merged with the ideological left-wing protests against Bevin's foreign policy. Thus Rhys Davies at the Party Conference of 1948 charged that he had never heard Zilliacus criticize the foreign policy of any government except Britain's. Nor could Davies understand the attacks on America. He was opposed to dollar imperialism—but he was also opposed to British and to rouble imperialism. He put all totalitarian governments in the same category. "There is no dictatorship of the proletariat; it is a dictatorship of the ruthless over the helpless, a dictatorship of the cunning over the simple, whether it is a dictatorship of the Pharaohs, the Czars, the Kaisers, the Hitlers, the Mussolinis, or the Stalins."[115] Similarly, at the same conference, Victor Yates regretted that there was no alternative put forward between the Zilliacus Amendment and the NUM resolution declaring loyal support for the government's policies; he went on to dissociate himself from Zilliacus' proposal that 10 per cent of German production should be set aside for reparation payments after industrial production in Germany had reached 70 per cent of the pre-war level. "I have always believed that the policy of reparations is quite anti-Socialist." Yates did not, however, seem to share Rhys Davies's willingness to condemn the Soviet Union, for he described as a "dreadful statement" another delegate's comment on the Soviet Union as "that brutal militarist clique".[116]

The crude model, delineated earlier in this chapter, of a party divided between an explicitly socialist and predominantly intellectual and middle-class Left, to whom foreign policy *was* and should be the reflection of its internal programme, and a cautious, realistic, largely working-class Right, continuing save with a few adjustments the international commitments of Conservative and coalition governments, can hardly be sustained.

The conception of a socialist foreign policy may or may not have been valid; the embodiment of that conception in specific governmental decisions in the world which faced the Labour Government of 1945 may or may not have been possible. What is clear is that the Combined

[115] *LPCR, 1948,* p. 192.   [116] *Ibid.,* p. 194.

Lefts did nothing to demonstrate that the conception was coherent or its execution feasible. They were unable to offer any mutual consistent set of alternatives to the foreign policy of the government. The foreign policy critics offered no agreed proposals of their own. Each group might claim to propound a "socialist foreign policy", but none could express it in terms acceptable to the rest. On Germany, the critical test of the early post-war years, the Left found themselves separated from the Centre Left, and could muster only the committed pacifists as allies. Socialism offered no unified response to the cause of European unity; the Combined Lefts were as initially as divided as the rest of the party. The guardians of the more specifically radical tradition of the party had to content themselves with a short-lived victory over the length of national service and a series of empty calls for world government. The more explicitly socialist critics of Labour's international policy were often isolated from the radical and pacifistic elements. The Cabinet, when challenged, could rely on the help of the pacifists and the world government enthusiasts to vote down the critics of the Anglo-American alliance, and on the Centre Left to help sustain the principle of conscription.

Figure 17 shows both the merits and the inadequacies of the simple distinctions of class, occupation, and education which have often been adduced to explain Labour's conflicts over foreign policy. It shows, in summary form, those issues on which particular social categories responded in a distinctive way. The two broad columns show which groups behaved in a markedly different manner from the rest of the party over conscription and foreign policy. Neither the foreign policy critics nor the conscription rebels, however, were homogeneous; and the narrow columns show which of the demographic categories were conspicuous amongst the political subgroups comprising each of the main rebel groups.

Criticism of Bevin's foreign policy, it is true, came largely from the Professions and the University graduates. In short, the differences in the Labour Party were structural. The opposing groups were not simply groups of men distinguished by conflicting opinions or some psychological characteristics (though, naturally, that cannot be ruled out). The dispute between Bevin's supporters and his critics conformed, remarkably closely, to the picture of a struggle between Hampstead intellectuals and pragmatic, earthy Trade Unionists. Small wonder that there was often so much bitterness between the two sides.[117]

Yet, as was shown in the 1955–9 study, it is too facile to see the contest between Left and Right simply in these terms. By the 1955 Parliament it was the Miscellaneous Occupations—the journalists, the clerks, the political organizers—who had become the mainstay of the Left. Moreover, if we identify the University graduates with the "intellectuals" it is clear that the intellectuals of the party were not a homogeneous group either in terms of composition or political belief. It has already been shown that the U4's were older, more senior, and more likely to represent constituencies of the Celtic fringe than the U1's, U2's, and U3's. It has also been demonstrated that the two groups differed sharply in their attitudes to conscription; moreover, the U4's were more likely to be found amongst the Left, the U1's, U2's, and U3's amongst the Centre Left. In addition the Left were recruited predominantly from older Members without war service. The bright young men from public school and Oxford and

---

[117] For a description of the attitude of trade unionists to middle-class intellectuals see Bremner, *op. cit.*, p. 279: "There is some liking and admiration. There is some resentment of the great verbal facility of these comparative newcomers. There is some scorn of them as not being 'practical men'. And there is the class difference. Most of these intellectuals are middle class, and many have not been in the Labour Party long enough to be trusted (as, for example, Mr. Attlee is trusted). There is the belief that these intellectuals are not as firmly loyal or as reliable as the old guard. And there is some suspicion that some are less convinced Labour Party supporters than opportunists, intent on using the Party to further their own careers."

	Foreign policy			Conscription		
	The combined lefts	Ultra left and left	Centre left	All opponents	Ideological pacifists	Other opponents
Professions	× × × × × ×				×××××	
Misc. occupations						×××××××
Workers						×××××××
University graduates	× × × × × ×				×××××××	
UI (+U3)	× × × × × ×		××××××			
U4 (+U2)		× × × × × ×		× × × × × × × ×		×××××××
Under 5l	× × × × × ×		××××××		×××××××	
5l and over		× × × × × ×				×××××
Scotland and Wales				× × × × × × × ×		
War service	× × × × × ×		××××××			
No war service		× × × × × ×		× × × × × × × ×		

Fig. 17. "All Opponents" refers to Members voting against conscription on either the Amendment to the Address (1946) or on either the Second or Third Readings of the National Service Bill (1947).

The entries for the University classes relate to U1 + U3, and U4 + U2 on foreign policy, and to U1 and U4 alone on conscription.

Cambridge, who came into the party in 1945, the core of the Centre Left were more amenable to the apparently harsh logic of events than their secondary school and redbrick colleagues.

Yet in the next Parliament, and especially after 1951, the Broader Left was to be re-mobilized; this development, which brought the Labour Party 10 years of factional conflict, is traced in the next chapter.

CHAPTER 5

The Labour Party: Foreign Affairs and Defence,
1950–5

"... many reforming ships are manned by mutineers." (HAROLD LASSWELL, *Psychopathology and Politics*.)

The factional conflicts that were, in one form or another, to disturb and divide the Labour Party for more than a decade, and almost to destroy it, began in the narrowly divided Parliament of 1950. Before the election there had been a controversy, often concealed, between those who looked for a programme of consolidation and those who wished to see a more militant, more dramatic attack upon the capitalist system. The election statement "Labour Believes in Britain", although a compromise, had leant more towards the Right than the Left. The statement had called for a new instalment of nationalization, but the industries mentioned were neither numerous nor especially important.

When the House met in early March the government had only one basic task—to survive. Yet the dispute went on: had Labour's near defeat been caused, as the Right and the pragmatists averred, by the alienation of the (so-called) moderate floating voter, or, as the Left argued, by the estrangement of those who resented the compromises which had been made.[1] In the House of Commons, however, the government's tiny majority and the vigour of the Conservative offensive helped to sustain discipline during the early months.

At the Labour Conference of 1949, Crossman, it will be recalled, had spoken of the pride which members of the party could feel at "four years of foreign policy". But in the same speech he had warned against an excessive emphasis on armaments. "I know quite well", said Crossman, "that we have got to have armaments ... What I am asking for is that the Cabinet ... when it weighs up the relative priorities, should see that a Socialist gives priority not to armaments, but that it regards them as only the second line of defence."[2] This difference over the priority to be given to defence, as against other forms of expenditure, was to become the first of the many conflicts which were to divide the Labour Party in the 1950s.

During the election campaign the publication of *Keeping Left*,[3] a successor to *Keep Left* (with a somewhat changed sponsorship), attracted little attention amidst the charges and counter-charges of the official party spokesman. Yet the language of *Keeping Left* helped both to explain the mellowing of opinion which had taken place amongst the Centre Left after 1946, and foreshadowed the questions which were to divide the party after 1951.

[1] See the discussion in *Tribune*, 3, 10, and 31 Mar. 1950, and *NS & N*, 4 Mar. 1950.
[2] *LPCR, 1949*, p. 193.
[3] *Keeping Left*, London, 1950.

83

Keeping Left looked back to its predecessor's analysis of post-war international relations. Its protests, the authors of *Keeping Left* claimed, had come too late to be effective, and its proposals were outdated, or at least postponed, by the American offer of Marshall Aid and by Russia's refusal to co-operate in the European recovery plan. The British Government, it was argued, could have done more in the first 18 months of peace to prevent the final breakdown of Big Three co-operation; but, however blame was to be distributed, the fact remained that the foreign policy proposed in *Keep Left* had ceased to be valid after the summer of 1947.

The tenor of the references in *Keeping Left* to America was distinctly more charitable than the tone of the earlier pamphlet. In 1947 *Keep Left* had warned that "America, wedded to free enterprise has swung to the Right when the rest of the world is going Left. . . . American liberalism is weak and divided", but in 1950 its successor could rejoice in the re-election of President Truman and aver that his programme, the Fair Deal, was "based on the three moral principles which inspire our socialism". After admitting that it was most unlikely that "the American Labour Movement will ever adopt an explicitly socialist programme", the pamphlet opined that over a wide field the Truman Administration and the Labour Government had the same interests, the same ideals, and the same enemies.[4] In 1947 *Keep Left* had urged that Britain should take the lead in the creation of a Third Force, based on the socialist countries of western Europe and the British Commonwealth. Three years later *Keeping Left* observed that most of western Europe had swung violently to the Right and was a great deal more reactionary than "capitalist" (*sic*) America.[5]

These developments help to explain why, after 1947, the Centre Left had abandoned its hopes of a Third Force and muted its criticisms of the government's foreign policy. Yet when it looked to contemporary and future problems, the pamphlet pointed at what were to become the great divisive issues of the fifties—the scale of military expenditure, German rearmament, and nuclear weapons.

The nature of the government's foreign policy—which *Keeping Left* now conceded to be inevitable—had imposed a rearmament programme which, if continued, would commit Britain to an expenditure of £1000 million a year and possibly far more. Britain's worldwide political and military commitments constituted a "crushing burden". Britain was using far more of her national wealth than she could safely afford in order to sustain her foreign policy. Armaments were not the first priority; the greatest danger to the West came from its own political and economic tensions. A policy which gave priority to arms expenditure and so intensified the "social crisis" would, in fact, increase the West's insecurity. Communism was more likely to triumph through the social and economic disintegration of the Western nations than through open aggression.[6]

To meet the hazards entailed by excessive rearmament, the pamphlet made three proposals: Britain should seek to break the atomic deadlock by putting forward new plans for prohibiting all weapons of mass destruction and should announce in advance her own readiness to forego them; a ceiling should be placed on the Defence Estimates, a figure of 6 per cent of the national income being suggested; and, though it was not possible to abolish conscription at once, a form of selective service might, it was recommended, be introduced.[7]

Economic commitments at home, however, were not the sole reason for reducing the priority given to arms production. The revolt of the coloured peoples was the major fact of the post-war world, and outside Europe the Russians held the ideological initiative almost everywhere. Full employment and fair shares had to be applied on a world scale which could only be

[4] *Keeping Left*, London, 1950, p. 25.   [5] *Ibid.*, p. 26.   [6] *Ibid.*, p. 22.   [7] *Ibid.*, pp. 22–23.

done by a permanent system of aid from the richer to the poorer countries. Economic help, moreover, must proceed hand in hand with political and social emancipation. Britain had not yet found, either for her own colonies or the coloured peoples as a whole, "a full constructive answer to the Russians". If a backward nation were to liberate itself by revolutionary action and did not interfere with its neighbours, Britain should offer it recognition and help.[8]

If the need for further British rearmament met with scepticism, the authors found German rearmament totally unacceptable. A rearmed Germany would seek to recover the eastern territories lost to Poland, it would destroy the hope of any real democracy in Germany, it would be exploited by Communist propaganda, and in France would enable the Communists to pose as the only national party—"In order to gain Germany as an ally we should lose France". Finally, a rearmed Germany would rule out the chance of any peaceful and genuine solution of the German problem.[9]

Keeping Left thus presaged what were to become the major themes of Labour's dissident section during the next few years. The struggle over the scale of British rearmament, the thesis that economic strength at home and economic development in the colonies should take precedence over the enhancement of military power; the specific problem of German rearmament; the question of nuclear weapons—all of these issues, which were soon to become a source of rancour and conflict, were foreshadowed in the pamphlet. At the same time, the friendly references to the United States and the acceptance of the Anglo-American alliance showed that the authors had moved a considerable way from the anti-American asperities and the Third Force visions of 1947.

THE KOREAN WAR AND REARMAMENT

The renewal of internal party conflict and the defeat of the Labour Government can be traced to the Korean war.[10] From the North Korean attack came a train of occurrences, unexpected at the time. Fears that the invasion of South Korea heralded a policy of increasing belligerence by Russia, and that it might be the prelude to a general war, caused a dramatic and upward reappraisal of the armaments programme. So far from reducing the arms burden, the NATO governments now felt constrained to accelerate the rate of rearmament. The same fears provoked a scramble for raw materials and a rapid rise in their prices which led to the British balance-of-payments crisis of 1951 and a heavy increase in the cost of living. The expansion of the arms programme had to be paid for; taxes were raised in the 1951 budget, and charges—whose symbolic significance far outstripped their real importance—had to be made for some forms of treatment under the National Health Service.

The imposition of charges upon teeth and spectacles was the precipitating cause, real or ostensible, of Aneurin Bevan's resignation from the Cabinet in 1951; but the scale of rearmament soon superseded the new health charges as the main issue of the contest.

Before this had happened, however, the Korean war had already stimulated and reactivated

[8] *Ibid.*, pp. 23–25.   [9] *Ibid.*, p. 21.

[10] Korea, a former colony of Japan, had been partitioned after the war with a Communist government ruling the North, and a client-administration of the United States, recognized by the United Nations, governing the South. In June 1950 the North Korean army crossed the partition line, the 38th parallel, into South Korea. Almost immediately the Security Council met and called upon the North Koreans to withdraw. When the North Koreans refused, President Truman ordered American forces, under the auspices of the United Nations, to defend South Korea. The United Nations welcomed American intervention and called on all member states to help. Britain offered naval assistance almost at once, and later sent a military contingent.

the suspicions and fears of the United States which had for the past 3 years, lain dormant in some sections of the Labour Left. Thus the direct effects of the Korean war were to rob the Labour Party of electoral support and to exacerbate the conflict amongst party militants and MPs.

The feelings released by the events of the Korean war can only be understood in the context of America's general policy in the Far East. In 1949 the civil war on the mainland of China ended in a victory for the Communists, and Chiang Kai Shek and the Nationalist Army withdrew to Formosa. Formosa had been under Japanese control between 1895 and 1945, but under the Cairo Agreement of 1943 it had been decided that it should revert to China after the defeat of Japan. The status of Formosa became a rallying-cry for the Left during the 1950s. America's defence of the island, and of the Nationalist regime there, provoked deep hostility.

Britain, acting for practical rather than ideological or moral reasons, recognized the Chinese Communist regime at the beginning of 1950, a decision warmly welcomed by the Labour Left. The American Administration, assailed by the Republicans for having allowed the Communists to win, refused recognition. Virulent hatred of the new China seemed to be the dominant emotion in America. The President was unwilling or unable to accept the logic of events and open diplomatic relations with the new government. Nevertheless, the Americans made no immediate move to protect Formosa. Not until late June, after the North Koreans had struck, did President Truman order the Seventh Fleet to defend Formosa against Communist invasion, and in doing so he also announced that the Seventh Fleet would act against any attempt by the Nationalists to attack the mainland. If Formosa was to be protected, it was also to be neutralized.

Nevertheless, there remained the question of recognition, and of the disposal of China's seat at the United Nations, which carried with it permanent membership of the Security Council, and hence the right to veto any decision of the Council. China continued to be represented at the United Nations by the nationalists; Britain followed up her act of recognition by supporting, later in 1950, the seating of the Chinese Communists.[11] America voted against, and after the outbreak of the Korean war her attitude hardened still further. In their attitude to recognition and the UN seat, both the Labour Left and the Americans demonstrated an affinity that underlay their disagreement; both regarded recognition and admission to the UN as expressions of moral approval rather than as pragmatic decisions. The American style of politics, especially the style of the American Right, had much in common with that of the British Left.

There was a widespread belief in Britain, by no means restricted to the Left, that the Chinese Communists were little more than agrarian reformers. Mao Tse Tung was seen as a potential Tito; Communist China might temporarily ally herself with the Soviet Union from motives of expediency and Communist solidarity, but she could, in time, if treated with understanding and generosity by the West, be detached from the Soviet alliance. The Americans were seen as so obsessed with the menace of Communism as determined to destroy a popular, national movement.

The rift over Far Eastern policy, already apparent in 1949, helps to explain the growing disenchantment of the Centre Left with the United States. Later developments, such as the crossing of the Yalu river, and the American initiative for rearmament, were to stimulate their latent animosity. So, too, were left-wing fears that elements in the United States were seeking an all-out war with China.

[11] When the issue came up in 1951, after China had intervened in Korea, Britain abstained.

Though Britain's support of American intervention in Korea incurred the censure of a few on the Left, it also met at first with the approval of most, especially of the Centre Left of 1945–50. American military help to South Korea, under the auspices of the United Nations, was represented by the British Government as an act of collective security—an interpretation widely accepted in the Labour Party. It was not until later, when American policy appeared to threaten China, that acquiescence turned to doubt, and doubt, amongst some, to open or qualified hostility.

Meanwhile, discussions had been going on between the British and American governments about the rearmament programme. The Americans pressed strongly for an increase in British rearmament and in September 1950 the Prime Minister announced the introduction of a new programme to last 3 years and to cost £3600 million. In November the government announced that the period of national service would be increased from 18 months to 2 years. Growing pessimism about the international situation led to pressure for a further increase in rearmament over and above the £3600-million level. In January 1951 the government announced a new and bigger rearmament plan to cost £4700 million over 3 years; in February Mr. Aneurin Bevan, as Minister of Labour, wound up for the government in the debate on the new defence programme and asserted that it was within Britain's capacity.

In April the budget of Hugh Gaitskell (who had succeeded Sir Stafford Cripps as Chancellor 6 months before) destroyed whatever hopes there had been of maintaining the unity of the Labour Party. Gaitskell had the unpopular task of paying for rearmament; fresh taxes were imposed, and in order to meet the claims of hospital expansion some charges were imposed on certain forms of medical treatment. The National Health Service, of which Bevan could claim to be the father, seemed to be the first victim of rearmament. The principle of the free health service had been impaired. Bevan fought the proposals in the Cabinet and lost. In the meantime he had publicly declared, in a speech in Bermondsey, that he could never remain a member of a government which charged people for medical treatment.

On 21 April Bevan resigned as Minister of Labour. With him went Harold Wilson, then President of the Board of Trade, and John Freeman, Parliamentary Secretary at the Ministry of Supply.

Bevan's letter of resignation disclosed that the dispute stretched beyond the substantively minor, if psychologically important, question of health charges; the proposed level of rearmament, wrote Bevan, was physically unattainable in the coming year without grave extravagance in spending.

In his resignation speech Bevan developed his attack on the rearmament plans. Echoing the words of *Keeping Left*, Bevan argued that "the weapons of the totalitarian states are, first, social and economic, and only next military"; if the Western economies were disrupted by excessive military expenditure, and the standard of living reduced, the Communists would have established "a whole series of Trojan horses in every nation of the western economy".[12]

Wilson's resignation speech, delivered the day after Bevan's, emphasized the difficulties in carrying out the rearmament programme, particularly those imposed by the shortages of raw materials.[13] John Freeman's letter of resignation also questioned the feasibility of the government's rearmament programme.

The resigning Ministers were not objecting to the principle of rearmament; they were not pacifists. They were objecting to the proposed level of rearmament, to the cuts made in the social services to finance rearmament, to the government's order of priorities which, to the

[12] HC Deb. 487, cc. 34–43.   [13] *Ibid.*, cc. 228–31.

critics, put military power above economic strength and social progress. In the Bevanite critique can be discerned an echo of the conscription controversy of 1946–7, when Crossman and his allies had accepted the principle of conscription but had quarrelled with the proposed length of service. The two sides disagreed in their assessment of the Communist challenge; the government saw primarily a military, the ex-Ministers a social and economic, threat.

The day of Bevan's resignation, 21 April, marked the beginning of years of discord—of disputes that were to torment the Labour Party long after Bevan himself had made his peace with the party leadership.

The remnants of the Keep Left group rallied round Bevan to become the nucleus of the Bevanites—a source of continuing and energetic, though not always cohesive, opposition to the Front Bench for the next few years.

In July *Tribune* published a new pamphlet, *One Way Only*,[14] which contained a foreword written by the three ex-Ministers. The tenor of the pamphlet was strikingly similar to that of *Keeping Left* published 18 months before. Whilst accepting that some measure of military strength was required to deter the Russians, it rejected the need for Atlantic rearmament on the scale proposed by the NATO governments. The policies of the West were based on a gross overestimate of Russian strength and of the Russian willingness to risk a general war. The rearmament of the Atlantic Powers should be subordinated to a World Plan for Mutual Aid— a plan approved by the Labour Conference in 1950 but now to be crippled by the claims of arms production. Part of the resources and labour to be devoted to rearmament should be allocated to the plan, and Britain should take the lead by diverting resources from its own rearmament programme. Like *Keeping Left*, the pamphlet called for the extension of the principle of fair shares to the international sphere. Britain and the West should help the colonial peoples by economic and technical aid to complete their revolutions, and not collaborate with reactionary forces to suppress popular national movements. The pamphlet warned of the dangers of an arms race between the Great Powers, and presaged the calls for summit meetings which were to be made repeatedly in the Labour Party in the years ahead by demanding a "supreme effort . . . to negotiate a settlement with Russia in the next two years".[15]

In its attitude to the United States, the pamphlet again echoed the sentiments of *Keeping Left*. It described as an "absurd belief" the notion that the United States must be regarded as a homogeneous bloc of massed reaction. "No one can doubt that both the aim of the great American aid policies since the end of the war, and the political force behind them, were strongly progressive."[16] All foreign policies, socialist or otherwise, must contain elements of compromise. "The idea that a Socialist government should seek co-operation only with other Socialist governments is a stupid illusion. . . . It is a policy for hermits, not for Socialists."[16] Today, however, the Anglo-American alliance was under strain; a new temper was rising on the other side of the Atlantic. A wild anti-Communist crusade, to be conducted by every means from witch-hunts to atom bombs, was preached by the extreme elements on the American Right.[17] The American Administration was yielding, step by step, to these pressures; in turn, the British Government's resistance to the demands of the American Administration was growing weaker. Exports of rubber to China had been stopped, and at the UN the British delegate was no longer pressing the issue of Chinese representation. The Americans were willing to risk an extension of the Korean war, were prepared to bring Franco's Spain into NATO, and were championing the idea of German rearmament. What was needed was a series of independent

[14] *One Way Only*, London, 1951.
[15] *Ibid.*, p. 4.   [16] *Ibid.*, p. 11.   [17] *Ibid.*, p. 11.

British initiatives to reassert British independence and "rectify the lop-sided nature of the alliance and to secure certain specific purposes".[18] These purposes were the achievement of an armistice in Korea and, ultimately, a negotiated settlement of the Far Eastern problem; the Germans should not be rearmed and Franco should continue to be excluded from NATO. Peace proposals should be put to the Russians which should include the World Plan for Mutual Aid, though the latter, however, should go forward whether or not the Russians agreed to it. Western rearmament programmes should be scaled down so as to release resources for the plan, and raw materials should be allocated amongst the Atlantic powers on "a more realistic and comprehensive scale".[19]

Once again, a different system of priorities to the government's was offered; whereas the Labour Government saw the military threat as the most urgent peril, the authors of the pamphlet saw the misery of the underdeveloped nations and poverty at home as the greatest danger.

KOREA AND THE FAR EAST, 1950–1

Early in July the North Korean advance was contained around the Pusan bridgehead in the south-east of the country. A rapid build-up of United Nations forces began; and in September the UN Commander, MacArthur, struck at the North Koreans. The UN forces drove out the invaders, re-occupied Seoul, capital of South Korea, and pushed on beyond the 38th parallel into North Korea. By October the UN armies had at one point reached the Manchurian border. There were those (including the British Government) who urged that the UN forces should not begin a general advance to the Yalu river, but, disregarding their advice, MacArthur pressed on and began what was to have been his final offensive.

The United Nations troops encountered massive Chinese forces. The UN army was pushed back hundreds of miles, beyond the 38th parallel; Seoul fell once again. Then the United Nations rallied and in May 1951 crossed the parallel once more. Truce talks began at Panmunjon 2 months later, and dragged on for nearly 2 years before an armistice was signed.

No fewer than eleven motions on Korea were tabled in the 1950–1 Parliament, but six of them attracted fewer than five signatories. The most controversial was a one man EDM tabled by S. O. Davies, the left-wing Member for Merthyr Tydfil, who demanded that Britain should withdraw all its naval forces from the area and recognize the claim of the Korean people for "the unification and independence of their country". This was an extreme and unrepresentative motion; others, however, better reflected the thinking of the Labour Left in Parliament and the country.

The distinguishing mark of all but one of these more popular EDMs was their vagueness. Thus in a motion tabled less than 3 weeks after the outbreak of the fighting, Sydney Silverman and 15 Labour colleagues urged the government to use "its best endeavours to limit the area of conflict" and to bring about an end of the fighting under the auspices of the United Nations; it added for good measure an exhortation to the government to urge the withdrawal of Americans from Formosa and to obtain the admission of Communist China to the United Nations.[20] Eight members who had originally signed the motion withdrew their names at the request of the Prime Minister.[21] Another, tabled by Emrys Hughes and 15 of his colleagues in February 1951, urged that further efforts should be made to obtain a cease fire and a permanent settlement

---

[18] *Ibid.*, p. 12.   [19] *Ibid.*, p. 13.   [20] EDM 45/50.
[21] See R. J. Jackson, *Rebels and Whips*, London, 1968, p. 91.

"by the withdrawal of all armed forces"; this motion also regretted the action of the United Nations in branding China as an aggressor (a decision supported by Britain) and strongly opposed any form of sanctions against China likely to prolong the war.[22] At the end of May, Emrys Hughes, Sydney Silverman, and 12 other Members repeated the call for negotiations for a cease fire and the withdrawal of foreign armies.[23] A month later, Sydney Silverman put down an EDM, signed by 17 other Members, which earnestly hoped the government would take the initiative in securing, by international agreement, the freedom and independence of Korea.[24] Each of these motions was tabled by acknowledged left wingers; but the demands were not so much distinctively left wing (with the possible exception of the EDM which regretted the "branding" of China as an aggressor) as remote from reality. They showed the Labour Left at its rhetorical best and its practical worst.

In contrast to these long and cloudy resolutions was one which was as brief as it was specific. This EDM[25] was put down in mid-November 1950 by Michael Foot when General MacArthur was opening the offensive which, he hoped, would take him to the Manchurian border. It urged the government to seek an immediate agreement on the line beyond which the UN forces would not advance "with a view to bringing the fighting to an end as quickly as possible". Although heavily supported by the Left, the motion was not in itself hostile to the government. Moreover, it became clear from the foreign affairs debates held before Christmas not only that the government themselves were urging this course on the Americans, but that even the Conservatives were thinking of such a policy.[26] The Left could say publicly what the government had to urge in private.[27]

The signatories of the Korea motions can be arranged in a Guttman scale—into a Left and a Centre Left. The value of Yule's Q for 8 of the 10 possible pairs of motions ranged from 0·75 to 0·96. The value of two pairs (EDMs 29/*51* and 66/*51*, and EDMs 84/*51* and 5/*51*) was 0·46. Two of the EDMs involved, 66/*51* and 84/*51*, which generally, in combination with other motions, yielded rather lower values of Q, were discarded leaving two of the "rhetorical" motions and the more specific 5/*51*. Of the 22 Members who signed either or both of the two remaining "rhetorical" motions, 14 also signed EDM 5/*51*. Members who signed these "rhetorical" motions were deemed to constitute the Left on this question, and the 26 who signed EDM 5/*51* without signing either of the other two motions, the Centre Left.

Both the Left and the Centre Left drew disproportionately from the middle-class occupations, the University graduates, the Co-operators and the Constituency sponsored, and the under-50's. The support of the Centre Left came, more than that of the Left, from the Professions, the University educated, and the youngest Members. There was also a modest tendency for the Left and the Centre Left to draw on the Left and Centre Left of 1945–50 respectively, but the numbers involved are too small to warrant any special note being taken.

KOREA AND THE FAR EAST, 1951–5

Few of the more clearly left-wing EDMs tabled in the next Parliament won much support. EDM 4/*51*, tabled by Sydney Silverman, called on the Conservative Government to declare that fighting in Korea should cease on the armistice line already agreed and that Communist

[22] EDM 29/*51*.   [23] EDM 66/*51*.   [24] EDM 84/*51*.   [25] EDM 5/*51*.
[26] See HC Deb. 481, cc. 1177 and 1437 for the comments of Eden and Attlee and 482, c. 1459 for Mr. Bevin's.
[27] Ian Mikardo, however, displayed some scepticism about the sincerity of the two Front Benches. See HC Deb. 481, c. 1252.

China should be "accorded her rightful place" at the United Nations. Seventeen backbenchers signed this motion. Nearly 3 months later, at the end of January 1952, Sydney Silverman and 16 colleagues called on the government to take no further part in the fighting unless North Korea violated the cease-fire line already agreed, and again urged the admission of Communist China to the United Nations,[28] whilst 10 Members signed a motion put down by Barbara Castle which called on the government, in view of the delay in reaching an armistice, to see that Britain was directly represented at the peace negotiations.[29] Altogether, 30 Members had signed one (or more) of these three EDMs.[30]

Negotiations with the Communists had begun in July 1951 but soon reached deadlock, the chief cause of dispute being the fate of those North Korean and Chinese prisoners of the United Nations who did not want to be repatriated to their homeland. The United Nations insisted that they could not send these prisoners back against their will; and the deadlock remained until at the end of March 1953, the Chinese Prime Minister, Chou En-lai, suggested a new formula for resolving the dispute. On 1 April Churchill gave a cautious welcome to the proposals and said that they did not in themselves seem inconsistent with any of the principles laid down by the United Nations.[31] On the same day, 4 North Staffordshire Members, headed by Ellis Smith, and 2 other MPs sponsored a motion which welcomed Mr. Chou's proposals and called on the government to use its influence with other members of the United Nations to exploit this opportunity for "the rehabilitation of Korea".[32] Ninety-four Labour MPs signed the motion.[33]

The Professions and Miscellaneous Occupations came out disproportionately in support of the more obviously left-wing EDMs—as did the CLP sponsored and the University graduates. On the other hand, the Ellis Smith motion appealed preponderantly to the Workers, the Trade Unionists, the older MPs, and, amongst the graduates, to the U4's. The differences in the nature of the support attracted by these motions were very sharp.

It was the traditional Left which expressed most clearly and openly the anxieties which the Korean war, and especially American policy, had aroused. But it is clear that the Worker/Trade Unionist element were also uneasy, and were willing to take advantage of any reasonable opportunity for negotiation.

Fears about America's intentions in the Far East and the acquiescence of the Conservatives and Labour's Front Bench in this policy helped to provoke a demonstration on the floor of the House. Just before leaving office, Herbert Morrison, as Labour's Foreign Secretary, had taken part in the negotiations which led to the signing of the Japanese Peace Treaty. The treaty came up for discussion in the House of Commons shortly after the change of government.

The Labour Front Bench were, of course, as fully committed to the treaty as the new Conservative Government, and their spokesmen exhorted their backbench followers to accept it. However, the treaty was heavily criticized from the Labour benches; representatives of Lancashire and the Potteries feared the renewal of Japanese competition. The treaty, said Arthur Irvine, gave a fillip to Japanese industry which might be detrimental to Lancashire and to the interests of British industry,[34] but the agreement was also indicted on broader grounds. "The

[28] EDMs 4/51 and 16/51.   [29] EDM 77/51.

[30] The value of Yule's Q for the three pairs of motions ranges from 0·70 to 0·91.

[31] HC Deb. 513, c. 1219.   [32] EDM 82/52.

[33] This motion has not explicitly been treated as part of a scale: instead, those signatories who did not sign one or other of the Silverman or Castle EDMs have been analysed separately. The value of Yule's Q for EDM 82/52 and the three Silverman/Castle motions ranges from the low figure of 0·25 for EDMs 4/51 and 82/52, to 0·62 for EDMs 16/51 and 82/52.

[34] HC Deb. 494, cc. 956–61.

main engine behind the Treaty", declared *Tribune*, "is military calculation. . . . Though the first line of attack had come from the spokesmen of Lancashire and the Potteries, concerned with the threat of Japanese competition, the argument about Britain's trading interests was not the most vital."[35] Sydney Silverman, after mentioning that two mills in his Lancashire constituency of Nelson and Colne had had to close because of unfair Japanese competition, went on to argue that the treaty deferred a genuine and lasting settlement in the Far East,[36] whilst Arthur Irvine feared that the treaty was a symbol of the build-up of military force to the east and west of Russia—a build-up which she might construe as a threat to her safety.[37] In the division, 35 Labour MPs, including Bevan, Wilson, and Freeman, went into the lobby against the combined forces of the Labour Front Bench, and those who heeded them, and the Conservatives. The 35 included 5 Members, 3 of whom came from Lancashire, who were not normally associated with the Left, but all of the remaining 30 were to rebel with Bevan in the rearmament debate a few months later. Moreover, all of those who expressed fears of unfair Japanese competition in the debate were, with one exception, associated with the Left at this time.[38] Only a small number of MPs were involved in this rebellion, and, probably for this reason, only one statistically significant association emerged—that of sponsorship. The CLP sponsored were more prominent in the rebellion than the Trade Unionists—a contrast which is the more impressive given the industrial character of some of the objections to the treaty. The occupational breakdown did not yield any significant relationship; but more of the Professions and the Miscellaneous Occupations (especially the latter) rebelled than of the Workers and the Business Members.

It is not easy to offer a simple definition of "Leftness" for the 1951–5 Parliament, for Bevan often attracted pacifists and others, unconnected with the regular Left, on particular issues. The best approach is to divide the party into three groups based on behaviour in floor revolts. The Left has been defined by reference to the attitudes of Members in three rebellions—the vote against the Japanese Peace Treaty of November 1951, the "57 Varieties" demonstration against

TABLE 20. LEFTISM, DEFENCE POLICY, AND THE FAR EAST

	Left		Other Defence and Nuclear Critics		Rest		Total
	No.	%	No.	%	No.	%	
Left (4/*51*, 16/*51*, 77/*51*)	18	45	6	11	5	4	29
Welcome for Mr. Chou's proposals (82/52)	10	25	17	30	41	33	68
None	12	30	33	59	79	63	124
Total	40	100	56	100	125	100	221

$\chi_4^2 = 42 \cdot 03$. Significant at $0 \cdot 1\%$.

[35] *Tribune*, 30 Dec. 1951.   [36] HC Deb. 495, cc. 919–30.   [37] *Ibid.*, cc. 956–61.
[38] The one exception was Harry Hynd, of Accrington, who voted for the treaty. The left wingers who spoke were Ellis Smith, Stross, Sydney Silverman, Irvine, and Harold Davies.

the scale of rearmament 4 months later, and the "Abstention of the 62" on nuclear weapons in March 1955. Members who rebelled (or in the Abstention of the 62 abstained) in any two of these three protests have been termed the Left. They numbered 40 in all.

A second category consists of Other Defence and Nuclear Critics. Members who, without qualifying for the Left, rebelled on either the 57 Varieties revolt or the Abstention of the 62 or on the nuclear weapons clause of the Atomic Energy Bill have been allocated to this class, which contains 56 backbenchers. The remaining 125 Members are called the Rest.[1] As might be expected, the signatories of the more left-wing Far Eastern EDMs were drawn, quite disproportionately, from the Left, as defined above. The Other Defence and Nuclear Critics, however, responded much like the Rest (Table 20).

NEGOTIATIONS WITH RUSSIA, 1950–1

The last negotiations with the Russians at Foreign Minister level had taken place in 1949 and proved fruitless. In the election campaign of 1950, Winston Churchill spoke of his desire for a meeting with the Russians at the highest level; whilst he saw the American possession of the atomic bomb as the surest guarantee of peace, he hoped there might be found "some more exalted and august foundation for our safety than this grim and sombre balancing power of the bomb". This suggestion was quickly denounced by Labour Ministers as an election stunt and "soapbox diplomacy". Attlee, in his final election broadcast, announced that Britain was prepared to discuss with Russia and other nations the menace of the hydrogen bomb, but reminded his listeners of the Russian rejection of the Western proposal for international control of atomic energy, and added: "The difficulty does not lie in method nor in the choice of persons to discuss these high matters. All that is required is the will."

Thus the first call for a high-level conference had come from the Conservative leader, and had, not surprisingly, been denounced by the Labour's official spokesmen as an election gimmick. Attlee seems to have been sceptical of the value of such conferences. "The fashion of Summit Conferences in peace-time, with all their attendant publicity seemed to him to have, more often than not, more risk than advantage."[39] Nevertheless, the cry for a high-level meeting was taken up later in the year by sections of the Labour Party. The Korean war, and the ominous signs of international tension, inspired the wish and prompted the demand for a new conference of the Great Powers. The Left, in particular, cherished a belief which was widespread in the Labour Movement that most disputes could be resolved by rational discussion. The successive calls for summit conferences made during the next few years reflected this faith. Negotiation was posed as the alternative to war. At the Margate Conference Harold Davies moved a composite resolution which called upon the government, inter alia, "to strive to end the differences between the five great powers, to which end a Conference should be called immediately". Seconding the motion, Mr. Casasola of the Foundry Workers Union asked: "After a war what happens? You have got to come to the conference table and end it and discuss your difficulties. . . . Why not come to the conference table first and remove the difficulties with which you are faced?"[40]

Like Churchill's election call, this demand from the Labour Left met with little sympathy from the Foreign Secretary. Russia, he said, could sit down at the table with Britain tomorrow, and Britain would forget the past; but after asserting a preference for negotiation through the

[39] Lord Francis-Williams, *A Prime Minister Remembers*, London, 1961, p. 149.
[40] *LPCR, 1950*, p. 142.

United Nations rather than through a meeting of the Great Powers, he went on to remind the delegates of the tortuous and fruitless negotiations of 1947.

During October and November, fears grew that the actions of the UN Commander, General MacArthur, would draw Communist China into the Korean war, and perhaps result in the outbreak of a general war. In mid-October the Foreign Ministers of the Communist bloc countries met in Prague and made some proposals for solving the German problem—proposals which were rejected, in effect, by the Americans. Early in November the Russians suggested that a conference of foreign ministers should be held to consider the Prague proposals. Ten days later, on 13 November, Mr. Bevin told the House of Commons that the Prague proposals would not serve as the basis for such a conference.

Amongst the Left feeling grew that the West should negotiate with the Communist countries. In December a *Tribune* editorial called for negotiations with both China and Russia. Whilst acknowledging that Russian intransigence might oblige the West to embark on rapid rearmament (including the rearming of Germany), *Tribune* thought to do so without making a "positive reply" to the Russian proposal for a meeting of the four Great Powers would be giving a gratuitous victory to the Russians.[41] *Tribune*'s tone, however, continued to be restrained. On 29 December, though it found the latest Western reply to Russia "determinedly cautious", the journal declared that the reply held the door for negotiations firmly open, and added that ". . . even the slenderest chance of a general détente with Russia should be seized".[42] Meanwhile, in mid-November, Ian Mikardo, together with 5 other signatories of the Foreign Affairs Amendment of 1946, had tabled a motion which, whilst appreciating that the earlier Russian proposals had been found to be unacceptable, urged the government to put forward alternative proposals for a four-power conference.[43] The signatories came largely from the Left (24 of the 36 signatories still on the backbenches 18 months later voted with Aneurin Bevan in the floor revolt against rearmament), but included a few men of the Right, such as Roy Jenkins and Austen Albu. Moreover, the list of signatories was almost identical with that of the preceding EDM, tabled the same day, which had called upon the government to seek agreement on a line, in Korea, beyond which the UN armies would not advance.[44]

A day later Ellis Smith tabled another motion, longer and more rhetorical, than EDM 6/51, but similar in substance. This motion recorded its appreciation of the government's efforts to strengthen the authority of the United Nations, and went on to call for an early meeting of the Foreign Ministers' Conference and for the implementation of Resolution C of the UN General Assembly which had appealed to the Great Powers to renew their efforts to "compose their differences and establish a lasting peace."[45]

On 18 November the *Daily Telegraph*, reporting the Mikardo EDM (together with that on Korea tabled at the same time), averred that the presence amongst the signatories of so many of Mr. Bevin's most persistent critics from the last Parliament suggested a fresh stirring of dissatisfaction within the socialist ranks. On 22 November the same newspaper reported that a sense of frustration over the course of foreign policy was growing amongst Labour MPs, who felt that the government should take the initiative to resolve the deadlock between East and West. It noted that many signatories of Ellis Smith's EDM had been amongst the most loyal supporters of Ernest Bevin; though neither this EDM nor the earlier motions on East-

---

[41] *Tribune*, 15 Dec. 1950.   [42] *Ibid.*, 29 Dec. 1950.   [43] EDM 6/51.

[44] See p. 90. All but two of the signatories of the Korean EDM signed the call for a new four-power conference; and all but one of the signatories of the latter motion signed the Korean EDM.

[45] EDM 7/51.

West negotiations and Korea could be regarded as hostile, some backbenchers were saying that no fresh impetus could be expected from Bevin in his present state of health. On 24 November, in a leading article entitled "Another 'stab in the back' ". the *Daily Telegraph*, after describing the three EDMs as "a major operation without anaesthetic", asserted that about a third of the backbench Labour MPs were apprehensive lest Ernest Bevin should no longer be fit "for an office of so momentous responsibility".[46]

In December the West made new proposals to the Russians for a deputy foreign ministers' meeting, a decision which came as a surprise to Ernest Davies, the Under-Secretary of State for Foreign Affairs; this circumstance suggests that backbench pressure had induced the British Government to take the initiative with its allies in proposing a conference.[47]

The difference between the two motions lay in their sponsorship and their supporters. The second EDM was put down by Ellis Smith, who though sometimes associated with the Left, was less closely identified with it than Ian Mikardo. Though Smith's fellow-sponsors included the left-wing Dr. Barnett Stross, the remaining 4 were all Trade Unionists and none of them were men of the Left. Presumably, the second motion was put down to enable those Members in favour of a high-level conference to say so without the embarrassment of associating publicly with the Left and perhaps, incidentally, destroying their credit with Ernest Bevin. It was as though two groups of people both trying to arrive at the same place, chose to travel in different buses. Forty-six Members signed this motion. Only 3 MPs signed both—even though the sentiments expressed were almost the same.

The Mikardo EDM drew its support more or less from the normal sources of the Left—the graduates, the CLP and Co-op. sponsored, and the under-50's, but more from the Miscellaneous Occupations than the Professions. Three-quarters of the backbenchers who had served in the previous Parliament came from the "Broader Left".[48] The backing for Ellis Smith's motion came in striking fashion from the traditional sources of the Right—from Trade Unionists, the Workers, the Elementary educated, and the older Members.

Only 3 of the 28 survivors of the 1945 House who signed Smith's motion had belonged to the Broader Left—but it is significant that 14 of them had opposed or had had reservations about conscription.[49] Ellis Smith's motion mobilized an equal and opposite force to that recruited by Ian Mikardo. When the two motions are combined and their supporters are compared with the rest of the party, few differences emerge; but those few are intriguing. The Miscellaneous Occupations came out most strongly for negotiation, closely followed by the Workers, whilst the Professions lagged behind.[50] Moreover, the Members with war service supported the motions less strongly than those with none. It seems as though the cause of negotiation, providing it could be detached from the Left, could muster considerable support amongst the normally loyal sections of the party.

The circumstances in which the two motions were tabled, and especially the contrasting nature of their support, strongly suggest that the second motion was deliberately put down to show that support for negotiations with Russia was not confined to the Left or "the intellectuals" of the party.

[46] *Daily Telegraph*, 24 Nov. 1950.
[47] See Rose, *op. cit.*, p. 152.
[48] Members of the Left and Centre Left and Dual Abstainers in the 1945–50 Parliament.
[49] Here defined as those who voted against conscription or abstained two or three times.
[50] Though when the motions are combined no statistically significant association is found between attitude and occupation.

NEGOTIATIONS WITH RUSSIA, 1951–5

In the next Parliament there was further agitation within the Labour Party for high-level negotiations. This agitation was, moreover, often linked with the conflict inside the party over German rearmament. We have already seen how *One Way Only* had called for a supreme effort to negotiate with Russia. In April 1952 *Tribune* deplored the West's refusal to consider seriously a recent Russian offer, and asserted that the aim of negotiation had been replaced by the goal of obtaining Russia's unconditional surrender. The Labour Party leadership were criticized for not taking the initiative in pressing for genuine negotiations "in which both sides give as well as take".[51]

In January 1953 Dwight Eisenhower assumed office as President of the United States, and in March Stalin died. In April Eisenhower expressed the hope that the new Russian leaders would be willing to negotiate with the West; and the Russians, in turn, indicated their wish for new discussions. On 11 May the British Prime Minister, Churchill, announced in the House of Commons that he favoured a "conference on the highest level between the leading powers" and that it should take place without long delay. There should be no ponderous or rigid agenda, and the conference should be confined to the smallest possible number of persons and powers.[52] *Tribune* greeted this declaration with enthusiasm. Both Churchill and Attlee, wrote J. P. W. Mallalieu, had "made speeches which a few weeks ago would have been inconceivable by either".[53]

Eden, the Foreign Secretary, had fallen ill in April, and at the end of June, Churchill, who had been temporarily undertaking Eden's duties, had a stroke. It was rumoured that the Americans and some of Churchill's Cabinet colleagues had never liked the notion of a summit conference, and were using the Prime Minister's illness as an excuse for postponement and, if possible, avoidance of the meeting. In July *Tribune* thought the Big Four negotiations were in danger. The forces of reaction in the United States and elsewhere were opposed to any form of negotiation with the Soviet Union. The task of the Labour leadership, and the government, should be to see that a four-power conference was called.[54]

At the end of September Tom O'Brien, after a private talk with Churchill, who was recuperating in the South of France, alleged that the cause of the delay was to be found in political opposition at home rather than the Prime Minister's illness, an interpretation rebutted by a special Downing Street statement.[55]

In October the issue was discussed at Labour Party Conference; Attlee moved a long resolution on behalf of the National Executive which, inter alia, deplored the West's failure to maintain the initiative in efforts to break the deadlock between East and West. Denis Healey, from the Right, found himself in the unfamiliar role of opposing the platform; there was the danger, he warned, that the Labour Party would use Churchill's advocacy of four-power talks as an excuse for "dodging the consequences of a decision we ourselves took on German rearmament when in power". Attlee, he charged, had told the House in July that the Labour Party wanted a summit conference without an agenda which would not be restricted to the problem of Germany but could deal with other issues such as disarmament. "This idea is the idea that Churchill put forward on 11 May, and up to the moment that Churchill put it

---

[51] *Tribune*, 18 Apr. 1952.   [52] HC Deb. 515, c. 897.   [53] *Tribune*, 15 May 1953.
[54] *Ibid.*, 3 July 1953.
[55] This statement reaffirmed Churchill's beliefs in a four-power summit, but explained that because of French and American insistence the talks would take place at Foreign Minister level.

forward Clem Attlee and every leader of the party had been pouring cold water on the idea." Healey concluded by exhorting the party to "show some honesty and courage in facing the facts".[56]

In the 1950–1 Parliament separate EDMs, expressing the same demand but attracting different support, had been put down. In 1953 the same pattern recurred over the same issue.

On 7 May, 4 days *before* Churchill himself suggested a new four-power conference, Ellis Smith tabled a motion urging the government to take the initiative "with a view to bringing about a basis of agreement which will lead to a Five Power Conference". The six sponsors included Barnett Stross, Ellis Smith's co-sponsor of 2½ years before; Harriet Slater, who had just been elected to the House for Stoke North; Dai Grenfell, a trade unionist who had voted with the Bevanites in the defence floor revolt of 1952; a trade unionist and ex-Minister, Ness Edwards—and, as sixth name, Harold Wilson.[57] At the beginning of July, when the Left were arguing that the chances of a negotiated settlement were being sabotaged, Wilson and four other regular Bevanites put down an EDM which asked the government to make it "its prime concern" that an early conference with the Soviet leaders should take place;[58] and in November (after the three Western Powers had sent identical notes accusing the Russians of not wanting genuine negotiations at present), Wilson, his four Bevanite co-sponsors of the July EDM, and Ellis Smith, put down a further motion. This EDM rejected the British Government's contention that the Soviet Union did not wish to enter into serious negotiations and regretted that the Western Powers had both rejected the Soviet proposals and laid down rigid pre-conditions for a meeting. It went on to ask the Prime Minister to propose, at his forthcoming Bermuda meeting with Eisenhower and the French Premier, Laniel, that a five-power conference should be held without pre-conditions on either side. Thus the EDM supported the Soviet view that Communist China should take part in the conference. Thirty-eight Members signed this motion, nearly all of them veterans of the 57 Varieties protest.[59] Again, the Professions and the Miscellaneous Occupations subscribed more frequently than the Workers to the Bevanite EDMs; while, in turn, the Workers signed the EDM of mixed sponsorship more generously than the Professions. The behaviour of the Elementary educated and the graduates and the CLP sponsored and the Trade Unionists paralleled that of the two main occupational groups; and, as in 1950, when the three EDMs are conflated, the Workers seem on this evidence to have felt more strongly about negotiations than the Professions. Unwilling to sign a purely Bevanite demand, they came out in substantial numbers for an EDM of more catholic sponsorship.[60]

Table 21 shows the responses of the various ideological groupings within the Labour Party to the "summit conference" EDMs.

Support for the Bevanite EDMs came to an overwhelming degree from either the Left or the Other Defence and Nuclear Critics, whilst the signatories of Ellis Smith's motion were drawn more evenly from the various backbench groups. What deserves special mention here is the lack of prominence of the Professions amongst the signatories of either the Bevanite motions or Ellis Smith's EDM.

These motions, like those of 1950, testify to the widespread desire for negotiations with the eastern countries. This desire sprang, not only from the specifically socialist tradition of the party, but also from the pacificist tradition, which, as we have seen, was more widely diffused—

---

[56] *LPCR, 1953*, p. 160.   [57] EDM 96/52.   [58] EDM 115/52.   [59] EDM 13/53.

[60] The value of Yule's Q for the two Bevanite EDMs (115/52 and 13/53) is 0·91; the value of Yule's Q for the two pairs involving EDM 96/52 is 0·21 and 0·35.

TABLE 21. LEFTNESS, DEFENCE POLICY, AND SUMMIT TALKS

	Left		Other Defence and Nuclear Critics		Rest		Total
	No.	%	No.	%	No.	%	
Bevanite EDMs (115/52 or 13/53)	25	63	9	16	2	2	36
Mixed 96/52 only	11	28	22	39	26	21	59
None	4	10	25	45	97	78	126
Total	40	100	56	100	125	100	221

$\chi_4^2 = 100 \cdot 26$. Significant at $0 \cdot 1\%$.

and, of course, to a wish for a more flexible approach to the Russians which was felt beyond the borders of the Labour Party.

THE BEVANITE REVOLT

Both Far Eastern policy and the issue of negotiations with Russia had been the subject of EDMs in the short-lived Parliament of 1950. Strictly speaking, the dispute about British rearmament began with Bevan's resignation in April 1951; but no EDMs on this topic were tabled, and the only public demonstration on the question took place when Labour was in opposition in the next Parliament. The Bevanite floor revolt against rearmament began what was to be, even by the standards of the Labour Party, more than 6 months of bitter strife and harsh recrimination. It culminated in the autumn of 1952 in the sweeping Bevanite gains in the constituency party elections to the National Executive, and in a stern decision of the Parliamentary Party which outlawed organized factions within the party. Thereafter the scale of British rearmament lost its importance as a source of conflict within the party; its place was taken by the struggle over the rearming of Germany and later by the cleavages over nuclear weapons.

The Bevanites, with some pacifist allies, made their demonstration at the end of a defence debate in March 1952. Some substance had already been given to the Bevanite charge that rearmament on the scale contemplated would overstrain the British economy by the new Conservative Government's decision to re-phase the programme which would now take 4 years instead of 3. The government had concluded that the original plan—the famous £4700 million programme—could no longer be attained in the original 3 years.

In February the government published its first Defence White Paper[61] and tabled a motion calling for the House's approval. The Parliamentary Labour Party resolved to abstain on the motion for approval but to offer an amendment expressing lack of confidence in the government's capacity to carry out the new, adjusted programme. In short, the PLP, by its abstention, was prepared to accept the measures and by its amendment to question the capacity of the men. The party leadership could not disavow the policy which they themselves had begun; but some pacifists opposed to rearmament on principle, and the Bevanites who had long criticized its scale, could not let the programme pass without challenge.

[61] Cmd. 8475.

In the debate Churchill announced that it would not be possible to fulfil the rearmament plans for 1952 laid down by the Labour Government. Physical factors and the claims of the export drive were the cause.[62] It fell to Crossman to put the main Bevanite case. He chided the Labour Front Bench for the wording of the official Amendment which accepted the Tory policy but condemned the Tory administration of that policy—"of all the things on which I would hesitate to challenge the Prime Minister the last would be his competence to carry out a defence programme".[63] Crossman accepted the need for rearmament and cited his votes against conscription; indeed, he admitted that the claims of defence were sometimes overriding needs. Nevertheless, in present conditions rearmament should be content with a lesser place; its effects on the supply and prices of raw materials and the strain imposed by new military expenditure on a fully employed economy were a source of hazard. "We must now re-think our armaments programme, not in terms of an imminent war as the main danger, but in terms of the imminent bankruptcy of the free world outside the USA as the immediate danger we have to face." Where he disagreed with the Prime Minister was on priorities; defence should be measured against three other priorities—national solvency, national independence, and the Welfare State.[64] W. T. Williams, one of the authors of *Keeping Left* and a former Baptist Minister, accepted the need to deter the Soviet Union, but argued that rearmament was reducing the standard of life and restricting exports "for largely irrelevant purposes". Like *One Way Only*, Williams wanted the resources at present intended for rearmament to be diverted to "Marshall Aid on a world scale".[65] Carmichael, the former ILP Member for Glasgow, Bridgeton, like Crossman, expressed disquiet about the effects of rearmament on Britain's economic strength, and her export markets. ". . . real strength depends on physical stability, financial security and a powerful moral force within the country."[66] Wigg, an ally of Crossman in the days of *Keep Left*, spoke in support of the official amendment; it would not be right for him to have voted for the programme a year ago and to renounce it now.[67]

When the official Labour amendment was put to the vote, 53 backbenchers (including Bevan, Freeman, and Wilson) abstained; then when the government motion was taken, these 53, and a further 4 who had voted for the Opposition amendment, went into the lobbies against the government.[68]

The rebels, soon dubbed the 57 Varieties because of the alleged (or real) diversity of motives inspiring their votes, seem to have consisted of two sections—those absolute pacifists who were opposed to armaments on principle, and the others, mainly Bevanites, who had no objection to arms in principle but who quarrelled with the level of rearmament.

Of the 57, 39 had been backbenchers between June 1946 and May 1949—the 3 years which stretched from the conscription EDM to the debate on the Atlantic Pact. From the EDMs and division lists of the earlier Parliament it is possible to trace the origins of this coalition. First, there were the critics of Ernest Bevin's foreign policy—those MPs falling into the Left and Centre Left[69] categories on the foreign policy scale and those who abstained on both of the

[62] HC Deb. 497, c. 446.

[63] *Ibid.*, c. 481. Presumably, to judge from the context, Mr. Crossman meant that it would be the first thing on which he would *hesitate* to challenge the Prime Minister.

[64] *Ibid.*, cc. 480–93.

[65] *Ibid.*, cc. 508–14.

[66] *Ibid.*, cc. 529–33.

[67] *Ibid.*, c. 501.

[68] The four were Ellis Smith, Barnett Stross, Cecil Poole, and Dai Grenfell.

[69] None of the Ultra Left survived the general election of 1950.

key foreign affairs divisions of the period, that on the amendment to the Address in 1946 and that on the NATO pact in May 1949. These groups will be collectively termed the Broader Left.[70]

The backbench survivors of the 1945 Parliament consisted then of:

(1) *Foreign Policy—the Broader Left*

  49 MPs of whom *29* rebelled comprising:

    The Left   16 MPs of whom *11* rebelled.

    The Centre Left   20 MPs of whom *11* rebelled.

    The Dual Abstainers 13 MPs of whom *7* rebelled.

The next category consists of those who were opposed to, or seemed to have reservations about, conscription, but neither by signature nor abstention on the two key votes opposed the government's foreign policy. Some opponents of conscription had, of course, already criticized Bevin's policies either overtly or implicitly; such Members (11 in number) have already been accounted for under the Broader Left.

(2) *The Opponents of Conscription*

  44 MPs of whom *7* rebelled comprising:

    The Pacifist Hard Core[71] 13 MPs of whom *2* rebelled.

    The Pacifist Moderates[72] 13 MPs of whom *2* rebelled.

    The Pacifist Abstainers[73] 18 MPs of whom *3* rebelled.

(3) *The Remainder*

  65 MPs of whom *3* rebelled.

This leaves a further 11 Members who joined the backbenches after June 1946 but before 1951. Some came in at byelections, and the data for these is incomplete; some were elected in 1950 and naturally we have no indication from the sources studied of their attitudes in the years from 1946 to 1949. We do, however, have the evidence of the EDMs on the Far East, tabled in 1950–1. Forty-five Members entered the House between June 1946 and the end of the 1950 Parliament, and of these 10 joined the rebellion. Four of these 10 had signed one or both of the two Left-wing EDMs and a further 4 had signed the specific Centre Left EDM 5/*51*. Only 2 signed neither of these Far East motions.[74] In contrast, none of the 35 loyalists had signed any of the Left EDMs, and only 4 signed the Centre Left EDM 5/*51*.

Thus the first major Bevanite revolt shows a considerable degree of continuity with the left-wing groupings of the 1945 Parliament, and amongst the newcomers there is a striking overlap between the signatories of the Far Eastern EDMs and the rearmament dissidents. Yet, as interesting as the continuities, are the differences. Thirty of the Left and Centre Left were no longer on the backbenches, most of them having been defeated or retired. Fourteen, who were still backbench MPs, took no part in the rebellion. Some of these, like Bessie Braddock and Woodrow Wyatt, had clearly and publicly moved to the Right; a few, such as Reeves and Edelman,

---

[70] The term Combined Lefts of 1945–50 refers to the Ultra Left, the Left, and Centre Left, as defined in Chapter 4, and differs from the Broader Left in that it excludes the Dual Abstainers. It affords a convenient way of describing the three left-wing foreign policy groupings.

[71] Those who opposed the National Service Bill of 1947 on the Third Reading.

[72] Those who opposed the National Service Bill of 1947 on the Second Reading and/or voted against the government on the anti-conscription Amendment to the Address in 1946.

[73] Those who abstained on two or three of the above divisions.

[74] One of these two signed EDM 66/*51*—the "discarded" motion. One of the loyalists had signed EDM 84/*51*.

took part in later revolts. Most of the remainder appeared to have withdrawn permanently from the Left; in the later disputes they gave few signs or none to show that they were opposed to the leadership. Of the hard-core pacifists who obeyed the Whips on this occasion, 4 were to rebel with Bevan on the issue of nuclear weapons in March 1955; the other 4 conformed to party decisions except on the specific question of conscription.[75] Of the more moderate anti-conscription Members, some, like Mrs. Mann, became fervent loyalists; others rebelled occasionally on subjects such as nuclear weapons and conscription, but otherwise were not conspicuous in revolt. Indeed, few of the Second Reading opponents of the Conscription Bill were still in the House by 1955.

Thus the main elements of the first major Bevanite revolt consisted of the residues of five groups—the Foreign Policy Left, the Centre Left, the dual abstainers, the opponents of conscription and, amongst the newcomers, the Far Eastern Left.

The clearest relationship between rebellion and social characteristics is provided by sponsorship. Only an eighth of the Trade Unionists defied their Front Bench compared with more than a quarter of the combined forces of the Co-operators and the CLP sponsored. It is, nevertheless, clear that the Trade Unionists were more conspicuous in this rebellion than they had been in the foreign affairs demonstrations of the 1945 Parliament. University graduates also supplied a disproportionate share of the rebels (over half), whilst the Elementary educated, in particular, conformed well to party discipline. The younger Members were more likely to rebel than their seniors; a third of the under-50's made their way into the Bevanite lobby, whilst less than a fifth of the over-50's joined them.[76] The occupational breakdown affords the clearest

TABLE 22. THE 57 VARIETIES

	Occupation and ideological sources				
	Workers	Miscellaneous Occupations	Business	Professions	Total
The Broader Left Former Left, Centre Left and Dual Abstainers	3	9	3	14	29
Critics of conscription Anti-conscription amendment; Second and Third Reading Rebels and Abstainers (two and three times)	5	2	—	—	7
Rest 1945–50 Parliament	1	1	—	1	3
1946–50 entrants	3	4	—	3	10
Total	12	16	3	18	49[a]

[a] Balance made up of ex-Ministers, etc., and 1951 entrants.

[75] Three of the 11 who did not rebel in 1952 had died or retired by 1955.
[76] Significant at 10 per cent when four age groups tested.

contrast with the foreign policy demonstrations of the earlier Parliament. The differences in the behaviour of the four occupational classes were *not* statistically significant, though both the Professions and the Miscellaneous Occupations came out in larger numbers than the Workers.

It was, not surprisingly, the pacifist appeal of the protest which accounted for the increased representation of the Workers, whilst the Professions and Business Members were predominantly drawn from the critics of Ernest Bevin's foreign policy.

GERMAN REARMAMENT

No issue so fiercely divided the Labour Party in the Bevanite era as the question of German rearmament. Already, by 1950, the United States Government had started to press for some form of German contribution to Western defence, and, it will be recalled, the notion of German rearmament had been unequivocally rejected by the authors of *Keeping Left* in the same year.

For a while the party was able to maintain an uneasy unity on the subject. In February 1951 Clement Attlee, as Prime Minister, laid down four conditions which had to be met before Britain would agree to German rearmament. The rearming of the NATO countries must precede that of Germany; the armed forces of the democratic states must be built up before the creation of the German military units; German units should be integrated with the Western defence forces so as to prevent the growth of a German military threat; and, finally, the Germans themselves must agree.

Until the Attlee conditions had been fulfilled, the party could avoid a total schism on this question. Soon after the 1951 election EDM 14/51 was tabled; as far as the Labour Party was concerned it was not highly provocative for it merely deplored the refusal of the Foreign Secretary, Anthony Eden, to give an assurance that Parliament would be consulted before Britain committed herself to support an actual measure of German rearmament. In May 1952 the occupation of West Germany came to an end with the signing of the Bonn Convention; another motion called for new four-power talks on Germany and, referring to the fourth of the Attlee conditions, demanded that fresh elections should be held in West Germany before a German military contribution was made.[77]

The Convention and the European Defence Community Treaty[78] were debated in Parliament at the end of July when Mr. Shinwell moved an official Labour amendment designed to avoid internal party conflict; it accepted the principle, subject to proper safeguards, of a German military contribution to "international collective security" but regarded the present time as inopportune as the Western powers were still trying to negotiate the German problem with the Russians. The amendment was naturally rejected by the Conservative majority, the division being marked by a few Labour abstentions. Mr. Bellenger, one of the abstainers, stigmatized the amendment as a face-saving compromise.

In June 1953, after the uprising of the East German workers, Michael Foot and Arthur Irvine called on the government to recognize that the revolt called for a complete reconsideration of the European Defence Community proposals.[79]

The 1953 party conference passed a resolution adding a new condition which would have delayed German rearmament until further efforts had been made to achieve the peaceful reuni-

[77] EDM 78/51.

[78] The Community was to be the means by which German forces were to be integrated with those of the other Western allies.

[79] EDM 111/52.

fication of Germany. On 9 February 1954 William Warbey put down an EDM which called on the government to propose a settlement at the Berlin four-power conference which would preclude any of the powers from entering into a military alliance with Germany.[80]

The breakdown of the four-power conference in the same month meant that the party would now have to face up to all the divisive implications of the issue. The leadership was itself split, with Hugh Dalton being the leading non-Bevanite opponent of German rearmament. The Parliamentary Party met on 23 February and by almost the narrowest of margins approved a motion in favour of German rearmament.[81] The next day the National Executive of the Party declared, by a comfortable majority, that the further efforts to achieve peaceful reunification stipulated by the 1953 conference had been made and frustrated by the Soviet Union.

In this situation the NEC announced the support of the Labour Party for a German contribution to European Defence. In June NEC issued a pamphlet in favour of German rearmament to which the Bevanites published a speedy reply.

At the end of August the French National Assembly rejected the European Defence Community—hitherto the cornerstone of all plans for German rearmament. The British Government promptly put forward new proposals permitting German rearmament which were embodied in the London and Paris agreements, and approved by the other allies, including the French.

Meanwhile the issue had been bitterly debated at the 1954 Labour Party Conference. Again, by the narrowest of margins, the leadership triumphed; the Woodworkers Union, who had opposed German rearmament at the TUC a month before, switched their votes and saved the day for the National Executive. The debate was marked by the change in allegiance of a prominent Bevanite, Desmond Donnelly, who began his long march to the Right with a public disavowal of his former colleagues.[82] The leadership had secured the authority of conference, albeit by a narrow and dubious majority, for German rearmament.

In November the London and Paris agreements came up for debate. The Parliamentary Labour Party decided by 124 votes to 72 not to oppose the treaties; in short, the party was to abstain—a concession made to the considerable minority within the party who were bitterly hostile to German rearmament. Six Labour MPs forced a division and voted against the treaties; however, the old ILP veteran turned Moral Re-armer, John McGovern, who had taken part in the revolt of the 57 Varieties, voted for the government. All 7 were suspended from the Parliamentary Party.

Two months after the ratification debate, a further motion appeared on the Order Paper. In January 1955 Moscow Radio put out a statement proposing free elections in Germany and German reunification. Elements within the Labour Party seized upon this statement as evidence of a Russian change of heart and as affording a further opportunity to reconsider—and hence to delay—German rearmament. On 25 January Sydney Silverman, with pacifist and left-wing co-sponsors, called on the government to propose that the four-power negotiations should be resumed before the final ratification of the London and Paris agreements.[83]

Meanwhile, on 9 February, Aneurin Bevan asked that an official motion be put down calling

---

[80] EDM 34/53.

[81] A motion expressing approval of German rearmament was carried by 113 to 104 after a motion moved by Harold Wilson to delay a decision until the five-power conference had taken place had been lost by 111 votes to 109 (*The Times*, 24 Feb. 1954).

[82] *LPCR, 1954*, p. 104.

[83] EDM 22/54.

for immediate talks with the Russians. Attlee was opposed to the use of summit talks as a means of delaying German rearmament, and did not approve of the suggestion for an immediate four-power conference. The Parliamentary Party turned down Bevan's proposal by 93 votes to 70.[84]

A week later Aneurin Bevan, with the backing of John Strachey and Michael Stewart, both men of the Centre, tabled a long motion which, after a reference to thermo-nuclear weapons, deplored the government's refusal to discuss the future of Germany with the Soviet leaders before the Paris treaties had been ratified by all the countries concerned. Altogether 117 Labour MPs signed this motion (EDM 35/54).

The motion was, of course, a direct reproach to the leadership; the party had already agreed not to press for immediate talks, but Bevan had, in defiance of the majority decision, tried to muster support for his unofficial motion. When the full implications were realized, 5 members, including E. G. Gooch, a member of the NEC, withdrew their names. At a further meeting of the Parliamentary Labour Party, a resolution moved by Attlee, which censured Bevan for his conduct, was carried by 132 to 72.

Altogether 109 MPs signed one or more of the six German rearmament EDMs. The motions can be divided into two—the four which were tabled before the PLP meeting of February 1954, which first committed the party to support of German rearmament; and the two which were tabled in January and February 1955 after the Moscow broadcast. Table 23 shows the numbers signing in the two periods.

TABLE 23. GERMAN REARMAMENT

Signed in both periods	Signed in first period only	Signed in second period only	Did not sign	Total
62	12	35	112	221

Overall, the Professions and Miscellaneous Occupations were most hostile to German rearmament, as were the CLP sponsored and the University graduates. Amongst the graduates the U1's (public school and university) were less averse to German rearmament than the other University Members. Welsh and Scottish Members signed more than English MPs, and the younger Members more than the older.

Of the Members who revolted with Aneurin Bevan in the rebellion of the 57 Varieties, all but 2 signed. One of these non-signatories was John McGovern, who voted with the Conservatives when the matter was debated in the House. Of those who had not rebelled, 58 out of 169 signed—almost exactly one-third.

The importance of the German rearmament issue within the Labour Party lay in the fact that opposition to it stretched far beyond the normal Bevanite ranks. Men of the Centre and Right, never linked with the Bevanites, found it hard to stomach the deliberate re-militarization of Germany.

It has often been said that the large minority against German rearmament was a coalition of Bevanites, pacifists, Jewish Members, and ex-servicemen. This cause mobilized an alliance that stretched well beyond the traditional Left, and it was this which gave the issue its peculiar importance in the struggles within the Labour Party. On no other question did the leadership

[84] *Daily Telegraph*, 10 Feb. 1955.

come so near to defeat. *The Economist*, describing the coalition in unflattering terms, called it "an oddly assorted collection of Labour groups—the lunatic left, the ordinary Bevanites, the bloc of Jewish MPs, ex-servicemen of both wars, some MPs who are unexpectedly emotional on this subject without being emotional on anything else, and many of the party's old women of the male sex".[85]

Table 24 shows the reaction of the Left and the other ideological groupings to the German rearmament EDMs.

TABLE 24. LEFTNESS, DEFENCE POLICY, AND GERMAN REARMAMENT

German arms EDMs	Left		Other Defence and Nuclear Critics		Rest		Total
	No.	%	No.	%	No.	%	
Signed three or more	29	73	12	21	2	2	43
Signed two	6	15	17	30	8	6	31
Signed one	4	10	11	20	20	16	35
All Signers	39	98	40	71	30	24	109
All Non-Signers	1	3	16	29	95	76	112
Total	40	100	56	100	125	100	221

$\chi_6^2 = 132 \cdot 21$. Significant at $0 \cdot 1\%$.
Signers against Non-Signers. $\chi_2^2 = 80 \cdot 16$. Significant at $0 \cdot 1\%$.

Presumably, this group of rebels embraces those whom *The Economist* described as "the lunatic left and the ordinary Bevanites". The third group identified by *The Economist*, the Jewish MPs, showed themselves, not surprisingly, to be hostile to the rearming of Germany. All of the Jewish backbenchers signed at least one motion. Six of them belonged to the Left, but in their protest against German rearmament these 6 were joined by 8 other Jewish MPs, though 3 of these Jewish Members, belonging to the Right of the party, signed only the moderate EDM 14/51.

For the pacifists, a group not mentioned by *The Economist*, the evidence is less clear cut; nearly half of those who voted against conscription in 1953 belonged to the Left. Nineteen of the remainder were on the backbenches for the whole of the controversy, and of these no fewer than 15 MPs signed one motion or more. But of the 15 survivors of the votes against conscription in 1946–7, not hitherto accounted for, only 6 signed.

Forty-one signatories (including those who voted against conscription in 1946–7 but not in 1953) still remain; the ex-servicemen constituted a higher proportion of these than they did of the non-signatories, the association being established at the 5 per cent level.

Of the non-Left, the Workers were much under-represented, but the relationship was not statistically significant. Graduates signed more than non-graduates, and amongst them the combined forces of the U2's, U3's, and U4's, were more hostile to German rearmament than the U1's (public school and Oxford or Cambridge).

The division of the six EDMs into two classes makes it possible to check whether findings based on the first set of motions are duplicated by those based on the second group. Broadly speaking they are—the main differences being that the Workers and the Elementary educated came out rather more strongly, though still lagging well behind relative to the other groups, for the Silverman and Bevan motions than for the earlier EDMs.

It is also possible to apply Yule's Q to these motions (Table 25).

TABLE 25. GERMAN REARMAMENT EDMs

Motions Tabled November 1951 to February 1954

		+	−	Total
Motions tabled January–February 1955	+	*a* 62	*b* 35	
	−	*c* 12	*d* 112	

$$+ = \text{Signers.} \quad - = \text{Non-Signers. Yule's } Q = \frac{ad - bc}{ad + bc} = 0\cdot 89.$$

Table 25 shows the very high consistency in signing: all but 12 of the 74 who signed in the first period did so in the latter. Q attains the very high value of $0\cdot 89$, confirming the validity of the scale.[86]

CONSCRIPTION

In 1953 the dispute over conscription was resumed. The Conservative Government presented an Order, under the National Service Act, renewing conscription for a further 5 years. Alfred Robens, from the Labour Front Bench, indicated that as a protest against the government's decision to seek an extension for such a long period, the party would officially abstain; they would not, however, vote against the government because the effect of carrying such a vote would be the immediate end of conscription.[87] Nevertheless, some backbenchers decided to challenge the government. Again, a variety of criticisms of the government's measure were voiced. Some Members, like Robens, objected to the extension being made for 5 years but, unlike him, were willing to vote against the Order. Stephen Swingler asked for any inquiry into conscription, mentioning as proper topics for such an inquiry the use of manpower in the armed forces and the economic cost of compulsory service.[88] Jimmy Hudson, the veteran pacifist, saw conscription as violating the fundamental liberties of youth "in an area of the spirit. . . . A man must be free to decide between himself and God, or the best that is in him,

---

[86] Yule's Q for the five pairs of motions involving the very mild EDM 14/51 gave generally low values, falling to as low as $0\cdot 33\%$. The values for the remaining ten pairs of motions were high, never falling below $0\cdot 65\%$, and in one case reaching $0\cdot 89\%$.

[87] HC Deb. 520, c. 1645.

[88] *Ibid.*, cc. 1613–17 and 1631–7.

what line he shall take regarding a duty which the State may decide to enforce upon him."[89] Carmichael, an ex-member of the ILP, argued that the international situation was not as tense as it had been 6 or 7 years before; Britain's empire had shrunk and so the need for a conscript army had diminished; the production of atomic weapons made a large army an anachronism. He also attributed the rise in juvenile delinquency to the unsettling effects which the expectation of the call-up had on young men.[90] His ex-ILP colleague, John McGovern, who announced that he had been opposed to conscription "before I accepted the policy of the UN based on the philosophy of the Labour Party policy", thought a 2-year period of service too long, and spoke of the corrupting experience of service life.[91] Julian Snow, who also thought a 5-year extension was too long, questioned the government's use of the armed forces in colonial areas like Kenya and Guiana, and emphasized industry's need for manpower.[92] The pertinacious champion of world government, Henry Usborne, saw a supra-national authority as the only alternative to national service; he would, therefore, divide the House, even though this alternative was not "instantly practicable".[93] In short, opposition to the Order was supported by diverse arguments, and though these reasons were sometimes simply auxiliary weapons in the pacifist armoury to strengthen an argument based on moral or religious grounds, they sometimes represented genuine non-pacifist motives for voting against the renewal of the government's powers.

Forty Labour MPs voted against the Order. Of these, 25 had been backbenchers when the National Service Act of 1947 was passed, and 18 of them had opposed the Bill on either Second or Third Reading. But no fewer than 22 Members, who were still backbenchers and who had voted against the earlier Bill, did not go into the lobbies against the Order; this 22 includes 9 of the 21 surviving backbenchers who had opposed the Third Reading of the 1947 Bill. Whilst absence from the House may account for some of the apparent changes of heart, it seems likely that some Members had by now accommodated themselves to the practice of conscription.

Nevertheless, whatever individual changes in attitude occurred, opposition to conscription, as in 1947, cut across the normal social boundaries of the party. No association between attitudes to conscription and occupation and sponsorship has been established. But although the Elementary educated were as likely to protest against the Order as the University graduates, amongst the graduates the U4's had, as in 1947, a greater tendency to vote against conscription than the U1's, U2's, and U3's.[94]

However, the opponents of conscription were much more closely identified with the various left-wing demonstrations and revolts than they had been in the 1945–50 Parliament. Twenty-three of the 39 opponents of the conscription Order who had been backbenchers when the Bevanites challenged the government and their own leaders on rearmament, voted with the rebels. The same number abstained with Aneurin Bevan over the issue of nuclear weapons in 1955. As Table 26 shows, nearly half of those defined as Left voted against the Order compared with a handful of the Rest. In 1946–7 Crossman and his friends had striven to divorce the two issues of foreign policy and defence; in the 1950's the two questions were inextricably confused. All-out pacifists opposed the rearmament programme; the Bevanites, arguing not for no rearmament at all but simply for less rearmament, found themselves in the same lobby. Moreover, some left wingers who had supported conscription in 1947, such as Swingler, Stross, and Harold Davies, were now prepared to vote against it.

[89] *Ibid.*, cc. 1617–25.   [90] *Ibid.*, cc. 1613–17.   [91] *Ibid.*, cc. 1625–30.   [92] *Ibid.*, cc. 1637–40.
[93] *Ibid.*, cc. 1603–4.
[94] This association is provisional only, being significant at the 10 per cent level.

TABLE 26. LEFTISM, DEFENCE POLICY, AND CONSCRIPTION

Conscription	Left		Other Defence and Nuclear Critics		Rest		Total
	No.	%	No.	%	No.	%	
Voted against Conscription	17	42	15	27	7	6	39
Did not vote	23	58	41	73	118	94	182
Total	40	100	56	100	125	100	221

$\chi_2^2 = 32\cdot70$. Significant at $0\cdot1\%$.

NUCLEAR WEAPONS

In 1952 the Americans tested their first hydrogen bomb. In March 1954 further tests, which aroused greater fears than the early experiments, were carried out. Reports of a heavy fall-out and fears of genetic injury aroused deep alarm. Within the Labour Party there was widespread concern at the prospect of further testing.

At the end of March, 5 North Staffordshire MPs and John Parker called on the British Government to take any initiative it considered advisable to prevent the explosion of any more thermo-nuclear bombs and further research and development for military purposes. Their motion also asked the Five Great Powers to submit proposals for the future of atomic control and a reduction in military spending.[95]

Although this EDM remained on the Order Paper for only 2 days, 108 signatures were collected. The sponsors withdrew the motion on 1 April after Mr. Attlee and his Shadow Cabinet colleagues tabled an official motion which, pointing to the grave threat to civilization posed by the hydrogen bomb, declared it would welcome an immediate initiative by the government to bring about a meeting of the Big Three to consider again the problem of controlling and reducing armaments. In the ensuing debate the government accepted the official Labour motion, which was passed by the House without dissent.

Meanwhile the government had introduced a Bill to transfer the control and development of atomic energy in Britain from the Ministry of Supply to a new public corporation, the Atomic Energy Authority. The Bill itself was innocuous and did not arouse great controversy, but when it came up for Third Reading at the end of April, Frank Beswick moved an amendment which would, if passed into law, have required the government to seek specific approval from both Houses before any thermo-nuclear bombs were manufactured by the Authority.

Beswick, whilst admitting that he was against British production of the hydrogen bomb, emphasized that his clause raised the issue not of unilateral disarmament but of parliamentary control. "The question is shall there be an executive order given in secret or shall there be a full and proper debate with a democratic decision openly carried out."[96] Eric Fletcher, who seconded Beswick's motion, also laid stress on the need for

[95] EDM 50/53.
[96] HC Deb. 526, cc. 1795–6.

parliamentary control;[97] both George Darling and Aneurin Bevan argued in a similar vein.[98] George Strauss, speaking from the Front Bench, charged that unilateral renunciation of the hydrogen bomb by Britain was inherent in many of the speeches, despite the emphasis on parliamentary control. He argued that it would be wrong to carry the clause when international discussion on the control of nuclear weapons might soon take place; it might appear to others that Britain was limiting her right to manufacture the hydrogen bomb.[99] He suggested, therefore, that it would be wise not to vote on the matter. Nevertheless, Beswick pressed the Amendment to a division and was supported by 65 Labour MPs (including Aneurin Bevan who had just resigned from the Shadow Cabinet). Three Whips who also voted for the Amendment were promptly asked to resign their office.

The Amendment appealed to three distinct sections; there were the pacifists who would have voted against any form of armaments; there were some Members prepared to accept conventional weapons who abhorred the manufacture of thermo-nuclear bombs; finally there were those Members who, without necessarily opposing British manufacture of the hydrogen bomb, insisted that it should not be done unless parliamentary approval had been obtained after open debate.

Twenty Members who took part in the revolt were never associated with the Left in any other floor revolt during the 1951–5 Parliament. They included such Members as Ernest Davies, George Darling, Harry Hynd, and Arthur Blenkinsop. Pacificism hardly accounts for the votes of these 20, for only 2 of them had voted against national service a few months before as against 12 of the remaining 34.[100] Most of these 20 were presumably seeking to maintain the principle of parliamentary supremacy.

Almost the same proportion of the Professions and the Miscellaneous Occupations went into the lobby against the pleas of the Labour Front Bench; once again it was the Workers (together with the small Business section) who lagged behind.

The second demonstration over nuclear weapons was a much more serious affair. It came soon after Bevan had been rebuked by the Parliamentary Party for putting down the unofficial motion which had deplored the government's refusal to negotiate with the Russians before the ratification of the Paris treaties. The Annual Defence White Paper was to be debated in March, and an official party amendment was tabled to the Prime Minister's motion of approval. The amendment criticized the deficiencies in the equipment and organization of the services and went on to acknowledge that, until world disarmament had been attained, it would be necessary to deter aggression by relying on the threat of thermo-nuclear weapons. Thus any Member who supported the official amendment would be expressing approval of the use of nuclear arms.

Bevan himself did not oppose the British manufacture of the hydrogen bomb, but he differed from the government and his own Front Bench about its possible use. The government had appeared to countenance the use of thermo-nuclear weapons by Britain even if a country attacking her employed only conventional armaments. Bevan tried to find out the circumstances in which the government would be prepared to use nuclear weapons. Unable to obtain the precise account he sought, he asked whether the Labour Front Bench would countenance the use of the hydrogen bomb against a conventional attack. He wanted an assurance "that the

---

[97] *Ibid.*, cc. 1803–9.
[98] *Ibid.*, cc. 1823–6 and 1829–33.
[99] *Ibid.*, cc. 1837–40.
[100] Eleven rebel Members were not continuously on the backbenches during the Parliament.

language of their amendment . . . does not align the Labour movement behind that reckless-
ness, because if we cannot have the lead from them, let us give the lead ourselves".[101] Attlee
was not present in the Chamber when Bevan spoke; when the Labour Leader wound up for
the opposition, Bevan rose and repeated his question, a question to which Attlee gave no
clear answer.

Some Labour Members regarded the hydrogen bomb as differing in kind from all other
weapons. "I feel", said G. A. Pargiter, who had never hitherto been identified with any important rebel group, "I have gone pretty far down the slippery slopes to hell in the acquiescence
which I have given up to now in the manufacture of weapons, and of the atom bomb, and I
feel that it has to stop somewhere."[102] Maurice Edelman, who had signed the Foreign Affairs
Amendment in 1946, argued that the immense destructiveness of the hydrogen bomb and its
genetic effects made it something more than a super-efficient atomic weapon. "I do not believe
it is morally right to acquiesce in any circumstances in the production of instruments which
make the generation which survives a hydrogen bomb war into monsters."[103]

Tom Driberg, who had put down an amendment of his own (which was not called) which
refused to assent to "the development of a weapon of immense and indiscriminate destructive
power", did not agree with his old leader, Bevan, when "he seemed to brush aside one of the
central themes of this debate . . . the rights and wrongs, the ethics of the hydrogen bomb and
of nuclear warfare, as in some way secondary or irrelevant to our main discussion". Like
Edelman, he saw the hydrogen bomb as a weapon apart; nor could he see that Britain had any
advantage in possessing it. "Surely we have somewhat different and I hope higher values; it is
not by nuclear might that we shall impress and influence our friends and allies. India does not
have the hydrogen bomb . . . . Yet India has played a notable part in world diplomacy and international politics in the last year or two."[104] The pacifist, Victor Yates, attacked the whole philosophy of nuclear deterrence, and after saying that he could not see very much difference
between the two parties on this issue, announced that he would abstain.[105]

The abstainers consisted of some, like Edelman, Pargiter, and Driberg, who regarded the
hydrogen bomb as an instrument of war that was uniquely wicked; of those who, like Bevan,
were willing to accept British manufacture of the bomb, but were not prepared for Britain
to use thermo-nuclear weapons against an attack launched with conventional forces; and the
pacifists, traditionally opposed to all armaments, conventional, atomic, and thermo-nuclear.

Some familiar allies, however, were missing. Wilson had taken Bevan's place on the Shadow
Cabinet a year before, and whatever views he had on this issue he was bound by rules of collective responsibility. Only a week before the demonstration, Crossman, together with George
Wigg, had argued in the *New Statesman* for Britain's possession of the hydrogen bomb.
"On balance therefore, we believe that Britain should remain a member of NATO and make
one supreme effort . . . to find a basis for peaceful co-existence. If this is to be our role, it is
difficult to deny Mr. Attlee's contention that Britain must share in the possession of the ultimate
deterrent."[106]

John Freeman, explaining his support for the official Labour amendment, thought Bevan's
question to Attlee and the government "misleading" and "unworthy of the penetrating analysis
which preceded it . . . I thought that the specific point on which Mr. Bevan focused his difference with the Labour Front Bench lacked both the logic and substance of his formidable

[101] HC Deb. 537, c. 2122.   [102] *Ibid.*, cc. 1922–7.
[103] *Ibid.*, cc. 1946–53.   [104] *Ibid.*, cc. 2142–50.
[105] *Ibid.*, cc. 2162–6.   [106] *NS & N*, 26 Feb. 1955.

case against the government.''[107] Nevertheless, Freeman found the choice of Crossman and Wigg to remain in NATO unacceptable on both political and strategic grounds.

Bevan's misconduct, which closely followed the censure administered to him by the Parliamentary Party for defying party decisions, led to the withdrawal of the party Whip and almost to his expulsion for the national party. His challenge once more focused public attention on the disunity of the Labour Party at a time when a general election was believed to be near.

The 62 abstainers differed considerably from the 57 rebels of 3 years before. Only 30 of the 57 joined Bevan in making this demonstration.

TABLE 27. THE BEVANITE REVOLTS

	Rebelled March 1952 and abstained March 1955	Rebelled March 1952; did not abstain March 1955	Abstained March 1955; did not rebel March 1952	Total
The Broader Left, 1945–50	19	9	9[a]	37
Anti-conscription, 1945–50[108]	2	5	6	13
The Rest, 1945–50	—	3	5	8
New entrants, 1946–50 (incl.)	6	4	5	15
1951 and later	1	1	5[b]	7
Ex-Ministers, deaths,[c] etc.	3	4	2	9
Total	31	26	32	89

[a] Four not available to rebel in 1952.   [b] Three not available to rebel in 1952.
[c] Deaths refers to Members rebelling in 1952 who died before 1955.

Table 27 shows the interrelationships between the two chief Bevanite rebellions and the connection they bore with the factional groupings of the 1945 Parliament. Continuity was most marked amongst the members of the Broader Left and the post-1946 entrants, and was curiously absent amongst the opponents of conscription. Nor, indeed, were the consistent rebels of the Broader Left notably more pacificistic than those who revolted in 1952 but obeyed the Whip in 1955; 8 of the 19 "dual" rebels had voted against conscription at some stage in 1946–7, but so had 4 of the 9 who did not abstain in 1955. What is also striking is the "compensation" tendency. Thus 9 MPs of the Broader Left who revolted over rearmament in 1952 did not abstain in 1955, but these losses to the Bevanite cause were offset by 9 members of the Broader Left who, not rebelling in March 1952, did abstain in 1955. The same rough compensation applied to the other ideological categories.

Within the Broader Left the behaviour of the Foreign Policy Left is noteworthy. Sixteen were backbenchers during the whole of the 3 years which spanned the two revolts; 13 took part in at least one revolt. Twenty were on the backbenches for one or both of the revolts; 17 rebelled on at least one occasion.

Perhaps the most notable feature of this protest lies in its social composition. The earlier Bevanite revolt had followed the pattern of the 1945 Parliament with the Professions, the Miscellaneous Occupations, the CLP sponsored, and the University graduates being the most

[107] *NS & N*, 12 Mar. 1955.
[108] Anti-conscription as defined on p. 100.

conspicuous amongst the rebels. In this revolt the familiar relationships disappear. Educationally there was no significant difference between the behaviour of the various groups; the demonstration against nuclear weapons appealed impartially to graduates and non-graduates, the
Elementary and the Secondary educated, the graduates of Oxford and Cambridge and their
provincial brethren. The most striking aspect of the occupational breakdown lies in the
distinctive behaviour of the Miscellaneous Occupations and in the similarity of the Professions
and the Workers. Nearly two-fifths of the Miscellaneous Occupations abstained compared with
only one fifth of the other two main occupational groups. The nuclear issue had helped to
create a new and unfamiliar cleavage within the party.

In examining the relationship between the two rebellions, we have already noted the tendency
for the rebels to recruit sufficient newcomers from each of the ideological groups of the 1945–50
Parliament to compensate for their losses. This compensation tendency did not extend to the
occupational categories. Thus 7 of the 10 members of the Broader Left who had revolted in
1952 but conformed to party decisions in 1955 were Professionals; in contrast, only two of the
new recruits from the Broader Left were from this category. The Miscellaneous Occupations
gained from both the two-way traffic of the Broader Left and from those members, elected
in and after 1951, who joined the demonstration. All but one of these belonged to the
Miscellaneous Occupations class.

The only other variations in support are found amongst the sponsorship groupings; the Co-
operators and the CLP men did furnish a larger proportion of their members than the Trade
Unionists, but the difference is only significant at the 10 per cent level, and hence cannot be
regarded as firmly established. Otherwise the abstainers were, socially, very much a cross-
section of the party.

ANTI-COMMUNISM AND ANTI-FASCISM

It was not the Left, however, who made all of the running in foreign affairs. Five EDMs—
two of which were signed by more than 60 Labour MPs—strongly criticized the Soviet
Union or other Communist countries. Two condemned the persecution of Roman Catholics
in Poland;[109] one called for a UN inquiry into the massacre of Polish officers at Katyn;[110]
another saluted the East German workers for their rising of 1953; and the fifth condemned
anti-semitism in Communist countries.[111]

All that these motions had in common was their criticism of communism. The motion
addressed to the East German workers might have been expected to appeal to the Trade
Unionists with special force, and, indeed, this motion was overwhelmingly trade unionist in
both its sponsorship and its signatures. Similarly, the motion condemning anti-semitism might
have been expected to attract greater support than other anti-Soviet motions from the Left of
the party, and this, indeed occurred, though, surprisingly, it had little appeal to Jewish Members. The value of Yule's Q for the various pairs of motions is, not unexpectedly, often very
low; indeed, Yule's Q for EDMs 95/51 and 109/52 has a value of $-1 \cdot 0$, indicating that none
of the Members who signed the EDM calling for a UN inquiry into the Katyn massacre signed
the motion on the East German rising of 1953. An examination of the occupational and political
character of the East German EDM shows that it drew quite disproportionate support from
the Workers and from the Rest rather than the Left. EDM 53/52 on anti-semitism also received
disproportionate Worker support, but not to the same extent as the previous motion; the Left

---

[109] EDMs 6/53 and 8/53.   [110] EDM 95/51.   [111] EDMs 109/52 and 53/52.

on this EDM mobilized something like their due share. The three other motions appealed, in occupational terms, to a cross-section of the party.

When all five motions are combined their signatories are seen to have been drawn, in contrast to most of those dealing with foreign policy, predominantly from the Trade Union/Worker section of the party. Two-thirds of the Workers signed compared with two-fifths of the CLP sponsored and the Professions. Similarly, the Elementary educated were much keener than the University graduates. The associations between anti-communism and occupation, sponsorship and education were unusually sharp, reaching the 0·1 per cent level of significance.

In total contrast were the supporters of Anti-fascist EDMs. Two were critical of Franco's Spain.[112] One protested against the rehabilitation of the Krupp family,[113] and the fourth objected to the re-interment of executed German war criminals.[114] These motions appealed to much the same sort of Members as those who opposed German rearmament and British defence policy in 1952—the University cum Professions cum Constituency-sponsored Members— but not to the Workers, the Trade Unionists, or the Elementary educated.[115]

Table 28 shows the relationship between the three main ideological categories into which the party has been divided and signature of the anti-communist and anti-fascist EDMs.

TABLE 28. FLOOR REVOLTS, ANTI-FASCISM, AND ANTI-COMMUNISM

	Left		Nuclear and Other Defence Policy Critics		Rest		Total
	No.	%	No.	%	No.	%	
Anti-fascist only	12	30	8	14	7	6	27
Anti-communist only	4	10	22	39	70	56	96
Both	5	13	8	14	13	10	26
Neither	19	48	18	32	35	28	72
Total	40	100	56	100	125	100	221

All signing anti-fascist motions against All Others. $\chi_2^2 = 12·54$. Significant at 0·5%.
All signing anti-Soviet motions against All Others. $\chi_2^2 = 23·70$. Significant at 0·1%.

Two-thirds of the Rest subscribed to the anti-communist EDMs, but less than a quarter of the Left. On the other hand, nearly half of the Left signed the anti-fascist motions compared with less than a sixth of the Rest. The Nuclear and Other Defence Policy critics were in between the other two blocs on both issues. The Left evidently feared a recrudescence of the brutalities of the recent past; the loyalists responded to the cruelties of the present.

[112] EDMs 17/52 and 6A/53.   [113] EDM 66/52.   [114] EDM 43/53.

[115] The value of Yule's Q ranges from 0·03 for EDMs 17/52 and 66/52 to 0·70 for EDMs 66/52 and 43/53. In short, the anti-Franco EDMs were not signed by the same Members as the anti-German EDMs. Because of the small number of signatories of all but EDM 66/52, it is not easy to compare the occupational and political composition of the various groups of signers. What does seem clear is that the anti-German motions, coming as they did during the struggle over German rearmament, received disproportionate support from the Left, whereas the anti-Franco motions cut across the normal political boundaries. The Workers were clearly under-represented in all four motions.

ANTI-COLONIALISM

Sympathy for colonial peoples has long been a distinctive feature of the British Labour Movement. Deriving partly from such non-socialist sources as nineteenth-century radicalism, and partly from Marxism in both its pure and vulgarized forms, anti-colonialism has emphasized both the political oppression of the native population by the European powers and their economic exploitation. The legacy of Fabianism on colonial affairs has been less clear; some of the early Fabians, repelled by the Little England views of the radicals, had sympathized with imperialism at the turn of the century, whilst others had been resolute critics of British colonial expansion. The Society was, for example, deeply divided over the Boer War.

In 1940 the Fabian Colonial Bureau was set up under the auspices of the Fabian Society. The Bureau sponsored research on colonial problems, collaborated with friendly MPs, and developed relationships with organized groups of various kinds in both Britain and the colonies. Whilst the bureau was not unresponsive to the abstract principles of democracy and personal freedom espoused by the heirs of radicalism or to the theme of capitalist exploitation, it emphasized in its research and propaganda the immediate, the specific, and the practical, rather than the remote, the general, and the theoretical; in short, it was more concerned with achieving particular economic improvements than a total reconstruction of the colonial economies, with gradual advance towards self-government rather than with the sudden withdrawal of British rule.[116] Sections of the Labour Party, as of the Liberal Party before them, have maintained a special vigilance in defence of the rights of subject peoples; they have detected, exposed, and denounced harsh punishments and arbitrary rule, and economic neglect and backwardness. Between 1945 and 1951, when Labour was in office, this tendency was inhibited by the claims of party loyalty and the government's colonial record. Mr. Attlee's Administration had already shown their goodwill to the people of the colonies by conceding independence to India, Pakistan, Burma, and Ceylon. Having had Asia on account, so to speak, the apostles of African emancipation were prepared to wait. Some aspects of the colonial policy of the Conservative Government, elected in 1951, however, encountered strong resistance and criticism from elements within the Labour Party; and on specific questions these elements could coalesce in opposition to Conservative policy.

Both *Keeping Left* and the *Tribune* pamphlet *One Way Only* had stressed the importance of the colonial revolution; both had emphasized the revolutionary struggle for national independence and the need of the emerging nations for technical and economic assistance. This concern for the peoples of the Third World was reflected in a series of motions tabled between 1950 and 1955.

Only one anti-colonial EDM appeared on the Order Paper during Labour's term of office.[117] This, couched in the language of Christian and humanitarian socialism, was sponsored by Richard Acland and Fenner Brockway and was signed by 111 Members; it reaffirmed the confidence of the House (or more accurately of the signatories) in the course of Commonwealth and colonial policy in the preceding 5 years and, acknowledging that difficulties might be encountered where different peoples had reached different stages of development, called on

---

[116] For a valuable account of the work of the Fabian Colonial Bureau and more generally of attitudes within the British parties to colonial affairs, see D. Goldsworthy, *Colonial Issues in British Politics, 1945–1961*, Oxford, 1971.
[117] EDM 38/51.

the white races the world over to free themselves "from the conception of racial superiority" and to accept the brotherhood and equality of men. It appealed most of all to the Miscellaneous Occupations who mustered nearly two-thirds of their Members in support, and least of all to the Business group. Though the Workers lagged behind both the Miscellaneous Occupations and the Professions they signed in surprisingly large numbers—mobilizing more than two-fifths of their group. Education, however, provided a clearer division; more than half of the University graduates signed, but only a third of the Elementary educated. The attitude of the Women is also noteworthy, with 10 out of the 12 supporting the motion.

COLONIAL BRUTALITY

Of the motions put down in the next Parliament, no fewer than four referred to real or alleged brutality by British troops or administrators. The best-supported, put down by Tom Driberg, and drawing 131 signatures, protested against collective punishment imposed on Malayan villages during the campaign against the terrorists.[118] A second, tabled by Brockway, who had agreed to organize "Left pressures" within the movement on colonial affairs,[119] expressed disquiet at measures taken against the Africans during the Mau Mau revolt in Kenya, drew attention to the high proportion of killed to wounded, and called for a parliamentary inquiry.[120] A third objected to the bombing of Africans by British aeroplanes;[121] and a fourth, signed by only 9 Members, expressed concern at the treatment of Kikuyu prisoners.[122]

A simple quantitative scale was constructed to measure feelings over this aspect of colonialism. The evidence of the EDMs indicates that sensitivity to harshness and brutality was found in almost all sections of the party. It is true that the CLP-sponsored provided a disproportionate number of the keenest Members (that is those signing two or more of the four EDMs), but they also supplied as big a proportion of the totally apathetic as the Trade Unionists. Curiously, the clearest division emerges from the regional breakdowns, the Scottish and the Welsh Members displaying the greatest indignation: indeed, outside the Left, 16 of the 21 Scottish and Welsh MPs signed the colonial brutality EDMs compared with fewer than half of the 104 English Members. Amongst the different age groups, the oldest Members showed least concern. Nevertheless, the most interesting feature of these EDMs lies in their widespread appeal.[123]

ARBITRARY RULE

Feelings about the imposition of arbitrary rulings led to two more demonstrations. One declared that Seretse Khama should be allowed to resume the chieftainship of his tribe from

[118] EDM 63/51.
[119] A. F. Brockway, *Outside the Right*, London, 1963, p. 82.
[120] EDM 124/52.   [121] EDM 28/53.   [122] EDM 77/52.
[123] The value of Yule's Q between the Malaya EDM 63/51 and the three African EDMs, treated as one motion, is 0·62. Its value for various pairs of motions involving EDM 63/51 ranges from 1·00 (obtained from EDM 63/51 and EDM 77/52—a motion with very few signatories) to 0·40. The value of Yule's Q for the pairs of the three African motions ranges from 0·28 to 0·84. The lowest value was obtained for the pair involving the Bevanite motion EDM 30/53 and EDM 124/52. The occupational composition of the signatories of the African motions and the Malaya EDM is not dissimilar. Politically, the Left were a little more prominent amongst the signatories of the African EDMs than amongst the Malaya EDM, but the difference is not marked. Amongst the African EDMs, however, EDM 30/53 was distinguished by receiving very little support from the Rest. EDM 30/53 replaced EDM 28/53, which had expressed the same sentiment at greater length. The two EDMs have been treated as the same motion.

which he had been removed by Patrick Gordon-Walker, Commonwealth Relations Secretary in the Labour Government.[124] Then in May 1953 Fenner Brockway put down a motion which censured the government for appointing one Rasebolai Kgamane to exercise chiefly powers in the Bamangwato reserve of Bechuanaland after a meeting of the tribal council had refused to elect him as chief. Sixty-three Labour Members and some Liberals signed this EDM.[125]

An occupational breakdown of these motions discloses a notable contrast to the widespread appeal of the "anti-brutality" EDMs. The Miscellaneous Occupations were easily the most concerned; nearly two-fifths signed one or other motion, whilst less than a quarter of the Professions and a seventh of the Workers did so.

These motions, moreover, registered a strong appeal on the Left, as is disclosed by Table 29; but it is interesting that the Other Defence and Nuclear Critics contributed no more signers, proportionately, than the Rest. Political anti-colonialism could clearly attract some Members who were normally numbered with the Right and Centre of the party.

TABLE 29. LEFTISM, DEFENCE POLICY, AND ARBITRARY RULE

Arbitrary rule	Left		Other Defence and Nuclear Critics		Rest		Total
	No.	%	No.	%	No.	%	
Signers	24	60	11	20	22	19	57
Non-Signers	16	40	45	80	103	81	164
Total	40	100	56	100	125	100	221

$\chi_2^2 = 29 \cdot 951$. Significant at $0 \cdot 1\%$.

Occupation provides the main dividing line in support for two residual EDMs that do not properly belong with either of the previous scales. One protested against the arrests in South Africa of Mr. Solly Sachs and other trade union leaders,[126] and another of Fenner Brockway's put down during the Queen's visit to Bermuda in 1953 deplored the Governor's failure to invite any coloured person to the state dinner held for her and the Duke of Edinburgh.[127] The Miscellaneous Occupations again led the way, rallying more than twice as many of their Members, proportionately speaking, as the Workers, and more than the Professions. The reticence of the Workers is reflected in the sponsorship breakdowns—the CLP Members signing more generously than the Trade Unionists.

ECONOMIC ANTI-COLONIALISM

Two bread-and-butter motions won extensive support. Nearly 200 MPs—or most of the backbench party—signed a motion tabled by Jim Griffiths of the Front Bench which, inter alia, asked the government to seek agreement in Kenya for a policy which would allow Africans to acquire land in the White Highlands.[128] The association between occupation and

[124] EDM 11/51.   [125] EDM 100/52.   [126] EDM 102/51.   [127] EDM 10/53.
[128] EDM 97/51.

attitude in this case is tentative and not fully established; but, once again the Miscellaneous Occupations were the most keen, and the Workers the most apathetic.

Finally, a motion tabled by Richard Acland in March 1954 called for an effective international plan for World Mutual Aid which would, the motion stated, mean sacrifices from Britain and a diversion of resources from defence. The motion's preamble referred to the by now familiar argument that the defence of democracy would depend as much upon "moral, social, political and economic as upon military policy".[129] In spite of its distinctively Bevanite wording, 139 MPs signed this motion; the wording may help to account for the strong association between sponsorship and attitudes, and education and attitudes, for Trade Unionists and the Elementary educated again signed less generously than their fellows.

Like the protests against arbitrary rule, the mutual aid motion appealed with special force, to the Left; but the Other Defence and Nuclear Critics also signed in large numbers. Although this EDM attracted particular support from the Left, it also, like those on arbitrary rule, obtained considerable backing from the Centre and Right (Table 30).

TABLE 30. LEFTISM, DEFENCE POLICY, AND MUTUAL AID

	Left		Other Defence and Nuclear Critics		Rest		Total
	No.	%	No.	%	No.	%	
Signers	34	85	39	70	46	37	119
Non-Signers	6	15	17	30	79	63	102
Total	40	100	56	100	125	100	221

$\chi^2_2 = 35 \cdot 86$. Significant at 1%.

Anti-colonial feeling, in either its economic, or political or humanitarian form, was thus spread much more widely throughout the backbench party than opposition to rearmament or anti-Americanism. The friends of the subject peoples could often mobilize support which extended far beyond the traditional Left, and could even cut into the Trade Union/Worker section of the party. Not all aspects of anti-colonialism appealed to the same groups, however; indignation at harsh punishments, and military operations conducted with seeming carelessness for human life, was found virtually throughout the party. So, too, was support for the motion on the disposal of land in Kenya, which, admittedly, enjoyed official patronage. On the other hand, support for mutual aid at the expense of the defence effort and living standards at home corresponded more closely to the traditional strength of the Left. Opposition to arbitrary rule and to colour discrimination was distinctively linked with the Miscellaneous Occupations. It is striking that the EDMs dealing with *political* anti-colonialism appealed to the same groups in this Parliament as in the next.[130] The stability of the links between opinions and occupation is noteworthy. Whatever the variations in the responses of individual MPs, specific groups displayed a striking continuity of attitude.

[129] EDM 41/53.

[130] See S. E. Finer, H. B. Berrington, and D. J. Bartholomew, *Backbench Opinion in the House of Commons, 1955–59*, London 1961, p. 40.

THE IDEOLOGICAL GROUPINGS AND THEIR SOCIAL CHARACTERISTICS

So far the social characteristics of various groups of enthusiasts, such as the political anti-colonialists, and of particular rebel factions, like the dissidents of the 57 Varieties demonstration have been examined. The division of the party into three categories, on the basis of participation in floor revolts, crude though it may be, permits an overall view of the relationship between social characteristics and backbench rebellion, and affords a comparison with the foreign policy factions of the 1945 House.

Table 31 shows the occupational breakdown of the three groups—Left, Other Defence and Nuclear Critics, and the Rest. More extended comment is offered later,[131] but the most striking feature is the behaviour of the Workers who, overwhelmingly loyal in the 1945 Parliament, now, though still not as conspicuous as other occupational groups, were to be found in considerable numbers in the floor revolts. Moreover, the Miscellaneous Occupations had overtaken the Professions as the most rebellious group. Generally, the differences in the behaviour of the various occupational groups are so reduced, compared with the 1945 House, as to be explicable in terms of chance.

TABLE 31. LEFTISM AND DEFENCE POLICY BY OCCUPATION

	Left		Other Defence and Nuclear Critics		Rest		Total	
	No.	%	No.	%	No.	%	No.	%
Workers	10	15	15	21	43	63	68	100
Miscellaneous Occupations	12	23	17	33	23	44	52	100
Business	4	15	6	22	17	63	27	100
Professions	14	21	17	25	36	54	67	100
Unknown	—	—	1	14	6	85	7	100
Total	40		56		125		221	

$\chi_6^2 = 5 \cdot 20$. Not significant. Unknowns omitted.

Sponsorship, however, does yield a clear association; the Trade Unionists were significantly more loyal than the CLP men, but even they, though still falling behind the CLP Members, were more rebellious than in the 1945–50 House. Only one Co-operator was found amongst the Left but 8 (out of 15) were Other Defence and Nuclear Critics—behaviour which presaged their susceptibility to the unilateralist appeal in the next Parliament. Neither the educational nor the age breakdowns yielded any associations at an acceptable level of statistical significance.

[131] See below, p. 123 and Ch. 9.

THE SOURCES OF THE IDEOLOGICAL GROUPINGS,
1951–5

The past voting history of the rebels in the floor revolts over rearmament and nuclear weapons has already been traced; in the same way it is possible to examine the voting (and signing) backgrounds of the three ideological groupings.

Table 32 shows the origins of the groupings in summary form.

TABLE 32. THE LEFT AND DEFENCE POLICY GROUPINGS, 1951–5

1945–50	Left		Other Defence and Nuclear Critics		Rest		Total
	No.	%	No.	%	No.	%	
Left	8	57	5	35	1	7	14
Centre Left	11	55	4	20	5	25	20
Dual Abstainers	5	45	2	18	4	36	11
Anti-conscription	2	11	8	42	9	47	19
Rest of Right	2	3	18	25	52	72	72
New entrants	9	15	14	24	36	61	59
Ex-Government, etc.	3	12	5	19	18	69	26
Total	40	18	56	25	125	57	221

Anti-conscription embraces those MPs who voted against conscription but did not belong to the Broader Left; the Rest of Right contains all members of the 1945 Rest except those who voted against conscription.

The Centre Left, though contributing nearly as many as the Left to the Left of 1951–5, also supplied considerably more to the Rest. The contribution of the Dual Abstainers is also noteworthy; the opponents of the National Service Bill of 1947 were inconspicuous amongst the Left, but not surprisingly were prominent amongst the Other Defence and Nuclear Critics. Backbenchers recruited since 1945 were slightly more right wing than the party as a whole.

CONCLUSION

In the 1950's the challenge of the Left (using this term in its looser sense) to the party leadership was more persistent and far more vociferous than hitherto. To account for this we have to look (the influence of great personalities apart) at the diplomatic and military courses followed by the two super-powers, but especially by the United States.

Between 1945 and 1950 Russia and her satellites seemed to be aggressive, imperialist, intransigent; the diplomatic and political offensive Russia launched against British interests in 1945, the deportations in eastern Europe, the imposition of totalitarian control over Russia's border states, the refusal to co-operate in the Marshall Plan, the Czech coup, the expulsion of Yugoslavia from the Cominform, and the Berlin blockade, contrasted harshly with the generosity of Marshall Aid and the idealism of Point Four. From 1950, however, American initiatives were increasingly of a military kind, and appeared to be prompted by an anti-communism compounded, in equal quantities, of cynicism and passion. *Keeping Left* had distinguished between the "Good America" embodied in the American labour movement, and on occasion, in the Truman Administration, and the "Bad America"—the Right, the reactionaries in Washington.[132] From the beginning of the Korean war it seemed as though, however honourable the intentions of the Truman Administration might be, it had had repeatedly to yield to the clamour of the Pentagon, to the stubborn disobedience of its generals, to the narrow prejudices of conservative Congressmen, and the shrill cries of a public conditioned by the hysterical anti-communism of the demagogues of platform and press. "The Communist offensive in Korea", declared the *New Statesman* in its first issue after the crossing of the 38th parallel, "has, in short, given American Imperialism just the opportunity it desires. The effect on the balance of political forces in the United States must be wholly deplorable."[133] At first, whatever doubts might be expressed by those on the farther fringes, most of the Left endorsed America's resistance to the North Korean attack and Britain's support of the United Nations action. When it seemed that America sought to conquer the whole of North Korea and use the episode as a means of enlarging and prosecuting her quarrel with Communist China, opinion changed quickly.

> "... I and many people in this country, [said F. Elwyn Jones, later to join Aneurin Bevan in the revolts of 1952 and 1955] have grave anxieties about the conduct of American diplomacy in the Far East and the exercise of American military power. The result of the way in which American diplomacy has been conducted in recent months has, unfortunately, been to cause the Far Eastern countries to view all that we do, and particularly what the Americans do with the gravest suspicion."[134]

A succession of American decisions, each objectionable in itself, began to assume the shape, so familiar to the Left, of conscienceless imperialism. The American demand for new and rapid rearmament in the NATO countries; the pressure to bring about the rearming of West Germany; the threat to bomb the Manchurian airfields; the reluctance to negotiate with the Soviet Union; the development and testing of thermo-nuclear weapons; the acquisition of military bases in Spain—all of these indicated to the left-wing mind that the alliance had almost lost its original justification and its moral purpose.

Moreover, the changes of leadership that took place served only to blemish further the image of the United States and to refurbish that of Russia. Many of the Left had written off the Truman Administration in despair long before the election of 1952; but amongst some a trace of sympathy for the Democrats remained, and the virtual replacement of Truman by John Foster Dulles destroyed this lingering friendship. The death of Stalin, the early renunciation of the dictator's more extravagant designs by the new leaders and their apparent desire to reach a fair and peaceful settlement cast Russia in a new and softer light.

The special target of the Labour Left was the United States—capitalist, imperialist, and militarist; the British Conservative Government and the Labour leadership, regarded as the too willing allies and apologists of America, shared what opprobrium remained. The Conservatives were presented as men who accepted most of the purposes of America's leaders, and who

---

[132] *Keeping Left*, p. 25.   [133] *NS & N*, 1 July 1950.   [134] HC Deb. 481, cc. 1234–5.

when they did not, lacked the independence and honesty to disagree with them. Though most of the Left accepted the Anglo-American alliance, they argued that Britain's bargaining power was great enough to permit her to disagree publicly with the United States and to refuse to collaborate in all of her initiatives. The Labour leaders might not, as the British Conservatives were usually alleged to, share the violently anti-Communist assumptions of the men who ruled America; but they were unwilling to diverge too sharply from American policy, too compliant to America's demands, too bound by undertakings made in government. Sometimes the Left were simply stating, openly, what the Labour leaders believed in private; more often they were attempting to take the Labour Party along a road which its leaders were reluctant to travel.

The Left of the 1945 Parliament, and their successors, would doubtless have maintained untouched their hostility to the United States, even if none of these events had occurred. But the decisive feature of the early fifties was the remobilization of the old Centre Left under a leader of extraordinary talent. The long-dormant suspicions of and latent hostility to the United States awoke anew; all that the Centre Left had said of the United States in 1946 seemed to be fulfilled a few years later. America was capitalist or she was nothing; driven by the logic of a system that could not find, in the tasks of peace, enough work to employ all of its citizens or to satisfy the greed of its owning class, she had to search unceasingly for new markets and new opportunities for investment, to expand still further her armaments industry, and to turn the defence of democracy into a world-wide crusade against communism. The Left were no longer isolated; the reawakening of the Centre Left brought additional numbers, intellectual strength, and men who were masters of the written and spoken word.

It would be an error, however, to emphasize the socialist character of the Bevanite critique of British foreign policy. It was the Left of 1945 who had maintained, unsullied, the socialist analysis of international discord, and who continued to recommend the socialist prescription. The original breach between the Bevanites and the Labour leadership had taken place over the *scale* of rearmament. There was nothing specifically socialist about the main criticism of the British rearmament programme, nothing that a non-socialist could not have accepted. In the United States, opposition to rearmament had been strongest on the Right; the terms in which the Bevanites denounced British rearmament were, socialist rhetoric and the concern for the social services apart, strikingly similar to those used by ultra-conservative critics of the American defence programme.[135]

"Republican interest in economy [writes an American historian] was quite pronounced in the November to April period, and it is interesting to note that in several of their statements linking fiscal responsibility to military spending, Republicans quoted various parts of Washington's Farewell Address, which warned against the dangers of overgrown military establishments."[136]

In Britain, too, right-wing critics of the arms programme were not lacking. Lord Blackford, a Conservative banker, referred to the

"ruinous rearmament programme which has been forced upon us . . . .I must say that for a long time past, [he went on] as soon as I heard that we were to spend £3,600,000,000 on increased armaments I thought it was more than we could afford; and when that figure was

[135] See M. R. Gordon, *Conflict and Consensus in Labour's Foreign Policy, 1914–1965*, Stanford, 1969, and R. J. Caridi, *The Korean War and American Politics*, Philadelphia, 1968.
[136] Caridi, *op. cit.*, p. 137.

increased to £4,700,000,000. . . . I thought it was absolutely impossible for us to meet that expenditure combined with the cost of the maintenance of the Welfare State. . . . I listened to his [Mr. Bevan's] spokesman Mr. Crossman, speaking in the Defence debate in another place, and I am bound to say that I thought he made a brilliant speech; but perhaps that was because I agreed with almost everything he said."[137]

In 1947 the Centre Left, in accepting the principle of conscription, had argued the policy of military realism; in 1951–2 the men around Bevan adopted the stance of economic realism. Their prescriptions owed little either to the rhetoric of radicalism or the logic of left-wing socialism.

Similarly, the broader differences about foreign policy between the Bevanites and the Labour Front Bench were essentially differences of judgement, which did not, in themselves, imply any fundamental conflict of political goals. The Bevanites insisted that the Labour Government had underestimated Britain's bargaining power with the United States; they discounted the government's fears that failure to respond to the American initiative would encourage a reversion to isolationism, and believed that both the British and American administrations overrated the Soviet military threat. In a world of imperfect information, where the motives and behaviour of other political actors could not be predicted, the best assessments were likely to be no more than intelligent guesswork.

Yet although the Bevanite attack on the level of military spending and on the bi-partisan foreign policy had nothing intrinsically socialist about it, the Bevanites contrived, consciously or unconsciously, to put it into a socialist context. Rearmament was pre-empting resources which could otherwise have been diverted to the expansion of the social services and the development of backward territories. American pressure for rearmament was prompted by ideological hatred of the Soviet Union and the internal contradictions of her highly developed capitalist economy. The desire to rearm West Germany, to bring Spain into NATO, the unwillingness to negotiate with the eastern bloc, testified to the designs inspired by re-actionary dogma and stimulated by the thrust for economic expansion.

In this way the Bevanites regained their socialist credentials; what began as a question of degree—How much rearmament can we safely afford?, was transformed into a difference of kind. The rearmament issue was the bridge that spanned the wide gulf separating the more flexible Centre Left from the doctrinaire Left. Nevertheless, the greater pragmatism of the Centre Left, their fundamental ambivalence towards NATO, their acceptance of some measure of rearmament, continued to offer potential sources of strain to the alliance.

In the 1945 Parliament there had been a strict divorce, except on the fringes of the Left, between the critics of Bevin's foreign policy and the pacifists. From 1950 onwards, however, the foreign affairs dissidents and the pacifists began to walk together. The Left contained some who, like Emrys Hughes, George Craddock, and Sydney Silverman, were zealous pacifists; but once defence rather than foreign policy *per se* had become the central point of division, many of those pacifists who did not share the economic and political postulates of either the Left or the Centre Left, became their collaborators. The Bevanites had made the *scale* of rearmament their first target of attack; inevitably they found themselves the fellow travellers of those who opposed the manufacture of arms on principle. British rearmament, the rearming of the Germans, negotiations with Russia, the development of nuclear weapons—these were issues bound to appeal to the pacifist heart, just as most of them did to the Bevanite head. Left, Centre

[137] HL Deb. clxxv, cc. 1230–3.

Left, and pacifists found themselves, by force of circumstance, merging into a single, if hardly united, opposition.

Despite the merging of the various opposition groups, there had paradoxically been in one sense a diffusion of the issues that divided the party. In the 1945 Parliament it was possible to construct a General Foreign Policy Scale based on backbench attitudes to the Anglo-American alliance. The Centre Left rejected Anglo-American collaboration up to the summer of 1947 or later; the Left still rejected the alliance after the Czech coup of 1948; but whichever year we take, a general line of cleavage can be traced dividing a minority of the party from the rest. Specific questions, like that of Palestine, Germany, Europe, and conscription complicate the picture somewhat, but it is still possible to trace a simple dividing line which other issues may disturb but not obscure. In the 5 years after 1950 no such simple cleavage can be distinguished; the Broader Left was itself initially divided over the Korean war; on four-power talks and German rearmament it was able to attract many who normally followed the lead of the Front Bench; the cohesion of the Bevanites was itself strained as their leader's behaviour seemed to become more wayward.

The picture is one of a succession of left-wing initiatives in which the Left were able to mobilize the support of many normally loyal Members or, alternatively, over which the Left was itself divided and confused.

Another feature was a change in the structural support of the Left Opposition of 1950–5. It has been seen how, on an issue like that of negotiations with Russia, members of the Trade Union/Worker/Elementary-educated section of the party could be recruited to the same cause as that of the Left. Moreover, in both of the main Bevanite revolts there had been a marked blurring of the old occupational divisions. The Workers were still under-represented, but more of them were found amongst the rebels than in the first post-war Parliament. To some extent the increasing prominence of the Workers can be explained by the tendency for the pacifists to merge with the Left in opposition to the leadership; but, in addition, a number of Workers, who had been elected after 1946 were themselves both left-wing and pacifistic.

Moreover, the well-known stereotype of a conflict between the left-wing Hampstead intellectual, and the down-to-earth manual worker, suspicious of folk with too much education and fine talk, however well it may have applied to the 1945 Parliament, becomes less and less appropriate during the 5 years after 1950. In the two later parliaments, the Miscellaneous Occupations came increasingly to the fore; on the Korean war they were certainly no less conspicuous than the Professions amongst the signatories of the leftish EDMs; the same is true of the EDMs on German rearmament, and on the issue of negotiations with the eastern powers the Miscellaneous Occupations were more prominent than the professions. They were also as likely to rebel as the Professions were in the revolt of the 57 Varieties. In the second Bevanite floor protest, that on nuclear weapons, they emerged clearly as the most radical group; and they occupied the same position on most of the anti-colonial issues. The left-winger of this period was no longer especially likely to be a lawyer or a schoolteacher, or a doctor; it was now equally probable that he would be a journalist, or a clerk, or a full-time political organizer. In the next Parliament, that of 1955–9, the Miscellaneous Occupations were to become the most distinctively radical of all the occupational groups.

The decline of the Professions amongst the Left, linked as it is to the recruitment of new parliamentary candidates and the defeat and retirement of older Members, is examined in detail in Chapter 9.

It is enough to say here that the changes, already taking place in the composition of the Left, were to culminate in its virtual transformation in the Parliament of 1955–9. In the great uni-lateralist controversies it was the Miscellaneous Occupations who became the scourge of the leadership. The Professions were to be, if not as reliable and united a group as the Workers, a force on whom the Front Bench could largely depend.

In the debate on the Foreign Affairs Amendment of 1946, Captain Crookshank, speaking for the Conservatives, had asked whether in taking so many "intellectuals" to its bosom the Labour Party might not be nursing a viper. He need not have worried; the viper had turned out to be a slow-worm.

CHAPTER 6

The Labour Party: Domestic Issues, 1945–55

"Parties of the Left tend to be composed of enthusiasts for particular reforms who hope by joining with others to achieve their aims, and of men and women who have through their individuality come to the front. . . .

"Their enthusiasm for their own special cause is apt at times to make them lose their sense of proportion." (CLEMENT ATTLEE, *The Labour Party in Perspective*.)

INTRODUCTION

If questions of foreign policy are of paramount interest to some socialist militants, it remains true that the chief purpose and justification of the Labour Party, both for many of its zealots and for its rank-and-file voters, lies in its commitment to social welfare and full employment at home. Yet some of the party's most articulate supporters lay as much, or even greater emphasis, on humanitarian and libertarian changes, as on the more prosaic issues like social security, jobs, and housing.

"My main concern [wrote Kingsley Martin] was to support the civilizers against the primitives, the thinkers who used their minds against the blimps who thought with their bowels. This involved support for all sorts of causes. If it seemed in the thirties to involve support mainly for the Labour Party, it was because in those days we imagined that when Labour came to power it would be able to carry out reforms over a wide field; we thought, perhaps not so foolishly, that its programme would include the abolition of capital punishment, the abolition of the House of Lords, and the abolition of blood sports, as well as the introduction of socialism."

Kingsley Martin was, of course, throughout his life passionately engaged in controversies about defence and foreign policy as well, and there were those like him, in the House of Commons—men such as Sydney Silverman—who combined a deep concern in such problems with a strong commitment to one or more of the numerous and often unpopular causes which elicit so much enthusiasm within the Labour movement. The partisans of these special causes are, however, by no means confined to the left-wing of the party; thus Reginald Paget's vehement opposition to capital punishment,[1] or Roy Jenkins's libertarian zeal could go hand-in-hand with firm support for the Labour leadership in its battles with the Left.

Apart from these non-material issues, which are largely peripheral to the political struggle,

[1] Though by 1972 Mr. Paget was expressing support for the use of capital punishment in Northern Ireland.

125

lie the purposes for which the Labour Party was founded and from which it derives its continuing rationale—the advancement of working-class living standards and the protection of working-class industrial organization. Demands for material betterment—for improvements in social security benefits and in the health and education services—figured prominently in the backbench motions of the period, especially in the years after 1951 when Labour was in Opposition. Although such demands commanded general assent within the party, they appealed to some Members with greater force than to others and sometimes with particular strength to specific sections of the party.

HUMANITARIANISM

Penal Reform

The cleavage over crime and punishment in the House of Commons has largely, though not wholly, reflected the division between the two main parties. Labour Members have always, preponderantly and sometimes overwhelmingly, supported a softening of the code of criminal punishment; Conservative Members have, to a disproportionate degree, sought to maintain the rigours of the existing law.

The Labour Party Conference voted for the abolition of the death penalty in 1934, but when in office in 1948 the Labour Government resisted, with ultimate success, an attempt to abolish capital punishment.

In 1947 the Home Secretary, Mr. Chuter Ede, introduced the Criminal Justice Bill, a long and detailed measure which, whilst abolishing birching and flogging, omitted all mention of the death penalty. In April 1948, on the Report Stage of the Bill, Sydney Silverman moved an amendment to abolish capital punishment for murder for an experimental period of 5 years.

On the Labour side there was sharp disagreement as to whether public opinion was ready for abolition. Silverman, moving the adoption of the clause, asked how public opinion was to be ascertained. "... we ... can only do it by getting a cross-section of our citizens ... Where can we find a better cross-section of the community than this elected House of Commons? ... We are not delegates. We are representatives. Our business is to act according to our consciences, honestly looking at the facts and coming to as right a judgement as we may."[2] Stanley Evans, a backbench Labour retentionist, argued that the abolitionists had no mandate. "However shocking it may be to sentimentalists, British public opinion is as sound as a bell of brass on this matter. ... Public opinion in this country is healthy and vigorous and free from neurosis."[3]

Silverman referred to the "melodrama and sensationalism" surrounding the death penalty, and the same passionate feelings were expressed by other Labour abolitionists such as Leslie Hale, Elwyn Jones, and Paget.[4] Both John Paton and Terence Donovan (later Mr. Justice Donovan) alluded to the experience of abolitionist countries "extremely varied in their history and traditions, their social and economic circumstances", as Paton put it.[5]

The Home Secretary, in advising the House to reject the clause, corroborated Evans's view of public opinion if in less pungent words "I have been surprised ... at the unanimity with which this feeling is expressed." He warned the House of the emergence in Britain of a new class of gangster and armed criminal. The police had the right to expect that the criminal who used arms or violence in his attempt to evade the police would be dealt with "with the utmost severity".[6]

[2] HC Deb. 449, cc. 980–7.   [3] *Ibid.*, cc. 1069–72.   [4] *Ibid.*, cc. 1032–8, 1064–8, 1090–4.
[5] *Ibid.*, cc. 1024–7, 1007–16.   [6] *Ibid.*, cc. 1082–90.

The amendment was carried on a free vote, but against the advice of the government, by the narrow margin of 23.[7] Two hundred and fifteen Labour Members voted for abolition and 74 (49 if only backbenchers are counted) opposed it. Thus amongst the backbenchers the abolitionists outnumbered the retentionists by more than 4 to 1.

Virtually every social grouping within the parliamentary party showed a majority for abolition—but there were big differences in the size of the majority. The Professions, the University graduates, the Constituency-Party sponsored, and the under-50's, were overwhelmingly in favour of abolition, whilst of those Co-operators who voted, not one opted for retention. Amongst the Workers, the Elementary educated, the Trade Unionists, and the over-60's, substantial minorities opposed the Silverman amendment. Not surprisingly, the intellectuals of the party displayed more enthusiasm than the working-class section. Once again, there was a divergence between the different political cultures of which the parliamentary party was composed.

Although the government did not put the Whips on, they did call upon the House to reject the amendment, and some Labour opponents of the new clause may have voted against it out of loyalty to their leaders. The Trade Unionist opponents of the clause would, no doubt, have been more influenced by considerations of loyalty than the Co-operators and the CLP Members. Nevertheless, when the issue came up again in 1953 and 1955, the Trade Unionist again displayed less support for abolition than their colleagues.

The House of Lords rejected the clause by an overwhelming majority, and the government therefore brought forward a compromise scheme, under which some, but not all, murderers would be subject to the death penalty. Even this measure was voted down by the Lords; and on 22 July Chuter Ede recommended the House to drop the compromise clause. The Bill had, except for the death penalty clauses, passed all its stages in both Houses. It would be a calamity if this Bill, "which effects very desirable and long urged reforms over the whole field of the administration of criminal justice" were to be lost. The government would explore "without delay" ways by which the death penalty could be limited without incurring the objections made to the recent compromise.[8] Committed Labour abolitionists, such as Donovan, Paton, Paget, and Silverman, protested at the government's decision, but the Whips were put on, and though a group of last-ditch abolitionists challenged the government, the decision to accept the Lords' verdict was carried by 215 to 34.

Altogether 97 backbench Labour MPs voted in both of the main divisions on capital punishment. Twenty-eight voted consistently for abolition and 19 consistently for retention; whilst 50 supported the Silverman clause in April but accepted the government's advice and voted to retain the death penalty in July (Table 33).

These votes form a perfect Guttman scale with the Consistent Abolitionists at one extreme and the Consistent Retentionists at the other.[9]

The absolute number who voted consistently for abolition is small; but on this scale the Workers, as in the April vote, were significantly less favourable to abolition than other Members. Indeed, only *one* Worker voted consistently for abolition. Similarly, the CLP men were more committed to abolition than the Trade Unionists, though the association cannot be regarded as firmly established. The educational differences were not statistically significant,

---

[7] Fifteen Conservatives voted for the clause which had been seconded by one of their number, Christopher Hollis.

[8] HC Deb. 454, cc. 707–11.

[9] For a description of Guttman scales, see Annex 1.

TABLE 33. CAPITAL PUNISHMENT DIVISIONS

April

		+	−	Total
July	+	28 *a*	— *b*	28
	−	50 *c*	19 *d*	69
	Total	78	19	97

$+$ = vote for abolition. $-$ = vote for retention.

$$\text{Yule's } Q = \frac{ad - bc}{ad + bc} = 1\cdot0.$$

though consistent with those derived from the analysis of the first division on the Silverman clause.

After the eventual excision of the clause,[10] 5 years passed before there was a new legislative initiative. This initiative was prompted by fears that an innocent man had been executed despite the official reassurance that "it could not happen". In 1949 the wife and child of Timothy Evans, a lorry driver living in Rillington Place, North Kensington, were found strangled, and in March 1950 Evans was hanged for the murder of his child. In 1953 John Reginald Christie, who lived at the same address as Evans, and had been a prosecution witness against Evans, confessed to the murder of six women. At once the suspicion was raised that Christie, and not Evans, had been guilty of the murder of Evans's child and wife, and this suspicion both strengthened the argument against the death penalty, and gave renewed fervour to the abolitionists. A week after Christie had been sentenced, Sydney Silverman attempted to introduce, under the Ten Minute Rule, a Bill to suspend the death penalty for 5 years. He referred to a newspaper report that Christie had confessed to the murder of Evans's baby and argued that retentionists could no longer dismiss the possibility of an irrevocable mistake.[11] The attempt was defeated by 256 to 195. One hundred and ninety-one Labour Members (including tellers) voted for the Silverman Bill and only 15 against.

Meanwhile the Home Secretary had agreed to ask Mr. John Scott Henderson, QC, to conduct an independent inquiry into the Evans–Christie case. The report, which was published on 14 July and asserted that Evans had, after all, murdered both his wife and his child, encountered deep abolitionist suspicions. On the same day Sydney Silverman, with the support of 20 Labour colleagues, put down a motion regretting that Scott Henderson's report could not be accepted and called for the establishment of a select committee to investigate the case.[12] On 29 July a debate was held on the matter. The abolitionists drew attention to what they regarded as discrepancies in the report, and were not satisfied with the Home Secretary's explanations. The next day Mr. Silverman tabled a further motion, repeating the demand for a select committee. Forty Labour MPs signed this EDM.[13]

[10] For a full account of this and other attempts to abolish the death penalty, see J. B. Christoph, *Capital Punishment and British Politics*, London, 1962.

[11] HC Deb. 517, cc. 407–11.

[12] EDM 121/52.   [13] EDM 128/52.

Two other EDMs relating to capital punishment were put down in this Parliament. One, with only 9 signatures, called for a review of the legal definition of insanity.[14] The other, put down in December 1954, with Sydney Silverman again as leading sponsor, expressed disquiet at the failure of the Home Secretary to reprieve a woman who, it was said, might have been insane, and urged the government to declare its policy upon the whole issue of capital punishment.[15] Fifty-three more Labour MPs added their names.[16]

The next opportunity for the abolitionists came in February 1955. The House was due to debate the recommendations of the Gowers Commission on Capital Punishment, and Silverman tabled an amendment calling for abolition of the death penalty for a trial period of 5 years. The debate was marked by the conversion of Chuter Ede, who had been Home Secretary when Evans was executed. "I was the Home Secretary who wrote on Evans' papers 'The law must take its course'. . . . I think Evans' case shows, in spite of all that has been done since, that a mistake was possible, and that, in the form in which the verdict was actually given on a particular case, a mistake was made."[17] The abolitionists again lost, but the vote was closer than in 1953 —245 to 214. The number of abolitionists on the Labour side rose to 195 whilst the retentionists in the party fell from 15 to 5.

It was the Workers, as in the free vote of 1948, who, through the EDMs, displayed least enthusiasm for abolition. Less than a fifth of them signed compared with about two-fifths of each of the other occupational groups. The sponsorship breakdown yields much the same result—the Co-operators and the CLP Members signed to a disproportionate degree, whilst the Trade Unionists tended to abstain. Educationally, the cleavage was even more pronounced; 44 per cent of University graduates signed but only 18 per cent of the Elementary educated. There was a consistent tendency for signing to diminish with advancing age. More than half of the under-40's were amongst the signers but less than a quarter of the oldest age group.

Table 34 shows how the EDM signatories behaved in the division lobbies. It is at once apparent from Table 33 that there was a marked relationship between attitudes to capital punishment, as revealed by the EDMs, and behaviour in the division lobbies. Eight Members signed three or more of the relevant EDMs; all of them voted consistently for abolition. Nearly three-quarters of those who signed two motions did so, just under two-thirds of those who signed one—but less than half of the non-signers. Moreover, of the 17 Members who voted for retention on either occasion or both, only one signed an EDM; of the 30 Consistent Abstainers, only 4 had signed. It is clear that keenness on this issue was closely connected with the *number* of motions Members signed.

Again, the correspondence is not absolute. Some abolitionist signatories may have been absent from the House for illness or other good reason in both debates. The single Retentionist and the 4 Consistent Abstainers who signed one EDM may have felt disquiet about particular decisions without having any special abhorrence of the death penalty as such.

The social characteristics of those who voted for abolition were similar to the relatively small band of enthusiasts who signed the EDMs. The clearest way of comparing the reactions

[14] EDM 114/52.   [15] EDM 16/54.

[16] The value of Yule's Q for the three of the six possible pairs of motions, i.e. all those pairs, except those involving EDM 114/52 which called for a review of the legal definition of insanity, ranged from 0·62 to 0·82. The value of the three remaining pairs of EDMs is much lower, ranging from 0·32 to 0·55. As there are only four Members who qualify by signing EDM 114/52, no violence is done to the findings by including its signatories in the humanitarianism scale. All the motions were characterized by disproportionately high middle-class and left-wing support.

[17] HC Deb. 536, cc. 2076–84.

TABLE 34. CAPITAL PUNISHMENT: EDMs AND VOTES

Votes	EDM signatories								Total
	Signed three or more		Signed two		Signed one		Signed nil		
	No.	%	No.	%	No.	%	No.	%	
Consistent Abolitionists	8	100	12	71	33	63	72	46	125
Non-consistent Abolitionists	—	—	5	29	14	27	42	27	61
Retentionists/Abolitionists	—	—	—	—	—	—	4	3	4
Consistent Abstainers	—	—	—	—	4	8	26	17	30
Retentionists Once or Twice	—	—	—	—	1	2	12	8	13
Total	8	100	17	100	52	100	156	100	233

Consistent Abolitionists were those who voted for abolition in both July 1953 and February 1955; those who voted for abolition on one occasion but did not vote at all in the other, have been termed Non-consistent Abolitionists; the handful who moved from retention in 1953 to abolition in 1955 have been called Retentionists/Abolitionists; whilst the terms Consistent Abstainers and Retentionists Once or Twice are self-explanatory.

Data grouped: Signed three or more and signed two combined. Consistent Abstainers, Retentionists/Abolitionists, and Retentionists Once or Twice combined. $\chi_2^2 = 17\cdot372$. Significant at 1% level.

of different social groups is to compare the distribution of the Consistent Abolitionists with that of the combined forces of the Consistent Abstainers, and the Retentionists, i.e., those who voted for retention on both occasions (one Member only) or voted for retention once and abstained on the other. Thus, the Professions mustered 47 Consistent Abolitionists against 7 Retentionists and Consistent Abstainers; the Miscellaneous Occupations 31 against 9; whilst only 30 Workers were consistently for abolition and 17 were Abstainers or Retentionists. Similarly, the Trade Unionists and the Elementary educated contributed fewer, proportionately, to the Consistent Abolitionists, and more to the Abstainers and Retentionists than the CLP and Co-operative-sponsored MPs, and the University graduates. Detailed figures showing the occupational breakdown can be found in Annex 3.

Between 1948 and 1955 the Labour Party moved from heavy support for abolition to near unanimity. The 49 backbench retentionists of April 1948 had been reduced to 4 by 1955.[18] This reduction can be ascribed partly to the process of retirement and replacement and partly to individual conversion. Of the 49, 8 had been replaced by Conservatives, and 7 further seats had, in effect, been lost to Labour, though not gained by the Conservatives, through the reduction of the total membership of the House which had accompanied the redistribution of parliamentary constituencies. Of the remaining 34, 10 had been replaced by new Labour MPs of whom 7 voted for abolition in 1955 and 3 were absent. Ten of the Retentionists of 1948 had moved over to the abolitionist side by 1955; a further 10 abstained or were absent.

The Workers contributed most in *numbers* to this fall in retentionist strength—not surprisingly since they had constituted the largest single bloc of the retentionists in 1948. Seven of the 13 Worker Retentionists of 1948, who were still in the House, switched to abolition in 1955, and

[18] One of the 5 Labour retentionists of 1955, Mr. Alfred Barnes, had been a Minister in 1948.

TABLE 35. CAPITAL PUNISHMENT, 1948 AND 1955

Change in Attitude by Occupation

	In House 1948 and 1955			1955 Replacement for 1948			Total			Grand total
	Abolition 1955	Abstention 1955	Retention 1955	Abolition 1955	Abstention 1955	Retention 1955	Abolition 1955	Abstention 1955	Retention 1955	
Prof.	2	1	2	1	1	—	3	2	2	7
M/O.	1	1	1	1	—	—	2	1	1	4
Bus.	—	3	—	2	—	—	2	3	—	5
W.	7	5	1	3	2	—	10	7	1	18
Total	10	10	4	7	3	—	17	13	4	34

a further 5 were now absent; 5 more Retentionist Workers had been replaced by 5 newly elected Workers who split 3:2 between abolition and abstention. The *proportionate* decline in retentionist strength was spread more or less evenly over the occupational groups. Table 35 shows in detail the changes in abolitionist sentiment amongst the different occupational groups.

The abolitionist ranks were further strengthened by the votes of those who, in 1948, had been compelled to abstain by virtue of their membership of the government. On the other hand, abolitionist support had been weakened by the defeat of many Labour MPs in 1950 and 1951. Against this there was the later growth of abolitionist sentiment in the Conservative Party, a development which, combined with the changes in the Labour Party, gave the abolitionists their limited victory in 1956 and, helped by some Labour gains, their greater success in 1964. The Workers fully shared in the general erosion of retentionist feeling within the Parliamentary Labour Party, but it remains true, judging by the abstentions, that the Workers were still, of all the occupational groups in the 1951–5 Parliament, the least committed to abolition.

Left-wingers like Sydney Silverman and Geoffrey Bing played a prominent part in the abolitionist campaign; and though they could attract vocal allies from the Right like Reginald Paget, it remains true that a special antipathy to capital punishment and a general left-wing orientation tended to go together (Table 36).

TABLE 36. Leftism, Defence Policy, and Capital Punishment EDMs

Capital punishment EDMs	Left		Other Defence and Nuclear Critics		Rest		Total
	No.	%	No.	%	No.	%	
Signers	22	55	22	39	28	22	72
Non–Signers	18	45	34	61	97	78	149
Total	40	100	56	100	125	100	221

$\chi_2^2 = 16 \cdot 13$. Significant at $0 \cdot 1\%$.

Hunting

Cynics have often averred that a penchant for brutality to people often goes hand in hand with kindness to animals. Whatever the general truth of this statement, it is not true of the Parliamentary Labour Party—at least in the years under discussion. The great majority of Labour MPs have been committed to softening the harshest severities of the law; and large numbers also have a deep dislike of the hunting of wild animals for sport.

The issue of hunting arouses two strong resentments on the Left; a deep dislike of cruelty, especially gratuitous cruelty, combines with a strong sense of class consciousness. Hunting, it is alleged, is the prerogative of the rich (an allegation strongly disputed by the partisans of hunting); it also involves the deliberate arousal of fear and the infliction of pain for pleasure. For the Left, it has, as an issue, the additional merit of being a largely rural pursuit—and the Labour Party draws most of its seats from the towns and the coalfields.

Two EDMs about hunting were put down in the 1945–50 Parliament. The first, in March 1948, declared that it was undesirable that petrol should be allocated for blood sports; 213

Labour MPs signed this motion (and an amendment which strengthened the main motion).[19] The second, which was prompted by the defeat a few days before of a Bill to make some forms of hunting illegal, called on the government to set up an inquiry into the law relating to cruelty to wild animals. It won the support of nearly 200 Labour MPs, as well as a handful of Conservatives, Liberals, and Independents, and the government did, in fact, appoint a committee of inquiry (EDM 22/48).

These motions, interestingly enough, did not appeal, disproportionately, to any specific section of the party. They gained roughly equal support from Members from all social backgrounds—from Workers and the Professions, from the old as well as the young. Only amongst the University graduates was there any difference in response; here those graduates who had been educated at a public school signed less often than those who had not.[20]

On 25 February Seymour Cocks introduced a Private Members' Bill to abolish most forms of hunting (though not fox hunting). The Minister of Agriculture opposed the Bill, and on a free vote the Bill was thrown out by 214 votes to 101. Nevertheless, 94 Labour backbenchers voted for it and only 29 supported the Minister. The Conservatives, perhaps prompted by something more than mere public spirit, turned up in large numbers to destroy the Bill.

Cocks and other Labour supporters of the Bill rested their case on the cruelty of hunting; to the argument that no form of control of deer was available which would not inflict more suffering than hunting, Cocks replied that if hunting were abolished, "alternative ways of killing the deer—and not cruel ways—will soon be found and adopted".[21] The speeches of the Bill's advocates were predictable; but a number of Labour Members, most of them representing rural or semi-rural constituencies, opposed the measure. These Labour opponents were at pains to remove the motion (not fostered by any of the speeches of the Bill's supporters in the House) that hunting was a rich man's sport. Mr. Stubbs of Cambridgeshire told the House that he had received hundreds of letters against a Bill which was "a direct and unwarrantable interference with country sports". Workers living in rural areas did not get the same opportunities for sport as people in towns. "What is wrong with a man and his dog going out on Saturday afternoon for a bit of coursing?"[22] Maurice Webb, representing the urban constituency of Bradford Central, referred to "the quite evident manifestation of angry opposition to this Measure in the countryside, and not merely there but in many great industrial districts in the North . . . where coursing is a pastime", and described a meeting with a deputation of "ordinary working men" from his own constituency, "These were not the idle rich, these were not playboys; they were ordinary working men who wanted to carry on this sport, and who denied that it was cruel." Expressing himself to be concerned "about great considerations of liberty which are involved in this matter", Webb argued that the House must be very cautious before making an "unnecessary intrusion" on individual freedom.[23] Victor Collins of Taunton argued that the alternatives to hunting were less humane. ". . . this is not a Bill to abolish hunting but a Bill for the promotion of cruelty to wild animals."[24] The Minister of Agriculture, Tom Williams, warned Members that people in the rural areas interpreted the Bill as "a townsman's attack upon the life of the country". Like Victor Collins, the Minister feared the abolition of hunting would lead to more cruelty, not less. Alluding obliquely to the fears that the Labour Party would alienate rural support, he hoped that ". . . we are not going to forfeit

---

[19] EDMs 40 and 40A/47.
[20] The value of Yule's Q for this pair of motions is 0·68.
[21] HC Deb. 461, cc. 2167–80.   [22] *Ibid.*, cc. 2205–6.   [23] *Ibid.*, cc. 2183–9.
[24] *Ibid.*, cc. 2243–8.

the goodwill we have so rightly earned, and go down to history as a party anxious to abolish the pleasures of others".[25]

The two EDMs had, of course, mobilized far more support than the Bill; the great mass of Labour backbenchers simply did not vote. The debate was held on a Private Members' Friday, and many had no doubt gone home to their constituencies. Many who were hostile to hunting may well have decided not to embarrass their own Ministers, and fears of electoral reprisals in rural constituencies may also have weighed with them. Yet despite the large abstention rate, voting in the division lobbies proves once again to have been related to the signature of EDMs (Table 37).

TABLE 37. BLOOD SPORTS: EDMs AND VOTES

Votes	EDMs							
	Signed both		Signed one		Signed nil		Total	
	No.	%	No.	%	No.	%	No.	%
Anti-hunting	67	71	23	24	4	4	94	100
Abstainers	80	42	60	32	49	26	189	100
Pro-hunting	9	31	7	24	13	45	29	100
Total	156	50	90	29	66	21	312	100

$\chi_2^2 = 36\cdot63$. Significant at $0\cdot1\%$.

We would expect those who signed the EDMs to contribute most to the anti-hunting vote and least to the supporters of the Minister, whilst the reverse should be true of those who signed none. These expectations are clearly borne out; the double signatories account for more than two-thirds of the Bill's supporters, less than half of the abstainers, and less than a third of the Bill's opponents. The non-signatories, however, constituted less than a twentieth of those voting for the Bill, a quarter of the abstainers, and nearly half of the Bill's enemies.[26]

A large number of Members, willing to sign EDMs which were directly or obliquely critical of hunting, were not prepared to defy their Minister's advice and vote for its abolition; but this decline in the strength of the anti-hunting lobby, it must be stressed, affected more or less equally all the main social groups. A breakdown of the Bill's supporters, by the main social categories, shows that like the EDMs, the Bill appealed to a cross-section of the party except amongst University graduates. Here, as with the EDMs, those graduates who had been educated at a public school gave less support than those who had not.[27]

[25] HC Deb. 461, cc. 2226–34.

[26] As mentioned below (see p. 135), and as shown in Annex 3, participation in the division was closely related to the proximity of Members' constituencies to London. The relationship between signing and voting still holds even when allowance is made for this factor. In the constituencies belonging to what has been defined as the Centre, the relationship is almost the same as that shown in Table 37. So, too, apart from a complication caused by the very small number—7—of the Minister's supporters, is the relationship for Members coming from constituencies defined as belonging to the periphery.

[27] This difference was not statistically significant, but the proportion of public-school MPs supporting the Bill was almost exactly the same as the proportion of public-school MPs signing the EDMs.

A disproportionate number of the Bill's opponents came from MPs representing county constituencies with a rural element, such as Buckingham and Chelmsford. This geographical bias helps to account for the behaviour of the U1's and U2's who may, on a hard-headed calculation of electoral interest, have decided not to let a peripheral issue like hunting impede the advance of socialism.

The Bill's opponents were drawn from the middle-class occupational groups—the Professions and especially Business, from University graduates (particularly the U1's and U2's), from the younger Members rather than the older, and most strikingly from the Constituency-Party sponsored, and not from the Trade Unionists. Indeed, all of the Bill's 29 backbench Labour opponents were CLP sponsored; not a single one came from the Co-operators or the Trade Unions. Moreover, the Left and Centre Left, on the foreign policy scales, contributed slightly more than their due share.

Thus although support for the Bill, as for the EDMs, came more or less evenly from all the social strata of the party, its foes came preponderantly from the non-working-class groups. The Professional, University-educated, CLP-sponsored Members were thus more likely to vote in the division (regardless of whether they were in favour of or against the Bill) than the Trade Unionists, Workers, and Elementary-educated men.

The explanation for this difference in participation almost certainly lies in the geographical distribution of Labour MPs. A full statistical examination of this factor can be found in Annex 3; here it may be briefly mentioned that attendance in the division was indeed closely related to the distance of the constituency from London. The nearer the constituency, the greater the likelihood of the Member voting. A breakdown of Members by sponsorship and voting shows that once allowance is made for distance, Constituency Party Members were little more likely than Trade Unionists to attend and vote.

It is improbable that this geographical factor, however, could explain the heavily middle-class character of the Bill's opponents. CLP Members were more likely to vote against the Bill irrespective of the location of their constituency.

There is here a remarkable difference between this question and that of the death penalty. Abolition of capital punishment was pre-eminently, in terms both of its leadership and its division lobby support, a middle-class crusade. The small group of Members prepared to vote in favour of hunting came disproportionately, and sometimes overwhelmingly, from the very classes that provided the most consistent and fervent opponents of the death penalty.

LIBERTARIANISM

Amnesty for Deserters

One other humanitarian issue is worthy of note—the question of an amnesty for deserters from the armed forces. This was hardly a purely humanitarian concern, however, for the issue was likely to be of special appeal to the pacifists in the party.

In June 1948 the elderly pacifist, Rhys Davies, tabled a motion welcoming the early reconsideration by the government of the question of an amnesty.[28] More than 100 Labour MPs signed this motion. Interestingly enough, and in contrast with feelings on the death penalty, this EDM appealed much more to the older, the Elementary educated, the Trade Unionists, and Co-operators than to the other sections of the party. Moreover, the differences were sharp;

[28] EDM 71/47.

only a sixth of the youngest age group signed compared with more than two-fifths of the over-50's; and a quarter of the University graduates compared with nearly half of the Elementary and Elementary/Secondary+ groups. Such a pattern stands in clear contrast to that disclosed by the capital punishment votes and motions.

This difference can be partly explained by the much wider appeal of pacifism. As is shown in Chapter 4, pacifist sentiment, as evinced by opposition to conscription, was spread more or less equally throughout all sections of the party. It is not surprising that pacifism and a less rigorous attitude to deserters should, to some extent, go together.

This factor can hardly afford a complete explanation, however; for though the Trade Unionist/Worker/Elementary-educated section were much more hostile to conscription than they were to the more distinctively ideological aspects of the government's defence and foreign policy, they were not more unfavourable than the rest of the party. Almost certainly the answer lies in the personal experience of the younger Members, and in the interrelationships (already discussed in Chapter 3) between war service, age, education, occupation, and sponsorship. Age and war service were closely linked; in turn, age was related to education, occupation, and sponsorship. Nearly half of the University men, but only a handful of the Elementary educated, had served in the armed forces; nearly a third of the CLP sponsored had served but only a tiny number of Trade Unionists. Not unexpectedly, when Members with war service, as a distinct category, are compared with Members who had none, the same sharp cleavage reappears; a sixth of those who had fought signed the motion as against two-fifths of the Members without war service.

Civil Liberties

A vein of radical libertarianism has always tempered the collectivist outlook of the Labour Party. There are many within the party who maintain special vigilance against abuses of authority—especially the *traditional* authorities such as the police, the security services, and the armed forces. This libertarian strand stands in contrast to another long-established element within the party—the strictly collectivist, managerial, "social engineering" tradition. A few of the EDMs reflected this libertarian concern.

International tension rarely provides a congenial temperature for personal liberty; and three divergent EDMs on civil liberties largely reflected the divisions within the party over the Cold War. In March 1948 the Prime Minister announced that Communists and Fascists employed in civil service posts with access to military secrets would be transferred to other, less sensitive departments, and that any for whom no suitable work could be found would be dismissed.

Forty-five MPs, led by Harold Davies, signed what was virtually a motion of censure on Mr. Attlee; their motion regretted his statement and suggested it was a departure from the principles of Democracy and Civil Liberty.[29] The signatories were drawn predominantly, but not entirely, from the Left of the party. Clearly there were a few Members outside the ranks of the Left who were disturbed by this potential threat to personal freedom.

The motion provoked an almost immediate retort from the Right who put down an amendment the next day, signed by 25 MPs, which congratulated the Prime Minister on his statement. Then a further, and more moderate motion, attracting only 12 signatures, was tabled by Mr. H. D. Hughes; his EDM recognized the claims of security but asked the government to consider measures to safeguard the liberties of those individuals who were affected.[30]

[29] EDM 35/47.   [30] EDMs 35A/47 and 38/47.

The internal security EDMs provide one of the few occasions when a salvo from the Left, on the Order Paper, led to an immediate retort from the Right. Hence, the three motions have been consolidated into a single qualitative scale, with Harold Davies's motion constituting the Left, the right-wing amendment (sponsored by Ernest Thurtle) the Right, and the middle-of-the-road motion of Mr. Hughes the Centre.

Only 76 Members expressed any opinion through the EDM machinery on the security issue. In spite of the small numbers, strong associations between atittude and social characteristics were found. The strongest association was found between age and attitude; the younger signatories (the under-50's) leant markedly to the Left, the older split evenly between Left and Right. The Professions and Business inclined to the Left, whilst the Workers and Miscellaneous Occupations were much more right-wing. The educational division followed similar lines— University graduates constituting more than half of the Left, non-graduates comprising most of the Right.

As has been suggested, opinion on internal security safeguards was linked to, though it did not exactly duplicate, the conflict over foreign policy—a relationship which is demonstrated in Table 38.

TABLE 38. INTERNAL SECURITY (CIVIL SERVICE) EDMs

Foreign policy	Left		Centre		Right		Total	
	No.	%	No.	%	No.	%	No.	%
Ultra Left	4	100	—	—	—	—	4	100
Left	13	93	1	7	—	—	14	100
Centre Left	10	63	6	38	—	—	16	100
Dual Abstainers	8	100	—	—	—	—	8	100
Rest	8	24	5	15	21	62	34	100
Total	43		12		21		76	

Data grouped. Foreign Policy Ultra Left, Left and Centre Left combined. Dual Abstainers omitted. Internal Security Left and Centre combined. $\chi_1^2 = 31 \cdot 765$. Significant at $0 \cdot 1\%$.

Admission of Aliens

In an Adjournment Debate on 19 June 1946, James Callaghan called for two changes concering immigration—one a matter of administration and the other of policy. He wanted foreign husbands of British women to be admitted on the same terms as the wives of British men; and whilst he disclaimed any wish to take down all the barriers to immigration, he called for a more liberal attitude towards the admission of aliens. "We are turning away from the shores of this country eligible and desirable young men who could be adding to our strength and resources. . . . It may be revolutionary to suggest that we ought now to become a country where immigrants are welcomed, but that is really the logical development of our present position in the world." Several Labour MPs, despite the lateness of the hour, stayed to support Callaghan—J. P. W. Mallalieu, Francis Noel-Baker, Sydney Silverman, Durbin, and Royle, with Pritt, the Independent Labour Member. All of them criticized the Home Office's administration of the aliens regulations. Silverman asked for an end to the position "which makes some people say that the British Home Office is the last stronghold of Fascism in Europe."[31]

On 25 June Callaghan put down a motion which drew the support of 80 Members and called for a progressive relaxation of restrictions on the immigration of aliens who, for various reasons, such as services to the allied cause, had a claim for favourable treatment; and went on to urge the government to adopt a more generous immigration policy for the future. Although more Professionals signed than Workers, and more of the CLP sponsored than of the Trade Unionists, the differences were not statistically significant. Within the University group, however, the Oxford and Cambridge Members (U1 and U3) were substantially more inclined to sign than the graduates of provincial universities (U2 and U4); moreover, there was an important age difference, the youngest Members being most enthusiastic (EDM 54/45).

Political Liberties of Civil Servants

In 1949 the Masterman Committee on the Political Activities of Civil Servants proposed that restrictions on the political activities of some Civil Servants be relaxed, but also recommended that stringent limitations be put on the political freedom of many junior and middle-rank civil servants as well as of members of the administrative class. Their report duly provoked an anguished EDM from more than 50 Labour MPs.[32] Analysis of the motion shows the familiar divisions of occupation, education, and age, with the Professions, University educated, and younger Members once again in the van. These divisions, however, mirror a strong regional distribution; MPs from London and the south-east signed, to a much greater extent than their colleagues. This regional division in turn probably reflects pressure, to some extent, from rank-and-file Labour Party workers employed in the Civil Service and the anxiety of MPs who foresaw some of their keenest constituency supporters being compelled to withdraw from active politics. This EDM, moreover, attracted disproportionate support from the Combined Lefts, who supplied 24 out of 51 signatories.[33]

The remaining libertarian motions constitute a miscellany of protests, defying generalization, some of them being of little intrinsic importance. One, put down in 1950, was really aimed at a Conservative MP who had sent a letter of complaint about a left-wing priest to his bishop.[34] An EDM of 1954 also, curiously enough, concerned a leftish clergyman; the motion prayed to overrule the action of the Secretary to the Duchy of Cornwall who, the motion asserted, had induced a Christian pacifist to withdraw his acceptance of a living in the gift of the Duchy because of his political opinions and activities.[35] The refusal of the American State Department to grant a visa to Sydney Silverman prompted an EDM,[36] and so did a decision by Bury Town Council to dismiss conscientious objectors from its staff.[37] Another, tabled in 1948, protested against the infringement of civil liberties in Ireland. These motions, however, are so influenced by partisan and religious considerations that they can hardly be accepted as genuine expressions of libertarian feeling.

[31] HC Deb. 424, cc. 343–54.

[32] EDM 55/49.

[33] *Keeping Left*, pp. 17–18, strongly criticized the composition of the committee. "As soon as its members were announced, it was clear that their report would be reactionary."

[34] EDM 44/51.

[35] EDM 45/53.

[36] EDM 70/52.

[37] EDM 98/52.

SOCIAL WELFARE

For most Labour voters, and for a large section of the movement, the Labour Party is primarily a vehicle for the extension of social welfare and the protection of trade union privileges. To these its ideological and humanitarian convictions have at best a secondary appeal, and for some, especially for ordinary Labour voters, these beliefs are at best unattractive and, at worst, repugnant.

Not surprisingly there were many EDMs concerned, not with specific ideological postures or the expression of moral principles, but with bread-and-butter questions of material well-being. Six main areas have been identified—social welfare benefits, education, health, housing, and the question of equal pay.

Pensions and National Assistance

Soon after the meeting of the new Parliament in 1945, Sydney Silverman collected more than 160 signatures for an EDM which requested the government to raise old-age pensions, by 7s. 6d. (37½p) for a single person and 12s. 6d. (62½p) for a married couple, without prejudice to the comprehensive social security scheme which was being prepared.[38] Another EDM, tabled in 1949, and much less well supported, asked the government to make old-age pensions payable to single women at the age of 55. There were virtually no differences in background characteristics between supporters of these EDMs and the non-signatories—a situation which contrasts markedly with the experience of later parliaments when demands for better welfare provisions were endorsed predominantly by the Trade Unionists, the Workers, and the Elementary-school Members. In the 1945 Parliament there was no clearly significant variation in the behaviour of MPs in different social and educational groups; what differences there were showed the Trade Unionists and the Workers to be *less* responsive than their colleagues.[39]

The relative indifference of the Trade Unionists can almost certainly be attributed to the trade-union tradition of loyalty; many Trade Unionists, though perturbed at the poverty of the pensioners, must have been reluctant to embarrass the government so early in the life of the Parliament.

Three social welfare EDMs were tabled in the succeeding Parliament. One in February 1951 called on the government to increase pensions and national insurance benefits and to ensure that they fluctuated in accordance with the cost-of-living index and to amend National Assistance Board regulations "in accordance with the people's needs".[40] A second was tabled the day after Gaitskell's budget speech in which he had announced that pensions would be increased for pensioners over 70. This EDM asked that increased allowances should be given to pensioners aged between 65 and 70 and called on the government to rescind the proposed charges for teeth and spectacles.[41] A third, put down a few days later, called for increased supplementary pensions.[42]

[38] EDMs 6/45 and 17/49.

[39] The association between sponsorship and attitude was significant at the 10 per cent level; there was no association between occupation and attitude.

[40] EDM 27/51.

[41] EDM 55/51.

[42] EDM 56/51.

These motions[43] did appeal preponderantly to the Workers and the Elementary educated. Nearly two-fifths of the Workers signed one or more of these EDMs compared with less than a fifth of the Professions and a sixth of the Businessmen. The Miscellaneous Occupations came out much more strongly than the Professions, but signed less often than the Workers. The figures for the University men and the Elementary educated mirrored those of their occupational counterparts.

The defeat of the Labour government the following October released a succession of social welfare EDMs. There were no fewer than seven which called for increases in either old-age pensions or national assistance scales or both.[44] The best-supported attracted 150 names; two of these EDMs, both strongly backed, had leftish sponsors.

There were only 40 Labour backbenchers who failed to sign any of these motions. Support was clearly associated with education, occupation, and region. The Elementary/Secondary+ and Elementary-educated groups were the most enthusiastic, whilst the University contingent were the least keen. Not surprisingly, the Workers were keener than both the Professions and the Miscellaneous Occupations, between whom there was little to choose. Amongst the regional groups, northern and Welsh Members were conspicuous in their enthusiasm for the social welfare EDMs.

The value of Yule's Q for the fifteen possible pairs of motions ranged from $-0 \cdot 20$ to $0 \cdot 71$. Generally, the values were relatively low. Despite these low values, the occupational distribution of support for five of the six motions is generally consistent, the Workers emerging as the keenest group for each of these five. The sole exception (EDM 46/51) attracted few signatories and was tabled by Front Bench Members.

TABLE 39. LEFTISM, DEFENCE POLICY, AND SOCIAL SECURITY

Signers	Left		Other Defence and Nuclear Critics		Rest		Total
	No.	%	No.	%	No.	%	
Three or more	18	45	16	30	31	25	65
Two	3	8	17	29	32	26	52
One	16	40	12	21	35	28	63
Nil	3	8	11	20	27	22	41
Total	40	100	56	100	125	100	221

$\chi_6^2 = 16 \cdot 07$. Significant at 2% level.

The Left, as Table 39 shows, provided the largest proportion of the heaviest signers; on the other hand, the Left and the Other Defence and Nuclear Critics were as numerous amongst the apathetic (the signers of one motion or none) as the Rest.

[43] Yule's Q yielded $0 \cdot 72$ and $0 \cdot 82$ for two of the pairs of motions. One pair (EDMs 27/51 and 55/51) gave a value of $0 \cdot 12$. All but 3 of the signatories of EDM 27/51 had, however, signed EDM 56/51 and would have qualified by virtue of these signatures.

[44] EDMs 24/51, 46/51, 47/53, 84/53, 93/53, and 7/54.

Education and Health

The attempt of the Conservative Government to enforce economies in the education estimates of local authorities provoked three EDMs protesting against the government's pressure.[45] Another very popular motion rejected the idea of achieving any economies either by reducing the school-leaving age or raising the age at which children began school;[46] and another with 14 signatures exhorted the government to press local authorities not to make economies in student grants.[47] The sponsors were not clearly identified with any ideological section of the party, and were nearly always former school teachers or dons.

The National Health Service attracted two EDMs. In March 1952, 71 Members declared that the House should proceed no further with the Conservative Government's Bill to impose new charges on users of the health service;[48] and the following December 41 MPs expressed alarm at the government's decision to reduce hospital staffs.[49]

These motions on health and education cut across the normal structural groupings of the party.[50] Indeed, only region, and in the case of education, seniority were related significantly to Members' concern. On the education motions, the backbenchers who had been elected in 1950 and 1951 were much more generous signers than their seniors; amongst the regional groups the northern Members felt most strongly on both health and education.

The contrast with the appeal of the motions on defence, foreign policy, and the death penalty was marked. Education and health appealed both to the Professions and to the Workers—to the former because of their own specialist interest in these services and to the latter as representatives of their beneficiaries.

There was almost no difference in the response of the various ideological groupings to these motions. The Left was not significantly keener than either the Other Defence and Nuclear Critics or the Rest.

Housing

Housing provoked a single EDM—one which drew more than 100 signatures. In April 1952 Mrs. Eirene White tabled a motion deploring the government's intention to reduce "still further" the standards for council houses.[51] The strongest support amongst the occupational groups, as with the social welfare EDMs, was found amongst the Workers; Trade Unionists were also much keener than both the CLP sponsored and the Co-operators, and the Elementary educated than the University graduates. The apathy of the graduates proves on inspection to have been largely due to the inertia of the U1's (public school and Oxford or Cambridge) who contributed only 4 signatures out of a potential 29. The Professional men and the Constituency sponsored, so zealous in matters of penal reform, were notably reticent in this as in some other areas of social welfare.

[45] EDMs 36/51, 91/51, and 46/52. [46] EDM 10/51. [47] EDM 39/51.
[48] EDM 52/51. [49] EDM 26/52.
[50] The value of Yule's Q for the two Health Service EDMs is 0·64. There is no significant difference in the occupational composition of the signatories of the two motions. The value of Yule's Q for eight of the ten possible pairs of motions on education ranges from 0·61 to 0·90. Examination of two EDMs (36/51 and 91/51) which, in combination with EDM 10/51, yield the relatively low values of 0·44 and 0·51 respectively shows that their occupational composition was not dissimilar from that of the signatories of the remaining motions.
[51] EDM 61/51.

The Left were, if anything, rather less attracted to this EDM than the Rest; and the Other Defence and Nuclear Critics displayed less interest than either of the other groups (Table 40).

TABLE 40. LEFTISM, DEFENCE POLICY, AND HOUSING

	Left		Other Defence and Nuclear Critics		Rest		Total
	No.	%	No.	%	No.	%	
Signers	12	30	22	39	61	49	95
Non-Signers	28	70	34	61	64	51	126
Total	40	100	56	100	125	100	221

$\chi_2^2 = 4 \cdot 79$. Significant at 10% level.

Equal Pay

Equal pay is a perennial issue in British politics. In July 1951 Douglas Houghton, former Secretary of the Inland Revenue Staff Federation, called on the government to announce a date by which a beginning would be made with the introduction of equal pay in the Civil Service. Forty-six Labour MPs and a number of Conservatives and Liberals signed this EDM.[52]

The defeat of the Labour Government 3 months later seemed to dispel any inhibitions Labour Members might have about pressing for equal pay. At the beginning of the first session of the new Parliament, Houghton repeated his EDM which on this occasion attracted nearly 120[53] signatures.[54] A similar motion was put down at the start of the next session,[55] whilst the sponsors at the beginning of the 1953–4 session peremptorily called for "tangible progress without further delay"—a demand subscribed to by more than 160 Labour MPs.[56] An earlier motion put down just before the budget of 1953 asked for the implementation of equal pay during the forthcoming financial year.[57]

In the 1951–5 Parliament the strongest associations were with education and sponsorship.[58] The keenest supporters were not the University members but the Secondary school men. The Elementary and Elementary/Secondary+ groups seemed apathetic; nearly half of their members failed to sign any of the equal pay motions as against just over a tenth of the Secondary educated. The Trade Unionists displayed less enthusiasm than their colleagues; fewer than a third of them were enrolled amongst the heavy signers (2–4 motions) compared with more than half of the Co-operators and the CLP backbenchers.

There was also a connection with the size of majority; MPs for marginal seats, perhaps sensitive to pressure from organized groups, signed frequently; the trend was not completely regular, however, so the relationship is blurred. Occupation and region yielded two tentative associations—both significant at the 10 per cent level. South-eastern MPs and Londoners signed often, probably because of the large number of women in the Civil Service in these

[52] EDM 85/*51*.

[53] Including the signatories of an amendment which would have widened the Motion's scope.

[54] EDM 1/51.   [55] EDM 1/52.   [56] EDM 2/53.   [57] EDM 63/52.

[58] The value of Yule's Q for the six pairs of motions ranges from 0·62 to 0·80. The educational composition of the two EDMs yielding the lowest value of Q (EDMs 1/51 and 1/52) is uncannily similar.

regions, whilst northern and Scottish Members signed more rarely. Of the occupational groups, the Workers were much the most lukewarm.

The division-lobby rebels, especially the Left, were clearly more concerned than the loyalists, as Table 41 shows. A third of the rebels were amongst the heaviest signers, compared with a sixth of the Rest.

TABLE 41. LEFTISM, DEFENCE POLICY AND EQUAL PAY

Signers	Left		Other Defence and Nuclear Critics		Rest		Total
	No.	%	No.	%	No.	%	
Three or more	13	33	18	32	20	16	51
Two	15	38	14	25	26	21	55
One	10	25	12	21	31	25	53
Nil	2	5	12	21	48	38	62
Total	40	100	56	100	125	100	221

$\chi_6^2 = 23 \cdot 07$. Significant at $0 \cdot 1\%$.

Fewer than 50 Labour MPs signed the equal pay motion of the 1950–1 session, so it is not surprising that there were few associations between type-class and attitude. Nevertheless, the figures are highly consistent with those for the later Parliament. The Secondary-educated and University graduates, the CLP sponsored and the Professional men were more concerned about the issue than the Elementary educated, the Trade Unionists, and the Workers.

Thus on the simple material issues such as social security payments, the Trade Unionists/ Workers/Elementary-educated group came into its own, generally supporting the EDMs more generously than the CLP/Professional/University section. On the social services, where professional feeling as well as material interests were engaged, no important differences can be discerned; and on equal pay, where egalitarian passion counted for as much as bread-and-butter concerns, the Trade Unionists and the Workers were the least enthusiastic.

Royal Grants

The question of royal grants recurred frequently in the nineteenth century. Radicals criticized the sums spent on the upkeep of the royal parks and palaces, on royal perquisites, and the Civil List. At this time radicalism was associated, not with programmes of public expenditure, but with retrenchment. The age of the social services had yet to come. Radicals stood for economy in government, and one place where economies might be made was in the expenditure devoted to the monarchy. In the early 1870's, some radicals, like Joseph Chamberlain and Dilke, went further and openly espoused republicanism; whilst many who made no open attacks on the institution of monarchy, kept a watchful eye for examples of royal extravagance or regal waste.

These attitudes to monarchy were transmitted to some members of the British Labour Movement. Radicalism entered the bloodstream of British socialism in two ways. Many of the pioneers of trade unionism and the ILP had been brought up in the radical tradition and had thoroughly absorbed the radical spirit. Their socialism began where their radicalism left off. The second source was more direct; many radicals joined the Labour Party with the split in and subsequent collapse of the Liberal Party during and after the First World War.

Whilst the number of professed republicans in the Labour Party was never large, suspicion of monarchy died hard; repeated criticisms were made of the alleged remoteness of the Royal Family from ordinary people, excessive ceremonial, and unnecessary expenditure.

George VI died in February 1952, 3 months after the Conservatives had returned to power. A Select Committee of the Commons was set up to consider what financial provision should be made for the new monarch and other members of the Royal Family. The Select Committee reported at the end of June and made a number of recommendations most of which were accepted by the government.

The government, following the Select Committee, proposed that the Queen should receive an annual salary of £475,000; that her husband, the Duke of Edinburgh, should be paid £40,000 a year; and that Princess Margaret, the Queen's sister, should, in the event of her marriage, receive £9000 a year over and above her existing salary. The government also proposed, in addition to certain payments which would be made for the Queen's younger children, that the Duke of Cornwall (later to become Prince of Wales) should be paid one-ninth of the revenues of the Duchy of Cornwall until he was 18, and £30,000 a year from the age of 18–21.

The Parliamentary Labour Party met on 8 July and decided to table two amendments to the government motion. One would have provided for a review of the Civil List every 10 years, and the second would have denied any payment to the Duke of Cornwall until he was 18. These amendments evidently came as a surprise, and appeared to be a response to backbench feeling. The allowance proposed for the Duke of Cornwall had provoked special hostility.[59]

Mr. Attlee, moving the official Labour amendments, conceded that public opinion liked "a certain amount of pageantry. It is a great mistake to make government too dull. . . . Therefore we on this side . . . believe that it is right to have a certain amount of pageantry, because it pleases people and it also counteracts a tendency to other forms of excitement."[60] Nevertheless, there was a case for "a fairly steady and constant review". Prices might fall, though he disclaimed any great optimism on this score; there might be changes, too, in the make-up of society and the conception of what was proper and convenient.[61]

Emrys Hughes, who led the critics of royal expenditure, began by describing himself, "like General Eisenhower", as a republican.[62] He moved an amendment to reduce the Queen's allowance to £250,000 a year, and expressed surprise that the government should have supported "the largest wage claim of the century". The cost of the British Monarchy was much higher than that of the American Presidency and the monarchies of the smaller European states.[63] James Carmichael, of Glasgow, was not, like Emrys Hughes, prepared to call himself a republican; he cited with approval the late John Wheatley,[64] who had once said that "he would never raise one finger to destroy a capitalist monarchy in order to replace it by a capitalistic republic". Nevertheless, Carmichael thought that pageantry was exaggerated and could be curtailed. It was wrong that the salary proposed for the Duke of Edinburgh should be higher

[59] *Daily Telegraph*, 9 July 1952.   [60] HC Deb. 503, c. 1328.   [61] *Ibid.*, cc. 1327–9.
[62] The debate took place during the week of the Republican Convention which nominated Eisenhower.
[63] HC Deb. 503, cc. 1343–6.
[64] Minister of Health in the 1924 Labour Government.

than the Prime Minister's, and wrong, too, that the House should vote a further £9000 a year to Princess Margaret in the event of her marriage without knowing anything about the means of her husband. Nor was it right that the House should, in 1952, provide a pension for the Duke of Cornwall's widow which was unlikely to be paid until the year 2000. "We are protesting against this; we are protesting against the amount of ritual which is going on." Carmichael concluded by chaffing Attlee with the speech he had made, as Leader of the Opposition, on the Civil List proposals made in 1937.[65] The themes of excessive display, the large number of palaces used by the Royal Family, and the psychological effect of these grants on industrial workers were taken up by Victor Yates and Ernest Fernyhough, both of whom, like Hughes and Carmichael, belonged to the pacifistic section of the party.[66]

In contrast to Hughes and his friends, Arthur Irvine, who had been associated with Aneurin Bevan in the revolt of the 57 Varieties, emphasized the value of the Crown to the Commonwealth. The Select Committee's report bore evidence of the "substantial economy" which had been made in royal expenditure. The vast majority of the British people liked pageantry and liked it very much. In the development of the backward countries, many of which were inside the Commonwealth, the Crown would be "a most beneficial and advantageous factor". It was a mistake to think that radical policies, even extreme policies, required the abandonment of traditional forms. His own Merseyside constituents would let none outdo them in loyalty to "this great institution of the monarchy".[67]

The government's resolutions were carried, reported to the House,[68] and then embodied in the Civil List Bill which received its Second and Third Reading within a fortnight. On the Second Reading, James Hudson repeated the charges of extravagance and called for a full-scale inquiry.[69] The debate on Third Reading was remarkable for the number of Members, closely linked with Aneurin Bevan, who spoke warmly of the monarchy. Jennie Lee, though critical of some aspects of royal expenditure and the functioning of the monarchy, stressed that "we ought not to have a shabby Royal Family and we ought not to have the job done too cheaply".[70] Ian Mikardo described the monarchy as "an institution valuable in itself", and declared that he would rather have the hero worship of monarchy than "the hero worship of strange people like film stars and others that goes on in some other countries".[71] Tom Driberg proclaimed that a constitutional monarchy "must represent in its dignity the true full dignity and the wealth of the great nation of which it is the symbolical head". Nor did he think that the British people would want to reduce the Royal Family to "what might be called a Scandinavian level and have them bicycling round London all the time".[72]

In the first debate there were five divisions. Two of these were official Labour amendments; one called for a 10-year review of the Civil List and the second opposed any provision for the Duke of Cornwall until he reached the age of 18.

There were also three unofficial backbench amendments. That tabled by Emrys Hughes, which sought to reduce the Queen's allowance to £250,000 a year, found 26 supporters from the Labour ranks (including tellers), but no fewer than 106 Labour MPs, including the Front Bench men, went into the lobby in support of the government. The second amendment, to cut the Duke of Edinburgh's allowance from £40,000 a year to £10,000 a year, attracted

[65] HC Deb. 503, cc. 1374–8.
[66] *Ibid.*, cc. 1387–91 and 1398–1403.   [67] *Ibid.*, cc. 1348–51.
[68] Which was, of course, the same body as the committee which had considered the proposals.
[69] HC Deb. 503, cc. 2009–15.   [70] HC Deb. 504, cc. 675–7.
[71] HC Deb. 503, cc. 696–9.   [72] HC Deb. 504, cc. 704–6.

the support of 57 Labour Members; whilst the third, which sought to omit altogether the sum of £9000 a year which was to be paid to Princess Margaret in the event of her marriage, rallied 114 backbenchers to the cause of socialist economy.

Scrutiny of the division lists shows a marked consistency in the pattern of voting. Twenty-one backbenchers, who voted in only one of the three divisions, have been excluded. A few Members abstained in one or other divisions but voted in two, and these abstentions have been treated as votes for the government. When allowance is made for these factors, only one Member voted "inconsistently"[73] as compared with his colleagues. Tables in Annex 3 show the distribution of the votes on the three divisions.

The votes cast in these three divisions form an almost perfect Guttman scale,[74] and it is possible to classify the party, on the issue of royal grants, into four groups:

The Left	26
Moderate Left	23
Moderate Right	34
The Right	31
	114[75]

The Left consisted of those Members who voted consistently for the reduction of the allowances in all three divisions; the Moderate Left supported the government over the Queen's allowance but voted for a reduction in the sum due to Prince Philip; the Moderate Right supported the allowances for both the Queen and the Duke but voted against the sum recommended for Princess Margaret on marriage. The Right voted consistently with the government.

There was a marked overlap between the Foreign Affairs and Defence Left of 1951–5[76] and the Royal Grants Left, as Table 42 shows.

TABLE 42. LEFTISM, DEFENCE POLICY, AND ROYAL GRANTS

	The Left		Others		
	No.	%	No.	%	Total
Left and Moderate Left	16	80	33	35	49
Moderate Right and Right	4	20	61	65	65
Total	20	100	94	100	114

$\chi^2_1 = 13 \cdot 561$. Significant at $0 \cdot 1\%$.

[73] In the sense that he voted for the reduction in the Duke of Edinburgh's allowance, along with 56 of his colleagues, but against the omission of the allowance for Princess Margaret—even though the dissident Labour element grew to 114 on this grant.

[74] For a description of Guttman scales, see Annex 1.

[75] The one MP who voted "inconsistently" has been omitted.

[76] Defined as those who rebelled with Aneurin Bevan on at least two out of the three major floor revolts of the Parliament—the Japanese Peace Treaty vote of November 1951, the 57 Varieties revolt of March 1952, and the Nuclear Weapons rebellion of March 1955.

Of much greater interest is that this overlap is almost wholly provided by what may be termed the irregular and pacifistic Left—men like Emrys Hughes, Sydney Silverman, Craddock, and Fernyhough. The friendly references which Bevan's nearest followers made to the monarchy in the Civil List debates have already been mentioned. Bevan himself occupied a Moderate Right position, voting to maintain both the Queen's and the Duke of Edinburgh's grants, but voting against the provision to be made for Princess Margaret's marriage. Tom Driberg went even farther and consistently supported the government. Many of Bevan's close associates did not vote, though, as has been noted, several of them spoke in the debate held a week later.[77]

Differences between the various social strata were small. Trade Unionists adopted a rather more left-wing position on this question than the CLP men, and the Elementary educated were slightly more radical than the graduates, though in neither case were the differences statistically significant. There was little variation in the responses of the Workers, the Miscellaneous Occupations, and the Businessmen; but the behaviour of the Professional men is notable. Less than a third of the latter took a Left or Moderate Left line, whilst half of the remainder did so.[78] There was, too, a noteworthy regional cleavage. Two-thirds of the Members from English seats took a Right or Moderate Right line, whilst nearly two-thirds of the Scottish and Welsh Members were found on the Left or Moderate Left. This regional contrast helps to account for the differences within the University group, the U4's being more hostile than the U1's, U2's, and U3's. The Professionals, the graduates from Oxford, Cambridge, and the public schools, and the English Members were to be found mainly in the monarchical camp. The vote against the government's proposals was a gut reaction, coming from those groups—regional and occupational—which constituted the real core of the Labour movement.

Opposition to royal grants was also closely linked with hostility to conscription and nuclear weapons. Twenty-four of those who voted against conscription in November 1953 voted in the royal grants controversy, and three-quarters of them were found in the Left or Moderate Left camp. Opponents of royal grants constituted the same proportion—three-quarters—of those who voted for Beswick's new clause on the Atomic Energy Authority Bill, and also of the men who abstained with Aneurin Bevan in 1955.[79]

Zeal for economy in the conduct of the monarchy was clearly linked with pacifistic feeling; the distinction between the radical and pacifistic section of the Left, and the more specifically socialist and modern section around Bevan, is sharp.

[77] There is the possibility, of course, that some of the Bevanites may have been influenced by fear of the presumed electoral unpopularity of resisting increases in the grants paid to the Royal Family. Even if this were true, however, the distinction between the hard-core Bevanites and the "irregular Left" would remain; the latter would either have differed from the Bevanites in their estimate of public reaction or, alternatively, would have been prepared to brave hostile public feeling. Either way, a clear difference of attitude is revealed. The issue of royal grants recurred in 1971. On this occasion a number of ex-Bevanites, including Crossman, voted against the proposed increase; the main burden of Crossman's complaint was the tax privilege enjoyed by the Queen. There was, interestingly enough, virtually no relationship between the behaviour of Members in the divisions in 1952 and the vote on the Civil List Bill in 1971. Moreover, the Welsh and Scottish Members were in no way conspicuous in the backbench Labour attack on the Civil List proposals. The opposition to the Civil List Bill came disproportionately from Members of the Tribune Group (in some respects the successors to the Bevanites) many of whom had been elected since 1959.

[78] Significant at the 5 per cent level when Professions tested against all other occupational groups combined.

[79] These figures relate to those actually voting in at least two of the royal grants divisions.

Royal Grants 1945–50

The issue of royal grants had arisen nearly 5 years before, when Labour was in government. There were only 2 divisions, however, and on one of these, which was called in rather curious circumstances, the Whips were put on. Moreover, a large number of Members abstained from one or other of the divisions. The data, therefore, are more ambiguous than those for 1952.

Princess Elizabeth, the heir to the Throne, married the Duke of Edinburgh in November 1947. A Select Committee of the House was appointed to consider what financial provision should be made for them. The committee was divided, a majority recommending an extra £25,000 a year over and above the sum then being paid to the Princess; the minority on the committee wanted the additional sum to be cut by £5000 to £20,000 a year.

At a meeting of the Parliamentary Labour Party, backbenchers actually defeated the government on this issue, by about 85 to 70 votes. The leadership, realizing that it was in no position to impose discipline, agreed to allow a free vote to Labour MPs when the proposal was discussed in Parliament.[80]

When the matter came before the House, Emrys Hughes moved an amendment which would have cancelled the whole of the extra sum proposed for the Princess; at the end of the debate the rebels belatedly, and somewhat half-heartedly, called for a division. The government put on the Whips and with the aid of the Conservatives overwhelmed the rebels by 345 to 33.[81]

The second amendment, moved by Maurice Webb, Chairman of the Parliamentary Labour Party, posed a bigger challenge. This amendment sought to give effect to the recommendation of the minority on the Select Committee who had wanted to reduce the annuity to £20,000. This, too, was defeated, but on a free vote and by a smaller margin. Without the help of the Conservatives, the government would have lost heavily.

One hundred and twenty-seven backbenchers voted in both divisions, and, as in 1952, the votes form an almost perfect Guttman scale. Twenty-two Labour Members voted against the government on each occasion; these twenty-two can be termed the Left. Fifty-one, who can be called the Right, supported the government both times, whilst the Centre comprised 53 backbenchers who voted with the government in the first division but against them in the second. There was also one Member, Mr. Reginald Paget, who voted with the rebels against the whole of the proposed new sum, and with the government against the recommendation to reduce the annuity by £5000. There were, in addition, 116 Members who voted in one, but not in both, divisions. Of these, the position of 83 who abstained in the first division but joined the rebels in the second, seems fairly clear. We cannot class them with the Left; but since they had had the opportunity to support the government in the first division but did not take it, we can assume that on this question they lie to the left of the Centre group.

With these data we now have four classes:

The Left	22
The Moderate Left	83
The Centre	53
The Right	51
	209

[80] See the *Daily Telegraph*, 18 Dec. 1947, and R. K. Alderman, Discipline in the Parliamentary Labour Party, 1945–51, *Parliamentary Affairs*, Summer, 1965. The *Daily Telegraph* described the meeting as stormy.
[81] HC Deb. 445, cc. 1747–58.

It must be stressed, however, that the interpolation of the Moderate Left (the 83 MPs who abstained in the first division and voted with government in the second) between the Left and the Centre, though reasonable enough, rests ultimately on an intuitive judgement, and the four classes cannot be regarded as constituting a strict Guttman scale. The three remaining classes—Left, Centre, and Right—do however, as mentioned above, form such a scale.

Analysis of the social and political characteristics gives a similar picture to that obtained from the 1952 votes. The greatest antipathy to the grants was displayed by the Workers and the Miscellaneous Occupations; the Business group were the most favourable, followed by the Professions. Only a tenth of the Workers were on the Right compared with nearly a third of the Professions and half of the Business Members. Likewise, the Trade Unionists and the Elementary educated were markedly more hostile than the CLP men and the University Members—though within the University section there was no difference between the various categories of graduates. Opposition was stronger amongst the Scots and Welsh than amongst backbenchers from English constituencies. As in 1952, opinions on royal grants were closely related to opinions on conscription and on foreign policy. The supporters of conscription were much more favourable than their pacifistic colleagues to the annuity; in the same way, the Foreign Policy Right were significantly more sympathetic than the Combined Lefts. Within the Combined Lefts (Foreign Policy) the Left and Ultra Left were disproportionately concentrated amongst the Royal Grants Left and Moderate Left. The Centre Left were conspicuous amongst the Royal Grants Centre.

Exclusion of the rather ambiguous group, the Moderate Left, does not alter this picture in any important way.

CONCLUSION

Broadly speaking, it would be true to say that the occupational, educational, and sponsorship cleavages on these domestic issues followed a crude ideological/material division. The middle-class element of the Parliamentary Party took the lead in the campaign against capital punishment, on the question of internal security, and on the political liberties of civil servants; the one material issue on which, to judge from the educational breakdown, they felt more strongly than the Workers, was the question of equal pay—which carried with it an important appeal of principle. On social welfare and housing, the Workers responded more strongly than the middle-class Members; and on education and health, where material interests merged with vocational pride, the two groups reacted in much the same way.

The ideological division in the party tended to follow the class cleavage; the Left provided the keenest abolitionists, a large and disproportionate share of those who protested at the report of the Masterman Committee, and, not surprisingly, the great majority of the critics of the Civil Service security measures. They were also more conspicuous than other groups in pressing the claims of equal pay; they were also enthusiastic supporters of one clearly material demand, the call for higher pensions and assistance rates, though here the heavy signers amongst the Left were drawn almost entirely from the irregular and pacifistic Left rather than from those closest to Bevan.

Of special interest are the deviations from the general pattern. The call for an amnesty for deserters from the armed forces came essentially from the Trade Union working-class element; towards hunting, the middle-class Members, in general, and the Left, in particular, displayed no special hostility; indeed, the vote against Seymour Cocks's Bill came overwhelmingly from the better-educated, non-manual section of the party.

On royal grants, the Professions took a less hostile view than the Workers and the Miscellaneous Occupations; and it was the irregular and pacifistic Left, not the Bevanites proper, who were prominent amongst the critics of royal expenditure.

As in the controversies over defence and foreign policy, the cleavage pattern was rather more complex than popular impressions would indicate. Whilst it is easy to identify some questions within the Labour Party as middle-class issues and others as working-class issues, there remains a broad and uncertainly defined policy area of confused identity and doubtful allegiance. In this policy area, middle-class ideology may meet and merge with proletarian class consciousness or, alternatively, middle-class calculation may clash with trade-union feeling; as happens much more frequently in the Conservative Party, a diversity of motives may create a temporary coalition of opposites; and such alliances, short-lived though they may be, help to temper the acerbity of the more sharply defined and long-enduring sectional disputes.

CHAPTER 7

The Social Composition of the Conservative Party

"Look at the Tory Party in the House of Commons. Eighty-six lawyers, more than 100 business executives or directors, twenty-six journalists, thirty-eight farmers. You can't say that *that* represents an 'upper-class' image."
(IAIN MACLEOD, interviewed by Kenneth Harris, *The Observer*, 26 Nov. 1961.)

1945–50

The defeat of 1945 left the Conservative Party at its weakest for a generation. Two hundred and thirteen MPs (including allies such as Liberal Nationals and "Nationals") returned to Westminster; not since 1906 had Conservative representation in the House of Commons fallen to such a low figure.

The length of the Parliament elected in 1935 was responsible for an exceptionally large number of voluntary retirements in 1945; as a result the newly elected Members constituted more than two-fifths of the backbench party—a remarkable number for a party which had suffered so heavily at the polls. The party had lost nearly all its industrial and semi-industrial seats; it now essentially represented the suburbs, the seaside resorts, and the countryside.

As in the Labour Party, certain Members such as Front Benchers, Whips, and occupants of certain politically sensitive posts, were excluded from consideration. Members who entered the House at byelections in and after 1945 have, however, been included.

The backbench Conservative Party, which consisted of 191 Members, has been analysed according to six different criteria—occupation, school, university, age, year of entry into Parliament, and region. It had been hoped to classify Members according to whether their constituencies were urban or rural. Unfortunately, because the constituencies are officially described in terms of the local government units existing in 1918, when the last major redistribution of constituencies took place, it was not possible to make any division between urban and rural divisions that would have been both meaningful and reasonably accurate.

First of all, Members were divided into four major occupational classes (Fig. 18) viz. Business, Farmers, Professions, and Miscellaneous Occupations. The Business class comprised all company directors, business executives, brokers, and underwriters: the Professional class all Members following a recognized profession. Miscellaneous Occupations covered journalists, publicists, political organizers, administrators (other than those employed in business), housewives, and a few Members who lived on private means.

Both the Business class and the Professions were broken down into three sub-categories. The distinction between the two largest business groups, directors of public companies[1] and

---

[1] Defined here as companies whose shares are quoted on the London Stock Exchange.

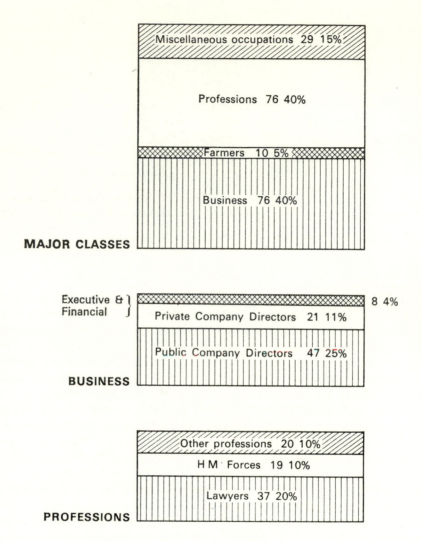

Fig. 18. The Conservative Party, 1945–50: by occupation.

directors of private companies,[2] corresponds very roughly to the division between big business and medium or small business. "Business executives and finance" was a small residual group of Members who held no directorships but who made their living in commerce, banking, or industry.

The Professions class comprised regular officers from the armed forces, lawyers, and members of other professions such as doctors and architects.[3]

[2] Defined here as companies whose shares are not quoted on the London Stock Exchange

[3] The problem of multiple occupation is important when attempting to classify Conservative Members. Some MPs claim to have an occupation in addition to that of company director; such Members are classified as belonging to the Business Group.

Secondly, Members were divided into four school categories (Fig. 19): Clarendon Public Schools, Other Public Schools, Non-Public Schools, and the Rest. The Clarendon Schools are the nine traditional English public schools and include the most expensive and exclusive public schools.[4] Four-fifths of the Members in this category went to one of the three leading schools—Eton, Harrow, and Winchester; and more than half came from a single school—Eton.

The Other Public Schools category contained those MPs educated at any other recognized British public school.[5] The Non-Public School group was a diverse class consisting of all Members (other than women and those educated in the Commonwealth) who had not had a public-school education. Some had attended private schools, some had been to old-established grammar schools, and others had been educated at secondary or elementary council schools.

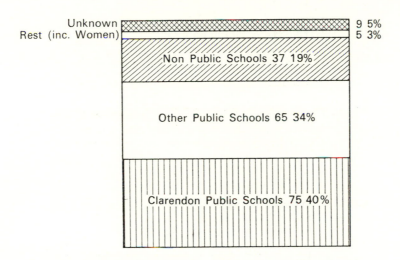

FIG. 19. The Conservative Party, 1945–50: by schools attended.

The Rest was a residual class containing the seven women MPs and six Members who were educated in the Commonwealth.

Next come the five University classes (Fig. 20): Oxford, Cambridge, Other Universities, Sandhurst, and Non-Graduates. The Other Universities group comprised Members who were educated at provincial, Scottish, Irish, or overseas universities. The Non-Graduates included Members from military, naval, or air-force colleges other than Sandhurst as well as those who had gone straight from school to a job.

Two further methods of classifying Members—according to age (Fig. 21) and length of parliamentary service—require no elaboration. As in the Labour Party, the Member was classified according to his age at 31 December 1949.

The party divided equally into two main occupational groups—Business and the Professions.

---

[4] So named because they were the subject of a Royal Commission enquiry under Lord Clarendon in 1864. The nine schools are Eton, Harrow, Winchester, Shrewsbury, Rugby, Charterhouse, Westminster, St. Paul's and Merchant Taylors'.

[5] Defined here as those schools represented on the Headmasters Conference or the Governing Bodies Association of Public Schools.

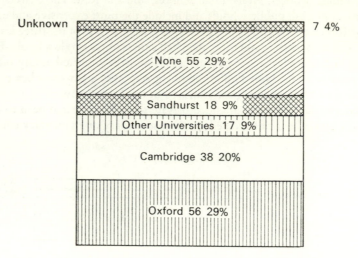

FIG. 20. The Conservative Party, 1945–50: by universities attended.

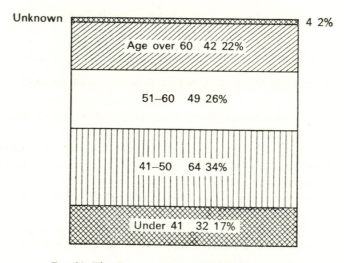

FIG. 21. The Conservative Party, 1945–50: by age.

Seventy-six MPs were Businessmen; exactly the same number belonged to the Professions. To these must be added 10 farmers and 29 MPs belonging to the Miscellaneous Occupations. The Business group was in turn divided into two main classes—the directors of public companies who numbered 47, and directors of private companies who came to 21. Nearly half of the Professional men were lawyers, a quarter were regular Service officers, and a quarter came from other established professions.

Educationally, the party retained its strong connection with the public schools. Two-fifths of the backbench Conservatives had gone to one of the Clarendon Schools, a category which contained the most famous and exclusive schools, and nearly three-quarters had been to a public school of some kind. A half had gone to Oxford or Cambridge, and less than a tenth to one of the provincial or Scottish universities; nearly a third, however, had not been to university at all.

The age structure of the backbench party resembled that of the Labour Party, the only difference of note being that Labour had a rather higher proportion of the over-60's.

A third of the backbenchers represented constituencies in London and the south-east. Twenty came from the West Country, and 33 from Scotland.

The Labour Party, as we have seen, was split into three distinct cultural groups—the University-educated CLP-sponsored Professional men, the Elementary-educated Trade-Union-sponsored Workers, and the Miscellaneous Occupations, who, though largely CLP or Co-operative sponsored, had a more mixed educational background. In the Conservative Party, the interrelationships between occupation and education were much less pronounced, the main differences occurring within the Business group. Thus the directors of public companies included more with a public-school education of some sort and more Members who had been to the Clarendon Schools. It must be stressed, however, that the numbers involved are not large. A strikingly high proportion of the public company directors had attended universities other than Oxford or Cambridge. The lawyers came overwhelmingly from Oxford or Cambridge whereas, not surprisingly, very few of the regular officers had had a university education. There were few differences in the school backgrounds of the other classes. The directors of private companies represented safer constituencies than members of other occupations—a divergence from the position in the 1955–9 Parliament.

The directors of private companies had less parliamentary experience than their colleagues and were a little younger; the lawyers were markedly younger but had actually served longer in Parliament than other Conservative backbenchers, indicating that lawyers tended to be elected at a younger age than Conservatives from other occupations.

Perhaps the most notable contrast emerges when the age structure of the various school groups is examined; nearly two-thirds of the Clarendon School men were under 50 compared with a third of the non-public-school Members. Etonians, clearly, were at an advantage; they could begin a parliamentary career at a much younger age than those who had had to establish themselves in life by their own efforts.

In the study of the composition of the Conservative Party in the 1955–9 Parliament the authors concluded: ". . . particular educational and social characteristics do not cumulate as markedly as they do in the Labour party, but blend and combine to produce a relatively undifferentiated and integral party."[6] This conclusion is even more applicable to the Conservative Party of 1945–50.

Table 43 (a)–(f) gives detailed figures of the composition of the Parliamentary Conservative Party. Regions have been defined in the same way as for the Labour Party, except that Wales has been merged with the Midlands.

[6] S. E. Finer, H. B. Berrington, and D. J. Bartholomew, *Backbench Opinion in the House of Commons, 1955–59*, p. 85.

TABLE 43. THE CONSERVATIVE PARTY, 1945–50

(a) *By Occupation*

	No.	%
Business		
Public company directors	47	25
Private company directors	21	11
Business executive and financial	8	4
	76	40
Farmers	10	5
Professions		
Lawyers	37	20
HM Forces	19	10
Other professions	20	10
	76	40
Miscellaneous	29	15
Total	191	100[a]

(b) *By Schools Attended*

	No.	%
Clarendon Public	75	40
Other Public	65	34
Non-Public	37	19
Rest (incl. Women)	5	3
Unknown	9	5
Total	191	100[a]

(c) *By Universities Attended*

	No.	%
Oxford	56	29
Cambridge	38	20
Other	17	9
	111	59
Sandhurst	18	9
None	55	29
Unknown	7	4
Total	191	100[a]

[a] Apparent discrepancies in addition due to rounding.

TABLE 43 (*continued*)

(d) *By Age*

	No.	%
> 60	42	22
51–60	49	26
41–50	64	34
Under 41	32	17
Unknown	4	2
Total	191	100[a]

(e) *By Year of First Entering Parliament*

	No.	%
Pre-war	83	43
1940–4	27	14
1945–9	81	43
Total	191	100

(f) *By Region*

	No.	%
Metropolitan	18	9
South-east	46	24
Eastern	9	5
Northern	14	7
Midlands and Wales	17	9
Western	21	11
Lancashire and Cheshire	23	12
Scotland	33	17
Ulster	10	5
Total	191	100[a]

[a] Apparent discrepancies in addition due to rounding.

THE 1950–1 AND 1951–5 PARLIAMENTS

As there was little change in the composition of the backbench Conservative Party between the election of 1950 and that of 1951, the figures for the two parliaments have been combined—as in the case of the Labour Party.[7]

[7] Except, as with the Labour Party, for age and year of entry into Parliament.

The election of 1950 had been marked by substantial Conservative gains, and that of 1951, which brought the Conservative Party back to power, had shown a further modest advance. The changes in individual membership of the party, however, did not bring any big change in its occupational and educational balance.

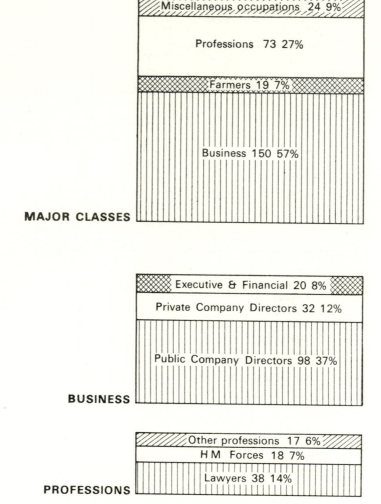

FIG. 22. The Conservative Party, 1951–5: by occupation.

Business somewhat strengthened its position, for nearly half of the backbenchers came from its ranks, with the directors of public companies being predominant. The Professions had fallen behind, and now numbered less than a third; the Miscellaneous Occupations had also lost ground, relatively speaking (Fig. 22).

There was little change in the educational origins of the party. The Clarendon Public Schools still supplied nearly 40 per cent of the backbench party, and the total public-school contingent comprised nearly three-quarters of the Members (Fig. 23). Nor was there much

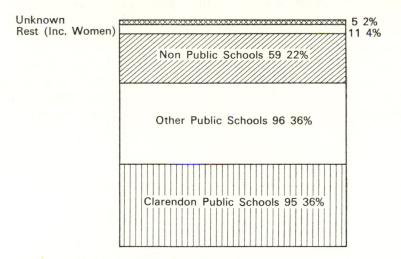

Unknown — 5 2%
Rest (Inc. Women) — 11 4%

Non Public Schools 59 22%

Other Public Schools 96 36%

Clarendon Public Schools 95 36%

FIG. 23. The Conservative Party, 1951–5: by schools attended.

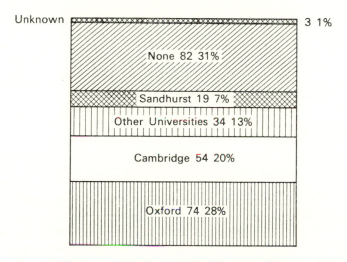

Unknown — 3 1%

None 82 31%

Sandhurst 19 7%

Other Universities 34 13%

Cambridge 54 20%

Oxford 74 28%

FIG. 24. The Conservative Party, 1951–5: by universities attended.

difference in the proportion of Members coming from the various universities. Oxford and Cambridge had much the same share as they had had in 1945, whilst the Other Universities rose a little (Fig. 24).

For this and the following Parliament it was possible, as a result of the redistribution of constituencies, which took place in 1948, to classify constituencies according to their degree of "urbanism". All borough constituencies in England and Wales were classified as urban, together with those county constituencies in which the proportion of people living in rural districts was less than a third; those in which the population living in rural districts constituted between a third and a half were classified as semi-rural; and constituencies where more than half the inhabitants lived in rural districts were termed rural. Population figures were derived from the 1951 census.

This method of calculation was not applied to Scotland because her local government structure and nomenclature differ from that of England and Wales. Scottish constituencies are shown separately and divided into burghs and counties. Ulster, because of its distinctive political culture and because it contains so few constituencies, has not been divided into urban and rural categories.

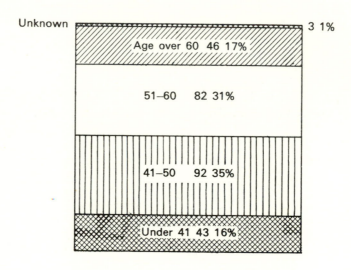

FIG. 25. The Conservative Party, 1951–5: by age.

The interrelationships between the various social characteristics resemble those of 1955–9 much more than they do those of 1945. Thus in 1951 more of the public company directors than of the directors of private companies had been to Oxford or Cambridge and the former, in contrast to the 1945 Parliament, tended to represent the safer constituencies, but, like the public company directors of 1945, more of them had been to a Clarendon School; moreover, only a fifth of them came from non-public schools compared with two-fifths of the directors of private companies. They were considerably older than the directors of private companies and had substantially more parliamentary experience. As in 1955–9, they were a better entrenched and more well-established group within the party than the private company directors.

The Clarendon School Members were considerably younger than their fellow Members, and the Public School group as a whole represented safer constituencies.

There is little cause in this study to differ from the way in which the Conservative Party in the 1955–9 Parliament was described. The party as a whole was much better integrated than was the Labour Party with its three distinct political cultures. Though there were overlaps between occupation and education, and between educational experience and age, these were nowhere as striking as those found in the Labour Party. As in 1955–9 the Business class, comprising more than half of the Parliamentary Party, turns out on inspection to have been a highly variegated group of Members, which suggests that we are unlikely to find in this period a distinctive "business" point of view within the Conservative Party at Westminster.

TABLE 44. BACKBENCH CONSERVATIVE
PARTY, 1950–1 AND 1951–5

(a) *By Occupation*

	%
Business	
Public company directors	34
Private company directors	13
Business executive and financial	6
	52[a]
Farmers	7
Professions	
Lawyers	16
HM Forces	7
Other professions	7
	30
Miscellaneous Occupations	11
Total	100

(b) *By Schools Attended*

	%
Clarendon Public	38
Other Public	34
Non-Public	21
Rest (incl. Women)	4
Unknown	2
Total	100[a]

[a] Apparent discrepancies in addition due to rounding.

TABLE 44 (*continued*)

(c) *By Universities Attended*

	%
Oxford	29
Cambridge	21
Other	13
	63
Sandhurst	7
None	29
Unknown	1
Total	100

(d) *By Character of Constituency*

	%
England and Wales:	
Urban	55
Semi-rural	8
Rural	23
	86
Scottish burghs	4
Scottish counties	7
Ulster	3
Total	100

(e) *By Region*

	%
Metropolitan	15
South-east	26
Eastern	5
Northern	8
Midlands and Wales	9
Western	10
Lancashire and Cheshire	12
Scotland	11
Ulster	4
Total	100

TABLE 44 (*continued*)

1950–1

(f) *By Age*[a]

	No.	%
> 60	28	11
51–60	58	22
41–50	104	40
Under 41	69	26
Unknown	2	1
Total	261	100

(g) *By Year of First Entering Parliament*

	No.	%
Pre-war	73	28
1940–4	29	11
1945	65	25
1950	94	36
Total	261	100

1951–5

(h) *By Age*[b]

	No.	%
> 60	46	17
51–60	82	31
41–50	92	35
Under 41	43	16
Unknown	3	1
Total	266	100

[a] Members were classified according to their ages as at 31 Dec. 1951.

[b] Members were classified according to their ages as at 31 Dec. 1955.

TABLE 44 (*continued*)

(i) *By Year of First Entering Parliament*

	No.	%
Pre-war	62	23
1940–4	18	7
1945	52	20
1950	81	31
1951–4	53	20
Total	266	100[a]

[a] Apparent discrepancies in addition due to rounding.

CHAPTER 8

The Conservative Party, 1945–55

"... that bought us the best, A perfect and absolute blank." (LEWIS CARROLL, *The Hunting of the Snark*.)

THE 1945–50 PARLIAMENT

The mood of introspection, induced by the defeat of 1945, had little effect on the parliamentary cohesion of the Conservative Party. Extensive changes were made in the party organization, one of the consequences of which was to purify and democratize the selection of candidates. Prolonged discussion took place about the formulation of a new party programme, a process which culminated in the adoption, with little dissent, of the Industrial Charter. These developments, however, were not marked by the rancorous disputes over policy, or the caballing against the party leadership, which had occurred after the last great Conservative defeat in 1906. The party trained its fire upon the socialist enemy; the austerities of the post-war years and the precarious situation of the British economy gave the party a plausible hope of returning to power at the next election.[1]

The EDMs illustrate the high degree of unity manifested by the party in the House of Commons. As has been noted, most of the backbench motions dealt with narrow, highly specific matters. Nearly a third were *Partisan*, condemning the Labour Government for actions such as its petrol-rationing scheme, for raising telephone charges, or acting unjustly towards Conservative client groups, like the farmers. The *Crossbench* EDMs were equally specific; support for the building of the Channel Tunnel, complaints about the Roosevelt memorial, demands on behalf of the publishing trade—motions such as these were typical of the Crossbench EDMs. Occasionally, a Crossbench EDM might concern a larger political question, such as self-determination for the South Tyrol, or the treatment of war pensioners, or retired civil servants; yet issues of this sort, important though they were, raised no questions of great significance for the development of Conservative policy.

The *Neutral* EDMs present much the same picture; protests against the requisitioning of land by the services, pleas for the remission of income tax for certain classes of servicemen and ex-servicemen, or for concessions to the Scottish hotel industry were characteristic of this type of backbench motion.

Indeed, taking divisions on the floor of the House and EDMs together, only three politically important issues divided the Conservative party in a public way—the Anglo-American Loan and the associated Bretton Woods Agreement, European unity, and the abolition of birching.

[1] For an account of the Conservative Party in the early post-war years see J. D. Hoffman, *The Conservative Party in Opposition*, London, 1964.

The American Loan

Since the seventies of the last century the Conservatives had been the party of empire. At first, while the party still clung to free trade, this had had no special economic implications. Since 1911, if not earlier, however, the Conservative Party had been, admittedly not with unswerving fidelity, the party of imperial preference. Joseph Chamberlain had called for the renunciation of free trade and the imposition of tariffs on foreign goods; and the introduction of this tariff would have permitted a preference to be given to goods produced in the empire by levying a rather lower charge upon them. With occasional hesitation, the Conservatives followed Chamberlain's doctrine.

It is difficult for us to grasp the emotional significance of this policy for many Conservatives in an earlier age.

> "The starting point of all my political thinking, [wrote Leopold Amery] from school days onwards, had been the British Empire or Commonwealth conceived as a unit and as the final object of patriotic emotion and action. That conception involved the desire, not only to maintain such unity as it possessed, but to make that unity more effective. . . . I regarded it as inconceivable that economic co-operation could be excluded from the picture. A union based on foreign policy and defence could have no meaning if it were not supported by co-operation for mutual welfare in peace and for the development of the economic resources of the whole."[2]

Amery saw, moreover, in such a union the answer to the social problems at home; the extension of social welfare, he thought, would only be possible in an expanding economy—and this, in turn, was not compatible with free trade. The continuance of free trade, which, Amery believed, implied a stationary economy, would foster the growth of class-based parties one of which would be committed to confiscatory socialism. Set against such a picture was Amery's vision of a Tory Party "true to a policy of Imperial greatness and social progress", not the party of a "mere negative *laissez-faire* anti-Socialism".[3]

The policy of imperial preference culminated in the Ottawa Agreements of 1932, negotiated for Britain by Joseph Chamberlain's son, Neville. So strong was the Conservative attachment to the cause of empire preference that Churchill, when discussing the draft of the Atlantic Charter with President Roosevelt, had to press for the excision of an apparently innocuous phrase which could have been interpreted as a prohibition against any discrimination in favour of empire trade.[4] Churchill, the erstwhile free trader, expressing the deeply held Conservative sentiment for imperial preference, referred later to "the comparatively small, modest Preference duties which have been built up in the British Commonwealth of Nations which have become part of our supreme common life and which are even more important to us as symbols of our indissoluble union than for their commercial advantages. . . ."[5]

The American Loan agreement came up for parliamentary approval in 1945 and was fiercely opposed by a section of the Conservative Party. The Front Bench advised abstention, but a number of Conservatives, such as Robert Boothby, spoke against the terms of the American Loan, and 74 Conservatives, accompanied by 21 Labour Members, voted against it. When the Bretton Woods Agreement Bill was taken, immediately after the approval of the Loan

[2] L. S. Amery, *My Political Life*, vol. 1, *England Before The Storm, 1896–1914*, London, 1953, p. 253.
[3] *Ibid.*, p. 255.
[4] W. S. Churchill, *The Second World War*, vol. 3, London, 1950, pp. 387–8.
[5] HC Deb. 430, cc. 21–22.

Agreement, 47 Conservatives, nearly all of whom had voted against the Loan, opposed the Bill.

One of the main grounds of opposition to the loan, and the Bretton Woods plan, lay in the damage which, it was alleged, the loan and the agreement would do to imperial preference, and empire trade. Robert Boothby argued that the proposals to eliminate discrimination in trade would "involve the break up of the British Empire. . . . If the Tory Party ceases to believe in the Empire, and the economic expansion and development of the Empire, it ceases to have any meaning in this country."[6] Lord Beaverbrook's son, Max Aitken, described the agreement as "a plan which will ditch Empire preference"[7] whilst Sir Thomas Moore opposed the agreement both because of its implications for empire trade and the harshness of the conditions imposed by the Americans.[8] Another Conservative, Christopher Hollis, based his argument on the serious deflation which, he argued, the terms of the loan would involve.[9]

Opposition to the loan agreement (or to the Bretton Woods plan) did not appeal with special force to any of the occupational or educational groups of which the party was composed; Public School men and Non-Public School MPs, University graduates and non-graduates, Business men and Professions, reacted in much the same way. Nor was there any evidence of a conflict between the generations; the 1945 intake and the pre-war Members voted in almost exactly the same proportions. The determined seeker after trends might note that the Midlands MPs, coming from the home of imperial preference, were more hostile to the agreement than Members from other regions—but the absolute figures are much too low for any confidence to be placed on this finding.

European Unity

Less uniformity prevailed in the Conservative response to an issue closely linked to that of empire—that of European union. In September 1946, Churchill, in his famous Zürich speech, exhorted Europe to unite, and soon after accepted the presidency of the European Movement. In March 1948 a crossbench EDM, calling on Britain, as a long-term policy to join in a federal Europe, was tabled, mustering nearly 200 signatures, more than 60 of them from Conservatives.[10] The motion was prepared by an *ad hoc* drafting committee[11] and had 3 Labour and 3 Conservative sponsors.[12] This EDM was actually debated in the House, an unusual occurrence.

In a foreign affairs debate in January 1948 the Conservatives showed themselves eager for British membership of or association with a United Europe. Ernest Bevin, in opening the debate, had spoken of the need for the closer integration of Europe. From the Conservative benches, Anthony Nutting accused the government of procrastination. "But how long", he asked, "has the time been ripe to organize Western Europe? I should have thought that the time was over-ripe."[13]

Conservatives were very sensitive to fears that closer integration with Europe might interfere with and hinder the relationship between Britain and the Commonwealth. Generally, however, they chose to evade the issue by asserting in the most general terms that some means could be

[6] HC Deb. 417, c. 461.   [7] *Ibid.*, cc. 682–5.   [8] *Ibid.*, cc. 642–6.   [9] *Ibid.*, cc. 522–31.
[10] EDM 33/47.
[11] See Ben Levy's reference to the committee, HC Deb. 450, c. 1349.
[12] R. W. G. Mackay, Leslie Hale, and Christopher Shawcross from the Labour Party, and Robert Boothby, Sir Peter Macdonald, and Peter Roberts for the Conservatives.
[13] HC Deb. 446, c. 410.

found of reconciling the old loyalties of Empire with the new obligations to Europe. Churchill himself set the pattern:

"We are sure that . . . this European policy of unity can perfectly well be reconciled with and adjusted to our obligations to the Commonwealth and Empire of which we are the heart and centre. I cannot believe that those difficulties will not be settled by patience and care. It is no help to draw sharp lines of contradiction between them. We need both as pillars in a world of reviving prosperity."[14]

Perhaps aware that he had skirted round the problem Churchill later adjured the House not to let the Debate "evaporate in benevolent and optimistic platitudes".[15]

Churchill's sentiments may have been magnificent but they hardly offered a solution; and with so august an example it was not surprising that Conservative backbenchers should have tried to wish the difficulties away. So Sir Peter Macdonald declared that it should not be beyond the wit of man to devise means whereby "the British Commonwealth can maintain its status as a Commonwealth and at the same time have a link with a United Europe".[16] In a later debate Sir Peter tried to rebut the charge that the apostles of federal Europe were "leaving the Commonwealth behind. . . . in the whole of my political life", he reminded the House, "I have been devoted to the interests of the Commonwealth."[17]

Boothby, who, as has been seen, was a stalwart empire preference man and yet an ardent European, found no obstacle to squaring this circle: ". . . what nonsense those people write and talk", he exclaimed, "who say that the ideas of the British Empire and Commonwealth and of a United Europe are contradictory or clashing ideas. On the contrary, they are entirely complementary."[18]

Some Members, whilst not indifferent to the claims of Europe, made clear that their first allegiance was to the Commonwealth.

"I for one [declared Colonel Hutchison] am glad . . . to hear creep into our consideration . . . the word 'commonwealth'. We await with interest the plan . . . to see how far that integration can be consolidated and be made compatible with the other aims, that is the closer integration with Europe with which I also agree. . . . By what logical process of thought [he questioned] can we be asked to create a custom union in Marshall-land which I should welcome and destroy it within our own Commonwealth—to build where our differences are so great . . . and to pull down among the Dominions and countries who share a common language, a common political thought, and who are tied by sentiment and common loyalties to the one Crown? . . . this country will take an imperial toss if she allows herself to be driven ever more closely into a European customs union, and at the same time driven away even further from her own Commonwealth."[19]

"For us in this House as a whole", said Anthony Eden expressing reservations about the federalist motion EDM 33/47, "the welfare of the Commonwealth and Empire must always be the first consideration. This is paramount";[20] and J. S. Maclay admitted frankly that he was "very nervous about the extreme idealist advocates of the federal idea".[21]

Two amendments were tabled, reflecting Conservative anxieties, about national sovereignty and older imperial ties. Between them they attracted 15 Conservative signatures; one accepted

[14] HC Deb. 446, cc. 554–5.   [15] *Ibid.*, c. 557.   [16] *Ibid.*, c. 488.
[17] HC Deb. 450, c. 1292.   [18] *Ibid*, cc. 1376–7.   [19] HC Deb. 446, cc. 472–5.
[20] HC Deb. 450, c. 1272.   [21] *Ibid.*, c. 1344.

co-operation with western Europe but explicitly rejected a federal union,[22] whilst the second insisted on the prior agreement of the other nations of the British Commonwealth.[23] Eleven months later the less drastic pro-European EDM 21/49 was put down; this welcomed the establishment of the Council of Europe, suggested a basis for the apportionment of representatives from different countries, and asserted that the British representatives should reflect the relative strength of the parties in the House of Commons. More than half of the 130 Members who signed this motion were Conservatives.

Support for these motions can be examined in two ways; the signatories of the federalist EDM can be compared with the rest of the party and the signatories of both the federalist motion and the more moderate EDM, which welcomed the creation of the Council of Europe, can be compared with those who signed neither.

A clear difference was established between the Businessmen and the Professionals on the federalist demand; less than a third of the former, but nearly half of the latter, identified themselves with the motion calling for federal union. Moreover, the small group of regular officers were even more pro-European on this evidence than the lawyers, though with such small numbers the differences are unlikely to, and do not, reach statistical significance. Similarly, the curious cleavage between Oxford and Cambridge, which was found on the subject of Europe in the 1955 Parliament,[24] also appeared in 1948. Almost half of the Oxford men signed the federalist motion against less than a fifth of the Cambridge educated; moreover only 2 of 16 backbenchers educated at provincial or Scottish universities subscribed to the call for federal Europe. As the association is significant at $2 \cdot 5$ per cent level, it is unlikely to have occurred by chance. In contrast, no significant associations can be found when the second test is applied—that is when the signatories of both the pro-European EDMs are set against the rest of the party.

Birching

The last question which divided the party concerned the retention of birching. The government's Criminal Justice Bill, introduced in 1947, provided for the abolition of both birching and flogging, thereby carrying out an intention of Sir Samuel Hoare, Conservative Home Secretary just before the war, which had met with heavy opposition within his own party. The Bill had been dropped at the outbreak of war. The Labour Government's attempt to abolish birching (which embodied a recommendation of the Cadogan Committee) was resisted by the Lords. The Upper House passed an amendment which sought to retain the birch; when the amendment came up before the House of Commons the government moved that it should be rejected, incurring the antagonism of a group of Conservatives led by Sir Thomas Moore. Sir Thomas confessed that he did not wholeheartedly concur with the abolition of flogging, but he was prepared to accept the return of birching as a compromise: "we, as a race are supposed to be geniuses for compromise". The Cadogan Committee had been guilty of illogical nonsense because they had favoured the retention of corporal punishment for attacks on prison officers but not for acts of violence against anyone else. Whilst agreeing that psychiatrists relieved much mental suffering, he deplored the excessive authority they had gained and described the Labour opponents of corporal punishment as "those well-meaning sentimentalists who support their Government in this monstrous policy".[25] Brigadier Rayner, of Totnes, shared Sir Thomas's view of psychiatrists: "Henceforward the young hooligan . . . will merely

[22] EDM 33/47A.   [23] EDM 33A/47.
[24] Finer *et al.*, *op. cit.*, p. 90.   [25] HC Deb. 453, cc. 1549–51.

be sent off to some fairly comfortable clinic where some of the psychiatrists . . . will try to find out where his sensitive little soul went wrong in his cradle days. . . . psychiatrists, when they were brought into the Army during the war, were pain and grief to the commanding officer, the M.O. and every decent chap in a unit."[26] When brutal crime was prevalent, he argued, it was wrong to do away with a punishment which might deter the brutal criminal.

Two Conservatives, Colonel Gomme-Duncan and J. C. Maude, put the case for birching in more temperate terms; they thought that fear of pain was a definite deterrent to some criminals, and Maude added that if judicial corporal punishment were totally abolished, prison sentences would become longer. A long prison sentence was often a very cruel punishment.[27] Quintin Hogg began from the proposition that he did not like flogging, but he thought the birch should be retained for occasional use.[28]

Sixty-three Conservatives (and 1 Liberal) voted, without success, to keep birching as a judicial penalty. In later years the demand to re-introduce birching was to be strongly linked to educational and age differences, but this was not so in 1948. Even the non-graduates, later to assume disproportionate importance in the ranks of the birchers, were only a little more in favour than the University men.

The only important issue, then, on which opinions were connected with structural features of the party, was the question of European union—and this had not, in the late forties, become as divisive a problem as it was later to be, largely because most members of the party avoided the full implication of the question. On the rare occasions when the party was disunited, its cleavages cut across the occupational and educational boundaries which played such an important role in the Labour Party. The consequences of this uniformity of response for the morale and long-term cohesion of the party can hardly be exaggerated.

1950–1

As in the 1945 Parliament, most of the Conservative EDMs were of a highly specific kind. Thirteen were designated as Partisan; and this category embraced such topics as the maladministration of British Railways,[29] the rise in the cost of living,[30] bigger meat rations for agricultural workers,[31] and an alleged breach of faith by the government in its naval re-engagement scheme.[32] Some were Crossbench: thus Labour and Conservative MPs joined hands to press for an inquiry into the divorce law,[33] for compensation for men who had been prisoners of war of the Japanese,[34] and an increase in the speed limit for heavy goods vehicles.[35] Rather more fell into the Neutral class—exemplified by such demands as EDM 22/50, which called for government assistance to the tourist trade, or EDM 49/50, which looked to a more permanent defence system for the NATO powers.

Four motions have been classified as Extremist; thus EDM 3/50 and 4/50 both called for the re-introduction of judicial corporal punishment; EDM 88/51 demanded the dismissal of the Dean of Canterbury—the "Red Dean"—whilst another EDM deplored the Foreign Secretary's refusal to assure the House that force would be used to protect British lives and property in Persia during the oil dispute with that country.[36] Three have been classified as "Convergent"; EDMs 32/50 and 35/51 called for the transformation of the United Nations into a world government and both, though largely Labour in their support, attracted a few Conservative signatures. The equal pay motion 85/51 has also been regarded as Convergent.

[26] HC Deb. 453, cc. 1551–3.   [27] *Ibid.*, cc. 1553–8.   [28] *Ibid.*, cc. 1561–2.
[29] EDM 68/*51*.   [30] EDMs 16/50 and 71/*51*.   [31] EDM 24/*51*.   [32] EDM 26/*51*.
[33] EDM 41/50.   [34] EDM 52/*51*.   [35] EDM 30/*51*.   [36] EDM 78/*51*.

Few of these EDMs, then, dealt with enduring and politically distinctive issues; like those of the previous Parliament, most were either partisan squibs, or ventilated the demands of pressure groups—particularly those groups such as the tourist industry or members of the armed forces—with which the Conservative Party has had a historic connection.

Moreover, there is some, but by no means conclusive, evidence that there was a systematic tendency for the 1950 intake and the younger Members to sign more frequently than the older. This means that where quantitative scales have been constructed an association between age and attitude, or between year of entry and attitude, may simply reflect a tendency of the younger and newly elected Members to sign more regardless of the issue. Fortunately, there is no reason to suspect that this tendency applies to any characteristics other than age and intake; it does mean, however, that the associations frequently found between age and opinion, and year of entry and opinion, may simply mean that the newly elected Members were habitually generous signers. For this reason, little reliance has been placed on such associations where quantitative scales have been employed. Where it has been possible to construct qualitative scales, however, this reservation does not apply.

Corporal Punishment

Two corporal punishment EDMs attracted only 33 signatures; it is not surprising, therefore, that no associations can be established. Urban Members signed rather more than their rural colleagues, and Londoners were more prominent than Conservatives representing constituencies in the Home Counties and provinces. Non-graduates signed marginally more than graduates; amongst the occupational groups, very few of the lawyers signed, whilst the Miscellaneous Occupations came out in relatively large numbers.

The Persian Oil Dispute

The quarrel with Persia provided an issue on which the Conservative Party could spontaneously unite in attacking the government. At the end of 1950 a dispute had arisen between the Persian Government and the Anglo-Iranian Oil Company about the royalties to be paid to the Persian Government. In the spring of 1951 Dr. Mossadeq, an extreme opponent of the company, became Prime Minister, and the Persian Parliament passed a Bill to nationalize it. The Persians refused to submit the problem to arbitration, and would not allow oil to be exported under the old terms. Mr. Attlee and his colleagues were severely criticized by the Conservatives for failing to defend British interests more vigorously. The alleged weakness of the government was in line with its record of impotence and vacillation in the Middle East, as the Conservatives saw it, and afforded another example of the policy of "scuttle and surrender" which the government had followed in India, Burma, and Palestine.

On 7 June Fitzroy Maclean and 5 other Conservatives tabled a motion which charged that the government's failure to provide "a firm or coherent policy in the Middle East" had gravely endangered British interests throughout the area, especially in Persia, and deplored the weakness shown by the government in their dealings with Egypt over the Suez Canal.[37] One hundred and fifty Conservatives expressed their support for the motion which, of itself, did no more than express the feelings held amongst both the party leaders and the backbenchers. A fortnight later, immediately after a debate in the Commons in which the Foreign Secretary, Herbert Morrison, had refused to say more than that the government would do all they could

[37] EDM 73/51.

to defend British lives, Maclean and 28 fellow-Conservatives put down a further EDM deploring Morrison's refusal to give a firm assurance that the government would take "the necessary measures to protect British lives and installations in Persia".[38]

The second EDM was expressing a stronger demand than the first, for it wanted a definite commitment from the government to use force, if need be, for the defence, not only of British citizens but of British property. In the debate Eden had called upon the government to pledge that troops would be sent, if need be, to protect British lives. He had asked for no similar promise to defend the company's installations.[39] The first motion echoed official Conservative opinion; the second went farther than the official spokesmen of the party were prepared to go. "Although our backbenchers were incensed and would have liked to recommend or even demand the immediate despatch of troops, Churchill was unwilling to commit himself to the details of any military operation about which he was quite ignorant", wrote Harold Macmillan.[40] When Churchill came to the 1922 Committee, Macmillan has recorded, he "spoke with great moderation and caution about Persia. It is clear that he thinks there may be a change for the better and that it would be foolish for the Tory Party to 'stick its neck' out. This was not to the taste of some of his audience."[41]

A qualitative scale was constructed, therefore, with the signatories of the second, less popular EDM, constituting the "Extremists", and the signatories of the first the "Moderates". There was a clear association between age and attitude, and as this scale is qualitative, considerable reliance can be put upon it. The younger Members chose not the less but the more belligerent standpoint. Nor is such a choice surprising; for the younger Members would have had no share in the pre-war policies of appeasement, but would have absorbed its lessons. To such men, Labour's policy of imperial retreat, its compliance with the demands of local nationalist leaders, may have been reminiscent of what, by then, was regarded as the disastrous course of the Baldwin and Chamberlain governments.

Atlantic Union and the Empire

One remaining issue may be mentioned briefly. In May 1951 Captain Ryder and 60 other Conservative backbenchers signed an EDM which welcomed the formation of regional defence pacts (such as NATO) but expressed the view that the long-standing association of Commonwealth and Empire remained "the first consideration of this country in its overseas commitments".[42] This motion quite explicitly put Britain's obligations to the Commonwealth above its new commitment to NATO. Another EDM, tabled in September 1950, urged the government to consult with the other NATO governments to find a basis for a more permanent defence union.[43] An attempt was made to compare the appeal of the proposed Atlantic grouping with the more traditional appeal of the Commonwealth. Details of the scale used are given in Annex 4; suffice it to say that no associations can be established. There are tantalizing hints again of the special Midlands nostalgia for Empire; urban Members seemed more empire-minded than the men of the shires, Cambridge Members more than Oxonians, and amongst the occupational groups the Miscellaneous Occupations were strongly pro-Empire, but no statistically significant results emerge.[44]

[38] EDM 78/51.   [39] HC Deb. 489, cc. 746–54.
[40] Harold Macmillan, *The Tides of Fortune*, London, 1969, pp. 344–5.   [41] *Ibid.*, p. 346.
[42] EDM 62/51.   [43] EDM 49/50.

[44] In the study of the 1955–9 Parliament, Cambridge Members were found to be more empire-minded than Oxford-educated MPs; in addition, the more extreme empire-minded members came disproportionately from urban constituencies.

Equal Pay

Twenty-five Conservatives signed EDMs calling for the introduction of equal pay for men and women employed in the public services or in teaching.[45] The only statistically significant relationship that was found (apart from year of entry) was with education, non-graduates signing to a disproportionate extent.

Thus few EDMs of real political importance were tabled; and most of those that were appealed (if we discount the factors of age and intake) with roughly equal force, to all sections of the party. The contrast with the Labour Party could hardly be more emphatic.

1951–5

The Conservative electoral victory meant that it was less easy to maintain the high level of unity that had distinguished the party between 1945 and 1951. In Opposition, the leadership can evade difficult choices by giving its backbenchers their head; there is no need (and this is particularly true of a Conservative Opposition) for the Front Bench to worry too scrupulously about the practical effects of a particular policy. But governments have to govern; and to govern, as Pierre Mendès-France has reminded us, is to choose. It becomes difficult to apply in government the brave slogans and simple injunctions of opposition.

It was not surprising, therefore, that the 1951 Parliament should have seen a number of Conservative revolts; there might have been more, prosecuted with greater vigour, had the majority been more substantial.

Some of the rebellions were clearly extremist in character; thus there were two EDMs and a private Members' Bill expressing the familiar backbench cry for the restoration of judicial whipping. There was an impatient demand for decisions about denationalization, a call for an inquiry into the structure of the National Coal Board, and with it a demand for a national fuel and power policy, and an anguished plea for the extension of imperial preference. In 1954 there was a request to the government to postpone a decision to the House, reached on a free vote, to increase Members' salaries. Most important of all, there was the formation of the celebrated Suez Group, who demanded the breaking off of negotiations with Egypt, which culminated in a floor revolt. The list of revolts hardly approaches the fratricidal level reached by the Labour Party in the same Parliament, but it testifies that the spirit of dissent within the Conservative Party had not altogether died during the 6 years of opposition. It slumbered, awaiting only the magic wand of official responsibility to bring it to life.

There were, too, a number of crossbench demonstrations. Some dealt with matters so specific and of such limited significance as barely to deserve mention: thus there was EDM 15/51 which wanted legislation to permit people to donate their eyes, in their wills, for corneal graft; or EDM 14/52 which protested about arrangements for hotel accommodation for the Coronation. Some concerned weightier matters; two EDMs[46] protested at the government's failure to give increased pensions to retired service officers; another[47] called for higher pensions for disabled veterans of the First World War; whilst EDM 44/54 called upon the government to give tax reliefs for the theatre.

[45] EDMs 10/*51*, 85/*51*, 96/*51*.   [46] EDMs 24/52 and 9/53.
[47] EDM 108/52.

Suez

Undoubtedly the most important revolt on the Conservative side was the rebellion of the Suez Group, a faction who called for a robust reassertion of Britain's imperial role. Under the Anglo-Egyptian Treaty of 1936 Britain had the right to maintain a military base in the Suez Canal area. In October 1951 the Egyptians denounced the agreement which still had 5 years to run. British forces in the Canal Zone were harassed, and anti-British riots took place in Egyptian cities.

The Suez Group was formed in 1952 just after the military leaders had deposed King Farouk. Harry Legge-Bourke, MP for the Isle of Ely, suggested to Julian Amery, son of the veteran imperialist Leo Amery and MP for Preston North, that they should be prepared to take independent action if the Conservative Government proposed to evacuate the Canal base. In the winter, Julian Amery called a meeting of like-minded Conservatives, which became known as the Suez Group.[48] The negotiations were protracted, and it was not until December 1953 that the critics surfaced. Forty-two Conservatives, headed by Captain Waterhouse, put down an EDM which, after referring to recent breaches by Egypt of the Anglo-Egyptian agreement on the Sudan, the refusal to permit ships bound for Israel to pass through the Canal, and the continued Egyptian acts of hostility towards Britain, urged the government to suspend negotiations with the Egyptians, to withdraw any terms that might have been offered, and to retain sufficient armed forces in the Canal Zone to defend the Canal.[49] The government nevertheless persisted, and finally reached agreement with Egypt; when the agreement was debated in the House in July 1954, 27 of the signatories went into the lobby against the government. Eleven did not vote, and 3 supported their Front Bench.[50]

The agreement provided for a base much reduced in size, to be manned by civilian technicians, and a 7-year treaty under which Britain would have, in certain circumstances, the right to reactivate the base. The military reasons for the agreement were explained by the Secretary for War, Brigadier Head. The advent of the hydrogen bomb had made the base of doubtful military value; the entry of Turkey into NATO had reduced the need for the Suez base. The base, moreover, was of little use unless Egypt would co-operate; British forces, especially the Army, were "overstretched and overstrained", and the withdrawal would permit the building up of strategic reserve. Britain could not afford the 80,000 men required to hold the Canal Zone; the government could not reject the best military advice and stay with fewer.[51]

The diehard rebels saw in the agreement a further sign of a weakening imperial nerve: ". . . we are becoming weary of our responsibilities . . . our burdens are becoming too irksome for us and we are really losing our will to rule",[52] declared Captain Waterhouse, the leader of the Suez Group.[53] Julian Amery warned that the consequences of this agreement would soon appear. Britain had agreed to "virtually unconditional evacuation of the Canal Zone". The pro-Egyptian party in the Sudan would be "immeasurably strengthened" by the decision.

[48] See L. Epstein, *British Politics in the Suez Crisis*, London, 1964, p. 43.

[49] EDM 20/54.

[50] One signatory had died; one MP who had been elected at a byelection 3 months after the motion had been tabled rebelled. The Labour Party officially abstained.

[51] HC Deb. 531, cc. 724–31.

[52] *Ibid.*, cc. 737–45.

[53] Waterhouse's phraseology bears an interesting resemblance to that used by Churchill on Indian constitutional reform in 1931, ". . . . We are suffering from a disease of the will. We are victims of a nervous collapse . . . .", quoted in Robert Rhodes James' article in *Churchill: Four Faces and the Man*, London, 1969.

The last element of stability in Egypt would go with the retreating British troops. In his closing words he echoed the faith in Britain's imperial purpose, so long proclaimed by his father. Those who opposed or derided the Suez Group now "may realize that this is not a fight in the last ditch but perhaps the beginning of a return to that faith in Great Britain's imperial mission and destiny without which, in my belief, our people will never be prosperous or safe or free".[54]

Other Conservatives could respond to Amery by looking to a different vision of empire. "This old conception of Empire [declared Brigadier Prior-Palmer] dies hard with us. People seem to forget that we have had three Empires, each one different from its predecessor. . . . Tremendous opportunities open before us . . . but it will not be done on the old basis and on the old conceptions."[55]

One erstwhile Suez rebel, Fitzroy Maclean, explained that despite his signature of the EDM, he was going to vote with the government. The government said that the strategic situation had changed, and that they were taking the only possible course. They had a mass of information which he, as backbencher, did not possess. He would not lay claim to greater foresight than the Prime Minister, and if, in changed circumstances, they could accept the agreement, so could he.[56]

The crisis over Middle East policy of which this was the first act, ranks as the most important the Conservatives had to face during the whole of their 13 years in office; yet it cut across every one of the familiar social and occupational groupings. All the fluctuations in support registered by different groups can be reasonably explained in terms of chance. Clarendon Public School men did not sign in significantly greater numbers than their Non-Public School colleagues, company directors more than professional men, graduates more than non-graduates. Military advice had weighed heavily with the government in concluding the agreement, and Members trained at military and naval colleges were, if anything, less conspicuous than others amongst the rebels. Western Members and East Anglian MPs signed in greater numbers than MPs from other regions, each contributing more than a third of their representatives; the behaviour of the Miscellaneous Occupations and of the Other Professions is also noteworthy—each providing nearly a third of their number; but it must be emphasized that these disparities could have been due to chance.

The decision to evacuate the Canal Zone was one of the most sensitive any Conservative government has had to take. It touched an imperial nerve, already exposed by 8 years of accommodation and retreat. To some Conservatives it seemed to endorse Labour's policy of abdication and withdrawal. Yet the evidence indicates that the upholders of the imperial tradition, the diehard defenders of empire, drew their support from no special section of the party, from no distinctive group or class. It will be recalled that in the 1955–9 study no firm associations between attitudes to the Suez affair and social characteristics were found. The continuity between the earlier revolt and the rebellions 2–3 years later is impressive. The contrast with the disputes over foreign affairs which took place in the Labour Party is once again complete.

Imperial Preference

The cause of empire preference died hard within the Conservative Party. The General Agreement on Trade and Tariffs which forbade any extension of imperial preference was resented by some sections of the party, which saw in GATT an attempt by American industry

[54] HC Deb. 531, cc. 771–82.   [55] *Ibid.*, c. 791.   [56] *Ibid.*, cc. 804–5.

to encroach into Britain's traditional export markets. At the Party Conference of 1952 a motion reaffirming belief in the principles of imperial preference, and urging the government to obtain changes in those articles of GATT which were injurious to empire trade and development, was carried overwhelmingly. Leo Amery, the old apostle of empire, declared that the only thing that barred Britain's escape from her economic Slough of Despond was GATT— "this lamentable agreement". Oliver Lyttleton, from the platform, told the conference that anyone who sought more empire trade and development was "pressing at an open door". Certain provisions of GATT were "crippling and hampering"; Britain could not raise duties on foreign goods without putting them on Commonwealth products. But he warned that the Sterling Area did more than half its trade with countries outside the Sterling Commonwealth. In commending the resolution he reminded the representatives that it required the fullest discussion with the Commonwealth, and would be raised at the forthcoming Commonwealth Conference.[57]

Several empire motions were tabled during this Parliament. Some were not particularly distinctive, merely calling, like EDM 75/51, for a Conference of Commonwealth and empire leaders to prepare measures to "open the way for expanded trade"; or like the signatories of EDM 15/54 sought to increase migration within the Commonwealth. More extreme than these EDMs was one tabled in April 1952, which urged the government to remove, wherever possible, all obstacles which prevented Britain from extending and increasing preferences within the Commonwealth and Empire[58]—a clear thrust at GATT. Forty-two Members signed the motion. The signatories of this more extreme EDM were compared with the signers of the moderate empire EDMs; but no significant associations were found. When the signers of all the empire motions, moderate, and extreme, are compared, however, with the non-signers, the Non-Public School men are found to be more frequent signers than their colleagues.

Colonial Affairs

There were two amendments, which between them attracted nearly 140 names, designed as retorts to the Labour EDM which had criticized the imposition of collective punishment on a Malayan village. The more popular EDM, supported by 128 MPs, welcomed the "inflexible determination" of the government to restore law and order in Malaya, and declared that the punishment was "appropriate, just and firm";[59] a second amendment, with 10 signatures, simply affirmed support for "all essential measures for the maintenance of law and order".[60] These amendments were not associated with either school or university background; but they did appeal disproportionately to particular sections disproportionately within the Business and Professional groups. Thus the directors of private companies and business executives subscribed more generously than directors of public companies. Amongst the Professional men, lawyers showed less interest than either of the other groups and, not unexpectedly, the regular officers were distinguished by an almost unanimous display of support.

Corporal Punishment

Both the motions calling for the restoration of judicial corporal punishment were tabled in the autumn of 1952. Sir Thomas Moore and 14 Conservative colleagues called for the restoration of birching in EDM 105/51, put down at the very end of the parliamentary session; and at the beginning of the new session, a week later, Moore repeated the EDM in the same

---

[57] *Daily Telegraph*, 10 Oct. 1952.   [58] EDM 64/51.   [59] EDM 63A/51.   [60] EDM 63AA/51.

terms. On this occasion, 69 Conservatives signed the motion including all 15 of those who had signed the previous week.

Support for corporal punishment was strongly associated with education and less markedly with age. The demand for birching was, above all, a non-graduate demand. Nearly half of the non-graduates signed the EDM, but only a fifth of their University-educated colleagues. Similarly, attitudes on corporal punishment were associated with school background; only one in eight of the Members from the Clarendon Public Schools expressed support for the re-introduction of birching, compared with nearly a third of Members from the Other Public Schools and two-fifths from the Non-Public Schools. However, it was a University education which seems to have been the decisive factor. Most MPs who had been to a public school (and especially those who had been educated at a Clarendon Public School) had gone to university; relatively few of the Non-Public School men were graduates. When the Other Public School and Non-Public School classes are broken down according to University attendance, a sharp distinction can be seen. Less than a quarter of MPs who proceeded from an Other Public School to University signed, compared with nearly two-fifths of those educated at Other Public Schools who had not gone to university. Amongst the Non-Public School MPs a similar difference emerges.[61] Amongst the graduates only a third signed; amongst the non-graduates nearly a half. Amongst the graduates the kind of university attended was also related to opinions on birching; the Oxford-educated expressed the least support, and the graduates of provincial and Scottish universities the most. The more exalted the educational background, the more prestigious the university, the less the support for birching.

Opinions on corporal punishment were also related to age. The under-41's expressed least support, the over 60's the most.

In February 1953 a Conservative backbencher, Eric Bullus, introduced a Private Members' Bill which aimed to restore birching as a judicial penalty. Supporters of the Bill cited the general increase in crime and an alleged rise in violent crime, there being considerable dispute over the comparability of official figures for the latter at different periods. The inconsistency of retaining corporal punishment for attacks on prison officers but not for any other kind of violent behaviour was again mentioned. The prisons were overfull, and, in any case, prison nowadays was not a deterrent. Some speakers referred to the fear in which women and old people lived in certain parts of the country.[62]

Sixty-five Conservative MPs supported the Bill on a free vote, whilst 38 complied with the Home Secretary's advice to reject it. The results are again highly consistent with those derived from the EDMs. Details of the attitudes of different groups to this Bill were given in the earlier study[63] and need not be repeated here; suffice to say that whilst the graduates voting divided equally, the non-graduates voted overwhelmingly for birching. Analysis of the votes by school, by type of university, and age, are all consistent with the inferences drawn from the EDMs, though on this evidence alone the associations could not be regarded as firmly established.

Home Affairs

Nationalization. The Conservatives had resisted most of the nationalization measures of the 1945 Parliament but they refrained from committing themselves to any extensive plans of

[61] There were too few Clarendon Public School Members who had not been to university to make this kind of analysis worth while.

[62] For the debate, see HC Deb. 511, cc. 754–840.

[63] S. E. Finer, H. B. Berrington, and D. J. Bartholomew, *Backbench Opinion in the House of Commons, 1955–59*, Annex 7.

de-nationalization. They were pledged, however, to restore the steel industry and some sectors of road haulage to private ownership. By April 1952 backbench discontent was being expressed at the government's failure to publish any plans for de-nationalization. At the same time there was considerable resentment about the immunity the nationalized industries enjoyed from effective parliamentary control. EDM 48A/51, an amendment to a Labour protest against fare increases in London, called on the government to introduce legislation to put the Transport Commission under stricter parliamentary control. A long EDM tabled by 3 Members of the "One Nation Group"[64] wanted an inquiry to consider the best means of combating the evils of monopoly in those industries which were to remain nationalized and also asked for early legislation to de-nationalize those industries that were not to stay in public ownership.[65]

The management of the coal industry also provoked backbench unrest, which took the shape of a long battle between the backbench Fuel and Power Committee, and the Minister. In March 1953 Sir Victor Raikes, the chairman of the committee, put down an EDM which at one time enjoyed the support of more than 120 Members; it viewed with acute concern a recent increase in the price of coal, called for an inquiry into the structure and administration of the National Coal Board, and adjured the government to provide a national policy "to make the most efficient use of our fuel and power resources".[66] The vice-chairman of the committee, Col. Lancaster, who had long been an advocate of decentralizing the Coal Board's structure, and the two honorary secretaries of the committee, Col. Crosthwaite-Eyre and Gerald Nabarro, were amongst the sponsors. "This motion", reported the *Daily Telegraph*, "reflects growing Conservative dissatisfaction with the absence of Government or Parliamentary control over the nationalized industries and of effective machinery to represent consumer interests. There is great anxiety over the rise in coal prices with the far reaching consequences this entails." The government wanted to avoid industrial conflict in the coalfields and took the view that the primary responsibility for changes in structure rested with the Coal Board.[67] Almost immediately the Cabinet discussed the motion and refused the demand for an inquiry. It was emphasized that the refusal was a collective decision of the whole government, not just that of the Minister of Fuel and Power.[67]

A few weeks later the Fuel and Power Committee met and resolved unanimously to raise the question of an inquiry and the adoption of a national fuel policy with the full backbench meeting, the 1922 Committee.[68]

On 23 April the committee met, the Minister Geoffrey Lloyd confronting his critics. According to the *Daily Telegraph*, he had a "personal success". The official statement published after the meeting was more prosaic. ". . . A full discussion took place . . . and the Minister addressed the Committee. The matter will continue to receive the close and continuous attention of the Committee but no special action will be taken as a result of the meeting." [69]

No significant differences were found in the support given to the call for an inquiry into the coal industry; and, similarly, the demand for better public control of the nationalized industries appealed indifferently to every section of the party except that the oldest and most senior Members signed less frequently than their colleagues.

Once again it is clear that political differences in the Conservative Party were not closely related to the occupational and social structure of the party.

[64] A backbench group set up in the 1950 Parliament to develop a Conservative approach to social and economic problems.
  [65] EDM 59/51.   [66] EDM 69/52.
  [67] *Daily Telegraph*, 13 Mar. 1953.   [68] *Ibid.*, 21 Apr. 1953.   [69] *Ibid.*, 24 Apr. 1953.

Social Policy. There were only two motions concerned with public expenditure for social purposes. EDM 61/52 expressed disquiet at the level of local authority expenditure and the heavy rate burden which resulted, and called on the government to hold an inquiry into every aspect of local government finance. It is not altogether clear whether the prime target of this motion was the level of social expenditure or its division between the national and local governments. Nearly a hundred backbenchers signed it, but, once again, detailed analysis fails to reveal any significant variations in support. EDM 31/53 asked for an examination of a scheme of house-purchase grants as a means of encouraging home ownership as an alternative to subsidized council housing. This EDM did have a disproportionate appeal to particular sections— to the non-graduates and the Non-Public School men; amongst graduates, the motion attracted a much higher proportion of men from provincial universities than from either Oxford or Cambridge, the support from the Oxford Members being notably low.

Only 30 Conservatives signed the two EDMs[70] expressing support for the principle of equal pay for men and women. The more recent entrants signed to a much greater extent than the older Members; but this difference, though it was very marked, could be attributed to a greater tendency amongst the Members of the 1950 and 1951 intake to sign more, regardless of the issues.

Members' Salaries. The issue of MPs' salaries, trivial in its financial implication, posed questions of principle for many Conservatives, which gave the matter special importance and aroused strong feelings. In 1946 MPs' salaries had been raised to the figure of £1000 a year; the rise in the cost of living in the next few years considerably reduced the real value of this salary, and some MPs, with no other source of income were suffering hardship. In 1953 the House of Commons appointed a Select Committee to examine the problem, and in 1954 this committee recommended an increase of £500 a year in the parliamentary salary.

The recommendation was popular with Labour Members, many of whom were largely or entirely dependent on their official salaries; but there was considerable repugnance to the proposed rise in the Conservative ranks.

The principle of unpaid public service had long been cherished by Conservatives. It had been alleged that the introduction of salaries for parliamentary service would attract to the House men prompted by no higher motive than the desire to make a comfortable living, men who had failed in other occupations, and men who, relying on their salaries for a livelihood, would be unduly responsive to the pressures of the Whips or the expectations of their constituency associations. In 1954 this sort of objection was voiced infrequently, but several reasons, many of them unheard in 1911 when payment of Members was introduced, were now advanced as grounds for delay. The issue was discussed in an Adjournment Debate on 13 May 1954, and 11 days later a further debate took place on a motion that the Select Committee's proposal should be accepted.

In the earlier debate, the Chancellor, R. A. Butler, indicated that the government would not accept the Select Committee's proposal for a flat rate increase in Members' salaries but suggested three alternatives.

In both debates some Conservatives argued that though some Members might experience hardship, there was even greater suffering amongst pensioners and other classes, outside the House. It was obviously essential, said Sir Thomas Moore, to defer any increase, "in fairness and justice to those who are less well off than ourselves".[71] "... let us", urged Jocelyn Simon

[70] EDMs 1A/51 and 24/53.   [71] HC Deb. 528, c. 109.

"postpone it until the needs of the neediest and hardest-pressed members of the community have been dealt with."[72] Simon also referred, along with other Members, to the widespread resentment amongst the electors which a rise in salaries would cause. ". . . it would be damaging", he warned, "to our political democracy to vote ourselves an increase first."[73] Major Anstruther-Gray argued that a salary increase would stimulate claims for higher wages,[74] and John Arbuthnot thought it wrong that the House should raise the salaries of its own Members "when the nation is just coming through an economic crisis".[75] Others, such as Sir Wavell Wakefield, wanted to postpone any increase until the next Parliament. Members had been elected on certain terms and conditions and it would be wrong to change these in the middle of a Parliament's life.[76]

The debate on 24 May turned on the form the increase should take, though some of the more general arguments advanced in the earlier debate were given a second airing. William Deedes offered an amendment, blessed by Butler in his speech of 11 days before, to the Select Committee's recommendation; this amendment would have substituted a variable expense allowance for the flat-rate increase envisaged by the committee.[77]

Robert Boothby, who spoke for the Select Committee's proposal, argued that the work of an ordinary MP had at least doubled in the last 30 years; it was no longer possible for a man to combine his duties as an MP with active participation in any other profession except journalism. "Good young Members are unobtrusively but steadily leaving this House, and this has been going on for a number of years."[78] Walter Elliot, a member of the Select Committee, spoke in terms, unusual for a Conservative, of the need for a House representative of the country's occupations. "We want a House which will represent the nation all through. It must represent the white-collared man, but it must also represent the black-handed man." To be representative, the House must offer an adequate livelihood.

The Select Committee's proposal for a salary increase was carried in the division by 280 votes to 166. Both parties allowed a free vote; the Conservatives split, 33 of them voting for the salary rise, whilst the Labour Party voted, solidly if unwhipped, in agreement with the Tory rebels. Despite the verdict of the division lobbies, opinion in the party remained predominantly hostile to the increase and next day a motion was tabled which called on the government to postpone implementation of the Commons' decision until the financial position of sections of the community with a "prior claim" had been eased. Fifty-six Conservatives signed this EDM.[79] Robert Boothby and 9 other Conservatives promptly put down an amendment which called on the government to implement the decision without delay.[80] One Conservative, Sir John Mellor, felt so strongly about the government's implied promise to accept the result of the free vote that he resigned the Conservative Whip.[81]

This controversy excited considerable ill-feeling in the Conservative Party. Robert Boothby asserted that "the roughest treatment" he ever had from the Tory Party came as a result of this incident. "There was a moment when I hardly dared face the party Committee, and addressed it with my hand on the door, in case immediate escape became necessary."[82]

Churchill seems to have been sympathetic to the call for an increase. "He grinned broadly", recounts Lord Moran, and records Churchill, after a meeting of the 1922 Committee as saying,

[72] HC Deb. 528, c. 133.   [73] Ibid., c. 132.   [74] Ibid., c. 80.   [75] HC Deb. 527, c. 1533.
[76] Ibid., c. 1558.   [77] HC Deb. 528, cc. 50–57.
[78] Ibid., cc. 37–46.   [79] EDM 71/54.   [80] EDM 71A/54.
[81] See R. J. Jackson, Rebels and Whips, London, 1968, p. 109.
[82] Lord Boothby, My Yesterday, Your Tomorrow, London, 1962. Also cited in R. J. Jackson, op. cit., p. 109.

"I was determined that the Committee should agree to a free vote in the House on Members' pay. They[83] were then certain to lose. . . ." The plight of some Members was such, Churchill told Moran, that they could not be sure of obtaining a square meal.[84]

On 4 June, however, Moran learnt that there was serious trouble in the party. "If they do nothing for Members who are worried about their income, I shall resign. I'm not going to run away. I don't mind a row with some of the bloody fools about the Tories. They didn't care a bloody damn about Old Age Pensions before this came up. Now it serves their purpose to think of them in connection with the pay of Members."[85]

Nevertheless, the government soon capitulated to backbench pressure. On 24 June Churchill announced that the government did not feel justified in raising MPs' salaries at the present time:[86] and on 8 July[87] the government proposed the introduction of a sessional allowance as an alternative to the salary increase.

Examination of the names of those who opposed the salary increase in the division reveals few associations that were clearly significant. The Members from the middle educational ranks proved to be most hostile; the Other Public School Members were significantly more opposed to the rise than both the Clarendon and Non-Public School backbenchers. The greater sympathy which the Non-Public School men displayed for Members without an alternative source of income is not unexpected; that evinced by the Etonians and other Clarendon School MPs is perhaps more surprising. Members educated at Oxford and Cambridge were less friendly to the rise than other graduates, though since the association only reaches the 10 per cent level it cannot be regarded as firmly established.

There were no significant differences between graduates and non-graduates; nor did any associations emerge from a scrutiny of the occupational, year of entry, or age categories. Analysis of the EDM reveals no significant relationships, but the breakdown by schools is consistent with the findings from the division lists. In short, once again analysis of the EDM gives a broadly similar result to that of the division list.

In order to facilitate comparison between the EDM and the division, discussion has concentrated on those MPs voting against the increase. When the 33 Members who voted with the Labour Party are compared with the opponents of the rise, the association between school and attitude disappears, whilst that between university attended, and attitude, is somewhat strengthened.

CONCLUSION

In the Labour Party it has been possible to distinguish a left wing marked by a certain continuity of doctrine and exhibiting in its opinions on diverse issues a common attitude or approach. The apostles of a socialist foreign policy usually stand for a more militant programme of common ownership at home, faith in nuclear disarmament, hostility to the American alliance, antagonism to the level of defence spending, have tended to be accompanied by a messianic belief in the reconstruction of society, in the establishment of a new economic and social order. The left-wing socialist would claim, moreover, that his opinions on what appear to be separate and distinct issues, are informed by a single and coherent doctrine.

Clearly it can be seen that such a picture has been true of the Labour Party since 1945 in a

---

[83] That is, the opponents of an increase.
[84] Lord Moran, *Winston Churchill: The Struggle for Survival, 1940–1965*, London, 1968, p. 577.
[85] *Ibid.*, p. 582.   [86] HC Deb. 529, cc. 595–6.   [87] *Ibid.*, cc. 2347–8.

broad, if rather blurred, sense. Even though the Left have often been joined on particular questions, such as German rearmament, or the Common Market, by men of the Centre and Right, it remains true that the Left have provided a semi-permanent hard core around which opposition to the leadership has developed. It was the Left who tried to rally opinion against America's policy in the Far East; who furnished the nucleus of support for negotiations with Russia; of opposition to German rearmament, to the manufacture of nuclear weapons, and later to the attempt to excise Clause Four from the party constitution.

Contemporary journalism has often tried to apply a similar pattern to the Conservative Party. Belief in Britain's imperial greatness, a yearning for colonial grandeur, are alleged to go hand in hand with support for capital and corporal punishment, for a niggardly attitude to the social services, and a desire to re-introduce the rigours of unrestricted capitalism. More recent controversies have added hostility to both coloured immigration and permissive legislation to the alleged syndrome of right-wing Conservatism.

In the earlier study it was observed that a syndrome or pattern of right-wing attitudes could only be found in the relatively narrow sphere of foreign policy. Belief in imperial preference, a desire for a more belligerent policy over Suez, and hostility to the United Nations, tended to march together. Though there was a statistical relationship between support for corporal punishment and right-wing views on foreign policy, the relationship was surprisingly modest; and some of the most prominent Conservative abolitionists had been vocal members of the Suez Group.[88] Moreover, within the realms of penal reform, there was virtually no correspondence, and certainly no statistically significant relationship, between attitudes to the death penalty and to corporal punishment, issues which are alleged to provoke a similar emotional response. In short, the views of Conservative MPs on birching seemed to be quite independent of their opinions on capital punishment.[89]

It is hard, therefore, to speak of a Conservative right wing in the late fifties. Rebel factions in the Conservative Party were usually temporary *ad hoc* coalitions of men who came together for one specific purpose; such coalitions dispersed after the controversy which gave rise to them had subsided. It was not possible to distinguish any permanently alienated group separated from their colleagues by differences over a range of diverse issues.

Examination of backbench motions and floor revolts in the 1951 Parliament suggests that this pattern held even more strongly in the early fifties than in the 1955–9 Parliament.[90] The Suez Group, for instance, on most questions reacted in much the same way as the rest of the party. Table 45 shows the relationship between membership of the Suez Group as defined by signature of EDM 20/53, and opinions on birching as defined by signature of the corporal punishment EDMs or votes on the Bullus Bill.

[88] Finer *et al.*, *op. cit.*, pp. 104–12.

[89] See H. B. Berrington, The Conservative Party: revolts and pressures, 1955–61, *Political Quarterly*, Oct.–Dec. 1961.

[90] Harold Macmillan, commenting on discussion in the Conservative Party after 1945 about new economic and social policies, writes: "But it would be wrong to suppose that those who adhered to traditional concepts, particularly on foreign or Imperial issues, were hostile to new ideas on economic or social questions. Indeed, for the policies which I advocated during these years I gained much support from friends whose orthodox Toryism no one could suspect" (Harold Macmillan, *Tides of Fortune, 1945–55*, London, 1969, pp. 300–1). Compare also Churchill's remarks about his backbench campaigns in the thirties. "On the German danger, as on India, I found myself working in Parliament with a group of friends. It was to a large extent composed differently from the India Defence League" (W. S. Churchill, *The Second World War*, vol. 1, London, 1948, p. 64).

Table 45. The Suez Group and Birching

	Suez					
	Suez Group		Others		Total	
	No.	%	No.	%	No.	%
Birching:						
For	18	19	77	81	95	100
Neutral	11	12	82	88	93	100
Against	7	23	23	77	30	100
Total	36	17	182	83	218	

For vs. Against. Not significant.

A preliminary glance at these figures might suggest that there was just a little truth in the left-wing caricature of the diehard Tory, for the Suez Group Members were marginally more likely to support the re-introduction of corporal punishment than their colleagues; but further inspection shows that they were marginally more likely to *oppose* judicial corporal punishment than their fellows. What appears to distinguish the Suez Group is a higher degree of commitment on this question; but even here the figures are not statistically significant.

The Suez rebels were also marginally more likely to have expressed support for the EDM which sought an inquiry into the National Coal Board. Again, these minor differences in support are not statistically significant; they could have arisen by chance. A similar pattern is found when the reactions of the Suez Group to the imperial preference and pro-colonial EDMs are examined—the more surprising because we might have expected belief in the assertion of imperial power to go hand in hand with faith in closer economic relations with the empire and with the vindication of British authority in the colonial territories.

Support for equal pay, too, seemed to cut across opinions on the Suez withdrawal, the National Coal Board, and corporal punishment. Indeed, the only relationship that was discovered out of the various combinations of issues which were tested[91] lay between the supporters of imperial preference and the upholders of colonial order. Threequarters of the empire preference signatories signed the pro-colonial EDMs as against one-half of the remainder of the party. This solitary association stands in stark and lonely contrast to the unrelieved flatness presented by the other issues.[92]

It would be easy to dismiss these negative findings as yet another example of academic industry that after much travail produces nothing of significance. On the contrary, the difference between the two parties in this respect is of great importance for the understanding of British politics.

[91] Suez: and corporal punishment, equal pay, nationalization (NCB), pro-colonialism, imperial preference. Nationalization (NCB): and corporal punishment, equal pay, imperial preference. Corporal punishment: and equal pay. Pro-colonialism: and imperial preference.
[92] For a study carried out in 1969 based on questionnaire responses which reaches broadly similar conclusions, see *Backbench Opinion* re-visited: the case of the Conservatives (R. C. Frasure, *Political Studies,* Vol. XX, September 1972).

B.O.H.C.—G

It has already been observed that the absence of any marked connection between occupational and social characteristics and distinctive political views within the Conservative Party (and also where these connections do occur their shifting nature) helps to explain the extraordinary unity and resilience of the British Right;[93] to this we must add, as a further cause, the almost complete absence of any significant overlap between the various rebel factions. To an even greater extent than in the 1955 Parliament, backbench rebellion in the Conservative Party, in this period, took the shape of the formation of *ad hoc* groups whose members dispersed as soon as the issue had been resolved or rendered nugatory by the passage of time.

[93] See M. Bremner, An analysis of British parliamentary thought concerning the United States in the post-war period, Unpublished Ph.D. thesis, London, 1950, fol. 325: "The comparative homogeneity of the Conservative Party is both a strength and a weakness. Certainly it permits the Conservatives to present a united front to the world more easily than their opponents can. Probably running the Conservative Party is an easier task, since the bulk of its Members are more alike than the bulk of Labourites. . . . "

CHAPTER 9

The Parliamentary Parties:
Continuities, Changes, and Reflections

"A representative person is one who will act in a given situation in much the same way as those he represents would act in that same situation. In short, he must be of their kind . . . thus a political party which begins to pick its personnel from unrepresentative types is in for trouble. . . .

"Political parties, like individuals, can have split personalities." (ANEURIN BEVAN, *In Place of Fear*.)

The use of the EDM as a source material has been heavily attacked by some commentators; it is said that EDMs offer confused and meaningless lists of names, of signatures subscribed from such a diversity of motives, and in such a variety of circumstances that it is not possible to use them for purposes of academic investigation. Considerable evidence has been presented in the preceding chapters and in the Annexes to show that for certain purposes the EDMs are an important and reliable source. There is a striking correspondence between the EDMs and the division lists, where the latter are relevant; it is hard to see how anyone can still maintain that EDMs are worthless as a source of data about attitudes within the parliamentary parties.

Yet a vindication of the value of the EDM does not rest on external corroboration alone. Even if no comparison with the division lists were possible, there would still be impressive internal evidence to support the validity of the EDM data. What is notable is the high degree of stability of the attitudes of different social and occupational groups as revealed by EDMs from one Parliament to another; and where changes do occur, as in the occupational composition of the Foreign Policy Left in the Labour Party, it is possible to trace these changes in floor revolts as well.

Figures 26–40 show the attitudes of the various occupational, sponsorship, educational, and university groups in the Labour Party to the more important issues in the four Parliaments which sat between 1945 and 1959.[1]

Whether or not an acceptable level of significance is reached, it must be stressed, depends to a considerable degree on the total number signing an EDM (or series of related EDMs), or participating in a floor revolt as well as on the proportions of different social groups behaving in a distinctive way; thus although no statistically significant relationship may be established, particular groups may still contribute disproportionately to certain factions. Again, even where relatively large numbers are involved, some groups may display greater enthusiasm than others

[1] Where no association between attitude and background factors reached the level of 10 per cent or better, the appropriate rectangle has been left blank.

for a particular demand, even though the results are not statistically significant. Thus an association was established in the 1950–1 Parliament between attitudes to world government and occupation; no association of this kind was found for the 1945–50 Parliament, but the results are consistent with those of 1950–1. Occasionally, as with the social welfare EDMs of 1945–50, the figures may, without a firm association being established, apparently diverge from those of a later period, but in no case do we find associations between type-class and attitude in one Parliament in clear contradiction to those of another. On conscription, penal reform, nuclear weapons, the political aspects of anti-colonialism, and (the experience of the 1945 Parliament aside) on social security payments, there is a marked degree of continuity in the pattern of group support.

Once again the Worker/Trade Union/Elementary-educated group leant towards the Right, often quite heavily so, on the ideological issues, yet even this contrast is tempered. On conscription they were as prominent as the middle-class Members, and on the issues of royal grants they were rather more critical than the Professions; and what support there was for hunting came almost exclusively from the middle-class section of the party.

OCCUPATION

The most important change that took place in this period is in the composition of what can loosely be termed the Left. In 1945 Ernest Bevin's critics were drawn, in a pronounced way, from the Professions; the Miscellaneous Occupations, though more rebellious than the Workers, were much more conformist than their Professional colleagues. In the Parliament of 1955–9 this had changed; the Miscellaneous Occupations had emerged as the most distinctively left-wing of the occupational classes. The relative conformism of the Miscellaneous Occupations in the 1945 House may, as is argued later,[2] have been partly due to the substantial number of Trade-Union-sponsored Members amongst their ranks. The retirement or defeat of these Members in 1950 and 1951 helped to change the political complexion of this group. The changing basis of the Left was already apparent by 1950; the Miscellaneous Occupations contributed as many (allowing for the difference in size of the two groups) to both of the "rhetorical" left-wing EDMs on Korea as the Professions. They were also more conspicuous than the Professions amongst the signatories of the Mikardo EDM calling for negotiations with Russia; and though anti-colonialism is hardly a distinctive badge of left-wing affiliation within the Labour Party, it is noteworthy that they signed the Acland/Brockway EDM 38/51 more generously than any other occupational group.

In the 1951–5 Parliament they seemed to be consolidating their position as the most left-wing class. In the revolt over the Japanese Peace Treaty, the nuclear weapons demonstration of 1955, and German rearmament, they were the most radical occupational group, even though the differences between them and their colleagues do not in every case reach statistical significance; and in the revolts of the 57 Varieties and over the Beswick amendment to the Atomic Energy Bill, they were no less conspicuous than their fellows from the Professions. By 1955–9 they were the most radical groups on unilateralism and anti-colonialism, and, less clearly, on the subject of German disengagement as well.

A second, less-marked but still important difference, lies in the changing attitude of the Workers to questions of foreign policy and defence. There were only 5 Workers amongst the

[2] See p. 188.

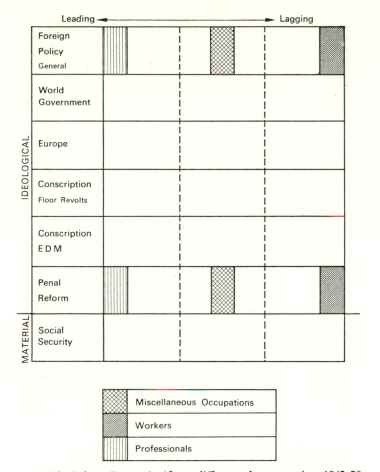

FIG. 26. The Labour Party: significant differences by occupation, 1945–50.

combined Lefts of the first post-war House; in later Parliaments they provided considerably more of the rebels, though they still lagged behind the other occupational groups.

THE OCCUPATIONAL SUB-GROUPS

Both the Professions and the Miscellaneous Occupations can be broken down into various occupational sub-groups. The Professions were divided into three categories—lawyers, school and university teachers, and members of other professions such as doctors and architects. In the 1945 Parliament there was virtually no difference in the foreign policy beliefs of these three classes; the three combined left-wing groups—the Ultra Left, Left, and Centre Left—accounted for just over 40 per cent of the Professions, taken as a whole, and for about the same proportion of each of the three component classes. In the 1951–5 Parliament, the lawyers seemed farther to the left than either the teachers or the "other professions". The numbers involved, however, are small, and the differences are not statistically significant.

Amongst the Miscellaneous Occupations the picture is clearer; the Combined Lefts of 1945–

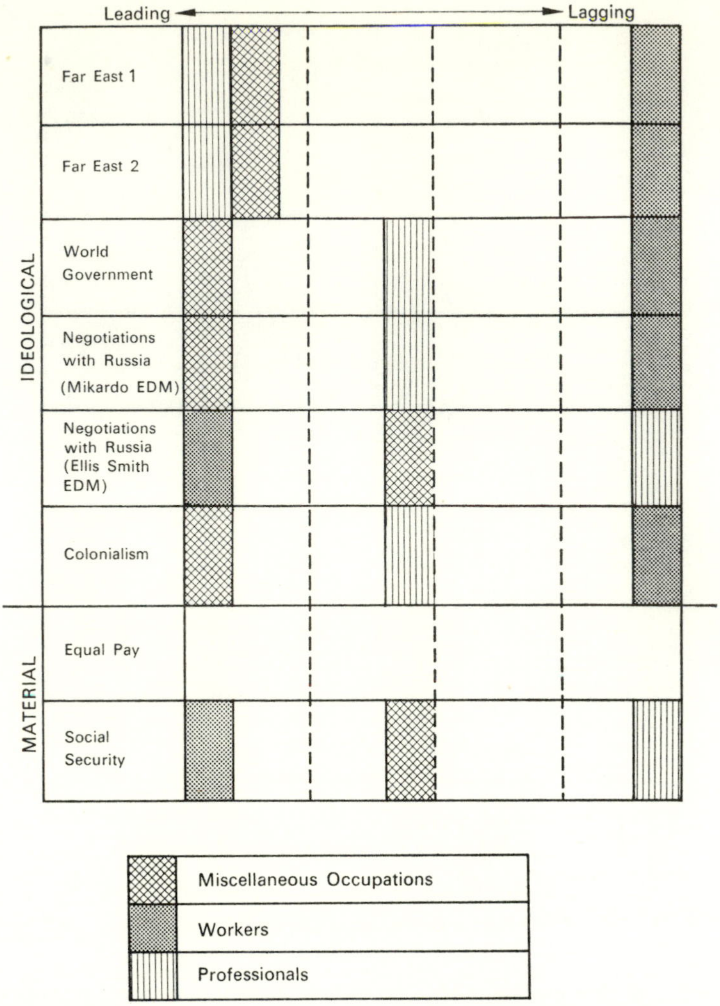

FIG. 27. The Labour Party: significant differences by occupation, 1950–1.[3]

50 comprised just over a quarter of the total. Of the journalists and authors, almost half adhered to the Left; of the trade-union and political organizers just over a tenth; and amongst the residue, less than a sixth. The importance of the trade union organizers in the 1945 Parliament and their virtual disappearance from later Parliaments, helps a little to explain the relative moderation of the Miscellaneous Occupations in the earlier period, and their swing to the Left in the 1950's. Of more importance was the presence, amongst the Miscellaneous Occupations of 1945, of a number of trade-union *sponsored* Members. Only 2 of the 18 sponsored Members were of the Left as against 16 of the 52 CLP and Co-operative Members. Indeed, the latter were almost, but not quite, as left-wing as the Professions. In the 1951 Parliament the journalists and authors were still the most left-wing of the sub-groups—but less markedly than before.

[3] Far East 1 compares the signatories of all relevant Motions on the Far East (including the "discarded" EDMs) with the non-signers. Far East 2 embodies the Left, Centre Left, and Rest as described on p. 90.

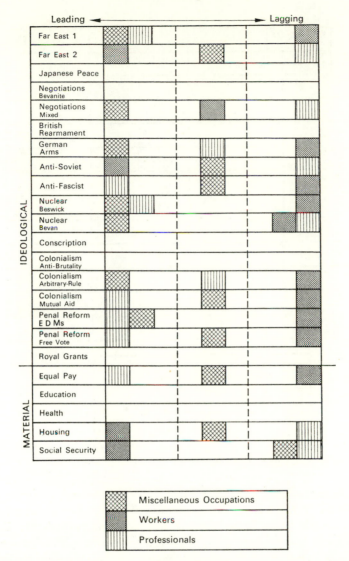

FIG. 28. The Labour Party: significant differences by occupation, 1951–5.[4]

SPONSORSHIP

The sponsorship breakdowns tended to reflect the occupational cleavages, but it is clear that until 1951 attitudes were less closely linked to sponsorship than to occupation, especially in the 1950–1 House. On the great divisive issues of the next Parliament, however, sponsorship was often a better test of support for the leadership than occupation. In the 57 Varieties revolt, the Abstention of the 62, and the rebellion over the Japanese Peace Treaty, Trade Unionists

[4] Far East 1 refers to the Left EDMs. Far East 2 compares the residue of the EDM on Mr. Chou's offer, i.e. those who signed 82/52 but not any of the Left EDMs, with the rest of the Party.

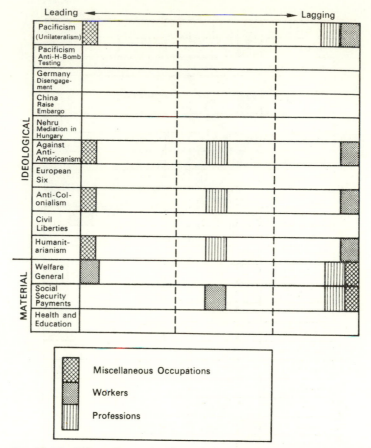

FIG. 29. The Labour Party: significant differences by occupation, 1955–9.

were significantly more loyal than other Members—even though differences between the various occupational groups were relatively subdued. The continuing strength of the Labour Right lay, not so much in the Workers *per se*, but more precisely in the Trade Unionists who overlapped with but did not exactly replicate the working-class section of the Party. Trade-union loyalty, rather than working-class pragmatism, was the sheet-anchor of the Right.

The Co-operators did not display the distinctive radicalism they showed in the 1955–9 Parliament. In the first post-war House they were farther to the right on foreign policy than the Constituency-sponsored. In the 1951–5 Parliament, however, though lagging behind the Constituency-sponsored on both the Japanese Peace Treaty and the level of British rearmament, they surpassed their constituency colleagues in their opposition to the arming of West Germany and to the British hydrogen bomb. Thus their anxieties over the nuclear question were already apparent before 1955. The election of five leftish Co-operators between 1953 and 1955 (some as replacement for Co-operators who had died or retired, others as "gains" from Trade Unionists or the Constituency-sponsored) swung the Co-operative Party in Parliament markedly to the Left. This movement towards the Left amongst the Co-operators in Parliament had been preceded by a pronounced left-wing emphasis in the Party Conference. The continuing

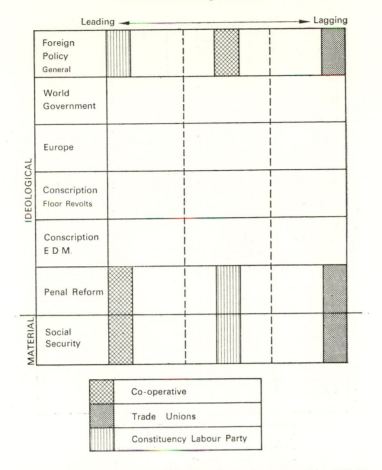

FIG. 30. The Labour Party: significant differences by sponsorship, 1945–50.

strength of the Left at the Conference had been a cause of some embarrassment to those leaders who saw the Party primarily as a means of promoting the welfare and advancing the ideas of the Co-operative movement.

"... the Party has been very largely drawn away from its original purpose into other fields. ... It has very largely been because those with strong views on matters which have little or no connection with the advancement of Co-operative philosophy or the defence of the movement's interests have used the democratic Constitution of the Party to push their own ideas. The result has been a source of embarrassment to the Co-operative Union and of downright annoyance to the Labour Party itself, which has sometimes seen its ally at best as an unwelcome ginger group and, at worst, as an enemy within the gates. ..."[5]

The Co-operative Party in Parliament is small, and the replacement of a few Members by others with distinctive political views, or individual changes of attitude by a few MPs, can

[5] Editorial in *Co-operative News*, 24 Apr. 1965, quoted in T. F. Carbery, *Consumers in Politics*, London, 1969, p. 237.

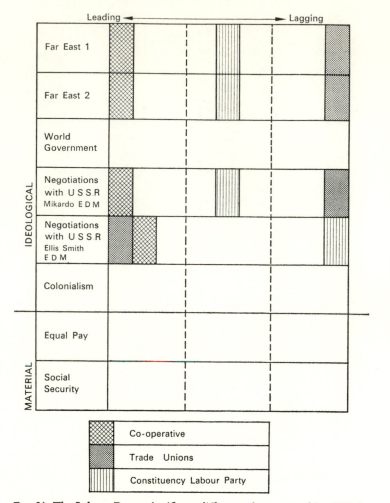

FIG. 31. The Labour Party: significant differences by sponsorship, 1950–1.

decisively change its ideological appearance. The situation in recent years has been unclear. T. F. Carbery argues that in the 1964–6 Parliament the Co-operative left-wing was not disproportionately large. Patrick Seyd, however, found on the Vietnam issue that the Co-operators once again took the most left-wing position.[6]

It is notable that by 1971 the Trade Unionists were better represented amongst the Left (as defined by membership of the Tribune Group) than in the backbench party as a whole. Of the sponsored Trade Unionists, 21 per cent were associated with the Tribune Group; of the CLP men, no more than 12 per cent. This change reflects, to some extent, the change in the ideological balance in the Trade Union Movement outside Parliament. All of the Trade Unionists belonging to the Tribune Group were elected in or after the General Election of 1959; the

[6] It must be stressed that given the small number of Co-operative MPs, their behaviour—though highly distinctive—contributed to only a minor degree to the marked statistical associations between sponsorship and attitude in the 1955–9 House.

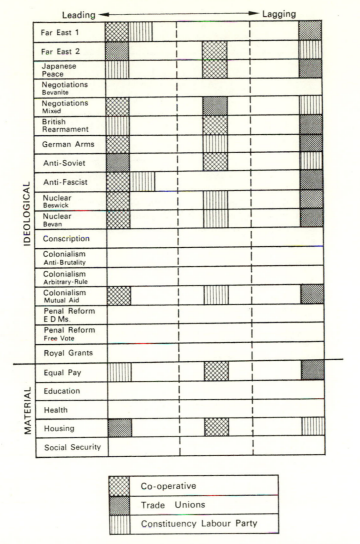

FIG. 32. The Labour Party: significant differences by sponsorship, 1951–5.

CLP members were recruited from the different parliamentary generations in a much more even way, as Table 46 demonstrates.

With the switch of emphasis from the "political" socialism of the early post-war years to the "industrial" socialism of the sixties, the social composition of the Left began to change.

EDUCATION AND UNIVERSITY ATTENDANCE

Not unexpectedly, sharp contrasts were found between the University graduates, and the Elementary educated on many issues, with the University graduates taking a more left-wing position on the ideological questions and the Elementary-school Members displaying more

TABLE 46. THE TRIBUNE GROUP 1971[a]:
SPONSORSHIP AND YEAR OF ENTRY

	Elected before 1959 (%)	Elected 1959 and after (%)
CLP	14	12
Trade Union	—	27

[a]The figures show the percentage of MPs in each category who were members of the Tribune Group. For membership of the Tribune Group see *Political Companion*, Jan./March 1972; principal Front Bench spokesmen, Whips, etc., have been excluded from the calculations.

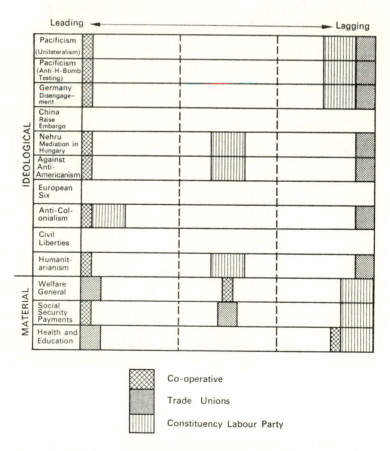

FIG. 33. The Labour Party: significant differences by sponsorship, 1955–9.

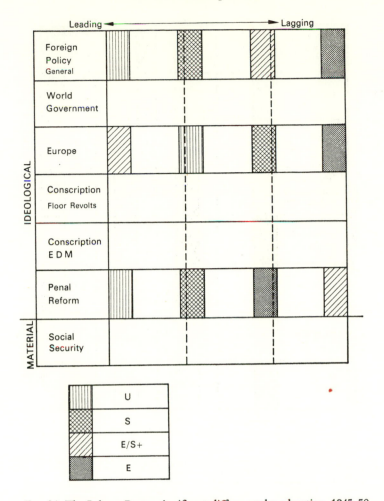

Fig. 34. The Labour Party: significant differences by education, 1945–50.

enthusiasm over the material issues. Generally speaking, the educational divisions paralleled the occupational cleavages. More surprisingly, differences were found amongst the graduates; it has already been shown that the U4's (secondary school and other universities) were generally older, and less likely to have served in the forces than other graduates; moreover, a substantial number of them sat for Scottish and Welsh constituencies, whereas almost all of the U1's, U2's, and U3's represented seats in England. These differences of age, experience, and geography were paralleled by differences of outlook. The U4's were more hostile to conscription, even though on many issues of foreign policy they were not more distinctively rebellious than other graduates. Indeed, in 1945–50 they (and the U2's) were less critical of the government's foreign policy, at least in the early years, than the U1's and U3's, though amongst those who did rebel the U2's and U4's were the more left wing. In 1951–5 the U4's were more likely than other backbench graduates to sign both the anti-fascist motions and the EDM welcoming Mr. Chou's initiative; they also subscribed much more freely to the social welfare motions.

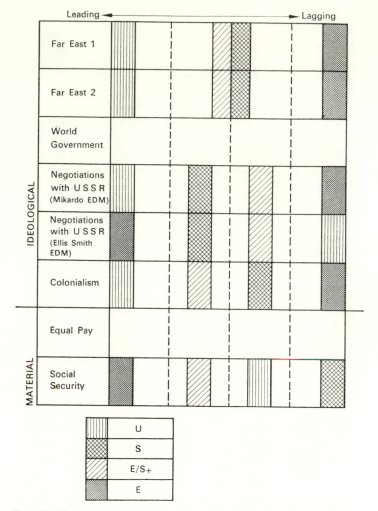

FIG. 35. The Labour Party: significant differences by education, 1950–1.

Moreover, there was a remarkable difference between the U4's and their graduate colleagues on the royal grants question. Generally, the U4's were characterized by a greater repugnance to measures of military preparedness, were more moralistic, and seemed to draw their inspiration from Victorian radicalism rather than twentieth-century collectivist beliefs.

The U1's (public school and Oxford or Cambridge) were socially the polar opposite of the U4's. On many issues they were indistinguishable from the U2's and U3's; on a few questions, however, they behaved in a way quite unlike any of the other groups of graduates.[7]

In the 1945 Parliament they (together with the U3's) comprised a disproportionately large number of the Combined Lefts. Yet in the 1951 Parliament they were less hostile to German rearmament and, moreover, signed the motions on health and housing less often than other

[7] Patrick Seyd showed that on Vietnam, in the 1964 House, the U4's were the most, and the U1's the least, radical.

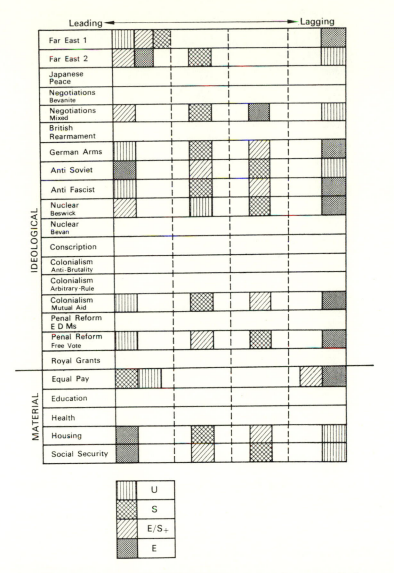

FIG. 36. The Labour Party, significant differences by education, 1951–5.

graduates; and, of course, like the U2's and U3's, they were considerably more right wing on some issues in the 1951 Parliament than the U4's.

There were 15 U1's amongst the Combined Lefts in the 1945 Parliament; of these 15 only 7 were "continuous backbenchers" in the 1951–5 House, most of the remainder having been defeated or retired (Table 47). Two of the 7 had moved clearly to the Right; 4 qualified as members of the 1951–5 Left, and 1 as an Other Defence and Nuclear Policy critic. Of the 9 U1's who were on the right in 1945, 4 were no longer backbenchers. The right-wing U1's survived the test of re-election little better than their colleagues.

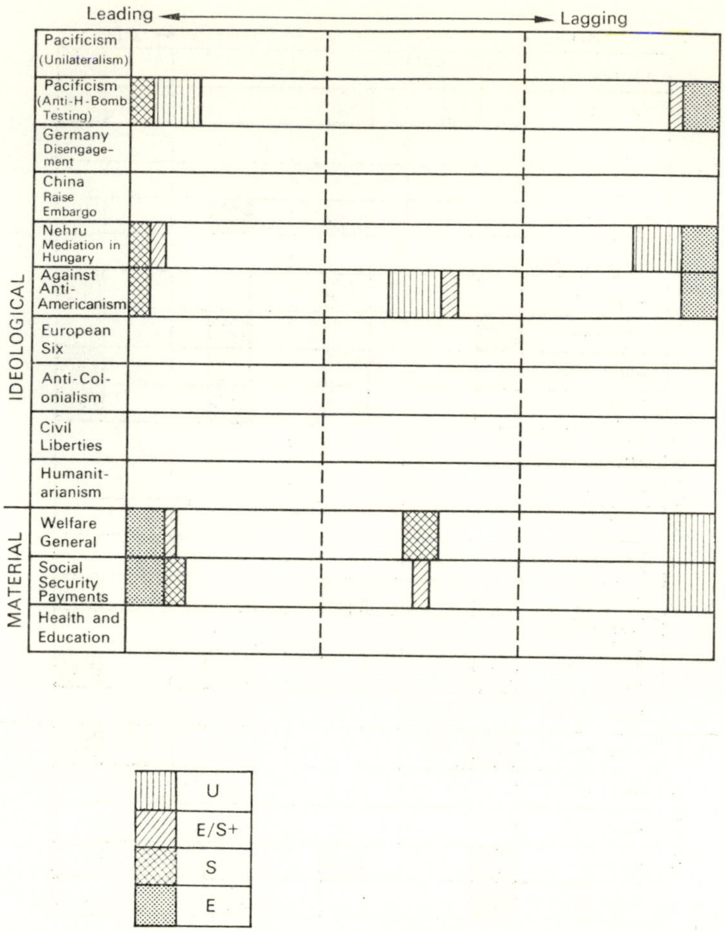

FIG. 37. The Labour Party: significant differences by education, 1955–9.

TABLE 47. U1's AND IDEOLOGICAL GROUPINGS, 1945–50 AND 1951–5

1945–50	1951–5				
	Left	Other Defence and Nuclear Critics	Rest	Out	Total
Combined Lefts	4	1	2	8	15
Rest	—	1	4	4	9
Total	4	2	6	12	24

As Table 48 makes clear, however, the Left made few recruits from those who entered the House after 1946.

TABLE 48. U1's, IDEOLOGICAL GROUPINGS, AND NEW BACKBENCHERS

1951–5	1945–50			
	Combined Lefts	Rest	New	Total
Left	4	—	2	6
Other Defence and Nuclear Critics	1	1	5	7
Rest	2	4	9(4)[a]	15
Total	7	5	16	28

[a] Ministers, etc., 1945–50, who joined the backbenches in 1951.

The numbers involved are small, and the figure for new Members amongst the Rest is inflated by the presence of 4 who had been Ministers in the 1945 Government and had joined the backbenches in 1951. Nevertheless, the U1's who made their way into Parliament in 1946 or later were considerably more right-wing than the U1's who came in with the victorious parliamentary party of 1945. The change in the political character of the U1's appears to parallel that of the Professionals.[8] The U1's of 1945 were like the Professional men of that cohort, a deviant generation.

In the 1955 Parliament a very marked division appeared between the U1's and the U4's on the issue of nuclear weapons. Only 20 per cent of the U1's could be classified as Left or Centre, whilst only 20 per cent of the U4's were classified as being on the Right. In addition, the U1's were very much more conformist than the other University graduates in the eight major floor revolts between 1951 and 1961.

The explanation probably lies, as for the much larger Professions group, in the formative experiences of the men who came into Parliament in 1945. Intellectual socialists in the 1930's were especially vulnerable to the appeal of Marxist doctrine or other left-wing variants of the socialist creed. Moderate solutions, pragmatic reformism, could no longer convince those dismayed by poverty at home and appalled by the collapse of democracy abroad. The apparent fulfilment of Marxist expectations during the Great Depression and the rise of fascism gave intellectual plausibility to extreme creeds.

For a short period, able young men from Oxford and Cambridge, drawn from prosperous families and educated at the most distinguished schools, formed the most conspicuous section of the Parliamentary Left, and, indeed, gave to the Left its intellectual leadership. This relationship, however, was short-lived; and their successors, elected later, proved to be much more moderate men.

THE CHANGING OCCUPATIONAL STRUCTURE OF THE LEFT

Of crucial importance to the changes in the Labour Party is the transformation of the occupational basis of the Left between 1945 and 1955. Most discussions of factionalism in the Labour Party have emphasized the broad division between working-class and middle-class Members;

[8] See pp. 199–208.

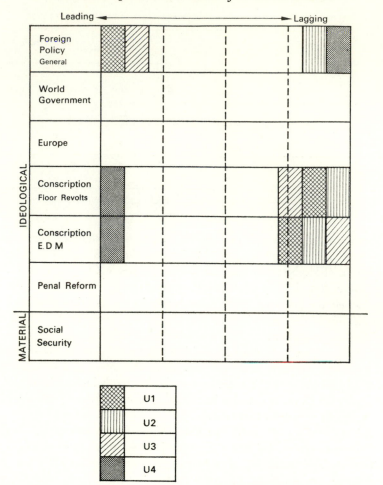

FIG. 38. The Labour Party: significant differences by university, 1945–50.

the former because of the primary concern with specific improvements in working–class living standards and *ad hoc* change, leant heavily to the Right. Middle–class Members, drawn to the party out of intellectual conviction or emotional attraction, tended to include many who saw socialism as the Vision Splendid, who thought in terms of abstract principles, a cast of mind which took them to the Left. In the earlier study, the authors showed that the division *within* the middle–class grouping was as significant as, or more so than, that between the workers and the middle–classes. The Professions were the dominant element in the Left before 1950; by 1955 this distinction had passed to the Miscellaneous Occupations. Indeed, from 1955 onwards, conflict within the Labour Party took increasingly the form of an alliance between the U1's, the Professions, and the Workers, against the Miscellaneous Occupations and the U4's. It is possible, as it was with the U1's, to trace in detail the change in the ideological character of the Professions.

A simple test of "leftness" is needed if the occupational composition of the Left in the 1955–9

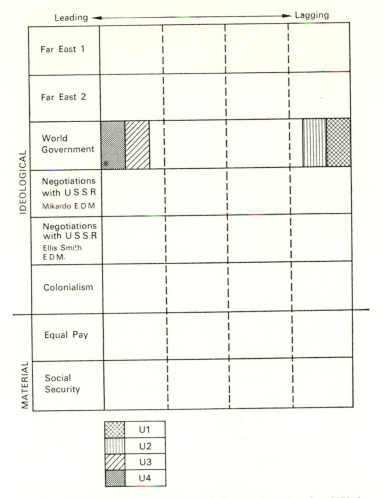

FIG. 39. The Labour Party: significant differences by university, 1950–1.

Parliament is to be compared with that of the Combined Lefts of 1945–50. To this end, Members have been classified as Consistent or Potentially Consistent Rebels, and as Non-Rebels, as explained in Chapter 1. Thus a Member who was continuously on the backbenches from November 1951 to March 1961, and who rebelled on at least one of the four specified occasions before 1955 and in at least one of the four specified revolts after 1959, has been termed a Consistent Rebel. The Potentially Consistent Rebels consist of two groups; first, there were those Members who were on the backbenches from 1951 to 1959 and who rebelled in at least one of the four floor revolts between 1951 and 1955; and, secondly, MPs who were backbenchers from 1955 to 1961 and who took part in at least one of the four revolts after 1959. The assumption is that Members who revolted in one of these periods would, had they been in the House then, have revolted in the other period as well.

On this basis, the 236 backbenchers of the 1955–9 Parliament can be classified as Table 49 shows.

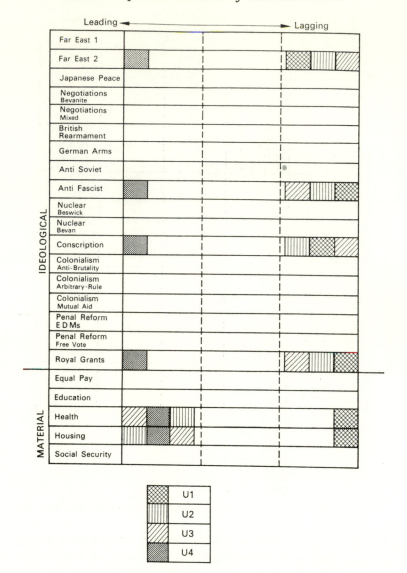

FIG. 40. **The Labour** Party: significant differences by university, 1951–5.

The composition of the Left had been affected, since 1946, in several ways. Some Members had been defeated, others had retired, died, or been expelled from the party; others had entered the House after 1946, at byelections, or in a General Election. Some former adherents of the Left apparently threw in their lot with the leadership; others, seemingly loyal to the Front Bench in the 1945 Parliament, became restive after 1950.

The backbench party of the 1945–50 Parliament included 70 Members of the Combined Lefts (Ultra Left, Left, or Centre Left on the Foreign Policy (General) Scale). Table 50 shows their occupational distribution.

TABLE 49. BACKBENCH REBELS, 1955–9, BY OCCUPATION

	Workers		Miscellaneous Occupations		Business		Professions		
	No.	%	No.	%	No.	%	No.	%	Total
Consistent and Potentially Consistent Rebels	19	24	23	39	8	38	20	29	70
Non-Rebels	50	64	25	42	12	57	36	52	123
	69	88	48	81	20	95	56	81	193
Non-consistent Rebels[a]	9	12	11	19	1	5	13	19	34
	78	100	59	100	21	100	69	100	227
Excluded[b]	1		1		3		4		9
Total	79		60		24		73		236

Data grouped. Consistent and Potentially Consistent Rebels against Non-Rebels and Non-consistent Rebels. Miscellaneous Occupations against Rest. $\chi^2_1 = 2 \cdot 778$. Significant at 10%.

[a] Members continuously on the backbenches from 1951 to 1961 who rebelled in one period but not in the other.

[b] Members not on the backbenches for the whole of either period.

TABLE 50. THE COMBINED LEFTS, 1945–50, BY OCCUPATION

Workers	Miscellaneous Occupations	Business	Professions	Unknown	Total
4	18	9	36	3	70

Table 51 shows how the occupational balance of the "Left" was affected by retirements, election defeats and so on, and by the election of new Members.

Apparent changes of belief were also responsible for the difference in the composition of the two left-wing groups. These are shown in Table 52. Table 53 shows the effects of all changes— conversion, backbench membership, and classification.

The process of defeat and retirement does little to explain the change in the structure of the Labour Left. It is true that considerably more Professional Members from the Left were defeated or withdrew from Parliament than of the other categories; but there were, after all, more Professionals amongst the Left in the first place. The increased prominence of the Miscellaneous Occupations was due almost entirely to the election of new Members; whilst that of the Workers was caused by the apparent conversion of some of them from loyal conformity to not infrequent rebellion—this increased restiveness itself being due to the greater salience of issues like rearmament and nuclear weapons.

TABLE 51. THE LEFT, 1945–50 AND 1955–9, BY OCCUPATION

Losses and Gains (Defeat, Election, etc.)

	Workers	Miscellaneous Occupations	Business	Professions	Unknown	Total
Losses						
Defeat and displace-ment	1	3	3	15	—	22
Retirement and expulsions	—	5	—	5	—	10
Deaths	—	—	1	—	1	2
Shadow Cabinet	—	1	—	—	—	1
Total losses	1	9	4	20	1	35
Gains						
Entry into House:						
1946–50	3	1	2	1	—	7
1951–4	—	4	—	—	—	4
1955	1	3	1	1	—	6
From Government or House of Commons Office to back-benches	—	1	1	1	—	3
Total gains	4	9	4	3	—	20
Net gains or losses through defeat, elec-tion, etc.	+3	—	—	−17	−1	−15

The Left of 1955–9 gained 9 recruits from Members in the Miscellaneous Occupations who entered the House between 1946 and 1955; on the other hand, the Professionals gained only 2. The Professional rebels of the 1955 Parliament consisted almost wholly of men elected in 1945 or before; more than a third of the Miscellaneous Occupations were recent entrants. The Worker element in the Left gained substantially from older Members who, rebelling with Bevan over rearmament or nuclear weapons, had died or left the House by 1959. We do not know how these Members would have reacted to the recrudescence of the dispute over the hydrogen bomb; but there were Workers, like Pargiter and Bernard Taylor, who remained in the House after 1959 and who did take part in the revolts of 1960–1.

In the earlier study the authors attempted to explain the divergence within the middle-class section of the party between the Professions and the Miscellaneous Occupations. A contributory factor, it was suggested, could be found in their rather different educational backgrounds; but the main grounds for the difference appeared to lie in the nature of the work performed by the two groups. The Professional men were all drawn from vocations—such as law, medi-cine, and teaching—whose members in their day-to-day work had a continuing responsibility for the welfare of their clients, and where (and this is especially true of law and medicine) a controlled judgement was required. The Miscellaneous Occupations worked under no such

TABLE 52. THE LEFT, 1945–50 AND 1955–9, BY OCCUPATION

Losses and Gains: Conversion

	Workers	Miscellaneous Occupations	Business	Professions	Unknown	Total
Losses						
To Non-consistent Rebels	—	—	—	3	—	3
To Non–Rebels	—	1	2	1	2	6
Total losses through conversion	—	1	2	4	2	9
Gains						
From "Rest", 1945–50, to Consistent Rebels	12	6	1	5	—	24
Net gains or losses through conversion	+12	+5	−1	+1	−2	+15

TABLE 53. THE LEFT, 1945–50 AND 1955–9, BY OCCUPATION

All Changes

	Workers	Miscellaneous Occupations	Business	Professions	Unknown	Total
Net gains or losses by conversion	+12	+5	−1	+1	−2	+15
Net gains or losses through changes in backbench membership	+3	—	—	−17	−1	−15
Total gains and losses	+15	+5	−1	−16	−3	—
The Combined Lefts, 1945–50	4	18	9	36	3	70
The Left, 1955–9	19	23	8	20	—	70

constraint. In this contrasting experience lay the main cause of their divergent attitudes. The Professional men tended to bring the caution and restraint of their workaday lives into their political controversies. Such an explanation does not, of itself, imply that the Professional Members reached *better* decisions; perhaps there are occasions when the leap of faith or the thrust of hope is needed. Nuclear disarmers might argue that hesitation and caution, in some circumstances, offer more hazard than the dramatic gesture or the sudden coup; but be that as it may, men from different occupations bring a different style to their reasoning processes, and have a different mode of reaching their conclusions.

The Miscellaneous Occupations bear a considerable affinity to Kornhauser's "freelance intellectuals".[9] Kornhauser argues that such men are much more disposed to join mass movements than intellectuals in corporate bodies, especially those in universities, citing in support of his thesis the importance of literary people in American Communist and fellow-travelling organizations and their relative insignificance in bodies like Americans for Democratic Action. He quotes the comment of Kingsley Amis, written in 1957,[10] that one way at university of distinguishing between the Marxist and the non-Marxist was to look at their likely occupation. "The Marxist wing included a strong faction of the more specifically literary and artistic intellectual which did not appear to the same degree in the democratic-socialist wing; a budding schoolmaster, let us say, was far less likely to be a Marxist than a budding poet was."

Kornhauser notes that the freelance is dependent on an anonymous and uncertain market; the forms of reward are less predictable, and recognition is more ephemeral, than for intellectuals in corporate bodies. Moreover, freelance intellectuals have fewer institutional responsibilities than intellectuals in professional organizations, and are therefore less likely to be committed to central values and institutions.

Freelance intellectuals, in short, are not likely to enjoy such stable rewards (whether these be psychic or material) as intellectuals in corporate bodies, and are not integrated into old and stable organizations. As a result, they are likely to contain in their ranks a disproportionate number of the socially alienated and discontented.

Some activists who in other, less stable, societies, would be drawn into overtly extremist movements, are in Britain attracted to the left wing of the Labour Party.[11] Some are Marxist or quasi-Marxists; there are others whose inspiration is religious or radical rather than specifically socialist; but whatever the differences in their formal beliefs, they are all deeply critical of the dominant institutions and values of British society. With some, this antagonism may have been expressed in a rigorous and coherent intellectual system; with others in a looser and more emotional form; but those who, on the Continent and in the United States, gravitate towards revolutionary movements, are in Britain more likely to be absorbed in the Labour Party and to occupy a position not unlike that which the radical wing of the Liberal Party did towards both its own leaders and the Conservative establishment.

Yet it is clear that whilst the Miscellaneous Occupations were the most distinctively left-wing group in the late fifties, 10 years before this role had been taken by the Professions. The school-teachers were more likely than the clerks, the lawyers more than the journalists, to criticize Britain's alignment in the Cold War. The explanation for this contrast probably lies in the early political experiences of the 1945 intake. Many of these men had grown to political maturity in the 1930's; the collapse of the second Labour government, the Great Depression, the rise of fascism, the Spanish Civil War—such events, and the interpretation put upon them, predisposed large numbers of young, active socialists to see politics in simple, Manichaean terms.

Most of the young Professionals, often fresh from the war, who came into the House in 1945, would have formed their opinions in the 1930's; but those who were elected later were more likely to have developed their political views at a time when the complexities of post-war affairs had become fully apparent. The Professionals of the 1945 cohort were a deviant group

[9] W. Kornhauser, *Politics of Mass Society*, London, 1960, p. 185.

[10] Kingsley Amis, *Socialism and the Intellectuals*, London, 1957.

[11] With the emergence of the New Left, this position may have changed substantially.

TABLE 54. POST-1945 ENTRANTS BY OCCUPATION

1955–9	Workers		Miscellaneous Occupations		Business		Professions		Total
	No.	%	No.	%	No.	%	No.	%	
Consistent Rebels	4	17	8	32	3	60	2	9	17
Non-consistent Rebels	3	13	5	20	–	–	5	22	13
Loyalists	16	70	12	48	2	40	16	70	46
Total	23	100	25	100	5	100	23	100	76

Data grouped. Miscellaneous Occupations plus Business vs. All Others. Consistent Rebels against Loyalists. $\chi^2_1 = 5\cdot86$. Significant at $2\cdot5\%$.

Two Members who came on to the backbenches in 1954 and rebelled once in that year but did not rebel again have been excluded.

who were no longer reinforced by the recruitment of new colleagues. New Professional men came into the House, but overwhelmingly and almost unanimously they adhered to the Centre and the Right. Table 54 compares the occupational backgrounds of those rebel and loyalist recruits who came into the party after 1945.[12]

The division of the backbench party of 1951–5 into the three broad political categories—Left, Other Defence and Nuclear Critics, and the Rest—permits a comparison of the responses of specific occupational groups to other issues. By pairing, for example, ideological orientations with the three most important occupational classes, nine sub-groups can be distinguished, i.e.

Left Professionals	Defence Professionals	Professionals of the Rest
Left Miscellaneous	Defence Miscellaneous	Miscellaneous Occupations of the Rest
Left Workers	Defence Workers	Workers of the Rest

The reactions of such groups as the Workers of the Left can be compared with the responses of the Left Professionals or of the loyalist Workers. In this way it is possible to tell whether a particular sub-group of backbenchers, in responding to a specific question, had more in common with their occupational class or their political grouping.

It is also relevant to examine the composition of each political-cum-ideological sub-group (e.g. the right-wing Professionals) in terms of other social characteristics, such as education. Thus the U1's were considerably better represented amongst the Professionals of the Rest than amongst the Professionals of either the Left or the Other Defence and Nuclear Critics. On the other hand, Members from Welsh and Scottish constituencies were most prominent amongst the Left Professionals. There were proportionately more of the more recent entrants amongst the Rest than amongst the Left; in contrast the small group of left-wing Workers boasted a

[12] In his unpublished study of attitudes to the Vietnam war in the 1964–6 Parliament, however, Patrick Seyd shows that the Professions were almost as left-wing as the Miscellaneous Occupations. The most radical position was taken by the small Business group, and the Workers were again the most moderate. It is not clear whether the radicalism of the Professions over Vietnam in this later Parliament was peculiar to the Vietnam issue or whether it reflected a more general left-wing orientation. It may, as is suggested later in this chapter, reflect a change in the character of the Professions because of the rapid expansion of higher education.

higher percentage of new Members than either the Defence Critics or the right-wing Workers—a fact which helps to explain the tendency of Workers and Professionals to converge after 1951. The right-wing Workers also claimed the largest proportion of sponsored Trade Unionists—but, given the massive trade-union dominance amongst the Workers, the differences were small, and even amongst the Left 7 of their 10 MPs were sponsored. The left-wing Workers included a larger proportion of Welsh and Scottish Members.

It is clear, pursuing the comparisons within the two most distant occupational groups—the Professions and the Workers—that Members generally had more in common, in their response to particular issues, with their ideological bedfellows than with other representatives of their own occupational group. Thus, amongst the Left, both Professionals and Workers were distinguished by a much higher degree of antipathy to both conscription and the level of royal grants than either the Defence Critics or the Rest. The same was true of colonial brutality; and, again, on colonial government both the Professions and the Workers on the Left seemed more concerned than their colleagues.

On capital punishment the Left were more hostile than either the Defence Critics or the Rest, irrespective of occupation; but support for abolition was also greater amongst the Professionals in each political category. Likewise, support for the Anti-Soviet motions varied by both occupation and political class, the subscription of signatures being much greater amongst Defence Critics and the Rest than amongst the Left, and, within each political category, greater amongst Workers than amongst the Professionals.

Two further features call for comment—the relatively high proportion (35 per cent) of right-wing Workers who signed Ellis Smith's call for a summit conference, and the contrast between the remarkable support given by the left-wing Workers to the social welfare EDMs and the apathy displayed by the Professionals of the Left. No other sub-group vied with the Workers of the Left in the way they demonstrated their attachment to the various tenets of the socialist syndrome—in their zeal for social welfare, their hostility to colonial injustice, their enthusiasm for economic aid to developing countries, in their support for international negotiation, in antagonism to royal grants, and their opposition to the death penalty—on most of these they outstripped all other groups, and in none were they far behind the most radical. Nor was this simply a reflection of a greater willingness to sign motions, for, on issues like conscription where opinion has been gauged by behaviour in the division lobbies, they enjoyed the same distinction. It was as though all the varied streams of the socialist tradition—trade-union concern for material improvement, radical opposition to militarism and royal expenditure, humanitarian interest in the fate of oppressed peoples abroad and in prisoners at home, had flowed together to form one great river. In contrast, their Professional colleagues on the Left, whilst evincing a similar support for the ideological issues, gave less backing than any other sub-group to the EDMs on social welfare and housing, and less than all but one to the motions on the health and education services. The Workers of the Left constituted a bridge linking the material purposes of the Trade Union section of the party and the ideological causes espoused by the various middle-class groups.

JEWS AND CATHOLICS

One distinctive group is of special interest—the Jewish Members. In the 1945 Parliament 14 out of the 24 Jewish backbenchers—or nearly two-thirds—were on the Left.[13] In the 1951–5

[13] Significant at well beyond the 0·1 per cent level.

period they were less conspicuously left-wing, but 6 of the 14 belonged to the Left according to the criterion used in Chapter 5.[14] The Roman Catholic section was much smaller. In 1945–50 the proportion of left wingers amongst the Catholics was almost the same as for the whole party; in 1951 none of the 12 Catholics were amongst the 40 Members of the Left.[15, 16]

There is no lack of theories to explain the clustering of Jews on the Left. The Jews are disproportionately represented in the Labour Party; not a single Jew sat as an official Conservative between 1945 and 1955, and yet 27 Jews were returned as Labour MPs in 1945, 21 in 1950, and 17 in 1951.[17] The number of Jews in Britain in the 1950's came to about 450,000, or just under 1 per cent of the population.[18] No one knows what proportion of them voted Labour, but even if all of them did (a most implausible assumption) it is clear that Jews were still, relative to their electoral contribution, considerably over-represented in the Parliamentary Labour Party.[19] Not merely, however, did Jews active in politics gravitate to Labour; they were heavily concentrated on the Left of the party. As a section not fully integrated in British society, still conscious of their "deviant" position, Jews are, in a sociological sense, a "marginal" group and hence less committed to the dominant institutions and values of the country.

To this sociological explanation may be added one that is overtly political. Identification of anti-semitism with the extreme Right (which in some countries, of course, preceded the 1930's) and the widespread interpretation of fascism as the last weapon of a desperate capitalism, would naturally impel politically minded Jews to the party of the Left—and within that party to its extreme wing.

The occupational background of the Jewish Members does little to explain their commitment to the Labour Left. It is true that Jews were heavily concentrated in the middle-class section of the party; only 1 of the 24 Jews was a Worker whereas no fewer than 14 were Professionals. However, if occupation and not race or religion had been the sole determinant of attitudes to foreign policy, we might have expected 7 of the 24 Jews (calculating to the nearest whole number) to have belonged to the Combined Lefts. In fact 14 did so.[20]

The picture, however unfair it may be, which many British socialists had of the Conservative Party as a party sympathetic to, or at least not hostile to, fascism[21] must have strengthened such a movement.

[14] Significant at the 2 per cent level.

[15] Jewish Members are defined as those listed by the appropriate post-election issue of the *Jewish Chronicle*; the names of Roman Catholic MPs are taken from the *Universe* of 3 Aug. 1945 and the *Scottish Catholic Herald* of 3 Mar. 1950 and 2 Nov. 1951.

[16] Mr. Delargy, a prominent Catholic Bevanite, was not on the backbenches for the whole Parliament, and hence does not figure amongst the 40 Left MPs.

[17] The number of Jewish Conservative MPs rose to 8 as a result of the General Election 1970; even so, they were heavily outnumbered by Labour's 31.

[18] See L. Epstein, *British Politics in the Suez Crisis*, London, 1964, p. 181.

[19] In 1970 the number of Jewish Conservative MPs rose from 2 to 8. Even so, the Jewish Conservatives were heavily outnumbered by the 31-strong Labour contingent.

[20] In the 1970 Parliament, however, the proportion of Jews in the Left (as defined by membership of the Tribune Group) differed little from that of the party as a whole.

[21] See pp. 48–49.

PARLIAMENTARY RECRUITMENT, SOCIAL BACKGROUND AND IDEOLOGICAL AFFILIATION IN THE LABOUR PARTY

So far we have examined changes in the occupational and social make-up of the dissident Left in Parliament; there is a sense, however, in which the backbench Labour Party represents (not necessarily in a precise way) the wider group of political activists with parliamentary ambition, who were, at the time, outside Parliament—in short, part of the more active section of the "political nation". Conclusions about the interrelationships between social background and opinion, and between one opinion and another within Parliament are perhaps inferences about the connection between, say, occupation and political attitudes, and between different attitudes in this wider group. How are the Members of this wider group—with their distinctive views and special experiences—recruited into the House? What, in short, is the relationship between the Parliamentary Labour Party and the broad circle of "available" men who aspire to Parliament themselves?

The social composition of a parliamentary party depends on three factors: the type of men who offer themselves for selection; the criteria used, consciously or unconsciously, by constituency parties and associations; and the concentration of candidates of different sorts in the constituencies that are actually won by the party. Unfortunately we have no reliable figures of those seeking adoption as Labour candidates; we do, however, know the distribution of candidatures (not candidates) between 1951 and 1964 amongst various occupational groups.[22] The Miscellaneous Occupations supplied about 30 per cent of the Labour candidatures, and the Professions about 37 per cent.[23] Both the Miscellaneous Occupations and the Professions were somewhat under-represented in the 1951 House compared with the figures for candidatures; this reflects the tendency of the safer seats to go to trade-union sponsored manual workers.[24]

Since the early fifties there has been a marked rise in the strength of the Professions, both within the PLP and, more broadly, amongst Labour candidates, a rise which reflects in two ways the expansion of higher education. As a result of improved educational services, young men from working-class and lower middle-class homes have been able to go to university, and the same expansion has provided them with posts in teaching and lecturing—two careers which are relatively easy to combine with part-time political work. The politically ambitious socialist can now often aspire to a professional career. He is no longer obliged to find employment as a white-collar worker or as a political publicist[25] or organizer.

There remains one other important feature of the changes in the composition of the Parliamentary Labour Party since the 1950's which has received little attention. The increase in the number of university graduates in the PLP is well known. It reached its peak in 1966 when more than 60 per cent of the Labour MPs were university trained, as compared with just over 40 per cent in 1950. What is surprising is that the proportion of public-school men in the

[22] Many candidates stood more than once; a candidate standing twice is counted twice, one standing three times is counted three times, and so on. See A. Ranney, *Pathways to Parliament*, London, 1965, p. 205.

[23] *Ibid.*, Tables 7–8. The figures given above refer to the occupational categories as defined in this study, not Ranney's, which uses a different method of classification.

[24] Apart from Ranney's there have been two major studies of the choice of parliamentary candidates—P. Paterson, *The Selectorate*, London, 1967, and M. Rush, *The Selection of Parliamentary Candidates*, London, 1969.

[25] The category "political publicists and journalists" includes not only those of established national reputation, but men who worked for relatively obscure left-wing papers and periodicals.

PLP actually fell from 21 per cent in 1950 to 17 per cent in 1966. Many commentators have spoken of the increasing middle-class predominance in the Labour Party. It must be emphasized that this middle class is of a rather different nature to the middle-class element which assumed the leadership of the Left in the 1945 House. It is, in short, more middle and less class.

The changes in the occupational composition of the party between 1951 and 1966 are shown in Table 55.

TABLE 55. THE PROFESSIONS
AND MISCELLANEOUS OCCUPATIONS IN THE
PARLIAMENTARY LABOUR PARTY, 1951–65

	Elected (%)	Defeated (%)
Whole Party	123	80
All professional	151	100
Teachers, lecturers, etc.	171	127
Miscellaneous occupations	118	72

The number in each category in 1966 is shown as a percentage of the same category in 1951.[26]

The Miscellaneous Occupations failed to keep pace with the expansion of the Parliamentary Party; even amongst the defeated candidates they fell behind. The Professionals grew by a half although the whole party increased by less than a quarter; and within the Professions the rise in teachers and lecturers was especially sharp.

Numerous motives can be distinguished in the choice of parliamentary candidates. Candidates might be chosen by virtue of their occupation or sponsoring body; thus some constituencies will choose trade-union sponsored Workers; until recently, these would have been drawn predominantly from the Right. Others might choose Oxford-trained Professionals who would also adhere preponderantly to the Right. Some will be chosen (though less often than might be expected) specifically for their ideological stance; with such a candidate, his occupation will, so to speak, be a byproduct of his political views. Others are selected for motives—local connections, personality, or factors connected with local in-fighting—which have little to do with any distinctive political opinions they may hold, or their social and educational background.

Sponsorship provides the most obvious link between selection and occupation; the tendency for sponsored trade-union candidates to be recruited from the ranks of manual workers (although less marked than in the past), naturally affects the occupational and ideological balance of the party. Preference may also be given to candidates from particular occupations for reasons other than those of financial help; and in so far as this occurs the effect will be similar to that of sponsorship.

The choice of candidates on overtly political grounds will affect the party's ideological balance and, secondarily, its occupational structure. Both of these effects may be termed

[26] Figures from D. E. Butler, *The British General Election of 1951*, London, 1952, and D. E. Butler and A. King, *British General Election of 1966*, London, 1966. The figures are not completely comparable with those given in this book, as Butler and King classify Members according to the nature of their first employment.

"systematic" and will presumably occur irrespective of the numbers of candidates of a specific ideological allegiance, or from a specific occupation, seeking selection. Presumably, however, the choice of candidates from the third group, those selected for reasons that have nothing to do with political opinions or their occupation or educational background, will bear some relationship to the numbers seeking candidatures. Thus the political complexion and occupational structure of a parliamentary party depends on an interaction between the deliberate ideological and social biases of the local selectors and the numbers in each group seeking adoption.

It seems probable that, allowing for the effects of office upon older Members, the proportion of the Left in the Parliamentary Labour Party has increased in the sixties; yet, as has been seen, the Miscellaneous Occupations have declined relatively to the Professions, a decline which reflects wider social changes. Presumably, the new Professionals (especially the teachers) are more left-wing than their predecessors; and bound up with this is the question whether an occupation attracts a particular type of person or whether it moulds a person according to a pattern deriving from its own necessities. Both factors may be relevant, though what weight should be attached to each is far from clear. What does seem evident is that the politically aspiring socialist, lacking the advantages of birth and inherited wealth, has both the capacity (in terms of the required educational qualifications) and the opportunity (in terms of the availability of posts) to enter the professions. It would not be surprising, therefore, to find a substantial change from the pattern of the early fifties.

To be a Member of the House of Commons, on the Labour side, is, for men of relatively humble origin and for those from higher social backgrounds who do not accept the British *élite's* values and assumptions, one way of obtaining prestige and power—or at least the sense of power; those who do not come from the favoured schools and prosperous homes from which the great majority of Conservative MPs are recruited, and those who do, who do not share the prejudices and traditions of the political establishment, may be termed a "counter-*élite*". For many of these a seat in Parliament is the only alternative to a life of social obscurity and political impotence. From the ranks of these political activists, together with the large contingent of trade-union sponsored candidates, the Parliamentary Labour Party is drawn. This counter-*élite* is both socially variegated and ideologically diverse; but its members are united by a common commitment to the Labour Party, perhaps the one vessel capable of carrying them all into the political haven. The ideological values and political styles of the Members of the counter-*élite* are related to their early background, their educational attainments, their social and vocational experiences; and though the PLP, because of the distortions of the selection process, may never exactly replicate in its own make-up, the composition of this counter-*élite*, there remains a close relationship between the two. The Labour Party in Parliament is likely to be a blurred reflection of the aspiring counter-*élite* in the country at large.

NINETEENTH- AND TWENTIETH-CENTURY CLEAVAGES

The nature of the Parliamentary Labour Party depends, therefore, on the conscious predilections, both social and ideological, of constituency selection committees, the operation of the sponsoring system, the type of men seeking a parliamentary career within the Labour Party, and, ultimately, on the decisions of the electorate. The interaction of these factors has produced in occupational terms a parliamentary coalition of Workers, the Professions, and Miscellaneous Occupations. Ideologically this coalition is an alliance of the Left, itself a mixture of Marxist and non-Marxist groups, dedicated to the common ownership of the means of production, and manifesting certain attitudes in other areas of policy, such as foreign affairs, which flow, or are supposed to flow, from the central socialist prescription, a Right committed to no more than economic interventionism and the extension of the social services, and a Centre, leaning now with the Right, now with the Left.

In organizational terms, it is a federation of the trade unions, the constituency Labour parties, sections of the Co-operative movement, and the Fabian Society. In another sense, it represents a tacit contract between its working-class voting supporters, hoping for higher living standards and more generous welfare facilities, and its predominantly middle-class activists, some of whom seek colonial emancipation and aid to the underdeveloped world abroad and libertarian and humanitarian reforms at home, whilst others, without neglecting these goals, look to aims of a more distinctively socialist nature.

Another view of the Labour Party, supplementing and not excluding the previous approaches, sees it as an alliance of two groups representing two distinct temporal strata of British politics—nineteenth-century radicals and twentieth-century collectivists. Nineteenth-century radicalism was pacifistic and moralistic in foreign affairs, anti-aristocratic, and critical of royalty at home; it offered no promise of material betterment to the lower classes and, indeed, championed economy in government. What radical leaders offered the radical voters was in John Vincent's words "great vicarious excitement . . . with an attack on authority, conducted as a public spectacle at national level."[27] Radicalism found a double pathway to the Labour Party—one immediate and direct, the other more circuitous. Many radicals, disheartened by the quarrels in the Liberal Party and dismayed by the Liberal Government's conduct of foreign affairs, joined the Labour Party during and after the First World War.[28] Long before this time, however, radicalism had penetrated the nascent Labour movement; the pioneers of the ILP, and the trade union leaders of the late nineteenth century had been saturated with the spirit of radical politics and religious non-conformity. Fabian socialism, in spite of its nineteenth-century origins, and trade unionism with its later commitment to governmental intervention in economic and social affairs, can be regarded as being essentially twentieth-century features.

It is clear that nineteenth-century radicalism remains vigorously alive within the Labour Party; with some, this radicalism has been combined more or less coherently, with the specifically collectivist policies associated, in varying ways, with Fabianism, neo-Marxism, and trade unionism. Others appear to emphasize their radical (and individualist) beliefs at the expense of contemporary collectivism. Indeed, a Cabinet Minister in the first Labour government, the late Josiah Wedgwood,[29] was so hostile to the compulsion inherent in modern collectivism that he had once opposed a proposal to raise the statutory age of leaving school. Another, and probably larger group, however, have partly discarded or escaped the influence of Victorian liberalism.

The most distinctively *radical* issue to arise during the decade after 1945 was the question of the grants to the royal family. As described in Chapter 6, some Labour MPs voted consistently for reductions in the amount of these grants; others voted for some reductions, but not all, whilst another group repeatedly voted to maintain the grants at the level proposed by the government. No issue arose which was so characteristically Victorian, so typical of individualistic radicalism. The money which would have been saved by the proposed cuts was negligible,

[27] J. Vincent, *Pollbooks: How Victorians Voted*, Cambridge, 1967, p. 47.

[28] See R. E. Dowse, *The Entry of the Liberals to the Labour Party, 1914–20* (Yorkshire Bulletin of Economic and Social Research, Vol. 13, No. 2, 1961).

[29] See R. W. Lyman, *The First Labour Government*, London, 1957.

and totally insignificant in the context of total government expenditure. Hardly one extra blade of grass or one further ear of corn would have grown as a result of these reductions. The proposals were essentially symbolic, and had little relevance to the purposes of collectivist change and social reform to which the Labour Party is primarily committed.

A second belief, which may, with rather less assurance, be regarded as belonging to the sphere of Victorian radicalism, is hostility to conscription. The nineteenth-century radicals were not only anti-aristocratic; they were also anti-militarist. Antipathy to conscription derived from several sources; but foremost amongst them was hostility to the spirit of militarism with its discipline, its conformism, its denial of personal liberty. Hostility to conscription passed from *laissez-faire* radicalism into the Labour movement, where it was reinforced by other fears; yet though pacificism, a repugnance to the use of armed forces, became a distinctive feature of the Labour Party, its origins lay in nineteenth-century radicalism rather than in collectivist socialism. "... the ideology of the Party", wrote Richard Crossman, 2 months before the outbreak of the Second World War, "springs from the Utopian Liberalism of Bright which Marx and Engels condemned so fiercely." Opposition to conscription had nothing socialistic in it. "Anti-militarism was the luxury of the Whigs, of the Liberal free-traders and of the nonconformist masses in the days when we possessed a monopoly of naval power."[30]

Victorian radicalism was, therefore, defined by reference to Members' votes in the divisions on royal grants in July 1952 and on the extension of national service in November 1953. Those occupying a Left or Moderate Left position in the royal grants controversy (essentially those demanding reductions in the grants to both the Queen and the Duke of Edinburgh), were regarded as Victorian radicals together with those additional Members who were absent from the divisions on royal grants but voted against conscription.[31] Sixty-eight of the 221 backbenchers who served throughout the Parliament were, on these criteria, classified as Victorian Radicals, and 153 as Twentieth-century Collectivists.[32]

In Table 56 the party has been divided into five strata or "layers" with each successive layer consisting of Members who do not qualify for inclusion in the preceding one. The Left constitute the topmost layer followed by the other critics of defence and nuclear policy, the most ardent humanitarians, the strongest protagonists of social welfare, and, finally, the rump of the party.

It is at once apparent that the Victorian Radicals were concentrated disproportionately on the Left; more than half of the latter, but less than a quarter of the Non-Left were Victorians. To put the matter the other way round, the Left constituted a third of the Victorians, but only a tenth of the Twentieth-century Collectivists.

Apart from the Left, the Victorians were strong amongst the other critics of defence and nuclear policy. Indeed, these two groups between them account for two-thirds of the Victorians.

[30] R. H. S. Crossman, Labour and compulsory military service, *Political Quarterly*, vol. X, no. 3, pp. 315–16.

[31] That opposition to national service is a satisfactory, if crude, criterion of Victorian radicalism is shown by the close relationship amongst Members voting on the royal grants issue between hostility to royal grants and hostility to conscription. Yule's Q has a value of $0 \cdot 71$.

[32] It is appreciated that these criteria will not, in the case of every individual Member, provide a wholly adequate classification; thus it could be argued that Michael Foot exhibits much more of the spirit of Victorian radicalism than of twentieth-century collectivism. Nevertheless, he occupied a Moderate Right positon on the royal grants question and did not vote against conscription in 1953. Similarly, Leslie Hale might, like Michael Foot, be regarded as displaying much of the ethos of nineteenth-century radicalism, and he had, indeed, served as a Liberal MP. Any simple criterion is open to objections of this kind, but the crucial question is not whether particular individuals are wrongly classified but whether any *systematic* distortion has been introduced.

TABLE 56. VICTORIAN RADICALISM AND TWENTIETH-CENTURY COLLECTIVISM

	Victorian Radicals		Twentieth-century Collectivists		Total	
	No.	%	No.	%	No.	%
The Left	23	58	17	43	40	100
Other Defence and Nuclear Critics	26	46	30	54	56	100
Humanitarians	2	8	22	92	24	100
Materialists	11	20	44	80	55	100
The Rump	6	13	40	87	46	100
Total	68		153		221	100

The Left and Other Defence and Nuclear Critics are as defined in Chapter 5. The Humanitarians were signatories of any one of the capital Punishment EDMs who did not qualify for the two preceding "layers"; the Materialists were those who signed either three or more EDMs on health and education or three or more EDMs on social security payments without qualifying for any of the three preceding layers; and the Rump consist of the remainder of the party.

The occupational breakdown is noteworthy. The prominence of the Workers and Trade Unionists amongst the opponents of royal grants has already been mentioned. Not surprisingly, they were also conspicuous amongst the Victorians. A third of the Workers were Victorians, as against a quarter of the Professional men; moreover, the Workers were not far behind the Miscellaneous Occupations.

The most striking findings, however, concern the regional and University groups. Victorian radicalism was pre-eminently a phenomenon of the Celtic fringe. Nearly half of the Victorians represented constituencies in Wales or Scotland; in contrast, only a ninth of the Twentieth-century Collectivists did so (Table 57).

Within the University section the U4's (secondary schools and other universities) were much more strongly Victorian than the U1's, U2's, and U3's. The former divided evenly between

TABLE 57. VICTORIAN RADICALISM AND REGION

	England		Wales and Scotland		Total	
	No.	%	No.	%	No.	%
Victorian Radicalists	38	56	30	44	68	100
Twentieth-century Collectivists	136	89	17	11	153	100
Total	174		47		221	

$\chi_1^2 = 30 \cdot 629$. Significant at $0 \cdot 1\%$.

TABLE 58. VICTORIAN RADICALISM AND UNIVERSITY EDUCATION

	U1, U2, U3		U4		Total	
	No.	%	No.	%	No.	%
Victorian Radicals	9	35	17	65	26	100
Twentieth-century Collectivists	42	72	16	28	58	100
Total	51		33		84	

$\chi_1^2 = 10 \cdot 2$. Significant at 1%.

Victorians and Twentieth-century Collectivists; the latter overwhelmingly belonged to the twentieth-century camp (Table 58).

This close link between University background and Victorian radicalism reflects, to some extent, the overlap between University education and region. A considerable proportion of the U4's, it will be recalled, sat for Welsh or Scottish constituencies.

A breakdown of the various ideological "layers" of the party by region and University background reveals some piquant features (Tables 59 and 60).

The Twentieth-century Collectivist element of the Left was overwhelmingly English, and its graduate section was drawn from the U1's, U2's, and U3's in a similarly overwhelming way. The regional imbalance amongst the Other Defence and Nuclear Critics is even more startling; more than half of the Victorian Radical Critics came from Scotland and Wales, but only one out of the 29 Collectivists.

In short, both the more narrowly defined Left, and the more numerous group who criticized the nuclear and defence policies of the party consisted of two elements. The Left contained the heirs of nineteenth-century radicalism, drawn disproportionately from Wales and Scotland, and led by intellectuals who had been educated at less prestigious schools and less prestigious universities; and also a specifically twentieth-century group who, to an overwhelming degree,

TABLE 59. VICTORIAN RADICALISM, REGION AND IDEOLOGICAL AFFILIATION

	Victorian Radicals		Twentieth-century Collectivists		Total
	England	Wales and Scotland	England	Wales and Scotland	
Left	13	10	15	2	40
		Fisher's exact test $\chi_1^2 = 4 \cdot 68$. Significant at 5%			
Other Defence and Nuclear Critics	12	14	29	1	56
			$\chi_1^2 = 18 \cdot 1$. Significant at 0·1%		
Humanitarians	2	—	20	2	24
Materialists	7	4	38	6	55
Rump	4	2	34	6	46
Total	38	30	136	17	221

TABLE 60. VICTORIAN RADICALISM, UNIVERSITY AND IDEOLOGICAL AFFILIATION

	Victorian Radicals		Twentieth-century Collectivists		
	U1, U2, U3	U4	U1, U2, U3	U4	Total
Left	3	7	9	1	19
	Fisher's exact test. $\chi = 20$. Significant at 1%				
Other Defence and Nuclear Critics	4	5	10	4	23
Humanitarians	1	1	8	2	12
Materialists	1	4	6	6	17
Rump	—	—	9	3	12
Total	9	17	42	16	84

represented English constituencies and were drawn predominantly from those who had either been educated at a public school, gone to Oxford or Cambridge, or done both. The critics of defence and nuclear policy outside the Left exhibit these same tendencies in a marked way.[33]

In the 1945 Parliament the Centre Left had put forward a critique of the government's foreign policy which was largely detached from traditional radical hostility to militarism and "power politics". From 1950 onwards the strictures of the Left exhibited more and more of the radical rather than the specifically socialist spirit. Criticism of the Korean war and of the rearmament programme, the demands for a summit conference, the rise of the unilateralist movement within the Labour Party, were witnesses to a resurgence of radical feeling. The struggle over nuclear weapons between 1955 and 1962 reflected, in its emphasis, the perennial radical hostility to armaments and power politics rather than the socialist analysis of imperialism and war, and the unilateralists' brief triumph at the Scarborough Conference of 1960 was a victory much more for the recurring voice of nineteenth-century dissent than for contemporary socialism. The more explicit, if paradoxically the more ambivalent, socialism of the Centre Left was superseded in its opposition to the foreign policy of the establishment by the modern form of a more enduring and more deeply rooted radicalism.

The succession of causes represented by Bevanism could attract such numerical strength as they did because they mobilized two distinct elements; the one, hard-headed, twentieth century, and English, whose leaders (Bevan apart) were drawn from *élite* educational backgrounds; and a more sentimental group, inheritors of the traditions of the old Liberal party, who either in combination with specifically socialist beliefs or alone, adhered to the enthusiasms of an earlier pre-socialist age.[34]

A comparison of the Left and Centre Left of 1945–50 is instructive (Table 61). Twenty-

---

[33] Finer *et al.* were over-hasty in dismissing a prominent Labour MP's comment that the real division in the party lay between Celts and Anglo-Saxons. These findings show that there was an important cleavage *within* the Left between these two territorial groups.

[34] This distinction parallels, to some extent, that made by A. H. Birch between *The Non-conformists* on the one hand and *the Idealists* and *the Planners* on the other. See his article "The Real Split in the Labour Party" in *The Guardian*, 17 Nov. 1960.

TABLE 61. THE LEFTS OF 1945–50 AND 1951–5

The Combined Lefts of 1945–50

The Left and Non-Left of 1951–5	The Left		The Centre Left		Total
	Victorian Radicals	Twentieth-century Collectivists	Victorian Radicals	Twentieth-century Collectivists	
Left	6	2	2	9	19
Non-Left	—	4	—	6	10
Total	6	6	2	15	29

nine of the Left Combined of the 1945 Parliament sat as backbenchers throughout the House of 1951–5. Of the 17 survivors of the Centre Left only 2 were Victorian Radicals, as against exactly half of the 12 survivors of the Left.

"Paradoxically", David Martin has put it, "it is the so-called left, with its apparently Socialist slogans, which provides clearest evidence of this inheritance from the anarchic tendencies of nineteenth-century liberalism", adding that the broad emphasis of these "anarchic socialists of the Left" rests on "foreign affairs and the whole question of violence".[35]

The difference between the two groups in the early post-war years was clear, for practical (as compared to symbolic) purposes resting essentially on the issue of conscription. Following Crossman, the collectivist Left were prepared at this time to forswear the long-lived hostility of the Labour Movement to compulsory military service. Many assented to conscription in a grudging and conditional manner—but assent they did. Important though this distinction is, it has often been latent rather than manifest; there were those, too, who, like Michael Foot, though supporting conscription and taking a moderate line on the question of royal grants drew clearly on both traditions, and the contrasts, moreover, were frequently softened or obliterated by the passage of time. The decision of the Conservative Government to abandon conscription in 1960 virtually erased that issue from the political agenda. In 1971, when the question of royal grants recurred, it was the Tribune group and survivors of the old Centre Left, like Crossman, who criticized most sharply the increase in the grants paid to the Royal Family. At some times the differences on the Left between the Victorian Radicals and the Twentieth-century Collectivists are clearly visible; at others, the two groups are almost indistinguishable in their responses to particular events or policies. Radicalism and collectivism are like roads starting in different places which now come together forming one long, broad highway, and now diverge, following their separate routes.[36]

There remains one important and interesting characteristic of the Victorians which has so far not been mentioned. Some of the Left subscribed heavily to the "material" EDMs such as those on social security payments and housing, others did not. To a remarkable extent, the division follows the simple dividing line of Victorian radicalism. The Radicals subscribed heavily to the "material" EDMs; the Twentieth-century Collectivists did not—indeed, only three of the 17 signed more than two of these motions. Paradoxically, those whose socialism

[35] D. Martin, *Pacifism*, London, 1965, pp. 89–90.

[36] It must be stressed that the difference between Radicals and Collectivists is one of degree. The whole Party united in opposing some of the Civil List proposals.

was most attuned to the inspiration of modern collectivism rarely concerned themselves with the bread-and-butter EDMs.

THE SIGNIFICANCE OF THE LABOUR LEFT

The Labour Party, by hallowed usage, is seen best as a tripartite alliance of Left, Right, and Centre. The Left—militant, dissident, doctrinaire—stands in almost permanent opposition to the party leadership; the Right—moderate, loyal, and pragmatic—provides the Front Bench with substantial and dependable backing. The Centre—pulled occasionally to the Left but more often to the Right—holds the balance of power.

Such a simple picture hardly does justice to the complexity of the Labour Party, to the variety of social groups from which it draws its mass vote and its activist cadres, or to the diversity of the historic strands of which it is composed.

The Left itself, though it displays a measure of continuity over the decades, as evinced by the general causes for which it fights, represents a loose and often changing body of opinion; its social make-up and the specific orientation of its policies, change in response to the emergence of new issues; so, after 1960, it tended, in practice, to merge with the pacifists from whom sections of the Left had stood firmly aloof in the late forties; and as has been shown, in the 1951–5 House, it was divided more or less equally into two sections—the heirs of Victorian radicalism on the one hand, and the spokesmen of modern collectivism on the other—whose members came from distinct social strata and whose socialist commitment had matured in different environments.

The importance of the Left lies in that, however unstable its membership over the years, at any one time it offers a stable core of support for or hostility to those controversial or potentially controversial proposals which are being canvassed almost continuously within the Labour Party. As new issues arise, the Left can ally with some hitherto alien section of the party; on capital punishment it can make common cause with university-trained professionals outside its own ranks; on conscription and defence policy, it can draw on that socially variegated group who feel most acutely that aversion to the use of armed force which is so widespread in the Labour Movement; on the economic development of the backward areas, it can mobilize the middle-class altruists of the Centre and Right; on German rearmament it can rally pacifists and ex-servicemen; and on social welfare and trade union rights is can co-operate with the Trade Unionist/Workers. In short, the rest of the party, the Non-Left, can be divided into middle-class and working-class groups whose members, aside from a perenially loyal core, can be detached by the Left on specific questions. Such an alliance may well blunt the blade of sectional cleavage; but, as over German rearmament, or more recently over the reform of industrial relations, it spells peril to the leadership.

CLEAVAGES IN BRITISH AND AMERICAN PARTIES

In the United States the bases of the cleavages which are found within the parties are pre-eminently geographical. Intra-party conflict represents the discordant claims of separate regions, the diverse interests of the several states, the special traditions and demands of congressional districts, the antagonistic claims—economic, ethnic, religious, and cultural—of the territorial units. In Britain these cleavages, though sometimes geographic, are predominantly social; divisions within the parties usually take the form of conflict between Members from different occupations and educational backgrounds. Amongst the regions the representatives of Celtic Britain sometimes stand out, special and separate, marked off from their English colleagues; more often they fail to respond in any distinctive way.

The huge extent and regional diversity of the United States, coupled with the relative homogeneity of its national legislators, make the latter, in so far as they are not the spokesmen of a party, the mouthpieces of their constituency or the agents of their region. In Britain the varying historic traditions and the distinctive opinions of which each party, but especially Labour, is composed, tend to be represented in a more subtle way, through separate vocational and educational groups, or even through the procession of the generations. The university-educated Professionals tend to embody the Left's enthusiasm for humanitarian penal reform and also the Fabian managerial tradition; amongst graduates the U4's, and amongst the territorial groups the Welshmen and the Scots, tend to be the guardians of the party's pacifistic conscience; and the party's special concern for social reform and the protection of trade union rights finds a natural representation in the Workers. In a two-party system, operating in a diverse society, any party must necessarily be a coalition. American parties are territorial alliances, whilst British parties are complex alliances, embodying distinct historical traditions and a variety of ideological beliefs which find partial expression in the distinct social groups from which recruits to the world of active politics are drawn.

The revolts which have been described in this study (as distinct from those expressions of opinion which, whilst sometimes in advance of, were not clearly contrary to, party policy) nearly always took the form of Extremist rebellions, as defined in Chapter 2. These revolts took what Mr. Crossman described as an L-shaped pattern; the rebels usually comprised a section of one party who were in conflict with an otherwise united House.

Some analysts have employed the concept of "marginality" to account for the propensity of certain individuals and groups to join movements or support causes at odds with the national consensus. It may be tentatively noted that the available data is consistent with this approach. With the near integration of the trade unions into the policy-making process after 1945, the rebellions often appeared to have the shape of a conflict between the representatives of the great corporate institutions of the country—business, trade unions, law, medicine, and education— and members of less accepted and less securely based sectors of the national life. It is true that in the 1945 Parliament the foreign policy critics were drawn disproportionately from the Professions and from those educated at the most prestigious schools and universities, but this pattern was short-lived; after 1955, and to some extent before, the U1's and the Professional men yielded their place to the Miscellaneous Occupations, to the secondary school and redbrick university graduates, and to the spokesmen of Wales and Scotland. In short, during the 1950's the critics came, to an increasing degree, from both the institutional and the geographical periphery. In the Conservative Party the evidence is less clear. The small size of the Miscellaneous Occupations category amongst the Conservatives makes it hard to draw definite conclusions. In a number of Extremist revolts, however, the figures are suggestive. The role of the directors of private companies after 1955 in right-wing revolts is also noteworthy. In each party those least integrated in the dominant institutions of the nation were most prominent in rebellion; moreover, as was argued in the earlier study, the Miscellaneous Occupations can be regarded as the most politicized group within each party—those Members for whom politics was often the great, and sometimes the only, activity.

INCLUSIVE AND EXCLUSIVE POLITICS

The pattern of cleavages in the Labour Party is far from simple. The ideological nature of these cleavages is complex, and their social character more variable than had been supposed.

There is, however, another criterion for classifying the divisions within a political party. In his study of Swedish politics,[37] *The Politics of Compromise*, Dankwart Rustow distinguishes three kinds of compromise. These three kinds of compromise, or more specifically of political situations which give rise to the compromises, are equally applicable to a political party. If the demands of the constituent sections are quite compatible with one another, the party will be able to press these demands simultaneously. The politics of such a situation may be styled "inclusive politics". Alternatively (and this applies especially to policies of public expenditure designed to help particular groups) the party can "split the difference" between the claims of rival sections; if it is possible to increase public spending by £200 million in a year, the protagonists of better schools and of improved hospitals can be conceded £100 million each. Finally, the situation of "exclusive politics" arises when the claims of different groups are incompatible with one another, and some kind of imposed decision—albeit a decision imposed by a majority—is required.[38]

Clearly it is easier for a party to preserve its unity if it can play the game of "inclusive politics" than if it is compelled to choose between incompatible policies. It has been argued that the Labour Party consists, in one sense, of people broadly committed to a wide range of policies; thus all members of the Labour Party believe in more generous social security provisions and in vigorous policies of expansion in education and the health service. Nearly all are opposed to the death penalty, all are in favour of equal pay for men and women, and most favoured the emancipation of Britain's colonial territories. Nevertheless, different groups varied in the keenness with which they pursued these objectives. For some, mainly Workers, the improvement of the lot of the under-privileged at home was the top priority; others would have given a high, though hardly first priority, to the abolition of the death penalty; some, like Fenner Brockway and Anthony Wedgwood Benn, were distinguished by their dedication to the removal of colonial injustices. From this aspect, the Labour Party could be regarded as a system of institutionalized log-rolling. Up to a point, at any rate, it was possible to satisfy the special demands of each of these groups; each group threw its support behind or gave its assent to the particular claims of the other sections.

At the other extreme are those issues where the demands are contradictory and incompatible. No legerdemain could reconcile the foreign policies of Ernest Bevin and his critics; no sleight of hand could bring together those who accepted the rearming of Germany and those who bitterly resisted it. Under such conditions the outward semblance of party unity simply could not be preserved.

In the 1945 Parliament, disputes over foreign policy belonged pre-eminently to the sphere of "exclusive politics". Similarly, the controversy between the irreconcilable opponents of conscription and the government partook of the same character; but a number of those who criticized the government's conscription policy would have been, and were satisfied, by a shorter period of service. For these the issue was of the "split the difference" sort. Disagreement about

---

[37] D. Rustow, *The Politics of Compromise*, Princeton, 1955, pp. 230–2.

[38] The distinction between "inclusive" and "exclusive" politics corresponds to the distinction between quantitative and qualitative differences outlined in S. E. Finer, H. B. Berrington, and D. J. Bartholomew, *Backbench Opinion in the House of Commons, 1955–59*, London, 1961.

co-operation with western Europe was also resolved by a "split-the-difference" technique, the supporters of integration being partially satisfied by British participation in consultative organs of European collaboration. In the social field there was no serious problem, for full employment was maintained and the government implemented the party's commitments to social security and a free health service.

In 1951 the party went into opposition; and it is clearly easier, for a party leadership without the responsibility of governing, to turn divisive questions, if it wishes, into the issues of "inclusive politics", to find forms of words satisfying to the whole or nearly the whole of the party. A leadership which is not overburdened with integrity can, with a little skill, successfully blur the real implications of policies. To their credit, the leaders of the Labour Opposition usually repelled this temptation, though their probity was hardly of much service to the party. For a time, they tried to turn the question of German rearmament into an issue of "exclusive politics"; they felt obliged to press for the party's assent to this measure, but eventually, by recommending the party meeting to instruct Members to abstain in the vote, they tacitly "split the difference". The divisions over the Japanese Peace Treaty and the manufacture of nuclear weapons belong to the field of "exclusive politics"; whilst those on equal pay, housing standards, social welfare payments, education, and the health service partook essentially of the character of "inclusive politics". So, too, ignoring the tiny handful who still defended the death penalty, did the question of capital punishment.

In the later years of opposition, issues like colonialism, penal reform, the social services, and welfare benefits, all belonged to the realm of "inclusive politics"; but the question of the hydrogen bomb, the party's commitment to common ownership as embodied in Clause IV of the Party Constitution, and some issues of foreign policy, could not be treated in this way, and deep rifts within the party were publicly displayed. Many of the real divergences were not exposed in opposition, however; the Labour Party needed the harsh test of government before it revealed the full extent of its inner contradictions. Trade-union and left-wing resistance to the incomes policy at one time threatened the government's survival; the resistance of the same alliance to the Industrial Relations Bill forced the government into a humiliating retreat.

In opposition, therefore, the leadership of a party can, if it wishes, evade the strict choices imposed by governmental responsibility by finding some formula which will appease all sections. In the early years of opposition, however, such action may be both distasteful and embarrassing; the memory of commitments made, and promises incurred so recently in government, will be a source of discomfort to the participants, and of disquiet to more detached observers. An opposition leader, however, who treats every question with the same caution and honesty as he would employ in government, is bound to transform most, if not all, issues into those of "exclusive politics".

In all of this the Left played a special part. In a curious sense the Left provided the knot which tied up the bundle of socialist attitudes. The syllabus of the Left embraced almost all of what were, outside the Left, the particular causes of distinct sections. Especially after 1955, but even to some extent before then, the party came more and more to adopt the nostrums of the Left, and in so doing to appease the special demands of each of the party's component groups.

These limitations apart, there is a strong tendency for the claims of different sections within the opposition party to "add up" rather than to cancel each other out. The social service lobby demanded a commitment to more generous programmes of social welfare; the Trade Union/

Worker group demanded increases in social security benefits and food subsidies; the feminists wanted the party to embrace the cause of equal pay with more than the customary verbal tribute; the advocates of negotiation with Russia wanted the party to declare forthrightly in favour of high-level talks; the proponents of colonial self-government and of economic aid to the underdeveloped countries desired to commit the party to the political liberation and economic advancement of the colonial territories, whilst the penal reformers sought to commit the party, in fact if not in name, to the abolition of capital punishment. The bland veneer of opposition might conceal any cracks in this facade, but the strains of government would soon reveal the fissures and breaches.

Yet, as has been seen, for some questions of foreign and defence policy, and, of course, on the very important issue of public ownership, an issue which, not being expressed through EDMs or floor revolts, lies outside the scope of this study, it was impossible to adopt the easy solution of accepting the claims of every vocal group. On rearmament, both British and German, on the development of nuclear weapons, on the Japanese Peace Treaty, and the maintenance of conscription, the undertakings made by the party when in office, and the sense of responsibility of its leaders, forbade such a course. Public dissension, and often open revolt, were the unavoidable outcome.

Like the Labour Party, the Conservatives could, whilst in opposition, disguise their disputes by treating potentially divisive issues as "inclusive". Indeed, the theory of opposition, as understood by Conservative leaders from Balfour to Churchill was framed on this assumption. So, from 1945 to 1951 the real nature of the choices involved in any genuine integration with Europe, was ignored; the potential conflict between the claims of empire and the call of Europe was overlooked. In office, however, the leadership could not escape commitment to specific policies, and so could not always avoid an open clash with backbench critics. The retreat from Suez, the refusal to restore corporal punishment, the disputes about MPs' salaries, and the administration of the coal industry, all resulted in public revolt. These disputes were often spirited and sometimes acrimonious; yet the Conservative Party never presented the picture of disunion offered by the Labour. Even when controversy dragged on, as over the government's fuel policy, or repeatedly recurred, as over birching, the quarrel remained limited and specific. The underlying unity of the party was never in question. To understand the difference between the parties we have to look at the pattern of the disputes, to examine the interrelationships amongst the various dissident groups, and to the relationship these groups bore to the structure of the parties.

CUMULATION AND DISPERSION

The unity of a party will, therefore, depend partly on whether it is in government or opposition. Parties in government are likely to suffer internal disunity because they cannot avoid taking decisions which have practical consequences; opposition parties do not have to define issues with the harsh clarity which the logic of office imposes.[39] Parties in opposition which *behave* as though they were in government, whose leaders are weighed down by the memory of responsibility recently incurred, or soon perhaps to be borne again, will suffer in a similar way.

A second factor affecting party unity is to be found in the extent to which various cleavages reinforce or cut across one another.

[39] See Jackson, *op. cit.*, p. 187 for a similar point.

In *Political Man*, Seymour Lipset has argued that cross-cutting politically relevant affiliations strengthen democracy by reducing the intensity of feeling involved in political choice.

> "... in contemporary Germany, a working-class Catholic, pulled in two directions, will most probably vote Christian Democratic, but is much more tolerant of the Social Democrats than the average middle-class Catholic. ... To the degree that a significant proportion of the population is pulled among conflicting forces, its members have an interest in reducing the intensity of political conflict. As Robert Dahl and Talcott Parsons have pointed out, such groups and individuals also have an interest in protecting the rights of political minorities."[40]

Lipset's thesis can also be applied to the structure of a political party. If social divisions, such as those of occupation and education, are superimposed upon one another, the party will be divided into distinct cultural groups; if some political divisions parallel the social divisions, then existing group tensions will become more acute; and if all, or nearly all, political divisions accumulate, the party will be divided into separate political sections. Such a party is likely to suffer from extreme internal disunity.

As has been observed, the differences between the Labour and Conservative parties in this regard are very marked. Social characteristics tend to accumulate in the Labour Party and to cut across one another amongst the Conservatives. Education and occupation reinforce one another on the Left but hardly on the Right; sponsorship (which does not exist in the Conservative Party) tends to follow the educational and occupational boundaries on the Labour side. Political disagreements often reflected cultural cleavages in the Labour Party but rarely did so amongst Conservatives; and there was some tendency (though it was far from complete) for the Left on one issue, in the Labour Party, to parallel the Left on another, whereas amongst Conservatives there was very little correspondence between the membership of successive rebel groups.

Reference has already been made to the social distinctiveness of the foreign policy critics of the 1945 Parliament. This distinctiveness increased the bitterness felt by members of the rival ideological groups. After 1950 there was some attenuation of these cleavages; the prominence of the Professionals became less marked, and although the Workers were still under-represented amongst the Left, they were to be found in greater numbers than before. The bitterness felt by the Right was focused upon the Bevanites proper (the core of whom corresponded to the twentieth-century element amongst the Left).[41] As has been seen, these men were primarily middle class.

The greater tolerance displayed by the Conservatives towards their rebels and the absence of formal rules proscribing dissent, can also be explained by the tendency, within the Labour Party, for political divisions to accumulate, and by the tendency amongst Conservatives for these divisions to cut across each other. As Lipset (citing Dahl and Parsons) observes, groups and individuals subject to cross-cutting loyalties have an interest in protecting the rights of

---

[40] S. M. Lipset, *Political Man*, London, 1963, pp. 88–89.

[41] This suggests that sometimes it is the *perception* of cumulative cleavages, whether or not this corresponds to the objective position, which is more significant than the objective situation. Gaitskell's reference to the Bevanites as "a group of frustrated journalists" may or may not have been true of the Bevanite leadership. It was hardly an exact description of Bevanite support in the PLP. The journalists amongst the Bevanites were the most visible (or, more precisely, the most audible) element; hence right wingers and middle-of-the-roaders may have perceived the Bevanites to have possessed greater occupational distinctiveness than they actually had.

political minorities. The more diffuse character of revolt in the Conservative Party means that a premium tends to be put on tolerance; anyone may be a rebel at some time.

Yet the Labour Party managed to avoid a total split. Although some features of the party made for disunion, others tended to moderate the keenness of the divisions. The Bevanites themselves failed to maintain their unity to the end of the 1951 Parliament; and, however exclusive and tight-knit they may have been in the earlier years, they were often joined in floor revolts by men whose inspiration was pacifistic rather than Left socialist. The composition of the Left on one issue was strongly related to but never duplicated the composition of the Left on another. On German rearmament the Left were joined by respectable men of the Centre and Right;[42] on the question of high-level talks, they found numerous, if distant, allies amongst the Trade Unionists; on colonial and humanitarian matters, men of the Left could look to other sections of the party for support.

In a paradoxical way the very factors that softened the divisions within the party made the position of the Labour leadership more precarious. An isolated, occupationally exclusive and ideologically distinctive Left might arouse passionate and bitter feelings within the party and might, by the very acrimony it aroused, stigmatize the party as divided and uncertain, but it could not threaten the Front Bench. A Left that was able on specific issues to mobilize men who were normally loyal, to attract Trade Unionists and the right-wing Professionals, presented the Shadow Cabinet with a grave problem.

We must consider, too, not only the extent to which various political groups within the party reflected occupational and other social boundaries, but the degree to which they cut across these frontiers. The Left of 1945–50 was primarily a faction of University-trained Professionals; but it never appeared to gain the support of even a majority of that section. In the post-1950 period, as has been noted, the social distinctiveness of the Left was diluted; and although on most issues the Left drew disproportionate support from the Professionals and the Miscellaneous Occupations, the leadership could always be sure of the backing of many individuals from these categories.

Nevertheless, the contrast between the two parties is striking; the greater social homogeneity of the Conservatives, the more integrated character of the party, the extent to which opposition to the leadership on one issue cut across opposition on another, all helped to make them a much more efficient electoral machine than Labour. As Angus Maude has written, the very multiplicity of tensions arising in the Conservative Party tends to make cohesion easier, as the tensions cancel one another out.[43] The much-vaunted social diversity of the Labour Party proved to be a handicap in the quest for power; different occupations and different classes sought divergent ends, proclaimed divergent values, and brought contrasting styles to politics. Lipset may well have exaggerated the harm done to a democratic society by cumulative cleavages; for cumulative divisions foster the development of stable groups of electoral support, and preserve the society from political fragmentation. The needs of a political party, however, differ fundamentally from those of a nation; the existence of stable factions, or of separate and clearly defined social groups, puts in peril its unity and at risk its hopes of winning or keeping power.

[42] As *The Economist* on 27 Feb. 1954 remarked, with some exaggeration, in commenting on the German rearmament controversy: "... In the meantime, Labour seems curiously cheered at finding an argument which cuts clear of the all too familiar Bevanite wrangle."

[43] A. Maude, *The Common Problem*, London, 1969.

ANNEX 1

Some Problems of Method

THE purpose of this Annex is to consider the problem of scale construction, to explain in greater detail the nature of the statistical measures employed, and to explain more fully the relationship between participation in floor revolts and signature of left-wing EDMs in the Labour Party which was described in Chapter 1.

THE PROBLEM OF SCALING

There is no doubt that, despite their usefulness, EDMs do not afford as rich a source of material as the roll-call votes of the American Congress or the votes of the Assembly in the French Fourth Republic. The limited number of serious EDMs, and the small number of Members signing some motions, means that it has not often been possible to employ the highly sophisticated techniques of scaling used in some American studies.[1]

A widely used scaling device is the Guttman technique, which unfortunately cannot frequently be applied to EDMs or, indeed, to divisions in the House of Commons.

The aim of Guttman scaling is to discover a single dimension running through the answers to a series of separate questions, or, in legislative terms, running through the responses of Members to a series of separate issues posed in legislative votes or resolutions. It may be, for example, that two divisions or roll-call votes dealing apparently with a common subject-matter in fact appeal to different motives. What appear to be two questions referring to the same issue of foreign policy may be dealing, in addition, with extraneous issues. Thus opposition to a European Federation may be prompted not only by belief in national sovereignty but by fears for the economic future of particular constituencies, or, more simply, adherence to unilateralism may be called forth by a desire to embarrass the party leadership for reasons other than a belief in the wickedness of nuclear arms. In such situations not one dimension is tapped but two, and attempts have been made, in studies of the American Congress, to cope with the difficulties that arise.

Let us illustrate the aim of Guttman scaling by taking a common dimension—weight. Suppose we were to ask a group of four people the following questions:

(1) Do you weigh 13 stone or more?
(2) Do you weigh 12 stone or more?
(3) Do you weigh 11 stone or more?

---

[1] See, for example, Duncan MacRae, Jr., *Dimensions of Congressional Voting*, Los Angeles, 1958, and the same author's *Parliament, Parties and Society in France 1946–58*, London and New York, 1967.

The responses to these questions might be as follows:

	Question 1 13 stone or more	Question 2 12 stone or more	Question 3 11 stone or more
A	Yes	Yes	Yes
B	No	Yes	Yes
C	No	No	No
D	No	No	Yes

Thus A, who weighs 14 stone, necessarily answers "Yes" to all three questions; B, who weighs 12½ stone, answers "No" to Question 1 and "Yes" to the other two; whilst C, who weighs only 10 stone, answers "No" to each question; D, who weighs just over 11 stone, answers "No" to Question 1 and 2, and "Yes" to Question 3. It would be possible to construct, with perfect confidence, a scale showing the position of each respondent along this single dimension of weight. A is clearly the heaviest, C the lightest.

It might be expected that, in any population, fewer people would subscribe to a more extreme statement than to a less extreme one. Taking the example of weight, we would expect more people to answer "Yes" to the question Do you weigh 11 stone or more? than to the question Do you weigh 12 stone or more?, and that more would answer "Yes" to the latter question than to Do you weigh 13 stone or more? Similarly, if we were to ask members of the Labour Party what proportion of the country's industry should be nationalized, more people would be prepared to agree to "*at least* 20 per cent" than to "*at least* 50 per cent", and more would assent to the latter figure than to 100 per cent.

In studies of the American Congress it has been possible to apply scaling procedures which array members along a single dimension—be it social welfare, race relations, or isolationism. To facilitate the exposition, however, let us take a simple example like the level of family allowances. Suppose there were a series of free votes in the House of Commons in which Members were able to vote for or against various levels of allowances. Some might want to reduce the present allowance; other Members would be prepared to accept the present level; others would want to increase the rate.

Empirical procedures have been devised to determine the extent to which legislators, in voting for a given proposition, are responding to the same issue or whether some are being influenced by another factor, e.g. a different political issue connected with the proposal, party feeling, or government advocacy of a given policy. Amongst these Yule's Q affords a simple way of finding out the extent to which a single dimension is being tapped by a series of votes.

Yule's Q involves a series of fourfold tables. To illustrate its use let us assume that out of the 500 MPs who were present 400 agreed to an allowance of *at least* 5s. (25p) per week for each child, 300 to one of 8s. (40p) per week, and 100 to one of 15s. (75p) per week. The next step would be to examine the responses of legislators according to the rate of family allowance they favoured. Logically, we would expect all those favouring a level of at least 15s. (75p) a week to have voted for a level of 8s. (40p) a week; and logically, all of the latter should have supported the level of 5s. (25p) a week. If these logical expectations are fulfilled, a perfect scale would emerge expressing a single dimension.

In fact, perfect scaling is unlikely to be found. Fortuitous motives and factors extraneous to the essential questions of policy are likely to intervene and deflect the votes of some legislators from the road of strict logic. In these circumstances we need to inquire how many Members did not vote according to expectations. Let us assume that of the 100 who agreed to 15s. (75p) a week all but 5 voted for one of 8s. (40p) a week, and that all but 3 voted for one of at least 5s. (25p) a week; let us also assume that of the 300 who voted for an allowance of 8s. (40p) a week, all but 10 voted for one of 5s. (25p) a week. We can then set up the four-fold Tables 62–64.

TABLE 62. FAMILY ALLOWANCE OF 5s. (25p) A WEEK

		+	−	Total
		a	*b*	
Family allowance of 8s.	+	290	10	300
(40p) a week	−	*c*	*d*	
		110	90	200
Total		400	100	500

(+ indicates support for, − opposition to proposal.)

The formula is $\dfrac{ad - bc}{ad + bc} = \dfrac{26100 - 1100}{26100 + 1100} = \dfrac{25000}{27200}$.

Therefore Yule's $Q = 0.92$.

TABLE 63. FAMILY ALLOWANCE OF 8s. (40p) A WEEK

		+	−	Total
		a	*b*	
Family allowance of 15s.	+	95	5	100
(75p) a week	−	*c*	*d*	
		205	195	400
Total		300	200	500

The formula is $\dfrac{ad - bc}{ad + bc} = \dfrac{18525 - 1025}{18525 + 1025} = \dfrac{17500}{19550}$.

Therefore Yule's $Q = 0.90$.

The value of Q depends on the numbers in the extreme cells *a* and *d* (those in our example who voted *consistently* for or against given levels of allowances) and the numbers in the two cells *b* and *c*. If the value of either *b* or *c* is small and that of *a* and *d* is large, the value of Q will be large; if either *b* or *c* are large, the value of Q will be small. The smaller either *b* or *c* is, the more "consistent" voting can be said to be—hence the logic of the measure.

TABLE 64. FAMILY ALLOWANCE OF 5s. (25p) A WEEK

		+	−	Total
		a	*b*	
Family allowance of 15s. (75p) a week	+	97	3	100
		c	*d*	
	−	303	97	400
Total		400	100	500

The formula is $\dfrac{ad-bc}{ad+bc} = \dfrac{8500}{10318}$.

Therefore Yule's $Q = 0\cdot82$.

In this example the value of Q is positive in every case; of course the value could be negative, e.g. in the case of EDMs if Members who signed one EDM tended not to sign another with which it was paired, Q would have a minus value.

There is no set value of Q for deciding whether or not two votes scale. Some researchers require a value of $0\cdot8$ or $0\cdot9$, and others are content with the value of $0\cdot5$ or $0\cdot6$. In the example cited, the value of Q never falls below $0\cdot82$, and most scholars would regard this as constituting a satisfactory level. The votes could thus be treated as a scale; Members would be assigned positions on the scale according to the way they voted. Those who voted with apparent inconsistency would be either omitted or given what on the balance of the evidence seemed the most appropriate place on the scale.

GUTTMAN SCALING AND EARLY DAY MOTIONS

This exact and highly sophisticated approach to the problem of scaling is not often applicable to EDMs. There are several reasons; as has been seen, the number of signatures obtained only partly depends on the demands expressed in the motion. The support enrolled depends also on the energy and motives of the sponsors. A relatively "extreme" EDM may be signed by more Members than a more moderate one because of the greater zest for collection evinced by the promoters of the former. Furthermore, the circumstances of the tabling of EDMs make it highly unlikely that the signers of an extreme motion will sign a more "moderate" motion which they would prefer to an even less congenial one. Thus Sydney Silverman and his fellow sponsors of EDM 26/1958, which called for the recognition of East Germany, were hardly likely to sign the amendment tabled by Messrs. Bellenger, Morrison, and J. B. Hynd, even though this amendment may have been marginally more to their taste than the German policy of the Conservative Government.[2] This amendment, whether or not it was more congenial than the policy of Mr. Macmillan, had clearly been put down as a riposte to the Silverman motion.

Moreover, the tabling of EDMs often takes place in a more confused and uncertain internal party situation than the calling of a roll-call vote in the American Congress. The European unity motions tabled on the Conservative side in 1956 did not refer to any specific government

[2] See S. E. Finer, H. B. Berrington, and D. J. Bartholomew, *Backbench Opinion in the House of Commons, 1955–59*, London, 1961, Annex 4, for a full description of this episode.

action which was being considered by the government. They called for closer British links with western Europe but made some concessions to Commonwealth interests, and about half of the Members who signed motions supporting Commonwealth preference signed the European unity EDMs. Logically, there was no inconsistency in this behaviour, since the European unity motions specifically mentioned the need to safeguard Commonwealth interests. Given this, and the attempts being made at this time to find some way of reconciling closer British association with Europe and the maintenance of the Commonwealth connection, it is not surprising to find so much apparent "cross-signing". In these circumstances, Guttman scales cannot be constructed.

Finally, there is the problem posed by the passage of time and rapid changes of attitude. For example, more Labour Members signed the more extreme "federalist" motion on European unity, tabled in March 1948, than signed the more moderate EDM tabled in the spring of 1949, which merely welcomed the establishment of *consultative* organs of western European co-operation. Perhaps the collection of signatures for the more moderate EDM was pursued less vigorously; but, probably, the explanation lies in the change of attitude to western European unity which took place in that period within the Labour Party.

For these reasons, Guttman's scaling techniques cannot always be applied to EDM data; yet this is far from saying that no valid conclusions can be reached about the distribution of political attitudes amongst the various social groups of which the parliamentary party is composed and of the interrelationships amongst the holders of these attitudes. Some of the scales used here have been of a *quantitative* kind, i.e. these scales were based on the number of Motions signed in a particular field of controversy. It does not seem unreasonable to infer that Members who repeatedly signed motions protesting at the exercise of capital punishment or defending the rights of individuals against arbitrary authority were more "humanitarian" or "libertarian", as the case may be, than Members who signed such motions rarely, or never. Indeed, it has been shown[3] that voting by Labour Members on the Street Offences Bill of 1959, a Bill which involved libertarian issues, was associated with the signature of a number of disparate "civil liberties" EDMs; and in Chapter 6 it has been shown that Labour Members who signed EDMs concerned with the death penalty or blood sports were more likely to vote against capital punishment or hunting than those who did not.

Nevertheless, this kind of validation is not always open to us; and where various motions have been combined into a single quantitative scale, Yule's Q can be used, not for Guttman scaling but to measure the internal consistency of support for any pair of motions in such a scale; and the social and political composition of the signatories of motions which, paired with other EDMs yield a low value of Q, can be compared with the composition of the signatories of the other motions.

As mentioned earlier, there is no set value of Yule's Q which the data must attain. On some issues Yule's Q reaches very high levels but on others much lower levels. Professor Aydelotte, in his study of voting in the early nineteenth-century House of Commons, has used a threshhold of 0·65. Moreover, Aydelotte has been able to restrict each pair of divisions to those Members actually voting and thus to exclude absentees and abstainers. With EDMs, absent Members are necessarily treated as non-signers, and the value of Yule's Q will presumably be correspondingly reduced below what it would have been if no Members were absent. For this reason it is not surprising that the value of Yule's Q is sometimes relatively low. The reader's attention has been drawn to the value of Q wherever relevant.

[3] Finer *et al.*, *op. cit.*, p. 42.

Some of the scales, however in both studies, were *qualitative*—i.e. the placing of Members on such scales depended on the *kind* of motions they signed as distinct from the *number*. These scales posed greater difficulty. As has been seen, this data was rarely suitable for Guttman scaling. Both in this and the earlier study the authors were sometimes compelled to impose their own categories upon the data, exercising their judgement as best they could. In their view the signatories of the Silverman motion on European disengagement in 1959 were more left-wing than those who subscribed to the Morrison–Bellenger amendment. Those Conservatives who signed motions supporting the adoption of specific responsibilities by the United Nations or its transformation into a world government with limited powers, were regarded as more internationalist than those who signed an amendment rejecting the proposal for a world authority and demanding that international co-operation be based on respect for national sovereignty. In imposing their own view of what constituted a more "extreme" or less "extreme" demand, or a more or less internationalist approach, the authors had, in the last resort, to apply their own subjective criteria. In so doing they may have misunderstood the real significance of a particular motion; two separate demands may have been unwittingly confused and forced into the pigeon-hole of a single attitude. Nevertheless, for all the more important areas of policy the scaling procedures were explained in detail. Criticism must be based not on wholesale denunciations of the source-material and technique but on the particular scales that were employed.

Despite the limitations, it has been possible to apply Guttman scaling procedures to a limited extent; thus in Chapter 5 the Left and Centre Left on Far Eastern policy in 1950–1 have been derived from a Guttman scale, and Guttman scaling techniques have been applied to the votes on the death penalty in 1948 and to the divisions on royal grants in 1952. An examination of the unilateralist EDMs in the earlier study shows that, using Guttman's technique, a Left and Centre can be clearly distinguished. It will be recalled that in the field of pacificism the authors distinguished a Left who called for the unilateral renunciation of the testing and/or manufacture of nuclear weapons; a Centre who opposed the establishment of missile bases in Scotland and/or hydrogen-bomb patrols by aircraft stationed in Britain; and a Right who limited their demands to a call for the strengthening of the United Nations.

When Yule's Q measure is applied to those Members who were ranked as either Left or Centre, a very high value of Q emerges, as Table 65 shows:

TABLE 65. LEFT PACIFICIST

		+	−	
		a	*b*	
Centre	+	45	70	115
		c	*d*	
Pacificist	−	2	119	121
		47	189	236

$$\frac{ad - bc}{ad + bc} = \frac{(45 \times 119) - (70 \times 2)}{(45 \times 119) + (70 \times 2)} = \frac{5355 - 140}{5355 + 140} = \frac{5215}{5495}$$

Therefore Yule's $Q = 0\cdot95$.

There were 119 MPs (those in cell *d*) who subscribed neither to the left-wing demand for unilateral renunciation of nuclear weapons nor to the Centre protests against missile bases and hydrogen bomb patrols, and 70 MPs (shown in cell *b*) who signed at least one of the Centre EDMs but did not associate themselves with any of the unilateralist motions. Of the 47 Left Pacificists, however, all but two signed one or more of the Centre EDMs. Thus, empirically, the Left category of the pacificism scale satisfies the most stringent of tests.

A much lower value of Q emerges when the Left Pacificists and the Centre Pacificists are separately put against the Right. This is hardly surprising given that one of the right-wing pacificist EDMs was tabled immediately after a left-wing amendment calling for the immediate and unilateral cessation of hydrogen-bomb tests and manufacture. It is hardly likely that Members favouring unilateral nuclear disarmament would have signed an EDM supporting multilateral disarmament when the multilateralist EDM was intended as a riposte to their own, even though signature of such an EDM would have been *logically* consistent with their own position.[4]

Had the multilateralist EDM been tabled before the unilateralist motion, the value of Q would presumably have been much higher, for many of those signing the unilateralist call would have had no inhibitions about signing the broader multilateralist motion.

A similar consistency appears when the *individual motions* comprising the Left and Centre categories are examined. In no case does the Q score fall below 0·67; often it reaches a figure of 0·80.

THE χ^2 TEST OF ASSOCIATION

The MPs have been divided into various social categories based on education, occupation, the character of the constituency, region, war service, and (where appropriate) sponsorship. The distribution of political attitudes amongst various social groups has been examined, and usually the χ^2 (chi-squared test)[5]—a standard statistical test of association—has been applied. The formula for this test is

$$\chi^2 = \sum \frac{(A - E)^2}{E},$$

where *A* equals the actual frequencies and *E* the expected frequencies, i.e. the figure which would be expected if there were no difference at all in the responses of different social categories. The greater the divergence between *A* and *E*, and the larger the number of items (MPs in this case), the more likely it is that an association will be found.

The χ-squared test can be illustrated by a simple example: let us assume that one of the parliamentary parties consists of two groups—the over-50's numbering 120 and the under-50's, who muster 80 MPs. Let us also assume that there is a division in the party over the question of legislation to forbid unofficial strikes with the older Members splitting 7 to 5 against the ban and the younger Members opposing such a ban by the margin of 7 to 1. There is a decisive majority in the party against such legislation but the younger Members are much more hostile than their seniors (Table 66).

The first step is to calculate what the expected distribution of pro-banners and anti-banners would be if there were no differences at all between the two age groups (the expected frequen-

---

[4] In the sense that any Member who desired unilateral nuclear disarmament would presumably welcome multilateral disarmament even more.

[5] "Chi" pronounced "ki"—the 'i' as in ice.

TABLE 66. EXAMPLE: UNOFFICIAL STRIKES BILL—
ACTUAL FREQUENCIES

	Pro–Banners	Anti–Banners	Total
Under–50's	10	70	80
Over–50's	50	70	120
Total	60	140	200

TABLE 67. EXAMPLE: UNOFFICIAL STRIKES BILL—
EXPECTED FREQUENCIES

	Pro–Banners	Anti–Banners	Total
Under–50's	24	56	80
Over–50's	36	84	120
Total	60	140	200

cies). This is shown in Table 67. The pro-banners constitute three-tenths of the total, the anti-banners seven-tenths. If there were no differences between the two age groups we would expect to find 24 of the under-50's (three-tenths of 80) and 36 of the over-50's (three-tenths of 120) supporting this proposed strike legislation.

Next we subtract the difference between the actual frequencies (shown in Table 66) and the expected frequencies (shown in Table 67), square the difference in each case, divide this product by the expected frequency in each case, and add the results.

Thus

$$\chi^2 = \frac{(10-24)^2}{24} + \frac{(70-56)^2}{56} + \frac{(50-36)^2}{36} + \frac{(70-84)^2}{84}$$

$$= \frac{196}{24} + \frac{196}{56} + \frac{196}{36} + \frac{196}{84}$$

$$= 8 \cdot 17 + 3 \cdot 50 + 5 \cdot 44 + 2 \cdot 33$$

$$= 19 \cdot 44.$$

The number of degrees of freedom is given by the product of the number of columns minus 1, and the number of rows minus 1. In this simple example there are two columns and two rows and there is, therefore, one degree of freedom; consulting tables of significance levels, we find that a table yielding a χ-squared value of $19 \cdot 44$ with one degree of freedom is significant at well beyond the $0 \cdot 1$ per cent level. In short, the odds against a distribution of opinions giving this value of χ^2 are more than 999 to 1. In this example the null hypothesis will therefore be discounted and the difference accepted as genuine.

It is customary to regard expected frequencies of 5 as being the smallest which can be permitted without serious error. With the aim of avoiding small expected frequencies, two devices have been employed in this study, as in the earlier book. Sometimes the whole category which gives rise to the expected small frequencies has been omitted; thus it has often been necessary to leave out the small Business or Co-operative category when testing for a difference between occupation and attitude or sponsorship and attitude within the Labour Party. Sometimes, however, separate categories or wings have been conflated; thus the U1's, the U2's, and the U3's have often been grouped and contrasted with the U4's; similarly, the various regions of England have sometimes been combined and compared with Wales and Scotland, and in Chapter 4 the Ultra Left, the Left and the Centre Left have been amalgamated, for these purposes, and compared with the Rest.

In 2 by 2 tables (i.e. those with two columns and two rows) in which expected frequencies fall below 5, Fisher's exact probability test can be used. A significance level can be obtained using published tables in the same way as with the χ-square test.

In this, as in the earlier study, a non-significant result was sometimes obtained after the application of the χ^2 test to a table. Further scrutiny sometimes suggested that a significant difference (or if a difference at a low level of significance were found one at a higher level of significance) might be reached by grouping some categories, or "wings". Thus on the royal grants issue the Left and Moderate Left were combined, as were the Right and Moderate Right; similarly, the Workers, the Professions and the Business classes were grouped and compared with the Miscellaneous Occupations for the Bevan floor revolt on the H-bomb. Again, the small size of some groups or wings is relevant here. Unfortunately, when the grouping is chosen because it is that which is most likely to yield significance, it is no longer true that the significance level measures the chance of erroneously rejecting the null hypothesis. In fact it will, in general, underestimate this probability (i.e. if, under such conditions, an association is just significant at the 5 per cent level, the odds will be less than 19 to 1 against its having occurred by chance). Nevertheless, the results of tests obtained from alternative groupings are often suggestive, and may sometimes be of value for future inquiry.

Any omissions or groupings which have been made are noted below the appropriate table together with the value of χ^2 and the significance level attained. The suffix attached to χ^2, e.g. χ^2_4, denotes the number of degrees of freedom.

In deciding whether or not differences have been established the following rule has been adopted:

(a) If the test reaches significance at the 5 per cent level (or better) it has been concluded that the difference is real and cannot be ascribed to chance.

(b) If the test is significant at the 10 per cent level but not at the 5 per cent level, the differences have been described as "provisionally accepted". Although such cases merit attention, the evidence is not strong enough to indicate unqualified acceptance.

(c) Differences at all other significance levels have been attributed to and can reasonably be explained in terms of chance.

It must be stressed that the choice of the 5 per cent significance level as the criterion for deciding whether or not differences are real is, in the last resort, an arbitrary, though reasonable, one, which most scholars accept. A table which gives a value significant at the 1 per cent or $0 \cdot 1$ per cent level is naturally even more convincing.

One objection to the use of χ-squared tests in this context is that the signatories are not drawn from a random sample of a population. It is indeed true that signatories of backbench motions are not members of a random sample. However, some statisticians would justify the use of χ-squared tests by regarding the behaviour of Members, when confronted with a particular motion, as one of a particular hypothetical sequence of observations in which motions with similar contents might have been presented to them.

Whether or not such a justification finds unanimous acceptance amongst statisticians, it seemed that tables reaching a significance level of 10 per cent were generally worth mentioning and that those reaching a significance level of 5 per cent were usually of clear substantive interest. For this reason, statistical significance at these levels has been taken as a prima-facie indication of the political interest of particular tables, though, as already mentioned, where the numbers involved in a table are very small, important percentage differences in tables which do not reach these levels of significance have also been thought worthy of attention.

DEFENCE AND FOREIGN POLICY FLOOR REVOLTS, 1951-61

As indicated in Chapter 1, Members' positions on the Foreign Policy and Pacificism EDM scales in 1951–9 have been compared with their behaviour in backbench floor rebellions between 1951 and 1961.

Eight important rebellions took place between November 1951 and March 1961. These were: (i) A revolt against the ratification of the Japanese Peace Treaty in November 1951. Thirty-five MPs voted against ratification whilst the Labour Front Bench and their followers, along with the Conservatives, voted for the Treaty.[6]

(ii) The Bevanite revolt of the 57 Varieties in March 1952. On this occasion 57 Labour MPs voted against the rearmament programme, thus flouting the decision of the Parliamentary Party.[7]

(iii) A revolt in favour of an amendment to the Conservative Government's Atomic Energy Authority Bill in April 1954, which would have required the government to obtain the specific approval of Parliament before making thermo-nuclear weapons. Sixty-five Labour MPs voted against the government in defiance of Front Bench advice.[8]

(iv) The Bevanite Abstention of the 62 in March 1955. Sixty-two Labour MPs abstained on an Opposition motion which censured the Conservative Government's defence policy. The rebels were, by abstaining, expressing their disapproval of official Labour policy on the hydrogen bomb—though the specific grounds for disapproval varied.[9]

(v) The abstention of 43 Members in February 1960. The Labour Party had put down a motion of censure on the government's defence policy. An unofficial motion deploring "a defence policy based on a nuclear strategy" was also tabled. When the vote was taken on the official motion, 43 MPs abstained.

(vi) A vote against the siting of Polaris submarines in Britain. On 16 December 1960 48 MPs voted in favour of a private Members' motion which censured the government for allowing Polaris submarines to be based in Britain.

(vii) The abstention of 72 MPs on defence policy in December 1960. In October the Scarborough Conference of the Labour Party had carried resolutions, against the leadership's advice, calling for unilateral renunciation of the manufacture or basing of nuclear weapons in Britain. Mr. Gaitskell, backed by a majority of the Parliamentary Labour Party persisted in

---

[6] See pp. 91–93.   [7] See pp. 98–102.   [8] See pp. 108–9.   [9] See pp. 109–12.

his policy of multilateral disarmament. On 13 December 1960 the House divided on an official Labour Party motion condemning the government's defence policy. Seventy-two Labour MPs abstained.

(viii) A vote on the Air Estimates in March 1961. On 8 March 24 Labour MPs forced a division against the Air Estimates, thus flouting a party decision.

DEFENCE AND FOREIGN POLICY EDMs, 1955–9

Pacificism

The pacificism scale used in *Backbench Opinion in the House of Commons, 1955–59* was employed as a measure of unilateralism; those who failed to sign any of the relevant motions were classified as being on the Right on this issue. The details can be found in Annex 3, pages 159–62.

Foreign Affairs

Members have been divided into Left, Centre, and Right Wing groupings on the issue of Foreign Affairs on the basis of EDMs tabled between July 1955 and February 1959.

The Left consisted of: Signatories of EDMs 9/55 and 15/57 who did not sign the Morrison/ Bellenger Amendment EDM 26A/58. Signatories of the Silverman EDM 26/58.

The Centre: Signatories of EDM 38/58 (the unified or "official" motion on German disengagement) other than those included in the Left.

The Right: Signatories of the Morrison/Bellenger Amendment EDM 26A/58 who did not sign the "unified" motion EDM 38/58.[10]

It must be stressed that these scales do not purport to measure the absolute size of any bloc. The size of the Left group on either scale could be increased or reduced by adopting either a more generous or a more stringent definition of Left. All that is being said is that, taking each issue in turn, those Members classified as Left are to the left of those classified as Centre and Right; that those classified as Centre are to the right of the Left, and to the left of the Right, and so on. The main table, covering those Members who were continuously on the backbenches from November 1951 to March 1961 and who were committed on foreign policy has been given in Chapter 1.

---

[10] Careful readers of the earlier study will note that the definitions of Left, Centre and Right there are not identical with those offered here. After consideration it did not seem appropriate to include the residue of those who signed EDM 60/57 as being on the Right. They have been regarded as uncommitted. The effect of this change is to reduce the right-hand side of Table 1 by 4 Consistent, and 4 Non-consistent, Rebels and 2 Non-Rebels. Their inclusion in the table would temper, though it would hardly blur, the contrast between the division lobby behaviour of Left and Right. However, inspection of EDM 60/57 (which opposed arming the West German forces with nuclear weapons) showed that it received quite disproportionate support from the Left, as defined above, or as defined by reference to 1951/5. Nearly three-quarters of the Foreign Policy Left, as defined above, signed as against a third of the Centre and the re-defined Right. Moreover, those signatories of this EDM, who remain members of the Right as re-defined, seem to have had special anxieties about German rearmament during the earlier controversy; nearly half had signed at least one of the relevant EDMs in the 1951 Parliament, compared with a quarter of those members of the Right who did not support EDM 60/57. In these circumstances, and given the character of the EDM's demand, it seemed wrong to class the residual signers of this EDM with the Morrison/Bellenger Amendment. To avoid further complication they were regarded as Uncommitted. Nevertheless, the effect of excluding them is to apparently strengthen a little the relationship between signing EDMs and floor revolts.

The Labour Party: Foreign and Defence Policy, 1945–55

FOREIGN AFFAIRS, 1945–50

Detailed figures showing the occupational breakdown of the various foreign policy groupings of the 1945 Parliament have been given in Chapter 4 (Table 10).

Examination of the signatories by sponsorship and education and age shows clearly that in addition to the Professions it was the Constituency sponsored, the University educated, and the younger Members who supplied most of Bevin's critics. This judgement, based on an examination of the signatures to backbench motions, is emphatically confirmed by analysis of votes and abstentions on two key foreign policy divisions. Tables 68–71 show the responses of Members to two important foreign policy divisions—that on the amendment to the Address of November 1946, and that on the NATO Treaty of May 1949. Backbenchers who abstained in both divisions are termed Dual Abstainers whilst those who supported the government on both occasions are described as Consistent Loyalists.

In each case where a comparison can be made, inferences drawn from analysis of signatures to motions are similar to those made from an analysis of division lobby votes and abstentions. The Professions, the Constituency sponsored, the University graduates, and the younger Members were more likely to abstain than the Workers, the Trade Unionists, the Elementary educated, and the older men. Associations have been firmly established between division-lobby behaviour and both occupation and education, whilst the association with sponsorship can be tentatively accepted. Although the association between age and abstention is not significant (probably because of the higher incidence of sickness amongst older Members), the figures are consistent with those derived from the motions.

Moreover, the ranks of the Dual Abstainers were almost certainly swollen by the involuntary absentees—those who were away because of illness, the claims of business, or absence abroad. As mentioned in Chapter 4, members of the Worker/Trade Unionist/Elementary-educated bloc, being older than their fellows, would have been more likely to be away from the House for reasons of sickness. If the involuntary absentees could be subtracted from the Dual Abstainers, the correspondence between the findings from the two sources—motions and division-lobby abstentions—might be even more marked. It is impossible to know precisely who the involuntary absentees were, but an inspection of Hansard can help us to identify some at least of those who were present in the House on or near the days of the divisions.

Some Members indicated their presence on the day of the debate on the amendment to the Address by asking oral questions, by speaking, or voting in other divisions; to these may be added those who similarly indicated their presence the following day. In the same way we can

TABLE 68. The Labour Party and Foreign Policy (Divisions) by Occupation

	Dual Abstainers		Consistent Loyalists		Total	
	No.	%	No.	%	No.	%
Workers	13	27	36	73	49	100
Miscellaneous Occupations	15	38	25	63	40	100
Business	7	24	22	76	29	100
Professionals	23	51	22	49	45	100
Unknown	1	25	3	75	4	100
Total	59	35	108	65	167	100

Unknown omitted. $\chi^2_3 = 8 \cdot 207$. Significant at 5%.

TABLE 69. The Labour Party and Foreign Policy (Divisions) by Sponsorship

	Dual Abstainers		Consistent Loyalists		Total	
	No.	%	No.	%	No.	%
Trade Union	13	25	38	75	51	100
Co-operative	4	29	10	71	14	100
CLP	41	41	60	59	101	100
Unknown	1	100	—	—	1	100
Total	59	35	108	65	167	100

Co-operative and Unknown omitted. $\chi^2_1 = 3 \cdot 375$. Significant at 10%.

TABLE 70. The Labour Party and Foreign Policy (Divisions) by Education

	Dual Abstainers		Consistent Loyalists		Total	
	No.	%	No.	%	No.	%
Elementary	10	19	43	81	53	100
Elementary/Secondary +	6	35	11	65	17	100
Secondary and Public School only	13	38	21	62	34	100
University	24	51	23	49	47	100
Women	3	33	6	67	9	100
Unknown	3	43	4	57	7	100
Total	59	35	108	65	167	100

Women and Unknown omitted. $\chi^2_3 = 11 \cdot 535$. Significant at 1%.
Elementary against University. $\chi^2_1 = 11 \cdot 507$. Significant at 0·1%.

TABLE 71. THE LABOUR PARTY AND FOREIGN POLICY (DIVISIONS) BY AGE

	Dual Abstainers		Consistent Loyalists		Total	
	No.	%	No.	%	No.	%
Over 60	15	30	35	70	50	100
51–60	11	26	32	74	43	100
41–50	20	43	27	57	47	100
Under 41	11	58	8	42	19	100
Unknown	2	25	6	75	8	100
Total	59	35	108	65	167	100

Data grouped. Under 41 and 41–50 combined. Unknown omitted. $\chi_2^2 = 4\cdot118$. Not significant.

distinguish Members who indicated their presence on either 10, 11, or 12 May 1949—the day of, the day before, and the day after the debate on the Atlantic Pact. There are good grounds, then, for believing that these Members were in fair health at the relevant time, and that those who abstained on both occasions were probably deliberate absentees. These Members will be called Class A. Class C Members are those who did not indicate their presence on the stipulated dates in either 1946 or 1949; whilst Class B consists of those who indicated their presence in either 1946 or 1949 but not in both.

Table 72 shows how strongly the "Dual Abstainers" of Class A were concentrated amongst the various left-wing groups.

TABLE 72. DELIBERATE ABSTAINERS AND INVOLUNTARY ABSENTEES IN FOREIGN POLICY. DIVISION BY FOREIGN POLICY (GENERAL) SCALE

	Ultra Left		Left		Centre Left		Rest		Total	
	No.	%	No.	%	No.	%	No.	%	No.	%
Class A	4	80	11	85	11	69	11	44	37	100
Class B	—	—	1	8	4	25	13	52	18	100
Class C	1	20	1	8	1	6	1	4	4	100
Total	5	100	13	100	16	100	25	100	59	100

Table 73 shows the extent to which Class A predominated amongst the Professions and Miscellaneous Occupations, and Classes B and C amongst the Workers (and the small Business group). In short, if we knew exactly who the deliberate abstainers were, we would almost certainly find the Professions and the Miscellaneous Occupations figuring even more conspicuously amongst them than these groups did amongst the broader class of Dual Abstainers.

TABLE 73. DELIBERATE ABSTAINERS AND INVOLUNTARY ABSENTEES IN FOREIGN POLICY. DIVISIONS BY OCCUPATION

	Workers		Miscellaneous Occupations		Business		Professions		Unknown		Total	
	No.	%	No.	%	No.	%	No.	%	No.	%	No.	%
Class A	6	16	10	27	2	5	19	51	—	—	37	100
Class B	7	39	4	22	3	17	4	22	—	—	18	100
Class C	1	25	1	25	2	50	—	—	—	—	4	100
Total	14	24	15	25	7	12	23	39	—	—	59	100

CONSCRIPTION, 1945–50

The findings derived from an analysis of EDM 53/45, which asserted that conscription should be ended as soon as possible, were, save in one respect, confirmed by an examination of the division-lobby critics of conscription. Some signatories of the EDM supported the government on the National Service Bill, whilst the Bill's opponents included some backbenchers who had not signed the EDM; but whatever individual differences there were in the make-up of the two groups, their social composition was much the same. Tables 74–80 compare the occupational composition of the EDM signatories with that of the division-lobby abstainers and rebels.

TABLE 74. CONSCRIPTION AND OCCUPATION

	EDM					Floor revolts					
	Signers of EDM 53/45		Non-Signers		Total	Division-lobby Opponents		Abstained Three Times		Others	Total
	No.	%	No.	%		No.	%	No.	%		
Workers	23	26	54	27	77	18	24	6	23	53	77
Miscellaneous Occupations	22	25	48	24	70	21	28	6	23	43	70
Business	14	16	28	14	42	11	14	5	19	26	42
Professions	26	30	60	30	86	25	33	5	19	56	86
Unknown	2	2	9	5	11	1	1	4	15	6	10
Total	87	100	199	100	286	76	100	26	100	184	286

Unknown omitted. $\chi_3^2 = 0\cdot184$. Not significant.

Data grouped. Opponents and Abstained Three Times against Others. Unknown omitted. $\chi_3^2 = 1\cdot054$. Not significant.

TABLE 75. CONSCRIPTION AND SPONSORSHIP

	EDM					Floor revolts						
	Signers of EDM 53/45		Non-Signers		Total	Division-lobby Opponents		Abstained Three Times		Others		Total
	No.	%	No.	%		No.	%	No.	%	No.	%	
Trade Union	25	29	62	31	87	19	25	9	35	59	32	87
Co-operative	8	9	14	7	22	11	14	1	4	10	5	22
CLP	53	61	123	62	176	46	61	15	58	115	63	176
Unknown	1	1	—	—	1	—	—	1	4	—	—	1
Total	87	100	199	100	286	76	100	26	100	184	100	286

Unknown omitted. $\chi_2^2 = 0 \cdot 497$. Not significant.

Data grouped. Opponents and Abstained Three Times against Others. Unknown omitted. $\chi_2^2 = 3 \cdot 931$. Not significant.

TABLE 76. CONSCRIPTION AND EDUCATION

	EDM				Floor revolts				
	Signers of EDM 53/45		Non-Signers	Total	Division-lobby Opponents		Abstained Three Times	Others	Total
	No.	%	No.		No.	%	No.		
Elementary	25	29	64	89	24	32	8	57	89
Elementary/Secondary+	7	8	27	34	9	12	3	22	34
Secondary and Public School only	13	15	32	45	11	14	3	31	45
University	28	32	60	88	23	30	7	58	88
Women	10	11	7	17	7	9	3	7	17
Unknown	4	5	9	13	2	3	2	9	13
Total	87	100	199	286	76	100	26	184	286

Women and Unknown omitted. $\chi_3^2 = 1 \cdot 597$. Not significant.

Women and Unknown omitted. $\chi_3^2 = 0 \cdot 327$. Not significant.

TABLE 77. CONSCRIPTION AND TYPE OF UNIVERSITY

	EDM					Floor revolts						
	Signers of EDM 53/45		Non-Signers			Division-lobby Opponents		Abstained Three Times		Others		
	No.	%	No.	%	Total	No.	%	No.	%	No.	%	Total
U1, U2, U3	9	32	38	63	47	7	30	3	43	37	64	47
U4	17	61	22	37	39	15	65	4	57	20	34	39
Unknown	2	7	—	—	2	1	4	—	—	1	2	2
Total	28	100	60	100	88	23	100	7	100	58	100	88

Unknown omitted. $\chi_1^2 = 6 \cdot 036$. Significant at $2 \cdot 5\%$.

Data grouped. Opponents and Abstained Three Times against Others. Unknown omitted. $\chi_1^2 = 7 \cdot 181$. Significant at 1%.

TABLE 78. CONSCRIPTION AND AGE

	EDM					Floor revolts						
	Signers of EDM 53/45		Non-Signers			Division-lobby Opponents		Abstained Three Times		Others		
	No.	%	No.	%	Total	No.	%	No.	%	No.	%	Total
> 60	27	31	59	30	86	31	41	6	23	41	27	86
51–60	23	26	50	25	73	21	28	10	38	42	23	73
41–50	23	26	51	26	74	12	16	3	12	59	32	74
41	7	8	29	15	36	7	9	6	23	23	13	36
Unknown	7	8	10	5	17	5	7	1	4	11	6	17
Total	87	100	199	100	286	76	100	26	100	184	100	286

Unknown omitted. $\chi_3^2 = 1 \cdot 991$. Not significant.

Data grouped. Opponents and Abstained Three Times against Others. Unknown omitted. $\chi_3^2 = 9 \cdot 345$. Significant at 5%.

TABLE 79. CONSCRIPTION AND REGION

| | EDM | | | | | Floor revolts | | | | | | |
| | Signers of EDM 53/45 | | Non-Signers | | | Division-lobby Opponents | | Abstained Three Times | | Others | | |
	No.	%	No.	%	Total	No.	%	No.	%	No.	%	Total
England	68	78	179	90	247	57	75	21	81	169	92	247
Wales	9	10	6	3	15	11	14	—	—	4	2	15
Scotland	9	10	14	7	23	8	11	4	15	11	6	23
N. Ireland	1	1	—	—	1	—	—	1	4	—	—	1
Total	87	100	199	100	286	76	100	26	100	184	100	286

Data grouped. Wales and Scotland combined. Northern Ireland omitted. $\chi_1^2 = 6\cdot09$. Significant at 2·5%.

Data grouped. Wales and Scotland combined. Northern Ireland omitted. Division-lobby Opponents and Abstained Three Times against Others. $\chi_1^2 = 11\cdot93$. Significant at 0·1%.

TABLE 80. CONSCRIPTION AND WAR SERVICE

| | EDM | | | | | Floor revolts | | | | | | |
| | Signers of EDM 53/45 | | Non-Signers | | | Division-lobby Opponents | | Abstained Three Times | | Others | | |
	No.	%	No.	%	Total	No.	%	No.	%	No.	%	Total
Civil Defence or Ambulance	5	6	11	6	16	4	5	2	8	10	5	16
Armed Forces	13	15	51	26	64	9	12	4	15	51	28	64
None known	69	79	128	64	197	61	80	18	69	118	64	197
Unknown	—	—	9	5	9	2	3	2	8	5	3	9
Total	87	100	199	100	286	76	100	26	100	184	100	286

Armed Forces against None. $\chi_1^2 = 4\cdot853$. Significant at 5%.

Division-lobby Opponents and Abstained Three Times against Others. $\chi_1^2 = 8\cdot288$. Significant at 1%.

The sponsorship, education, type of university, and war service breakdowns of the opponents of the National Service Bill (and of those who voted against the government on the Amendment to the Address which criticized conscription) are again very similar to the results obtained from the EDM. Thirty-two per cent of the EDM signatories were graduates and so were 30 per cent of the Members participating in the conscription floor revolts. Sixty-one per cent of the graduates who signed the EDM were U4's; the same group comprised 65 per cent of the graduate section of division-lobby rebels. Only in respect of age is there any serious discrepancy between the two sets of figures. The over-60's were considerably more, and the 41–50 age group considerably less, numerous amongst the division lobby rebels than amongst the EDM signatories; otherwise there is an extraordinary consistency in the results given by the two sources.

THE FLOOR REVOLTS, 1951–5

Four important floor revolts occurred in the 1951 Parliament—that on the Japanese Peace Treaty of November 1951; the rebellion of the 57 Varieties over the scale of rearmament in March 1952; the vote in favour of Beswick's amendment to the Atomic Energy Authority Bill in April 1954; and the Abstention of the 62 on the question of the hydrogen bomb in March 1955.

Sponsorship proves to have been the most important distinguishing characteristic of the dissidents in each of the four revolts; all of the sponsorship tables are significant at the 10 per cent level or better, with the CLP men and the Co-operators being more rebellious than the Trade Unionists. Education yields significant results for the Bevanite revolt over rearmament and for the rebellion on Beswick's amendment. Region and war service were only significant in the Bevanite rearmament demonstration. In the latter, too, younger Members tended to participate more than seniors; but when Bevan defied his Front Bench over the hydrogen bomb, he found more support amongst the over-50's than from the under-40's.

The pattern of revolt over the second protest on nuclear weapons was not as clear cut as that over the earlier demonstration; sponsorship was less clearly linked to rebellion than hitherto. It was the Miscellaneous Occupations, not the Professions, who behaved in the most distinctively radical way. The association between age and abstention was not firmly established and was, in any case, not regular; the behaviour of the under-41's, who supplied only one of the Rebels, is striking, however. On this issue, moreover, the ex-servicemen were more amenable than their colleagues to the Front Bench lead.

Generally, the dissidents in these revolts were much more of a cross-section of the party than Bevin's foreign policy critics had been. The similarity in behaviour of the four university classes is particularly striking. This is because, as argued in Chapter 9, what may loosely be called the Bevanite floor revolts saw the coming together of quite distinct ideological and social groupings.

ANNEX 3

The Labour Party and Domestic Issues, 1945–55

CAPITAL PUNISHMENT, 1953–5

In Chapter 6 it was shown that Members' hostility to capital punishment, as revealed by the EDMs, was closely related to Members' keenness, as revealed by the free votes on the floor of the House. It was also shown that the Members who felt most strongly about this issue came disproportionately from the middle-class occupational groups, the graduates, and the younger Members. As indicated in Chapter 1, there is no reason why we should assume that the social characteristics of the Members who feel most intensely about an issue will necessarily replicate in a precise way the characteristics of the broader group of lukewarm adherents. Nevertheless, a comparison of the backgrounds of Members who signed the four EDMs concerned with the death penalty, and those of the Consistent Abolitionists, shows that the same groups which were most prominent amongst the EDM signatories were also most conspicuous amongst the wider group of Consistent Abolitionists. Associations were established, on the basis of the EDMs, between attitudes to capital punishment, occupation, sponsorship, and education.

TABLE 81. CAPITAL PUNISHMENT, 1951–5, BY OCCUPATION

| | EDMs | | | | | Divisions | | | | |
| | Signers | | Non-Signers | | | Consistent Abolitionists | | Consistent Abstainers and Retentionists | | |
	No.	%	No.	%	Total	No.	%	No.	%	Total
Workers	13	17	57	37	70	30	24	17	40	47
Miscellaneous Occupations	24	31	32	21	56	31	25	9	21	40
Business	10	13	17	11	27	13	10	6	14	19
Professions	30	38	43	28	73	47	38	7	16	54
Unknown	1	1	7	4	8	4	3	4	9	8
Total	78	100	156	100	234	125	100	43	100	168

Unknown omitted. $\chi^2_3 = 11 \cdot 13$. Significant at 2·5%. Unknown omitted. $\chi^2_3 = 7 \cdot 904$. Significant at 5%.

245

Associations were established between attitudes, and both occupation and education, as well as that of age, on the basis of the free votes. No association was established between attitudes to capital punishment and sponsorship but the figures are consistent with those derived from the EDMs.

A distinction should perhaps be made between *fortuitous* non-signers and *less strongly motivated* non-signers. The wider group of Abolitionists presumably embraced many of the latter and included therefore a somewhat higher percentage of the Worker/Trades Union/Elementary educated categories. Nevertheless, the division lobby Abolitionists contained, like the EDM signers, a disproportionate number of men from the Professions, the University educated, the Co-operators, and the CLP sponsored.

Table 81 shows the breakdown by Occupation. Retentionists have been defined as Members who have voted for retention on one occasion or both, and for abolition on neither.

Working-class Members tended to be older than middle-class Members, and it might be argued that the relative lack of zeal for abolition displayed by the Workers in the division lobbies could be explained by the fact that this group contained a higher proportion of elderly Members than the middle-class categories, and hence a higher proportion vulnerable to sickness, which could be reflected in a lower attendance rate. However, even allowing for age the Workers were less likely to vote for abolition than the middle-class Members. For instance, among the over-51's 18 per cent of the Workers consistently abstained as against 8 per cent of the other three occupational classes; 41 per cent of the Workers who were under 51 voted for abolition on both occasions, compared with 57 per cent of the other three groups. The contrast between the Workers and the Professions is particularly marked.

Hunting

As indicated in Chapter 6, the social composition of the anti-blood sports group, as revealed by the free vote of 25 February 1949, closely matched that of the much larger category of Members who signed the two hunting EDMs. The opponents of hunting were drawn more or less evenly from most of the categories into which the party has been divided.

However, the picture is transformed when the Members voting *against* the Bill are taken into account (Table 82).

TABLE 82. BY SPONSORSHIP

	Anti-Hunting		Not Voting		Pro-Hunting		Total
	No.	%	No.	%	No.	%	No.
Trade Union	28	29	70	71	—	—	98
Co-operative	12	52	11	48	—	—	23
CLP	54	28	107	56	29	15	190
Unknown	—	—	1	100	—	—	1
Total	94	30	189	61	29	9	312

Anti-Hunting against Pro-Hunting. $\chi_2^2 = 18 \cdot 288$. Significant at $0 \cdot 1\%$.
Unknown omitted.

When opponents of the Bill are tested against supporters, significant associations are found between attitude and occupation, sponsorship, education, university, and age. This can clearly be ascribed to the distinctive characteristics of the Bill's opponents who were drawn disproportionately from Business and the Professions, University graduates, the under-51's, and amongst graduates the U1's and U2's. Not a single Trade Unionist or Co-operator was found in their ranks.

Divisions held on Private Members' Fridays can be notoriously misleading, however, for backbenchers whose constituencies are a long way from London may well travel back during the Friday. Thus a geographical bias could distort the figures; backbenchers voting are likely to consist to a disproportionate extent of MPs from the south-east and the Midlands. The geographic bias may well conceal one of an occupational and educational kind, for the northern Members were more often than their colleagues drawn from working-class vocations.

Backbenchers were therefore divided into two categories—those representing seats in the Centre and those from the Periphery. The Periphery was defined as Lincolnshire, Nottinghamshire, Derbyshire and Cheshire and all counties to the north, plus Devon, Cornwall and Wales. All other constituencies formed part of the Centre (Table 83).

TABLE 83. HUNTING AND DISTANCE FROM LONDON. VOTING ON ANTI-BLOOD SPORTS BILL

	All Voters		All Non-Voters		Total
	No.	%	No.	%	
Centre	81	54	69	46	150
Periphery	42	26	120	74	162
Total	123	39	189	61	312

$\chi_1^2 = 25 \cdot 7$. Significant at $0 \cdot 1\%$.

It can be seen that voting was, indeed, related to the distance between London and the constituency. More than half of the Centre cast a vote compared with a quarter of the Periphery. The further from London a Member's constituency, the less likely he was to attend and vote.

It was sponsorship which, on Seymour Cocks's Bill, provided the sharpest association between attitude and social characteristics. This characteristic has therefore been used to test whether or not the relationship between attitude and type class has been distorted by geographical factors (Table 84).

A comparison of Trade Unionists with the CLP sponsored *within* each area yields no association between voting *per se* and sponsorship. However, the crucial test is whether, after the regional factor has been held constant, any significant difference in opposition to hunting emerges between Trade Unionists and the CLP sponsored either on the basis of the division on Seymour Cocks's bill or the EDMs. Tables 85 and 86 show that taking the Centre and the Periphery separately no association between sponsorship and support of the Bill or between sponsorship and signature of the blood sports motions has been established. Moreover, within each

TABLE 84. VOTING ON ANTI-BLOOD SPORTS BILL BY SPONSORSHIP

The Centre

	Voters		Non-Voters		Total	
	No.	%	No.	%	No.	%
Trade Union	14	47	16	53	30	100
CLP	56	54	47	46	103	100
Total	70	53	63	47	133	100

$\chi^2_1 = 0 \cdot 55$.   Not significant.

The Periphery

	Voters		Non-Voters		Total	
Trade Union	14	21	54	79	68	100
CLP	27	31	60	69	87	100
Total	41	26	114	74	155	100

$\chi^2_1 = 2 \cdot 14$.   Not significant.

region the proportion of Trade Unionists[1] voting for the Bill was almost the same as of those signing the EDMs. In short, analysis of the EDMs gives similar results to analysis of the division, whether or not the regional factor has been controlled.

TABLE 85. SUPPORT FOR ANTI-HUNTING BILL AND DISTANCE FROM LONDON BY SPONSORSHIP

The Centre

	Anti-Hunting			Abstainers and Pro-Hunters		Total	
	No.	%	%	No.	%	No.	%
Trade Union	14	47	(29)	16	53	30	100
CLP	34	33	(71)	69	67	103	100
Total	48	36	(100)	85	64	133	100

$\chi^2_1 = 1 \cdot 88$.   Not significant.

The Periphery

	Anti-Hunting			Abstainers and Pro-Hunters		Total	
Trade Union	14	21	(41)	54	79	68	100
CLP	20	23	(59)	67	77	87	100
Total	34	22	(100)	121	78	155	100

$\chi^2_1 = 0 \cdot 13$. Not significant.

[1] Expressed as a percentage of Trade Unionists and the CLP sponsored combined.

TABLE 86. ANTI-HUNTING EDM AND DISTANCE FROM LONDON BY SPONSORSHIP

The Centre

	Signers			Non-Signers		Total	
	No.	%	%	No.	%	No.	%
Trade Union	26	87	(25)	4	13	30	100
CLP	77	75	(75)	26	25	103	100
Total	103	77	(100)	30	23	133	100

$\chi_1^2 = 1 \cdot 89$. Not significant.

The Periphery

	Signers			Non-Signers		Total	
Trade Union	52	76	(44)	16	24	68	100
CLP	69	79	(56)	18	21	87	100
Total	121	78	(100)	34	22	155	100

$\chi_1^2 = 0 \cdot 18$. Not significant.
The figures in brackets give the percentages of Trade Union and the CLP sponsored voting for the Bill or signing the EDMs.

When the supporters of hunting are compared with the opponents and the Abstainers, however, within the Centre, the cleavage between Trade Unionists and the CLP sponsored reappears (Table 87).

TABLE 87. HUNTING FREE VOTE AND DISTANCE FROM LONDON BY SPONSORSHIP

The Centre

	Anti-Hunting		Not Voting		Pro-Hunting		Total	
	No.	%	No.	%	No.	%	No.	%
Trade Union	14	47	16	53	—	—	30	100
CLP	34	33	47	46	22	21	103	100
Total	48	36	63	47	22	17	133	100

$\chi_2^2 = 7 \cdot 90$. Significant at $2 \cdot 5\%$.

The Periphery

	Anti-Hunting		Not Voting		Pro-Hunting		Total	
Trade Union	14	21	54	79	—	—	68	100
CLP	20	23	60	69	7	8	87	100
Total	34	22	114	74	7	5	155	100

Not testable.

Unfortunately, the total number of pro-hunters from the Periphery are too small to permit testing; however, the figures are consistent with those for the Centre. Thus it seems that *support* for hunting (as distinct from definite opposition to it) was related to sponsorship, and that this association stands even when the geographical factor is controlled.

ROYAL GRANTS, 9 JULY 1952

As explained in Chapter 6, three divisions on grants to members of the Royal Family have been used to construct a Guttman scale along which Members can be placed according to their zeal for economy in royal expenditure. The votes cast in each division have been compared with the votes cast in each of the other two. Yule's Q has been calculated for each table (Tables 88–90).

Yule's Q never falls below a value of 0·96, and the votes cast in these three divisions form an almost perfect Guttman scale. The 26 Members who voted consistently to reduce the grants are shown in cell *d* of Tables 88 and 90 and are included within the 49 in cell *d*, Table 89; these 26 Members comprise the Left. The Right consist of 31 Members shown in cell *a* of Table 89; they are included in the number shown in cell *a* in Table 88 and cell *a* of Table 90.

TABLE 88. *Div.* 200. Vote on Queen's Allowance

		+	−	Total
Div. 201 Vote on Duke of Edinburgh's allowance	+	65 *a*	− *b*	65
	−	24 *c*	26 *d*	50
Total		89	26	115

$$\text{Yule's } Q = \frac{ad - bc}{ad + bc} = 1\cdot0.$$

TABLE 89. *Div.* 201. Vote on Duke of Edinburgh's Allowance

		+	−	Total
Div. 202 Vote on Princess Margaret's allowance	+	31 *a*	1 *b*	32
	−	34 *c*	49 *d*	83
Total		65	50	115

$$\text{Yule's } Q = \frac{ad - bc}{ad + bc} = 0\cdot96.$$

TABLE 90. *Div.* 200. VOTE ON QUEEN'S ALLOWANCE

		+	−	Total
Div. 202 Vote on Princess Margaret's allowance	+	32 *a*	− *b*	32
	−	57 *c*	26 *d*	83
Total		89	26	115

Yule's $Q = \dfrac{ad - bc}{ad + bc} = 1 \cdot 0$.

+ = Vote in favour of grant.   − = Vote against grant.

These Members voted consistently in favour of maintaining the grants at the level proposed by the government. Twenty-three of the 24 in cell *c* of Table 88 form the Moderate Left, whilst the 34 in cell *c* of Table 89 constitute the Moderate Right.

1945–50

A Guttman scale was based on two divisions which took place on the proposal to increase the annuity paid to Princess Elizabeth. The votes cast in the first division can be compared with those cast in the second (Table 91).

TABLE 91. CIVIL LIST. *Div.* 51. VOTE ON AMENDMENT
TO CANCEL WHOLE OF EXTRA GRANT

		+	−	Total
Div. 52 Vote on amendment to reduce additional grant	+	51 *a*	1 *b*	52
	−	53 *c*	22 *d*	75
Total		104	23	127

Yule's $Q = \dfrac{ad - bc}{ad + bc} = 0 \cdot 91$.

+ = Vote for the government.   − = Vote against the government.

ANNEX 4

The Conservative Party, 1950–5

1950–1

Atlantic Union and the Empire

EDM 49/50, tabled in September 1950 urged the government, "in view of the great change in public opinion in Canada and the United States", to consult with these countries and other members of the Atlantic Pact to find a basis for a more permanent union "whereby a more permanent system of defence capable of guaranteeing peace might be built up". The motion was signed by 38 Members.

Two motions championed the more traditional Conservative cause of the Empire. Anthony Marlowe and three other Conservatives urged the government to convene an Empire Conference to investigate the possibility of creating an Empire Assembly, and to consider whether goods imported from dollar sources could be obtained from the Empire instead.[1] In May 1951, 64 Conservatives welcomed the formation of regional defence pacts (e.g. NATO) but expressed the view that "the long-standing association of the Commonwealth and Empire was essential to the successful operation of these pacts and remained Britain's first consideration in its overseas commitments."[2]

There was considerable cross-signing; 22 of the signatories of the Empire motions also expressed support for the EDM on the Atlantic defence system.[3] Forty Members, however, signed one, or both, of the Empire motions but ignored the EDM on Atlantic defence. These forty "Empire" backbenchers were compared with all those who signed the "Atlantic" motion.[4] As indicated in Chapter 8, there were no significant associations between opinions, as gauged on this scale, and social characteristics.

1951–5

Members' Salaries

It has already been explained that the social characteristics of the signatories of EDM 71/54, which called on the government to defer implementation of the Common's decision to grant a flat pay rise to MPs, were very similar to those of the backbenchers who voted in the division lobby against the salary increase. Tables 92–95 show, for purposes of comparison, the characteristics of the EDM signatories and the division lobby opponents.

[1] EDM 12/50.
[2] EDM 62/51.
[3] Such cross-signing was not, of course, inconsistent.
[4] Including those who signed one or both of the Empire EDMs as well.

252

TABLE 92. THE CONSERVATIVES AND MEMBERS' SALARIES BY SCHOOLS

	Signed EDM 71/54		Non-Signers	Voted against increase		Voted for increase or Absent	Total
	No.	%		No.	%		
Clarendon Public Schools	17	33	68	41	36	44	85
Other Public Schools	23	45	66	52	46	37	89
Non-Public Schools	11	22	46	21	18	36	57
Total[a]	51	100	180	114	100	117	231

$\chi_2^2 = 1\cdot203$. Not significant. $\chi_2^2 = 6\cdot541$. Significant at 5%.
[a] Members educated at Other Schools omitted from table.

The school, university, and age distributions of the EDM signatories are very close to those of the larger group who voted against the increase in the lobbies. The occupational similarities are less marked though such differences as there were can reasonably be explained by chance fluctuations.

TABLE 93. THE CONSERVATIVES AND MEMBERS' SALARIES BY UNIVERSITIES

	Signed EDM 71/54		Non-Signers	Voted against increase		Voted for increase or absent	Total
	No.	%		No.	%		
Oxford	13	42	53	35	45	31	66
Cambridge	11	35	37	29	37	19	48
Other	7	23	28	14	18	21	35
Total	31	100	118	78	100	71	149

$\chi_2^2 = 0\cdot164$. Not significant.
Oxford against Cambridge against Other. $\chi_2^2 = 3\cdot398$. Not significant.
Oxford and Cambridge against Other. $\chi_1^2 = 2\cdot77$. Significant at 10%.

TABLE 94. THE CONSERVATIVES AND MEMBERS' SALARIES BY OCCUPATION

	Signed EDM 71/54		Non-Signers	Voted against increase		Voted for increase or absent	Total
	No.	%		No.	%		
Public company	18	33	62	40	34	40	80
Private company	12	22	27	19	16	20	39
Business, financial and executive	5	9	12	6	5	11	17
Total all business	35	64	101	65	55	71	136
Farmers	4	7	14	12	10	6	18
Lawyers	5	9	29	16	14	18	34
HM Forces	5	9	9	8	7	6	14
Other professions	2	4	13	5	4	10	15
Total all Professions	12	22	51	29	25	34	63
Miscellaneous Occupations	4	7	20	12	10	12	24
Total	55	100	186	118	100	123	241

Business against Professions against Miscellaneous Occupations. $\chi_2^2 = 1 \cdot 606$. Not significant. Public Companies against Private Companies. $\chi_1^2 = 0 \cdot 951$. Not significant. Lawyers against HM Forces against Other Professions. Too small to test.

Business against Professions against Miscellaneous Occupations. $\chi_2^2 = 0 \cdot 1184$. Not significant. Public Companies against Private Companies. Not significant. Lawyers against HM Forces against Other Professions. $\chi_2^2 = 1 \cdot 684$. Not significant.

TABLE 95. THE CONSERVATIVES AND MEMBERS' SALARIES BY AGE

	Signed EDM 71/54		Non-Signers	Voted against increase		Did not vote	Total
	No.	%		No.	%		
Over 60	9	17	28	15	13	22	37
51–60	18	33	62	41	35	39	80
41–50	19	35	66	44	38	41	85
Under 41	8	15	28	16	14	20	36
Total[a]	54	100	184	116	100	122	238

$\chi_3^2 = 0 \cdot 67$ Not significant. $\chi_3^2 = 1 \cdot 773$. Not significant.

[a] Unknowns omitted from table.

ANNEX 5

The Bevanites

In Chapter 5 the Backbench Labour Party was divided into 3 groupings—Left, Other Defence and Nuclear Critics, and the Rest—according to the degree of Members' participation in certain floor revolts. The Left, as defined, is not identical with the Bevanite group because a number of pacifists or freelance Members sometimes joined in the Bevanite demonstrations. Moreover, there were some Bevanites who for various reasons (such as absence from the House or dissatisfaction with Bevan over his stand on the H-bomb issue in 1955) only rebelled on one of the selected occasions.

An attempt has been made to compile a list of Bevanites on the basis of private information. It has not been easy to draw up a definitive list because the different sources do not precisely agree. However, the names of 46 MPs who appear to have been associated with the Bevanites at one time or another in the 1951 Parliament have been collected. Thirty-five of these MPs rank as Left according to the criteria given in Chapter 5. The remaining 11 all qualify as Other Defence and Nuclear Critics. This means that 5 MPs of our Left were not Bevanites. The social composition of the 46 Bevanites has been compared with that of the 40 Left MPs and the reaction of the Bevanites to various issues has also been compared with the response of our Left to the same questions.

SOCIAL AND POLITICAL CHARACTERISTICS

In terms of social characteristics the Bevanites were somewhat more middle class than the Left and contained a higher proportion of university graduates, and amongst graduates, of the U1s. They also contained a rather higher proportion of middle-aged and English Members than did the Left. They were also more prominent among the signers of the German Rearmament EDMs, and not surprisingly more inclined to sign the Bevanite Motions on negotiations with Russia. They were a little less conspicuous among the heavy signers of the Social Security Motions, less inclined to take a left-wing stance on the issue of Royal Grants, and a rather higher proportion of them than of the Left belonged to the Twentieth Century Collectivists.

Glossary of Terms

THE LABOUR PARTY

1945–50 Parliament

The Ultra Left	5 Members	Members of the Labour Independent Group 1949–50.
The Left	26 Members	Members signing EDMs which reflected a neutralist position even after the Czech coup. Sydney Silverman was a prominent spokesman of this group.
The Centre Left	39 Members	Members who signed the Amendment to the Address on Foreign Policy in November 1946 not included in the above. R. H. S. Crossman and Michael Foot were prominent representatives of this group.
Combined Lefts	70 Members	
Dual Abstainers	25 Members	Those Members who abstained in two key Foreign Policy divisions in the 1945–50 Parliament (the Amendment to the Address in November 1946 and the NATO Treaty in May 1949) or actually voted against the NATO Treaty but did not sign any of the Motions or Amendments listed above. Sometimes, however, the term is used in a wider sense to include those already classified as Members of the Combined Lefts. This wider category consists of 59 Members.
The Broader Left	95 Members	This consists of the three groups comprising the Combined Lefts plus the Dual Abstainers.

1951–5 Parliament

The Left	40 Members	Members rebelling with Aneurin Bevan in at least 2 out of the following 3 floor revolts: Japanese Peace Treaty, Nov. 1951; British Rearmament (57 Varieties), March 1952; the Hydrogen Bomb, March 1955.
Other Defence and Nuclear Critics	56 Members	Members who rebelled in any *one* of the following floor revolts: British Rearmament (57 Varieties), March 1952; the Hydrogen Bomb, March 1955; Beswick's Amendment to the Atomic Energy Bill, April 1954.

1955–9 Parliament

The Left	51 Members	Members classified as Left-wing on both Defence and Foreign Policy, or as Left-wing on one and Centre on the other. See page 236 for the criteria on which Members were classified. An alternative classification based on behaviour in floor revolts is offered on pages 200–5. The Left defined in this way numbers 90.

256

BACKBENCH REBELLION IN THE LABOUR PARTY 1945-1955

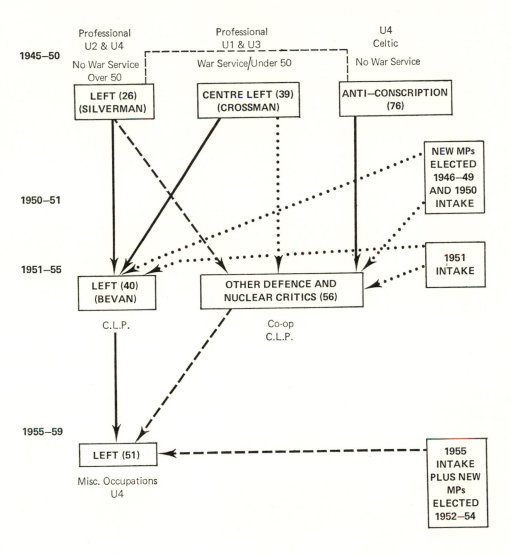

Left 1955–59 defined as in the Glossary

———— Strong contribution

– – – – Moderate contribution

• • • • • Contribution roughly proportionate to numbers

Name Index

Acland, Sir Richard   71, 114, 117, 186
Aitken, M.   167
Albu, A.   94
Alderman, R. K.   148n
Allen, S. S.   53
Amery, J.   174–5
Amery, L. S.   166, 176
Amis, K.   206
Anstruther-Gray, W.   180
Arbuthnot, J.   180
Attlee, C. R.   47, 48, 51, 69–70, 87, 90, 93, 96, 97, 102, 104, 108, 110, 114, 125, 136, 144, 171
Aydelotte, W. O.   2n, 230

Bagehot, W.   21, 28
Balfour, A.   223
Barnes, A.   130
Bartholomew, D. J.   3n, 11, 117n, 120n, 155n, 177n, 217n, 221n, 229n, 230n
Bassett, E.   11
Bealey, F. W.   2n
Bellenger, F. J.   102, 229, 231
Benn, A. W.   221
Benney, M.   2n
Berrington, H. B.   3n, 22n, 28n, 117n, 120n, 155n, 177n, 182n, 217n, 221n, 229n, 230n
Beswick, F.   14, 108, 148, 186, 216
Bevan, A.   67, 85, 87, 88, 92, 94, 98, 99, 104, 106–7, 109, 110, 111, 122, 145–7, 185, 217, 256
Bevin, E.   22, 47, 50, 51, 52, 55, 56, 67–68, 71, 76, 79, 80, 81, 94, 95, 102, 167, 186
Bing, G.   132
Birch, A. H.   217n
Blackford, Lord   121
Blenkinsop, A.   109
Blondel, J.   2n
Blumler, J.   2n
Boardman, H.   30
Boothby, R.   69, 166–8, 180
Braddock, B.   100
Bremner, M.   81n, 184n
Brockway, A. F.   114, 115, 116, 186, 221
Brooke, H.   22

Bullus, E. E.   177, 182
Butler, D.   2, 4n, 211n
Butler, H. W.   73
Butler, R. A.   179–80

Callaghan, J.   57, 137
Carbery, T. F.   192
Caridi, R. J.   121n
Carmichael, J.   99, 107, 144, 145
Carroll, L.   165
Casasola, R.   93
Castle, Mrs. B.   91
Chamberlain, J.   144, 166
Chamberlain, N.   18, 166
Chou En-lai   91, 189n, 195
Christie, J. R.   128
Christoph, J. B.   128n
Churchill, W.   50, 54, 56, 93, 96, 97, 99, 166–7, 172, 174n, 180–1, 182, 223
Cobden, R.   67
Cocks, F. S.   47, 71, 73, 78, 133, 150, 247
Collins, V.   133
Craddock, G.   122, 147
Crookshank, Capt. H. F. C.   64, 124
Crossman, R. H. S.   1, 7, 21, 27, 28, 56, 57, 58, 70–71, 72, 73–74, 76, 79, 80, 83, 88, 99, 107, 110–11, 122, 148, 214, 220, 256
Crosthwaite-Eyre, Col. O. E.   178

Dahl, R. A.   224
Dalton, H.   103
Darling, G.   109
Davies, E.   95, 109
Davies, H.   92–93, 107, 108, 136–7
Davies, R.   49, 72, 80, 135
Davies, S. O.   89
Deedes, W.   180
Delargy, H.   209n
Donnelly, D.   12, 13, 28, 103
Donovan, T.   126–7
Dowse, R. E.   213n
Driberg, T.   115, 145, 147
Durbin, E. F. M.   137

Subject Index

263